THE PSYCHOLOGY
OF LEARNING AND MOTIVATION

Advances in Research and Theory

VOLUME 11

CONTRIBUTORS TO THIS VOLUME

William P. Banks

Robert E. Christiaansen

Carolyn Cohen

D. James Dooling

Howard Egeth

Samuel Fillenbaum

Jeffrey A. Johnsen

Frank A. Logan

Lloyd R. Peterson

Leslie Rawlings

Stephen K. Reed

THE PSYCHOLOGY
OF LEARNING AND MOTIVATION

Advances in Research and Theory

EDITED BY GORDON H. BOWER

STANFORD UNIVERSITY, STANFORD, CALIFORNIA

Volume 11

1977

ACADEMIC PRESS New York · San Francisco · London

A SUBSIDIARY OF HARCOURT BRACE JOVANOVICH, PUBLISHERS

ACADEMIC PRESS, INC.
111 Fifth Avenue, New York, New York 10003

United Kingdom Edition published by
ACADEMIC PRESS, INC. (LONDON) LTD.
24/28 Oval Road, London NW1

LIBRARY OF CONGRESS CATALOG CARD NUMBER: 66–30104

ISBN 0–12–543311–5

PRINTED IN THE UNITED STATES OF AMERICA

CONTENTS

LEVELS OF ENCODING AND RETENTION OF PROSE
D. James Dooling and Robert E. Christiaansen

MIND YOUR p's AND q's: THE ROLE OF CONTENT AND CONTEXT IN SOME USES OF *AND, OR,* AND *IF*
Samuel Fillenbaum

ENCODING AND PROCESSING OF SYMBOLIC INFORMATION IN COMPARATIVE JUDGMENTS
William P. Banks

MEMORY FOR PROBLEM SOLUTIONS

Stephen K. Reed and Jeffrey A. Johnsen

HYBRID THEORY OF CLASSICAL CONDITIONING

Frank A. Logan

INTERNAL CONSTRUCTION OF SPATIAL PATTERNS

Lloyd R. Peterson, Leslie Rawlings,
and Carolyn Cohen

ATTENTION AND PREATTENTION

Howard Egeth

LIST OF CONTRIBUTORS

Numbers in parentheses indicate the pages on which the authors' contributions begin.

William P. Banks, Department of Psychology, Pomona College, Claremont, California (101)

Robert E. Christiaansen, Department of Psychology, Kent State University, Kent, Ohio (1)

Carolyn Cohen, Department of Psychology, Indiana University, Bloomington, Indiana (245)

D. James Dooling,[1] Department of Psychology, Kent State University, Kent, Ohio (1)

Howard Egeth, Department of Psychology, The Johns Hopkins University, Baltimore, Maryland (277)

Samuel Fillenbaum, Department of Psychology, Davie Hall, University of North Carolina, Chapel Hill, North Carolina (41)

Jeffrey A. Johnsen, Department of Psychology, Case Western Reserve University, Cleveland, Ohio (161)

Frank A. Logan, Department of Psychology, University of New Mexico, Albuquerque, New Mexico (203)

Lloyd R. Peterson, Department of Psychology, Indiana University, Bloomington, Indiana (245)

Leslie Rawlings, Department of Psychiatry and Behavioral Sciences, School of Medicine, University of Washington, Seattle, Washington (245)

Stephen K. Reed, Department of Psychology, Case Western Reserve University, Cleveland, Ohio (161)

---

[1] Present address: Bell Laboratories, Holmdel, New Jersey.

CONTENTS OF PREVIOUS VOLUMES

LEVELS OF ENCODING
AND RETENTION OF PROSE[1]

D. James Dooling[2] and Robert E. Christiaansen

KENT STATE UNIVERSITY, KENT, OHIO

I. Overview

In this chapter, we shall present a selective review of the research on constructive memory for prose and three original experiments which bear on current theorizing about memory. We follow Bartlett

[1] This research was facilitated by a Summer Research Fellowship from Kent State University to the first author. We are grateful to the following for their comments on a previous draft of the manuscript: Joseph H. Danks, Joseph S. Dumas, Larry L. Jacoby, and David C. Riccio. Thomas F. Keenan collaborated with us on the design and execution of Experiment 1. We are grateful to the following for assistance in conducting the experiments: Arlene Coleman, Heather Turnbull Miller, and David Payne.
[2] Now at Bell Laboratories, Holmdel, New Jersey 07733.

1

(1932) in studying the remembrance of meaningful material for long intervals and by using "errors" in retention to make inferences about the coding processes involved. Our results tend to support Bartlett's conceptions of abstract encoding and constructive retrieval. We demonstrate clearly, for example, that memory for prose becomes increasingly thematic with the passage of time. Our data also support the idea that comprehension of prose involves the activation of memory codes at various levels of abstraction. The higher the level of memory code, the longer it is remembered. We attempt to relate this "levels of encoding" idea both to Bartlett's theory of the schema and to Craik and Lockhart's (1972) "levels of processing" conception of memory. In addition, we argue that levels of encoding in prose retention do not form a strict hierarchy. Rather, they reflect flexible encoding processes that are context dependent.

II. Constructive Memory for Prose

After a brief review of Bartlett's theory and research, we shall present a selective review of recent research on constructive processes in memory. We shall organize the review along the lines suggested by Cofer (1977). He points out that constructive processes can occur at one of three points in time: (a) during comprehension of the material; (b) during the retention interval; and (c) during the retention test itself.

A. BARTLETT'S THEORY OF THE SCHEMA

In *Remembering,* Bartlett (1932) put as much distance as possible between himself and Ebbinghaus (1885/1964). Ebbinghaus knew that his own knowledge would enter into his memory experiments, so he sought to exclude it by learning nonsense. Bartlett, on the other hand, emphasized the role of prior knowledge in remembering. His subjects read materials that required cognitive interpretation, forcing them to make an "effort after meaning." Bartlett believed that the complex interaction between the stimulus materials and the subject's preexperimental knowledge was the very essence of remembering.

Verbal learning psychologists, in the tradition of Ebbinghaus, still argue for a more analytic approach to memory. They seek to minimize the effects of complex knowledge in the hope that basic principles of memory can be uncovered under carefully controlled conditions (see Murdock, 1974, pp. 4–5, for a clear statement of this view). But Bartlett would reject such an approach on the grounds that the experimental "controls" destroy the very process under investigation. On this point, we like Winograd's (1976) example that Einstein couldn't balance his checkbook. It is conceivable that an experimental psychologist who wished to study the cognitions of a mathematical genius would "simplify" the experiment by testing arithmetic ability. Such an effort would be doomed to failure, however, because the subsystem investigated is not representative of the total system to be studied. Bartlett's approach to remembering puts the highest value on the ecological validity of the empirical observations and the generality and scope of the subsequent theorizing.

Bartlett's experiments revealed many distortions in recall. Subjects who read about two Indians "hunting seals" by a river bank, for example, might recall that they were "fishing." Such errors demonstrate that memory storage is not verbatim and led Bartlett to characterize remembering as constructive. The information in memory is abstractly encoded, but is not erroneous. The meaning of the main ideas is preserved in a form that subjects can use as a guide for manufacturing a response. A particular recall, therefore, is the product of an integration between information acquired in a particular situation and more permanent general knowledge. With the passage of time, the relative contribution of general knowledge increases, leading to recall that is increasingly thematic and devoid of specific detail.

Bartlett (1932) clearly contended that memory recall did not represent a dredging up of lifeless traces in the form in which they were stored, but he was vague as to the nature of the information in memory. He is best known for his idea that information is stored in schematic form. But he was never comfortable with the term that is most closely identified with his theorizing on memory: "I strongly dislike the term 'schema' [p. 200]." Bartlett clearly rejected the idea that memory storage of prose could be characterized as an abstract outline, even though he is often cited for this very idea. He preferred to emphasize the diversity of memory codes available to subjects. He showed great interest, for example, in why certain details are remembered better than others, and attributed the recall differences more to interests and attitudes than to structural characteristics of the text. Bartlett also commented extensively on memory for the affective tone of a passage and noted numerous changes in recall with the passage of time. In short, Bartlett used the term "schema" loosely. He used it to cover a multitude of coding processes that defied neat packaging under a single rubric. His observations about memory recall, therefore, leave us with many challenging questions for research.

B. CONSTRUCTIVE PROCESSES DURING COMPREHENSION

Recent research on constructive memory has generally focused on the comprehension process. Often this has been by default, as there has been comparatively little work on memory changes across retention intervals, and even less on constructive activity during the test itself. Typical constructive memory experiments have involved a manipulation of comprehension processes at input that lead to creative, or at least nonliteral, remembering after a short interval. Numerous studies have demonstrated the basic phenomena that memory performance reflects some transformation of the information presented to subjects (for reviews, see Cofer, 1973; Pezdek, 1975). No one who has given even casual attention to prose retention holds that remembering is verbatim. All current researchers hold that subjects use their preexperimental knowledge during comprehension in ways that change the content of recall. If "constructive" means only the use of prior knowledge in storing a transformed version of the text, then just about *all* theories of prose retention are "constructive."

We would like to distinguish between weak and strong versions of constructive memory theory. The weak version holds that text is abstracted into memory by a set of rules. In other words, the text has an internal structure which is used by the comprehender to reduce the information load. The strong version, on the other hand, focuses on the comprehender's knowledge of the world. In addition to the perception of text structure, the comprehender apprehends an event in context. What is remembered depends more on what the reader knows than on the formal properties of the text itself. Our distinction parallels, to some extent, that drawn by Bransford, Barclay, and Franks (1972) regarding an interpretative vs. constructive approach to sentence memory. We have divided our brief review along such dichotomous lines, while realizing that individual researchers may fall somewhere on a continuum between the two views.

1. Abstractive Memory

Gomulicki (1956) challenged Bartlett's theory and data on remembering. He found very few memory distortions in recall and noted that almost all errors were errors of omission. Recall protocols did preserve the theme and important ideas of the passage. Such memory was attributed to an abstractive process. During comprehension, subjects store a reduced version of text content and reproduce this abstract at the time of recall. Zangwill (1972) has endorsed this view, while noting that Bartlett's constructive results were probably due to the unusual materials which he used. Like constructive theory, the abstractive view stresses the importance of preexperimental knowledge for remembering. The abstractive view emphasizes the idea that what is stored in memory is a transformed version of the text.

Recently a number of psychologists have approached prose retention from a perspective that can be considered a variant of the abstractive theory. Attempts have been made to characterize prose in linguistic terms and to demonstrate the psychological reality of the resulting formal structure. Kintsch (1976) and Meyer (1975), for example, have worked with the linguistic theories of van Dijk (1976) and Grimes (1974), respectively. They have been able to deduce a formal hierarchical structure for prose passages and to show that recall is related to the "height" of an idea in the hierarchy. Higher level, abstract ideas are remembered better than lower level details. Related work by Rumelhart (1977), Thorndyke (1975), and Bower (1976) has tended to focus on writing a grammar for simple stories that have a well-defined structure. Higher level constituents of such grammars tend to be correlated with both the content of recall and summaries of the stories written by subjects. These formal approaches to prose retention go beyond the Gomulicki-Zangwill approach in attempting to specify the units of abstraction in explicit terms.

Experiments which support an abstractive view tend to have certain features in common which differ from those common to Bartlettian research. Experimental passages are typically well organized and easy to comprehend, the retention intervals are short, and the subjects are motivated to perform accurately. The variables of interest tend to be those which can be conceptualized in linguistic or logical terms. More emphasis is given to the structural properties of the text than to the cognitions of the subjects. Such theories seem to operate on the principle that a well-organized, explicit theory of limited scope is preferable to a vague, amorphous theory which has wide generality. With Bartlett, we lean more to the opposing view.

2. Construction in Comprehension

A constructive approach to comprehension and memory begins with the assumption that the knowledge which subjects use in processing prose has not been adequately described by any formal system. The major concepts are more intuitive than linguistic and there is a heavy emphasis on the importance of contextual variables. Excellent descriptions of this position can be found in Bransford and McCarrell (1974) and Jenkins (1974). Our treatment of constructive processes during comprehension will be illustrated by some prior work by one of us.

Dooling and Lachman (1971) investigated the effects of comprehension on retention of prose by giving subjects vague, metaphorical passages that were difficult to comprehend. For example, some subjects read the following passage:

> With hocked gems financing him, our hero bravely defied all scornful laughter that tried to prevent his scheme. "Your eyes deceive," he had said, "an egg not a table correctly typifies this unexplored planet." Now three sturdy sisters sought proof, forging along sometimes through calm vastness, yet more often over turbulent peaks and valleys. Days became weeks as many doubters spread fearful rumors about the edge. At last from nowhere welcome winged creatures appeared signifying momentous success. (From Dooling & Lachman, 1971, p. 217. Copyright 1971 by the American Psychological Association. Reprinted by permission.)

Half of the subjects were given prior information with the title, "Christopher Columbus Discovering America." They were able to comprehend the metaphor and remember the passage better than a no-title control group. The title gave them the knowledge they needed in order to construct a coherent meaning for the passage. Unlike the no-title control group, they could relate a preexperimental schema to the information to be comprehended. The same exact text was processed very differently depending on whether or not subjects perceived the relevance of it to a body of prior knowledge. We consider this result constructive in the strong sense in that a particular cognitive state of the subject was the important controlling variable.

Constructive recall effects in the Dooling and Lachman experiment could not be attributed to events during the retention interval, for the interval was very short. The thematic effects, therefore, were due to processes that occurred either during comprehension, or recall, or both. Dooling and Mullet (1973) attempted to pin down the locus of such constructive effects by presenting subjects with a thematic title either before reading a metaphorical passage, or after, or not at all. A

TABLE I

RECALL OF VAGUE PASSAGES AS A FUNCTION OF THEMATIC TITLE PLACEMENT [a]

Dependent measure	Thematic title		
	Before	After	None
Correct sentences	3.0	1.4	1.2
Correct words	18.6	11.8	12.2
Thematic intrusions (words)	3.0	1.0	1.1

[a]Means not significantly different are underscored with a common line. (Adapted from Dooling and Mullet, 1973, p. 405. Copyright 1973 by the American Psychological Association. Reprinted by permission.)

summary of the results is shown in Table I. When the thematic title came immediately after reading the passage it was of no help. There was no evidence of a thematic effect which was specifically tied into the recall process. The results pointed to construction at input as the controlling process. Subjects who had comprehended the passage with respect to the thematic title recalled more words and sentences. They also made more thematic intrusion errors. The results do not necessarily imply that all constructive effects are determined by coding processes occurring during comprehension. A longer retention interval would surely have modified the results.

The two constructive memory experiments we have described here share with Bartlett the use of unusual stimulus materials. One could say that such experiments lack generality because the prose passages are not representative of those normally read by people. Spiro (1977), for example, has shown that constructive effects are dependent upon the presence of an inconsistency in the text. But this does not mean that constructive memory processes are absent when well-formed passages are read and remembered. Just as perception psychologists use visual illusions to demonstrate constructive processes that are a part of normal vision, it is necessary to use special materials in memory studies if the constructive nature of remembering is to be revealed. The absence of constructive errors on a memory test does not imply the absence of constructive cognitive processing of the text.

A second factor must also be considered in differentiating between results which support an abstractive vs. constructive interpretation of prose memory. As Spiro (1977) points out, most memory experiments induce an artificial accuracy set on the part of subjects. They see it as their job to memorize the material, not to experience new knowledge. The appropriate strategy, therefore, may be to isolate experimental information from more permanent knowledge structures. If new information is normally integrated with existing knowledge, then memory experiments may grossly underestimate the amount of naturally occurring constructive errors. Spiro has supported his observation by showing that subjects who did not believe that they were in a memory experiment made predicted memory distortions, while memorizers did not. Indeed, even casual observation of human memory in its natural state suggests that Bartlett was on target with his data on memory distortion. It seems to us that people are amazingly tolerant of recall errors in real life.

C. INTERVAL EFFECTS ON CONSTRUCTIVE MEMORY

Bartlett's experiments typically involved long retention intervals and he found that thematic recall errors increase with the passage of time. Changes in constructive errors with the passage of time cannot be attributed solely to comprehension processes during input. Bartlett's theory of memory is essentially one that focuses on changes in remembering across retention intervals. Yet a number of critics of the constructive view have studied only immediate recall (e.g., Gauld & Stephenson, 1967; Gomulicki, 1956). In this section we first demonstrate the phenomenon that memory performance becomes increasingly thematic with the passage of time. Then we describe experiments which have manipulated events within the interval to demonstrate constructive integration.

1. Thematic Errors across Time

Sulin and Dooling (1974) manipulated the subjects' knowledge of a topic in an attempt to show increased thematic errors with the passage of time. Subjects read a short biographical passage about either a famous or fictitious person. For example, the following passage is about a fictitious dictator named Gerald Martin:

> Gerald Martin strove to undermine the existing government to satisfy his political ambitions. Many of the people of his country supported his efforts. Current political problems made it relatively easy for Martin to take over. Certain groups remained loyal to the old government and caused Martin trouble. He confronted these groups directly and so silenced them. He became a ruthless, uncontrollable dictator. The ultimate effect of his rule was the downfall of his country. (From Sulin & Dooling, 1974, pp. 256–257. Copyright 1974 by the American Psychological Association. Reprinted by permission.)

By changing the name of the main character to Adolph Hitler, the subjects in the famous group were able to comprehend the passage

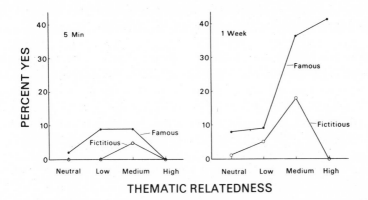

THEMATIC RELATEDNESS

Fig. 1. False recognition of thematic sentences for two retention intervals. (Adapted from Sulin & Dooling, 1974, p. 261. Copyright 1974 by the American Psychological Association. Reprinted by permission.)

with respect to their preexperimental knowledge about Hitler. Sulin and Dooling used a recognition test which consisted of seven sentences from the passage randomly intermixed with seven foil sentences. Four of the latter had nothing to do with the passage (neutral) but the three remaining foils varied in their relatedness to its theme (low, medium, high). For the Martin/Hitler passage, the high-thematic foil was *He hated the Jews particularly and so persecuted them.* Figure 1 shows the false recognition of foil sentences for two retention intervals. At the short, 5-min interval, there were few false recognitions and the famous–fictitious manipulation had no effect. At 1 week, however, there was a pronounced thematic effect. Subjects who had read about a famous person relied more on their preexperimental knowledge in making their recognition decisions. Retention became more thematic with the passage of time.

2. Manipulations within the Interval

Dooling and Christiaansen (in press) introduced a converging operation for the conclusions reached by Sulin and Dooling by adding a new manipulation during the retention interval. In addition to the famous and fictitious groups in the prior study, we used an after group. These subjects read one of the fictitious passages but were informed about the true identity of the main character just before their recognition test. With respect to encoding operations at input, they were in the same condition as the fictitious group. But at the time of the retention test itself, they had knowledge of the famous person just as the famous group did. We also added a control group, called the before group, who read the fictitious passage with fore-knowledge of its true main character. Figure 2 shows the percent yes responses to sentences that had not occurred in the passage for intervals of 2 days and 1 week. At the shorter interval, the after group performs about the same as the fictitious group. At a 1-week interval, however, the responses of this particular group have become more thematic. They appear to be using the new knowledge that had been introduced during the retention interval. At shorter intervals, when subjects still have some memory for the specifics of the material which they read, constructive activity appears to be limited to comprehension processes. But when lower level memory codes are lost with the passage of time, the subjects show increased construc-tion of their responses on the basis of their general knowledge of the topic.

Do the constructive effects depicted in Fig. 2 demonstrate cogni-tive integration during the retention interval? Or do they show only response bias effects on the retention test? Separating the locus of such thematic effects is a difficult task. In a follow-up experiment we compared the "after" manipulation for two different points within a 1-week retention interval. All subjects heard a fictitious version of an experimental passage under one of four conditions: (a) Before. The name of the famous main character was given prior to input. (In the previous experiment, the before group performed essentially the same as the famous group.) (b) Immediately after. The switch in main character was administered right after hearing the material. (c) Week after. The switch came just before the recognition test, as in the prior study. (d) Fictitious. No manipulation of main character.

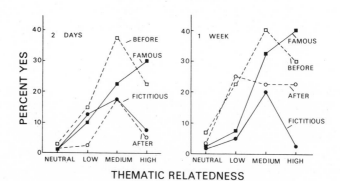

Fig. 2. False recognition of thematic sentences for various manipulations of main charac-ter comprehension. (From Dooling & Christiaansen, in press. Copyright 1977 by the American Psychological Association. Reprinted by permission.)

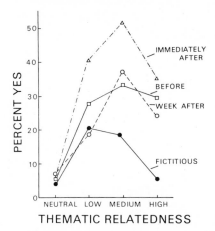

Fig. 3. False recognition of thematic sentences for various manipulations of main character comprehension. (From Dooling & Christiaansen, in press. Copyright 1977 by the American Psychological Association. Reprinted by permission.)

The results for false recognitions of foils are summarized in Fig. 3.
Clearly, the two different after conditions lead to pronounced differences in thematic errors. In fact, the manipulation of main character
immediately after comprehension led to the greatest amount of
constructive error. Compared to the before group, these subjects had
to perform a more difficult cognitive integration. The week after
group, on the other hand, presumably forgot part of the original
passage and did not have as much to integrate. The results show
constructive effects that interact with processes that occur during the
retention interval. Both Spiro (1977) and Loftus (1975) have also
shown similar constructive effects for an immediately after manipulation.

D.   CONSTRUCTION ON THE RETENTION TEST

A constructive view of memory calls attention to the cognitive
processes that occur at the time of the retention test. Over and above
comprehension and interval effects, what the subject is asked to do
will have important effects on what is actually produced. For Bartlett, a recall is created from the current knowledge state of the
individual. Little constructive memory research has focused on this
aspect of memory performance. Nor do we have any experimental
data which bear on the problem. We will confine ourselves to some
brief comments on the contributions of recall and recognition tests
to constructive memory performance. It is our view that recall tests

may underestimate constructive processing, while recognition tests can have the opposite effect.

1. Recall

The constructive view of memory depends largely on erroneous remembering for its data base. The abstractive view thrives on the fact that errors are so few in the free recall of prose. We have previously mentioned Spiro's (1977) observation that subjects may carry out encoding processes that isolate experimental material from their knowledge. Such an accuracy set probably has effects on the recall process itself. When under instructions to write down what they remember, subjects seem to be extremely conservative in setting their criterion for recall. In an unpublished experiment, conducted by Lachman and Dooling in 1967, recall instructions were manipulated for subjects who had read a passage under the same conditions. One group was told to write down all of the words that they could remember. The other was told to recall "the main ideas," using the words if they knew them. The latter group actually recalled significantly more of the exact words from the passage. Evidently, the "main ideas" aspect of the instructions caused them to loosen their criterion. These results are consistent with the view that there are performance constraints on the accuracy of recall which artificially limit the amount of constructive errors that will be obtained (Brockway, Chmielewski, & Cofer, 1974). For this reason, the recognition test has become the methodology of choice among constructive memory researchers.

2. Recognition

An experiment by Loftus and Zanni (1975) nicely illustrates constructive memory effects that come from the test itself. Working with a movie of an auto accident, they manipulated the wording of a question asked of those who witnessed the event. Asking subjects if they saw "*the* broken headlight" led to more false yes responses than a similar version which spoke of "*a* broken headlight." Recognition memory experiments, when used to assess prose retention, can have some of the properties of a leading question. If all of the items presented for binary recognition are new, then subjects have little choice but to make some constructive errors. The test situation itself contains the powerful suggestion that some of the items are old. We suspect that the fairly common practice of including more new than old items in binary recognition tests also artificially inflates the error rate. Subjects may take the test under the assumption that half of the items are old and thereby loosen their criterion for saying yes. The typical use of recognition tests may lead to overestimates of constructive memory processes. More analytic research is needed to separate out the contributions of the test itself to constructive memory results.

III. Levels of Encoding

Bartlett's constructive approach to memory has remained separate from other views of retention that have held a more predominant position in psychology. Radical differences between Bartlettian research and S-R associationism prevented any attempt at integration. More recently, it has been popular to conceptualize memory in information-processing terms by means of flow charts (Atkinson & Shiffrin, 1968). Such theories are also at odds with the constructive approach. They represent memory units as flowing from place to place. They do not address the multiplicity of encoding and retrieval processes discussed by Bartlett. Currently, however, much of the memory literature which was once described in associationistic or information-processing terms is now conceptualized within the levels-of-processing framework (Craik & Lockhart, 1972). It is our view that the levels-of-processing approach has a number of important commonalities with a constructive view of memory. By relating our prose retention results to both Bartlett and the levels of processing idea, we hope to point the way toward an integrated approach to human memory.

A. LEVELS OF PROCESSING FRAMEWORK

Craik and Lockhart (1972) suggested that flow-chart models be replaced by a levels-of-processing framework. Differences in retention are explained as due to different amounts of perceptual analysis. For purposes of immediate, rote memory, a low-level code that preserves the sound pattern of an item will be sufficient for accurate recall. At the other extreme, long-term memory for an item seems to require an elaboration of its meaning. There is a continuity of encoding processes from low to high. Task demands dictate the level of code that will be used. Differences in memory duration that were once attributed to structurally different memory systems are now seen as a result of different levels of processing. The more perceptual analysis an item receives, the longer it will be remembered.

The levels-of-processing framework has provided an adequate account of the data base which originally motivated researchers to postulate multiple memory stores and has explained memory phenomena that appear to be outside the scope of flow-chart models. The approach is also conceptually compatible with important theorizing about perceptual recognition (e.g., Neisser, 1967; Posner, 1969). In tying memory performance to perceptual processing, the levels-of-processing framework emphasizes the importance of encoding processes. Perceptual identification of any item to be remembered requires that the stimulus activate some subset of the subject's knowledge. As such, an item to be remembered is not a single entity to be stored and retrieved as a unit. The levels-of-processing framework is thus consistent with the idea that memorial information is encoded along many dimensions (Bower, 1967). Consider, for example, the extensive research program of Wickens (1972) on release from proactive interference. In numerous short-term memory experiments he has shown that subjects use a wide diversity of memory codes, everything from the lettering of words to their polarity on the semantic differential. Such encoding processes are selective, corresponding to the subject's perception of task demands (Underwood, 1972). Emphasis on coding processes entails the studying of how subjects use their preexperimental knowledge in remembering.

B. ELABORATIVE ENCODING

From the Craik and Lockhart analysis, it is clear that low level codes are those which preserve the critical sensory features of the stimulus, while high-level codes are semantic. Numerous experiments have since been conducted which have varied the low vs. high levels of encoding in support of the levels of processing notion. Too much of this research, however, has avoided the most interesting problem concerned with encoding processes, namely differences within the semantic domain. Experiments that have carried out coding manipulations within the semantic domain require a revision of the basic levels of processing idea along the lines of elaborative encoding for retrieval. A good example can be taken from a study by Barclay, Bransford, Franks, McCarrell, and Nitsch (1974). The point of their experiments was to demonstrate the flexibility of semantic encoding. For example, the word *piano* would be encoded very differently in the two following sentences:

a. The man lifted the piano.

b. The man tuned the piano.

For the first sentence, "something heavy" would be a good retrieval cue for the noun *piano*. For the second sentence, however, "something with a nice sound" is the better cue. The words of the sentences are encoded contextually; that is, the reader constructs and remembers an event for each instance. As such, the word *piano* is encoded differently in the two cases. Both encodings are, however, semantic encodings, and there is no a priori rationale for treating one as "higher" than the other. Differences in recall are due to the relationship between encoding processes and the conditions of retrieval (cf. Tulving & Thomson, 1973). R. C. Anderson and Ortony (1975) have provided additional experimental support for the same phenomenon.

Lockhart, Craik, and Jacoby (1975) have modified the levels of processing notion to accommodate semantic effects. They relate their revised ideas to Sutherland's (1973) conception of pattern recognition. In perceptual analysis there are different "domains" beginning with low-level structures concerned with sensory features and ending within the semantic domain. Items are perceived by processing through these different domains, as originally suggested by the levels-of-processing idea. But within each domain there is an optional amount of elaborative encoding that can be carried on. More specifically, coding processes within the semantic domain are "higher" than coding processes in other domains. But within the semantic domain there can be differences in terms of the "spread" of the encoding. The suggested model, therefore, is two-dimensional. Perceptual processing to the highest semantic domain means better memory. Further elaboration within the semantic domain can also lead to better memory.

To deal with differences within the semantic domain, it has proved necessary for levels-of-processing theorists to deal more thoroughly with retrieval processes. Tulving and Thompson (1973) have shown that memory for words is dependent on the relationship between encoding processes and the retrieval context. In other words, whether a semantic code is effective or not will depend on the conditions of retrieval. Moscovitch and Craik (1976) studied the relationship between depth of encoding and retrieval cues. Good remembering depended not only on the depth of encoding, but also on the relationship between the encoding and retrieval processes. Memory for a semantically encoded item is best when the item has been uniquely differentiated from other items and when retrieval cues reinstate the unique encoding. The original levels-of-processing idea has been extended within the semantic domain by identifying uniqueness as a property of encoding which leads to better remembering. By relating such encoding processes to retrieval processes Moscovitch and Craik come very close to a constructive view of memory.

C. BARTLETT'S THEORY AND LEVELS OF ENCODING

The levels-of-processing approach was developed within the verbal learning tradition. As such, it shares some of the pretheoretical assumptions and biases of an Ebbinghaus approach. The levels-of-processing work to date differs sharply from Bartlett's approach in its use of word lists and the scoring of performance for rote reproduction. While the differences between levels-of-processing and constructive memory approaches are real, we prefer to pass over them for our present purposes. We wish to highlight the similarities and perhaps encourage an integrated approach to human memory.

Bartlett was led to his research on remembering from studies of visual perception. It is a strength of the levels approach that memory is tied to perceptual processing. Both approaches call attention to the importance of preexperimental knowledge, semantic memory, in comprehension. The result is an emphasis on the variety of coding processes available to subjects for the processing of information. Recent developments within the levels approach have focused on memorability differences within the semantic domain. We expect that further work on elaborative encoding will contribute to our understanding of the higher level memory codes that were of central interest to Bartlett. When levels-of-processing researchers began to relate encoding processes to retrieval, we have the closest commonality with a constructive view of memory. Lockhart *et al.* (1975) describe recall as a process of reconstructing an item from contextual cues and the semantic codes available in memory. In agreement with Bartlett, retrieval is a constructive process.

The levels-of-processing framework began with the notion of a hierarchy of memory codes. High-level codes are remembered better than low-level codes. We think that this basic idea should be preserved in conceptualizing memorability differences within the semantic domain. Experiments on memory for prose have shown that high-level, abstract concepts are remembered better than specific details. The levels-of-processing theorists have not done much with higher level abstract codes because lists of unrelated words do not encourage the use of such codes in memory experiments. Prose comprehension, however, involves the activation of multiple memory codes at various levels of abstraction. The typical levels-of-processing experiment manipulates the encoding process such that a particular level of encoding is dominant for a specific experimental condition. Prose researchers, on the other hand, allow for subjective determination of the different levels of codes that are appropriate for the comprehension of a particular passage in context.

Broadbent (1970) has characterized Bartlett's theory as one of "hierarchical levels of processing." Bartlett did not limit himself to a single abstract memory code, the schema. He was very interested in understanding why some parts of a passage were remembered better than others and he explored a variety of memory codes in his experiments. In this informal sense, Bartlett's theory was hierarchical. But Bartlett did not view prose retention in terms of any fixed structure. Nor did he ever attempt to formalize his theoretical ideas in an explicit manner. Throughout his writings there is a stress on the variety and flexibility of encoding processes.

Our research on prose retention adopts the concept of levels of encoding, with the idea that higher level codes are remembered better than lower ones. The codes of interest, however, are those activated by the normal comprehension of prose. As such, we view high-level codes as those which are most abstract, those which subsume a major part of the ideas in a passage. Our concept of a hierarchy of memory codes, however, is context dependent. Like Bartlett, we see the formal structure of a text as only a partial determinant of memorability.

IV. Experiments on Memory Codes and Forgetting of Prose

We report three experiments that are concerned with the coding processes in memory for prose. Because we are not particularly interested in the ability of subjects to reproduce material by rote, our emphasis is on the "errors" which they make. Such errors contain important clues about how the information was encoded. By analyzing false recognitions for sentences from connected discourse at different intervals, we hope to be able to show how memory codes at various levels are forgotten. Like Bartlett, our focus is on constructive errors and how they increase with the passage of time.

A. EXPERIMENT 1

In this study, subjects are given one exposure to a brief passage and are tested on it at one of four different retention intervals: 7 min, 2 days, 1 week, or 1 month. The test requires a yes–no recognition decision on a single sentence. If the sentence is an old sentence from the passage, we expect that correct yes responses will decrease with the passage of time. We are more interested, however, in the recognition decisions for new sentences that were not in the passage. There are three different types of such foils, requiring three different levels of memory code for a correct no decision: paraphrases, thematically related sentences, and nonthematic sentences. Constructive yes responses to semantically and thematically related sentences should increase with the passage of time. For any given interval, however, we expect more yes responses to paraphrases than to thematic sentences. Paraphrases differ from true passage sentences with respect to low-level features that are easily forgotten. But thematic sentences differ from true passage sentences with respect to higher level memory codes that describe sentence meaning. Because the theme of the passage is a high-level abstract code, we expect few false recognitions of nonthematic sentences, even at the longest interval of 1 month.

1. Method

A total of 833 subjects participated in the experiment. Of these, we were able to test and use the data from 768. The design was totally between subjects with different numbers tested in each interval group: 7 min, 192; 2 days, 144; 1 week, 144; 1 month, 288. Return rates were quite high, ranging from 100% at 7 min, to a low of 94% at 1 month. It is unlikely, therefore, that interval effects were confounded in a major way by subject selection effects.

The data for the 7-min interval were taken from an experiment by Christiaansen, Dooling, and Keenan (1976). The 2-day and 1-week subjects were run together at input and assigned to retention-interval conditions haphazardly. The 1-month subjects were run at a different time. We are combining the data from these three studies into a single experiment because they are very similar in terms of subjects, materials, procedures, etc.

Three experimental passages of 10 sentences each were written for the experiment. We began by writing a neutral passage, as shown at the top of the next page.

Man's curiosity had led him to the challenge of the unknown. Those in charge had made careful plans for the attempt. The equipment had been meticulously checked and double-checked. Only the best men were chosen for the task. It was necessary to consider many variables in calculating a precise time for the event. When the day arrived, the participants were made ready and transported to the site. The beginning went smoothly and quickly. Midway, an unexpected occurrence caused danger and was skillfully avoided. The last part required total concentration and expertise. There was an historic moment of triumph when the goal was finally reached.

This passage could be given two different thematic interpretations, which was manipulated by presenting one of two different titles: (a) *The Climbing of Mount Everest*, or (b) *NASA Mission to the Moon*. For each thematic title, a more specific version of the passage was written by making appropriate lexical substitutions in each sentence. For example, the "unexpected occurrence" in the neutral passage becomes an "unexpected avalanche" in the specific version of the mountain passage, and an "unexpected meteor" in the moon version. These materials, therefore, give us a single 10 sentence passage with three versions for each sentence. All input materials and test sentences were drawn from this same pool of 30 sentences, as described below.

Each subject was given a single self-paced exposure to one passage. The passage was presented in mixed format such that specific and neutral sentences alternated. For any one subject, the passage theme was consistent throughout. That is, if given the moon title, all sentences were either neutral or moon-specific. Each subject was given only 9 of the 10 possible sentences to read. That is, one of the sentences from serial positions 2–9 was omitted without the subject's knowledge.

The test sentence for recognition represented one of four test conditions according to its relationship with the passage: (a) Identical. One of the sentences which the subject had actually read was presented. (b) Paraphrase. The alternate version of a sentence which was read was presented; that is, if the subject had read a neutral sentence, the specific version was tested, and vice versa. Paraphrases differ from identical sentences in terms of surface format. They are approximately the same, however, with respect to meaning and thematicity. (c) Thematic. This condition involved the presentation of a sentence which the subject had not read. It was the particular sentence which had been omitted at input for the particular subject to be tested. The thematic sentence differed from those read by the subject with respect to both surface format and sentence gist. It was similar, however, in overall topic. (*d*) Nonthematic. This was a sentence which the subject had not read, presented in a specific version which suggested the alternate topic. For example, if the subject had read nine sentences of the mountain passage with the "unexpected avalanche" sentence omitted, the test sentence would be: *Midway, an unexpected meteor caused danger and was skillfully avoided.* Such a sentence differs from those which the subject had read with respect to sentence format, sentence gist, and paragraph topic. The design was such that the same exact sentence could be the test sentence under the four different test conditions. Performance differences across test conditions, therefore, cannot be attributed to the peculiarities of the materials.

Subjects were typically run in groups of about 50 in a classroom. They were told that it was an experiment on language comprehension and to give the passage one reading in their normal manner. Following this self-paced input, subjects in the 7-min retention interval listened to a comedy record before the test. Other groups were informed that they should come back for a test at a later date and were given a sheet of paper with an appointment for the same time and place either 2 days, 1 week, or 1 month later. The test was identical for all groups. Each subject was given a small sheet of paper that had one sentence on it. They were asked to judge whether or not that sentence had been in the passage which they had read. After circling "yes" or "no," they were instructed to rate their confidence in their decision as "low," "medium" or "high." Testing was conducted with only one sentence per subject because Christiaansen *et al.* (1976) had found that the recognition test itself can introduce thematic errors.

2. Results

Each subject was given a combination score which represented both yes–no and confidence. A yes with high confidence was assigned a 6, with the lowest score of 1 for a high confidence no. The mean combination scores for the experimental conditions tested are shown in Table II. Percent yes responses are shown in parentheses. As is evident, we did not run all of the possible experimental conditions. The nonthematic test was given only at the 1-month interval. To do this we eliminated one-half of the input conditions for the identical test at 1 month. Because the nonthematic test always involved using a specific rather than a neutral test sentence,

TABLE II

MEAN YES-CONFIDENCE COMBINATION SCORES FOR EXPERIMENT 1[a]

Retention interval	Sentence[b] format	Test conditions[b]			
		Identical	Paraphrase	Thematic	Nonthematic
7 Min	Specific	4.50(71)	3.04(42)	1.91(12)	—
	Neutral	4.75(75)	2.79(33)	1.46(04)	—
2 Days	Specific	4.12(67)	3.79(54)	3.33(46)	—
	Neutral	4.25(71)	3.12(42)	2.58(33)	—
1 Week	Specific	3.75(54)	3.58(54)	2.88(33)	—
	Neutral	4.12(67)	3.75(58)	2.46(25)	—
1 Month	Specific	—	4.19(69)	[3.33(46)]	1.50(04)
	Neutral	4.12(67)	3.90(65)	3.04(38)	—

[a]Percent yes scores are in parentheses.
[b]For the identical and paraphrase tests, sentence format refers to the format of the sentence to be tested as it appeared in the passage. For the thematic and nonthematic tests, it refers to the format the sentence would have had if it had been in the text.

we tested only specific sentences in the thematic condition at 1 month. Because these data are not exactly comparable to the others in terms of counterbalancing, they are bracketed. Because of the two missing cells in the table, the best way to perceive the pattern of results is to look at the means (in boldface). These are also plotted in Fig. 4.

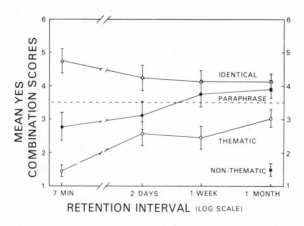

RETENTION INTERVAL (LOG SCALE)

Fig. 4. Mean yes-confidence scores for sentences in Experiment 1. (A maximum score of 6 represents a high-confidence, yes response.)

Analysis of variance on the data shown in Fig. 4 yielded a significant test X interval interaction, F $(6,336)$ = 2.31, MS_e = 3.20, $p <$ .05. (The single point for the nonthematic condition was omitted from this analysis and will be analyzed below.) Using planned comparisons with the .05 level of significance, we find the identical and paraphrase conditions significantly different at the two shorter intervals, but not at the two longer ones. The thematic condition is significantly less than paraphrase only at the 7-min interval, but it is significantly below condition identical at all four intervals. Both main effects were also significant in the analysis of variance in ways that can be inferred from the figure. A special analysis of variance was performed on the six cells at the 1-month interval (bottom of Table II). Planned comparisons showed that the nonthematic condition (1.50) was significantly lower than both of the thematic condition means (3.33 and 3.04). In general, the statistical analyses confirm what is apparent in the figure.

3. Discussion

If we were to look only at the identical function shown in Fig. 4, we might be tempted to conclude that subjects are slow to forget a sentence over a 1-month interval. An encoding interpretation of the data, however, suggests otherwise. We cannot make meaningful statements about memory for the sentence. Sentential information is represented in memory by a variety of memory codes that are more or less durable. The pattern of false-positive errors shows systematic changes in the retrievability of specific vs. general memory codes across time. An encoding interpretation of the identical function in light of the other data suggests that recognition test decisions are made on the basis of different information at different intervals. Subjects recognize a sentence by matching it against the codes available to them at the time of the test. If low-level codes are forgotten, there is a tendency to respond yes on the basis of high-level codes.

The data confirm Bartlett's conception of remembering in two important respects. First, thematic effects increase with the passage of time. As lower codes are forgotten, recognition decisions are increasingly based on semantic and thematic information. Second, the pattern of results shows constructive remembering. When subjects have forgotten the exact wording of a sentence, they do not take a random guess at the yes—no answer. Rather, they seem to piece together a response on the basis of whatever information they have available. In real life, a recognition based on very abstract codes will usually be good enough.

B. EXPERIMENT 2

Experiment 1 showed constructive test performance which was precipitated by a loss of lower level memory codes. In this experiment, we take a closer look at the memory codes available at a given retention interval by minimizing constructive activity on the test. Subjects are given a forced choice between two sentences. The tests can be made to vary in difficulty according to the specificity of the memory code needed for a correct discrimination. If a low-level code is needed for a correct response, subjects should perform better than chance only at short intervals. Discriminations on the basis of a high-level code should be possible at long intervals.

In conceptual terms, Experiment 2 is a replication of Experiment 1. We have, however, introduced a great number of methodological changes, including the forced-choice recognition test mentioned above. We have also used a new set of experimental passages, biographical paragraphs about American presidents (N. H. Anderson, Sawyers, & Farkas, 1972). The most significant change, however, has been the use of longer retention intervals: 1 week, 1 month, 2 months, 8 months. These should allow us to observe forgetting functions for high-level memory codes. We have chosen four different levels of encoding for the forced-choice test: sentence format, sentence gist, paragraph theme, and main character. We expect that performance on each of these discriminations will asymptote at chance in the order given above.

1. Method

The subjects at input were 861 students of general psychology. Of these, 744 were tested at one of the retention intervals. Return rates were as follows: 1 week, 97%; 1 month, 91%; 2 months, 88%; 8 months, 69%. Possible subject selection effects across intervals will be analyzed at the end of the Results section.

The input materials for any one subject consisted of two president paragraphs from N. H. Anderson et al. (1972). Both were about the same president, either Thomas Jefferson or Theodore Roosevelt. All paragraphs were selected from Anderson et al.'s A list, those which describe the president in highly favorable terms. Three such paragraphs were chosen for each president, with each subject reading two of the three. Within each paragraph a target sentence was designated for the later test. The sentence had to be a topic sentence in the sense that it clearly referred to the theme of the passage, but it could not be the first sentence of the passage because of the necessity of omitting it during input for half of the paragraphs. Fortunately, there were such redundant sentences in the materials to be used. The target sentence was always omitted during input for one of the input paragraphs. We also wrote an alternate version of each target sentence, so that subjects always read either Anderson *et al.*'s version or our own in one of the paragraphs. An example of the input materials for a typical student is shown below:

> After Thomas Jefferson left the presidency, he set out to accomplish one of the great ambitions of his life, that of setting up a university in his home state of Virginia. After this university was built, Jefferson served as the first rector. Jefferson's achievement was a great asset to the state of Virginia. It also served as a blueprint for the state universities which are so important in our educational system today.
>
> Thomas Jefferson was one of the most versatile men ever to ascend to the presidency, an acknowledged scholar, inventor, lawyer, and naturalist. Nicknamed "The Sage of Monticello," he had interests that ran the gamut from literature to astronomy to agriculture. While an ambassador abroad, Jefferson sent home many seeds and plants along with carefully gathered information on new farming methods which might improve U.S. agriculture. Jefferson's inventions were varied also, from an invention of the swivel chair to the design of a plow which won an international prize. *Jefferson refused to patent any of his inventions, desiring to make these items useful to the people of the country without restrictions.* (From Anderson, Sawyers, & Farkas, 1972, p. 181. Copyright 1972 by the Psychonomic Society. Reprinted by permission.)

To understand the types of test conditions used, it is useful to consider what each subject did *not* read during input. Referring to the materials shown above, the target sentence which we have italicized in the second paragraph is the correct alternative on each of four possible forced-choice recognition tests. The incorrect alternative is always a target sentence *not* read by the subject: (*a*) Sentence format. An alternative version of the target sentence, such as, *Jefferson never took out a patent on any of his creations because he wanted them to be freely available to all U.S. citizens.* A correct discrimination in this condition requires memory for some of the exact surface features of the sentence. (*b*) Sentence gist. The target sentence that was omitted from the first paragraph, namely, *Jefferson had always been vitally interested in education and he made extensive studies of several European university systems to draw the best features from each.* A correct discrimination here requires some memory for sentence gist apart from paragraph theme. Both alternative sentences are thematic with respect to the two paragraphs read by the subject. (c) Paragraph theme. A target sentence from a paragraph not read by this particular subject. A third paragraph about Jefferson and his views on slavery was in fact read by other subjects and had this target sentence: *After becoming President, Jefferson fulfilled one of his aims by bringing about a law which strictly prohibited any future slave trade in our country.* Subjects can perform correctly on this test if they remember the themes of the two paragraphs which they read. (d) Main character. A target sentence about the other president, Theodore Roosevelt: *Roosevelt took many measures to halt the destruction of the country's wilderness areas.* All the subject has to remember is which president was presented at input.

These four tests form a hierarchy in terms of abstractness. The most general concept for a subject is the main character. The information in both paragraphs is subsumed under this topic. Each paragraph, in turn, has its own theme. We were careful to select six distinctly different paragraph themes. Under each theme is a series of sentence meanings, which in turn are superordinate to certain surface aspects of the text. This hierarchy was intuitively devised for the particular input conditions of this experiment. We do not believe, for example, that "main character" will always be the highest or most abstract concept in a set of materials. What is most abstract will depend on the conditions of encoding.

The experimental design had three between-subject factors of interest: (a) four retention intervals; (b) four types of forced-choice test; (c) two different presidents. As actually run, however, there were only 24 of the 32 possible cells. We did not run the main character test at the two shorter intervals, nor the sentence format test at the two longer intervals. In addition to these factors, there were a number of counterbalancing factors that were not considered in any analysis: which of three paragraphs was omitted, which of two target sentences was omitted, which of two formats for the target sentence was read, two orders for the input paragraphs, and two orders of the test alternatives. With respect to all factors, each subject served in a unique experimental condition, though not all of the 1,152 possibilities were run.

Subjects were run in large groups in lecture halls. They were told to read the two paragraphs once in their normal manner and that "We are interested in reading and comprehension—not memorization." After everyone had finished reading the material, the subjects were told that the comprehension test would be given at a later date. They reached into an envelope and pulled out a reminder slip giving the date for their particular test. Tests for the first three intervals were all run in the same classroom during the fall quarter of 1975. The 8-month group was tested in a small laboratory room in May of 1976. All subjects were mailed a reminder a few days before the scheduled test. Those who did not show up were telephoned relentlessly and could be tested up to a week later than the scheduled date. Test instructions were written so that all subjects could be tested in a self-paced manner. Basically, subjects were told that one of the two sentences on the test actually occurred in the material which they had read. They were forced to choose one or the other and then to indicate confidence as low, medium, or high.

2.   Results

The recognition tests were scored for correctness and confidence, yielding a combination score with a range of 1–6. A score of 6 represented a high-confidence correct response, while 1 reflected a high-confidence error. The mean combination score for each level of test for the four intervals is shown in Fig. 5. Table III gives these mean plus percent correct in parentheses. Because of the incomplete design, we ran three overlapping analyses of variance for various subsets of the data. The primary analysis was done on the sentence gist and paragraph theme conditions across all four intervals. Two additional analyses were done for the test conditions that were run at

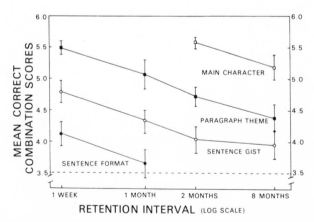

Fig. 5. Mean correct-confidence scores for the forced-choice test in Experiment 2. (A maximum score of 6 represents a high confidence, correct response.)

TABLE III

MEAN CORRECT-CONFIDENCE COMBINATION SCORES FOR EXPERIMENT 2

Test type	Interval[a]			
	1 Week	1 Month	2 Months	8 Months
Main character	—	—	5.57(95)	5.18(92)
Paragraph theme	5.49(94)	5.07(87)	4.71(87)	4.38(76)
Sentence gist	4.79(82)	4.34(72	4.03(64)	3.95(65)
Sentence format	4.12(65)	3.65(54)	—	—

[a]Percent correct scores are in parentheses.

only two intervals. In the second analysis we compared sentence format to sentence gist at 1 week and 1 month. The third analysis compared main character to paragraph theme at 2 months and 8 months. Our description of the results represents a generalization across these three analyses.

As predicted, the higher the memory code required for a correct discrimination, the better the overall performance. The main effects of type of test were clearly significant in all three analyses. It is also clear that there is consistent forgetting with the passage of time. The retention functions decrease monotonically for all four test conditions, though the sentence gist function does appear to be asymptoting above the chance level. As is evident from the graph, type of test and interval do not interact significantly. The various retention functions start out at different levels, but the rate of forgetting appears to be about the same for each of the memory tests at the four different levels. In addition, it is of interest to note the points in the retention interval where performance is still significantly above chance for a particular memory code. Simple t tests against the chance standard of 3.5 showed that sentence format was remembered better than chance at 1 week but not at 1 month. Sentence gist, paragraph theme, and main character are still remembered significantly better than chance at the 8-month interval. These results were confirmed when proportion correct was tested against .5 in χ^2 tests as well. Only one point on the graph, therefore, seems to reflect the total loss of the memory code measured: sentence format at 1 month.

The two different presidents read at input yielded results that were different in some respects. There was a main effect, reflecting the fact that Jefferson material was remembered better than Roosevelt (4.78 vs. 4.43). There was also one significant interaction involving the president variable, that of president x test type. For the four levels of memory code there are quantitative differences between the Jefferson and Roosevelt materials, probably reflecting the fact that Jefferson is better known. For both presidents, however, the test condition data order themselves as predicted.

Because we were only able to test 69% of the subjects at the 8-month interval, it is possible that our results could be compromised by subject selection effects. We attempted to assess this factor in two ways. First of all, we assumed that some of our no-shows at 8 months had dropped out of school. We corrected for this bias by removing the data at all intervals for all students who were not enrolled in the spring. But this did not affect the pattern of results. Second, we looked at course grades for General Psychology and found no differences which suggested that our sample of 8-month subjects was any more or less intelligent or conscientious than the others. We can not rule out the possibility of subject selection biases in our data, but we doubt that they could be of very large magnitude.

3. Discussion

The results provide clear support for a levels of encoding interpretation of prose retention. Abstract, general ideas are remembered better than more specific information at every retention interval. Another way of describing the data is to say that high-level codes are retained longer than low-level codes. The four levels of test which we administered do not, of course, exhaust the memory codes available to subjects after the comprehension of a prose passage. They do illustrate, however, the multilevel nature of prose retention. A Bartlettian interpretation of the data would go as follows: When subjects are asked to recall after a fairly long interval they must construct a response from the codes available. If they adopt a loose criterion for recall, they will reconstruct a passage that is correct in its general ideas but distorted in its details. A strict criterion, on the other hand, will lead to the construction of a substantially correct abstract that is brief and devoid of detail. Because Fig. 5 shows data from a forced-choice test, we have an estimate of the availability of memory codes without the normal constructive retrieval processes.

We did not expect the forgetting functions in this experiment to be substantially parallel, as they are in Fig. 5. We would have predicted that the rate of forgetting would be steeper for lower level codes. Taken at face value, the results would imply that differences in the memorability of various codes are entirely due to the comprehension process. Events during the interval have no differential effect. If a recall experiment should show different rates of forgetting for different memory codes, we would have to attribute the effect to constructive retrieval processes. While this explanation is somewhat plausible, we are not prepared to endorse it unequivocally. A number of factors suggest caution. First, we do not know how subjects use multiple codes in making a recognition decision. We doubt, for example, that they make a paragraph theme discrimination solely on the basis of theme. Retention of lower codes, such as sentence gist, format, etc., would also help in the decision. But we also doubt that all codes which are available are combined in an optimal fashion. In short, we do not believe that we have a pure measure for each code, so it is risky to speculate about the exact shape of the retention functions. Second, we would expect that interval effects would be minimal when subjects have isolated the experimental material from their general knowledge. Our experiment may have induced an artificial accuracy set which affected the shape of the curves. Third, our subjects read two short paragraphs that were easy to comprehend. Perhaps a greater memory load would have been necessary in order to obtain an interaction with the retention interval. Factors such as these, and many others, have to be thoroughly investigated before we can draw any general conclusions about the rate of forgetting for various memory codes (see Christiaansen, 1977).

C. EXPERIMENT 3

The first two experiments support the levels of encoding interpretation of prose retention. The data show the relevance of the levels-of-processing framework for the interpretation of connected discourse experiments. As such, our results are consistent with the prose work of Bower (1976), Kintsch (1976), Meyer (1975), Rumelhart (1977), and Thorndyke (1975). Each has demonstrated that higher level concepts are remembered better than lower level ones. Our data provide a replication of their experiments with a recognition memory technique and extend their conclusions in two important ways. First of all, we have shown code-specific forgetting with the passage of time. While others have shown similar effects for short intervals, the very long intervals employed in the present experiment have permitted a realistic test of differences among very general abstract memory codes. Second, our results support a constructive view of memory. Experiment 1 showed that subjects have a tendency to respond positively to sentence foils based on only vague, partial information. In Experiment 2, we provided a constructive interpretation for levels-of-encoding data.

While we believe that it is useful to view prose as being structured like a hierarchy, we wish to underscore the *as if* aspect of research strategies that emphasize prose structure. While there does appear to be something psychologically real about the levels of encoding idea, there is no support for the radical position that memory for prose is determined by its linguistic structure. In this section we describe an experiment that is meant to show the flexibility and variety of encoding processes in memory for prose. The aim is to illustrate limitations of a formal, hierarchical model of prose structure and to stimulate research on coding processes and context.

In Experiment 2, our highest memory code was "president." It was the most abstract in that it was the only discernible concept which applied to all of the material which the subject had read. In the present study we attempt to show that context affects the memorability of the president code. Subjects read a paragraph about a particular president in one of two different contexts. If there are seven other paragraphs about the same president, then remembering the president should be easy. But if the seven other paragraphs are about seven different presidents, a forced-choice president discrimination will be more difficult. In short, the same recognition test for the same sentence from the same paragraph will vary in difficulty according to the context of encoding.

In this experiment we also study an encoding variable that was not investigated in Experiment 2. We use president paragraphs that are either favorable or unfavorable to the president. If we present eight paragraphs that are very positive (or very negative) about a president, we expect favorableness to be a high-level encoding dimension for memory. Eight paragraphs of mixed favorableness, however, should make a recognition discrimination on the basis of favorableness more difficult. Favorableness was chosen for investigation for two reasons. First, affective variables seem to be important in human memory. Second, favorability is not easily categorized in logicolinguistic terms.

In this experiment, therefore, subjects read eight president paragraphs. The set of materials are either homogeneous with respect to president (one president), or mixed (eight different presidents). The favorableness dimension of the paragraphs is also manipulated in a similar manner. The homogeneous favorability paragraphs are all either entirely favorable or entirely unfavorable. The mixed favorability paragraphs consist of eight paragraphs with different levels of favorability. After a 6-week interval, subjects are given a forced-choice recognition test that requires either a president or a favorability discrimination. We expect that mixing the presidents at input will selectively lead to poorer performance on the president discrimination. Likewise, mixing the favorability dimension should lead to poorer performance on the favorability discrimination.

1. Method

There are 440 subjects who read the input materials. A total of 397 took the test, for a return rate of 90%.

Among the eight paragraphs read by a particular subject, the sixth was a target paragraph for the later test. It was about either James Monroe or William Howard Taft and was either very favorable or very unfavorable. The first sentence of each of these paragraphs was the target sentence for the test. All subjects read only one of these four possible target paragraphs. The foil for the forced-choice recognition test was taken from among the three target sentences that were not read at input. For the president test, it was the one about the alternate president with favorableness held constant. For the favorability test, it was the sentence at the other extreme of favorability for the same president. Context was manipulated by changing the seven filler paragraphs appropriately. The favorability ratings were provided by N. H. Anderson *et al.* (1972). Across the two context manipulations, target paragraph and test sentences were identical for each of four replications of the design.

The basic design was a 2 X 2 X 2 factorial with 44–53 subjects per cell. President was either homogeneous or mixed, as was favorability. Type of test was either a president or favorability discrimination. In addition, the following control variables were also included: The target paragraph at input was either favorable or unfavorable; the president in the target paragraph was either Monroe or Taft; on the recognition test, the correct alternative was in the first or second position equally often.

Subjects were run in large groups in a lecture hall for both input and test. They read the eight paragraphs once at a self-paced rate. After all subjects had returned the passage booklets to an envelope, they were informed that the "comprehension test" would be given in 6 weeks at the same day of the week, time, and place. A reminder letter was mailed out a few days in advance of the test date and an announcement was made in the General Psychology classes. Subjects who failed to show up for the test were contacted via announcement in class and allowed to take the test up to 1 week late. The test sheet was similar to that used in Experiment 2. Subjects were told to select the sentence which they had actually read 6 weeks earlier and rated their confidence on a 3-point scale.

2. Results

Correct-confidence combination scores ranging from 1 to 6 were computed as before and the means are summarized in Table IV. Percent correct are shown in parentheses. We were predicting a three-way interaction, that of type of test X favorability context X president context, but the interaction fell short of statistical significance. We therefore analyzed the two types of test separately to clarify the pattern of results that were obtained. Considering only the president test, where the subject had to choose between a Monroe sentence or a Taft sentence, where only one of these presidents had appeared in the input materials, the results are just as expected. Performance is better when all eight passages were about the same president, than when eight different presidents were mixed together (5.21 vs. 4.20), $F(1,166) = 29.76$; $MS_e = 1.66$; $p < .001$. Mixing the favorability of the material had no significant effect on the president discrimination. Nor was the interaction of the two context manipulations significant. We have shown here that perfor-

TABLE IV

MEAN CORRECT-CONFIDENCE COMBINATION
SCORES FOR EXPERIMENT 3[a]

| | President test | |
| | Favorability context | |
President context	Homogeneous	Mixed
Homogeneous	5.26(90)	5.16(91)
Mixed	4.29(75)	4.11(70)

| | Favorability test | |
| | Favorability context | |
President context	Homogeneous	Mixed
Homogeneous	4.97(89)	4.27(74)
Mixed	4.12(69)	4.21(72)

[a]Percent correct scores are in parentheses.

mance on the exact same paragraph on the exact same test is affected by the context in which the paragraph had been embedded.

With the favorability test, where the subject had to discriminate between a favorable vs. unfavorable sentence, we had hoped to reverse the effects described above. Mixing the favorability of the context had only a small and inconsistent effect, however. The effect for homogeneous vs. mixed favorability (4.55 vs. 4.24) was not quite significant, $F (1,166) = 2.68$; $MS_e = 1.70$; $p < .10$. But the effect of homogeneous vs. mixed president (4.62 vs. 4.17) was significant, $F (1,166) = 5.86$; $MS_e = 1.70$; $p < .05$, as was the interaction of the two types of context as seen in the bottom half of Table IV, $F (1,166) = 4.41$; $MS_e = 1.70$; $p < .05$. Only in the case of homogeneous president at input did the favorability context have the predicted effect.

3. Discussion

Our manipulation of context had the predicted effects on memory for the president. When a particular president was the common denominator for eight paragraphs, a sentence about him was easy to discriminate from one about another president. But the same test was more difficult when there was a variety of presidents presented at input. While there are a number of alternative explanations for such data, we interpret them as showing the effect of context in determining what will be a high-level memory code. A prose passage will be encoded for memory according to the structure of the situation in which it occurs. Meyer (1975) has shown a similar effect of passage context on the recall of a target paragraph.

Our enthusiasm for a contextualist interpretation, however, must be qualified by the data from the favorability manipulation and test. We had expected to show that this memory code was higher than the president code in one situation, but lower in another. Instead, it appears as though the president manipulation induced much stronger coding changes in memory. This could be due to our particular manner of manipulating the relative strengths of the two variables. Or it could be something intrinsic to the two different memory codes themselves. There is some suggestion in our data that the favorability code is dependent upon the president code. In other words, favorability is remembered as an attribute of a particular president. There may in fact be some sort of hierarchical relationship between a person variable such as president and an attribute such as favorableness.

V. General Discussion

A. BARTLETT'S THEORY REVISITED

Our experiments replicate Bartlett's best-known finding, that memory for prose becomes increasingly thematic with the passage of time. After a long interval details are forgotten, but general ideas persist. Our Experiment 1, in particular, supports Bartlett's conception of constructive memory. Subjects tended to falsely recognize sentences that were compatible with the memory codes available to them at the time of the test. While the other experiments did not deal with constructive retrieval, our emphasis on coding processes is compatible with Bartlett's concern for the effects of preexperimental knowledge on memory.

Our research suggests a modification of one form of schema theory. It is a mistake to think of a prose passage as represented in memory by a single abstract code, the schema. Rather, there appear to be multiple ways of encoding a prose passage and these codes vary in their abstractness. During the retention interval, lower codes are lost first and recall is achieved by a process of reconstruction from the available codes. From this point of view, the schema does not become more stereotyped with the passage of time. Rather, recall performance becomes more stereotyped because of the loss of lower level codes. Such observations do not seem to be radically different from Bartlett's theory.

In more general terms, we have also attempted to approach the study of memory from a Bartlettian perspective. He stressed the variety of memory codes involved in remembering and the complexities of the constructive retrieval process. He made sure that his data and theory were relevant for real-world remembering. It is possible of course to take an opposing position and to argue that a well-defined theory directed at one small aspect of the memory problem will lead to greater long-range payoffs. It is our view that such an approach has been tried in the recent history of memory research, with disastrous consequences. Too much of the data base for memory theorists consists of observations of a very unusual aspect of human memory, namely the rote recall of unconnected verbal items. It would seem to us that the first priority for the study of memory should be an expansion of the scope of memory experiments, with an eye to observing remembering under realistic conditions. Like Bartlett, we would caution against premature attempts to either fit memory into a highly formalized structure or to restrict the range of phenomena studied.

B. LEVELS OF ENCODING

We have attempted to relate Bartlett's ideas on remembering to the levels-of-processing framework (Craik & Lockhart, 1972). The two viewpoints emphasize the relationship between perceptual processing and remembering. Both emphasize the role of preexperimental knowledge in remembering. As levels theorists move toward a greater interest in retrieval processes, we see the possibility of a unified approach to memory research. Surely, we have not reached that point as yet. But neo-Bartlettians and modern verbal learners are both talking about memory with a common language, the language of encoding and retrieval processes.

The levels-of-processing framework provides a rationale for explaining memorability in terms of amount of perceptual processing. But when it comes to memory differences within the semantic domain, the hierarchy of memory codes gives way to flexible coding processes that are sensitive to contextual factors. We like this aspect of the levels view, but feel that it needs to be extended to account for prose retention. We have postulated that abstract memory codes are remembered better than specific ones. We share this view with most prose researchers. We do not know why abstract codes are remembered better, but could speculate about some possibilities. Perhaps abstract codes are comprehended better during input because there are less of them for any one passage. It is the nature of a hierarchy that there are more entries at the bottom than at the top. The amount of processing per concept may possibly be predictive of later recall. In a similar vein, we could postulate that abstract codes receive more presentations during input; that is, they are effectively presented to the subject more frequently because they are represented by a number of different lower concepts. A most interesting possibility to us is that abstract codes may be easier to retrieve. Our research does not address this issue in any meaningful way, but clearly such research is needed. We know little about the abstractness of retrieval cues and their effectiveness with various types of memory codes.

C. SPECULATIONS ON CONSTRUCTIVE MEMORY

It is our observation that humans yearn to have a perfect rote memory. Memory books based on mnemonic tricks seem to be selling well, and it is quite common to confer genius status on anyone who has an unusual memory for detail. These yearnings have found a responsive chord among most researchers on human memory who seem to take it as their goal to understand the process of verbatim recall. Educators, as well, have often been justly accused of teaching and testing rote memory, when the learning of ideas is viewed by everyone as the proper goal of education. Those of us who do research on memory have to spend endless hours at cocktail parties fending off otherwise educated people who want to improve their rote memories.

The collective anxiety about rote memory seems to us to come from a focusing on the things that we forget. We *do* forget a lot of details from time to time, often under circumstances that cause some inconvenience. But such instances are quite minor when compared to what we remember. Human memory is exquisitely suited for remembering most of the important information that we need to know to get on in the world. Each of us remembers our mother's name, how to tie a shoe, where we live, what our friends look like, as well as innumerable mathematical concepts, rules of language, standards of moral behavior, etc. What we remember is enormous. And even more remarkably, most of what we remember has been learned effortlessly and naturally. Our memories seem built for giving high priority to memory codes which have wide generality and importance. We seem to put stress on memory information that will allow us to be approximately correct most of the time, though rarely exactly perfect in terms of rote retention. It may be that the coding potential of the human brain has a limited capacity and that by giving abstract codes highest priority we are making very efficient use of our coding capacity.

Any conception of memory that discusses memory codes has to postulate some kind of constructive retrieval process. We do not recall and recognize memory codes. Our memory performance always represents a transformation between underlying codes and the information called for by the memory task. If we conceive of human memory as consisting of numerous abstract interconnected memory codes, then the distance between code and recall can be considerable, requiring very complex constructive activity. Examples of reconstructive errors are abundant in the research of Bartlett, our own research, and that of many others.

A major problem for such a constructive view of remembering is that rote memory seems to be common. Are there two types of memory processes, reproductive and reconstructive? We prefer to characterize all memory processes as constructive. At short retention intervals recall might appear to be rote. But in such a situation there are multiple codes available which make constructive retrieval very accurate. Retention also appears to be rote when we are dealing with the recall of highly overlearned material. Another way of describing this is to consider such rote recall as the product of a highly practiced skill. With practice, skills that once had to be consciously constructed in a very effortful manner become automated (Bartlett, 1958). From this perspective, rote recall is the result of a complex, overlearned constructive process that proceeds without effort or conscious awareness. Before we can hope to understand the automated retrieval of overlearned information (e.g., rote memory for word lists) we will have to learn a great deal more about simpler and more obvious constructive processes (e.g., memory for prose over long intervals).

REFERENCES

Anderson, N. H., Sawyers, B. K., & Farkas, A. J. President paragraphs. *Behavior Research Methodology and Instrumentation,* 1972, 4, 177–192.

Anderson, R. C., & Ortony, A. On putting apples into bottles—A problem of polysemy. *Cognitive Psychology,* 1975, 7, 167–180.

Atkinson, R. C., & Shiffrin, R. M. Human memory: A proposed system and its control processes. In K. W. Spence & J. T. Spence (Eds.), *The psychology of learning and motivation* (Vol. 2). New York: Academic Press, 1968.

Barclay, J. R., Bransford, J. D., Franks, J. J., McCarrell, N. S., & Nitsch, K. Comprehension and semantic flexibility. *Journal of Verbal Learning and Verbal Behavior,* 1974, 13, 471–481.

Bartlett, F. C. *Remembering,* Cambridge, Eng.: University Press, 1932.

Bartlett, F. C. *Thinking: An experimental and social study.* New York: Basic Books, 1958.

Bower, G. H. A multicomponent theory of the memory trace. In K. W. Spence & J. T. Spence (Eds.) *The psychology of learning and motivation* (Vol. 1). New York: Academic Press, 1967.

Bower, G. H. How people understand and remember stories. Paper read at the meeting of the American Psychological Association, Washington, D.C., September, 1976.

Bransford, J. D., Barclay, J. R., & Franks, J. J. Sentence memory: A constructive versus interpretive approach. *Cognitive Psychology,* 1972, 3, 193–209.

Bransford, J. D., & McCarrell, N. S. A sketch of a cognitive approach to comprehension: Some thoughts about understanding what it means to comprehend. In W. B. Weimer & D. S. Palermo (Eds.), *Cognition and the symbolic processes.* Hillsdale, N.J.: Lawrence Erlbaum Associates, 1974.

Broadbent, D. E. Frederick Charles Bartlett: 1886–1969. *Biographical Memoirs of Fellows of the Royal Society,* 1970, 16, 1–13.

Brockway, J., Chmielewski, D., & Cofer, C. N. Remembering prose: Productivity and accuracy constraints in recognition memory. *Journal of Verbal Learning and Verbal Behavior,* 1974, 13, 194–208.

Christiaansen, R. E. *Rate of forgetting of memory codes in retention of prose.* Unpublished doctoral dissertation, Kent State University, 1977.

Christiaansen, R. E., Dooling, D. J., & Keenan, T. F. *Prose retention: Levels of encoding and recognition test effects.* Unpublished manuscript, Kent State University, 1976.

Cofer, C. N. Constructive processes in memory. *American Scientist,* 1973, **61**, 537–543.
Cofer, C. N. On the constructive theory of memory. In F. Weizman & I. C. Uzgiris (Eds.), *The structuring of experience.* New York: Plenum, 1977.
Craik, F. I. M., & Lockhart, R. S. Levels of processing: A framework for memory research. *Journal of Verbal Learning and Verbal Behavior,* 1972, **11**, 671–684.
Dooling, D. J., & Christiaansen, R. E. Episodic and semantic aspects of memory for prose. *Journal of Experimental Psychology: Human Learning and Memory,* 1977, in press.
Dooling, D. J., & Lachman, R. Effects of comprehension on retention of prose. *Journal of Experimental Psychology,* 1971, **88**, 216–222.
Dooling, D. J., & Mullet, R. L. Locus of thematic effects in retention of prose. *Journal of Experimental Psychology,* 1973, **97**, 404–406.
Ebbinghaus, H. *Memory: A contribution to experimental psychology* (H. A. Ruger & C. E. Bussenius, trans.). New York: Dover, 1964. (Originally published, 1885.)
Gauld, A., & Stephenson, G. M. Some experiments relating to Bartlett's theory of remembering. *British Journal of Psychology,* 1967, **58**, 39–49.
Gomulicki, B. R. Recall as an abstractive process. *Acta Psychologica,* 1956, **12**, 77–94.
Grimes, J. E. *The thread of discourse.* The Hague: Mouton, 1974.
Jenkins, J. J. Remember that old theory of memory? Well, forget it! *American Psychologist,* 1974, **29**, 785–795.
Kintsch, W., Memory for prose. In C. N. Cofer (Ed.), *The structure of human memory.* San Francisco: Freeman, 1976.
Lockhart, R. S., Craik, F. I. M., & Jacoby, L. L. Depth of processing in recognition and recall: Some aspects of a general memory system. In J. Brown (Ed.), *Recognition and recall.* New York: Wiley, 1975.
Loftus, E. F. Leading questions and the eyewitness report. *Cognitive Psychology,* 1975, **7**, 560–572.
Loftus, E. F., & Zanni, G. Eyewitness testimony: The influence of the wording of a question. *Bulletin of the Psychonomic Society,* 1975, **5**, 86–88.
Meyer, B. J. F. *The organization of prose and its effects on recall.* Amsterdam: North-Holland Publ., 1975.
Moscovitch, M., & Craik, F. I. M. Depth of processing, retrieval cues, and uniquences of encoding as factors in recall. *Journal of Verbal Learning and Verbal Behavior,* 1976, **15**, 447–458.
Murdock, B. B. *Human memory: Theory and data.* Hillsdale, N.J.: Lawrence Erlbaum Associates, 1974.
Neisser, U. *Cognitive psychology.* New York: Appleton, 1967.
Pezdek, K. *Arguments for a constructive approach to memory* (Tech. Rep. 75-1), Amherst: University of Massachusetts, Cognitive Processes Laboratory, January 1975.
Posner, M. I. Abstraction and the process of recognition. In G. H. Bower & J. T. Spence (Eds.), *The psychology of learning and motivation* (Vol. 3). New York: Academic Press, 1969.
Rumelhart, D. E. Understanding and summarizing brief stories. In D. LaBerge & J. Samuels (Eds.), *Basic processes in reading: Perception and comprehension.* Hillsdale, N.J.: Lawrence Erlbaum Associates, 1977.
Spiro, R. J. Constructing a theory of reconstructive memory: The state of the schema approach. In R. C. Anderson, R. J. Spiro, & W. E. Montague (Eds.), *Schooling and the acquisition of knowledge.* Hillsdale, N.J.: Lawrence Erlbaum Associates, 1977.
Sulin, R. A., & Dooling, D. J. Intrusion of a thematic idea in retention of prose. *Journal of Experimental Psychology,* 1974, **103**, 255–262.

Sutherland, N. S. Object recognition. In E. C. Carterette & M. P. Friedman (Eds.), *Handbook of perception* (Vol. 3). *Biology of perception systems.* New York: Academic Press, 1973.

Thorndyke, P. W. *Cognitive structures in human story comprehension and memory* (Tech. Rep. p-5513). Santa Monica, Calif.: Rand Corporation, 1975.

Tulving, E., & Thomson, D. M. Encoding specificity and retrieval processes in episodic memory. *Psychological Review,* 1973, **80**, 352–373.

Underwood, B. J. Are we overloading memory? In A. W. Melton & E. Martin (Eds.), *Coding processes in human memory.* Washington, D.C.: Winston, 1972.

van Dijk, T. A. *Text and context.* London: Longmans, 1976.

Wickens, D. D. Characteristics of word encoding. In A. W. Melton & E. Martin (Eds.), *Coding processes in human memory.* Washington, D.C.: Winston, 1972.

Winograd, T. *A framework for understanding AI approaches to discourse.* Paper presented at the Twelfth Annual Carnegie Symposium on Cognition, Pittsburgh, May 1976.

Zangwill, O. L. Remembering revisited. *Quarterly Journal of Experimental Psychology,* 1972, **24**, 123–138.

MIND YOUR *p's* AND *q's*:
THE ROLE OF CONTENT AND CONTEXT
IN SOME USES OF *AND, OR,* AND *IF*[1]

Samuel Fillenbaum

UNIVERSITY OF NORTH CAROLINA, CHAPEL HILL, NORTH CAROLINA

The most important general lesson to be learnt . . . is that simple deductive relationships are not the only kind we have to consider if we wish to understand the logical workings of language. We have to think in many more

[1] This chapter was written while the author was supported by an NIMH Special Fellowship at the Institute of Human Learning, University of California, Berkeley. The research was supported in part by USPHS Grant MH-10006 from NIMH. For permission to include copyrighted materials from an earlier paper (Fillenbaum, 1976), the author is indebted to Springer-Verlag.

dimensions that than of entailment and contradiction, and use many tools of
analysis besides those that belong to formal logic . . . instead of restricting our
attention to the statement-making uses of language we must consider also
some of the many other uses it may have . . . and try to discover the answers
to questions of such form as "What are the conditions under which we use
such-and-such an expression or class of expressions?" [Strawson, 1952, pp.
231–232].

I. Introduction

Why study words like AND, OR, and IF, rather than such words as
HIPPOPOTAMUS, DESK, or CHEESE? In large part because of the
ubiquity and indispensability of the former sorts of terms. The
sentential connectives come from a small closed class, such that the
deletion or addition of any member significantly affects the re-
sources of the language in a way not true if some item is added to or
deleted from large open classes (Harman, 1975). The sentence operators serve a crucial role in language in that they allow the construction of complex propositions out of simpler ones and specify
the nature of the conceptual relations that obtain between these
constituent propositions, thus controlling the sorts of inferences that
may be drawn from the resulting complex propositions. As Johnson-
Laird (1975) has stated: ". . . it may be said that reasoning with
propositions is simply a matter of grasping the meaning of those
lexical items that happen to be connectives [p. 23]." But if we are
concerned with propositional reasoning, perhaps the job at hand is
more properly one for the logician rather than the psychologist. The
reply is simply that the logician's principal concern is not with
reasoning in natural language, and that there is no ground to believe
that the calculi of interest to the logician will map in any direct way
into the natural logic of everyday language (for what is perhaps still
the best treatment of the relevant issues, see Strawson, 1952).[2]

One might argue that in important respects the work of psychologists addressed to the study of sentence connectives has been
misguided. Consider, for example, the work on conditionals. Psychologists have often written as though the formula *If p,q* always has

---

[2] Indeed only recently do we find any serious concern about how to formulate questions
of the relevance of the antecedent to the consequent in IF . . . THEN propositions (Anderson & Belnap, 1976). von Wright (1957), in a paper "On Conditionals," does appear to be
concerned with normal uses of IF . . . THEN forms, and uses as one of his illustrations the
threat to a child "If you do not obey, I'll punish you [p. 142]." He points out that this may
be understood as "a prediction of what my behavior will be" or "subjectively [as a]
declaration of intention," noting that the latter type of conditional is very important in

some single analysis regardless of the properties of the p and q connected and, granting that the operator as used in the vernacular may be different in sense or use from the specification of its namesake in logic, much of the controversy about the interpretation of IF has been as to whether it could be better represented by material equivalence or a biconditional than by material implication; whether one needed to assume some sort of "defective" truth table such that the negation of the antecedent made the whole proposition irrelevant, etc. Such an endeavor seems in part misguided, in at least two ways. First, it is misguided because it appears very unlikely that there is one and just one analysis that will capture the various things that can be and are done by use of the conditional. Essentially the present argument is similar to that of Wason and Johnson-Laird (1972), viz., that the conditional "is not a creature of constant hue, but chameleon - like, takes on the color of its surroundings; *its meaning is determined to some extent by the very propositions it connects* [p. 92]." Our only quarrel with this formulation is to question whether what is involved is different meanings or senses of the operator or rather some single sense or logical representation with different contextually conditioned uses. We shall have more to say on this later, here we need only comment that such a distinction between sense and use(s) has been almost universally neglected by psychologists. Second, the common view is misguided because it seems primarily if not exclusively concerned with providing a truth–functional account of the connectives, i.e., an account where the meaning of a connective is defined in terms of the function which relates the truth values of constituent propositions to the truth value of the complex proposition resulting when that connective joins them. But as Johnson-Laird (1975) points out, there is a divergence in role "between logical calculi and the inferential machinery of everyday life." While the former are devised "for deriving logical truths," practical inference seeks "to pass from one contingent statement to another." Stated more generally, one must be concerned with the uses of connectives in the service of communication, one must direct attention to what is being done and understood by the employment of an operator in a sentence in context, one must consider the illocutionary force of the particular speech act in

---

ethics and law. But he explicitly refrains from considering that sort of use in his paper, even though one might argue that this intentional use is indeed the principal use of such "impositive" statements. Something similar occurs in Travis (1975) when he offers an analysis for conditionals and expresses the hope that his analysis will have some bearing for an account of conditional promises and threats, without actually considering the problems these might pose for his analysis.

which the operator occurs. Given some assumptions about the
logic of conversation, this may license or even require inferences
that are not legitimate if one considers only the truth–functional
relations of logic, and may block others which would be acceptable solely on truth–functional grounds. Consider an example
of the latter point: given the truth of p, the formula p or q is necessarily true; but someone who knows p to be true but rather than
asserting p asserts p or q would ordinarily be accused of misleading.
Because the assertion of a disjunction suggests that the speaker
does not know which of the disjuncts holds, and because a speaker
is supposed to be as informative as he can be, the speaker is misleading us by saying p or q when he already knows which of the
disjuncts actually obtained. To cite another example of the inade-
quacies of any simple truth functional analysis: consider that (not p
and p or q) logically entails q. But any speaker who asserts that "The
next president won't be Ford, it will be Ford or Carter" is certainly
not asserting $simpliciter$ that the next president will be Carter, but
rather substituting the assertion of the disjunction (that the next
president will be Ford or Carter) for the simple assertion of the first
disjunct (that the next president will be Ford).[3] Thus to deny p
"cannot be the same thing as to assert that p is false," as Wilson
(1975) states; such examples obviously pose problems for any
semantic or pragmatic theory.[4] The argument, of course, is not that

[3] On the other hand, to say something like "The next president will be Ford or Carter, and
it won't be Ford" may readily represent the steps in an argument leading to the conclusion
that the next president will be Carter. Hence the order of propositions in context may be
very important.

[4] Or consider again the divergence (cited immediately above) between p as implying p or q
and the conversational fact that the assertion of some proposition in a sense denies the
assertion of the disjunction of that proposition with any other proposition. Thus someone
who says "John flew to New York" because he knows that this is what happened, could and
probably would readily deny the correctness of something like "John flew to New York or
drove to Washington," just because that assertion leaves open or throws into doubt
something that he knows in fact to be the case, viz. that John flew to New York. Grize and
Matalon (1962) report, after Gréco, a vignette where subjects are told that a cat ran through
a room with two persons in it, the first of whom says "Un chat a traversé la pièce" while the
second says "Un chat ou un rat a traversé la pièce." Asked which of the two speakers told
the truth a majority of the subjects said that the first person "avait 'plus raison,' "
presumably because the first statement was more informative. It is of course unfortunate, for
all sorts of reasons beyond simplicity, that a truth–functional account does not work for the
logic of everyday speech. If it did, and if the conditional could be represented by material
implication, then anyone denying the blasphemy "If God exists there is evil in the world"
would be asserting that "God exists and there is not evil in the world," thus "dismissing
atheism and pessimism at one fell swoop," as the philosopher C. L. Stevenson pointed out
somewhere.

a truth–functional account is simply wrong or irrelevant, but rather that in principle it is at least of itself insufficient, and that there will be major problems, as yet hardly capable of being phrased, in articulating such an account with the required pragmatically oriented analyses. For clearly what is said generally should not only be true, but should be informative and have some point, in context. We need to be concerned not just with the role of the sentence connectives in intrapersonal reasoning in the setting of a monologue, but with their communicative uses in the interpersonal setting of (at least) dialogues.

This chapter will not provide a review of the literature, nor, unfortunately, can it offer any sort of general conceptual account for the connectives. Rather it will attempt to set out some of the major problems and issues in the context of illustrative studies, and will exhibit our ignorance by indicating the large gap between what has been done and what needs doing. We shall be interested in saying something about various employments of AND, OR, and IF, and in seeing what sorts of problems such uses pose for any conceptual analysis of these terms. Because in large measure we are just at the beginning in such an enterprise, our general strategy will be to treat AND, OR, and IF as more or less on a par, and we will have little to say about the possibility that, in contrast to their namesakes of propositional logic which are strictly interdefinable, these terms may differ in important respects, as implied by Karttunen's (1973a) analysis of the presuppositions of complex sentences which suggests that AND and IF may be similar to each other and different from OR with regard to presupposition filtering, or the possibility that AND and OR sentences are understood differently than IF sentences under negation and interrogation (with these operations characteristically bearing only on the second clause or proposition in the latter case). (For some comments as to possible differences between IF and such connectives as AND and OR, see Harman, 1975.) We shall have to be concerned with reasoning in natural language, with ways of going beyond what is said explicitly, and with the assessment of "fallacies" in reasoning. We shall be interested in presenting some uses to which the various connectives may be put in studying some general problems of psycholinguistics. In the final section of this chapter we shall mention some problems for the future, e.g., with regard to the presuppositions of complex propositions involving the sentence connectives, with regard to the role of negation, etc. The yield or payoff of this work should be at least twofold. To the extent that terms such as AND, OR, and IF play a crucial role in everyday discourse, then anything that can be said about their functioning should be of significance and value in its own right. To the extent that such terms may be used as tools to provide means for the study of general problems of understanding and communication, such as questions of the interaction of preexisting knowledge of ways of the world with current message content, their instrumental role is important. Finally, insofar as such work reveals something of the role of contextual factors in conditioning understanding and use, and forces us to be concerned with the part played by general assumptions about communication or conversational principles in understanding and reasoning in natural language, it may perhaps also serve as something of a model for other work in psycholexicology, for it hardly seems likely that the connectives are unique in these respects.

II. Some Uses of the Sentence Operators

The first thing that needs to be done is to demonstrate that terms such as AND, OR, and IF do not each have some single use but rather that each has at least a number of important different uses, and that therefore any attempt to discover *the* canonical use of each of these terms is a chimaerical enterprise. The argument here will have an *a fortiori* structure. If we can exhibit important differences in use just for the cases exhibited here and if there are other significant cases not even touched on, then the case for diversity should be all the stronger. Thus we shall show that subjects respond in systematically different ways to propositions involving unordered and ordered uses of AND (what Lakoff, 1971, calls symmetric and asymmetric AND) without even touching on a variety of other uses (of the sort discussed, e.g., in Schmerling, 1975). Or with regard to the conditional we shall show that subjects respond in systematically different ways to IF as employed in contingent universal propositions, as against temporal–causal propositions, as against its use in inducements (conditional threats and promises), without even considering other uses such as its concessive use "If poor, he is honest" or its suspensive use "She is pretty, if not beautiful" (Horn, 1972), its rhetorical use "If he wins the nomination, I'll eat my hat" (Yamanashi, 1975), or its performative use in the qualification of illocutionary speech acts "If I can ask, what do you mean by that?" (Heringer, 1971). This last case warrants some further comment since Heringer has spelled out a number of ways in which the IF used in the qualification of illocutionary acts differs from other IF's. Thus in the former case, in contrast to most other cases, there is no topical or causal connection between the antecedent and consequent clauses of the conditional, the IF clause does not make the utterance contingent or hypothetical, there are special constraints on tense and mood, and on possible paraphrases. Thus, prima facie, there are grounds for suspecting that people may handle sentences that employ this sort of IF differently than sentences using other IF's.

We shall now present some evidence that indeed AND, OR, and IF may each be used in a number of ways, and that subjects are sensitive and responsive to such differences. To show this, of course, is only to show that there is a problem. What is then required is some analysis which provides a conceptual account, whether of different senses and the conditions that control these, or of some underlying single sense and of the conversational–communicative principles that interact with that sense to license the various uses and understandings actually encountered.

Before proceeding, it might be appropriate to comment on an important and ill-understood precondition on most uses of all the sentence operators of everyday language, namely, the constraint of common topic (Lakoff, 1971; see also Wason & Johnson-Laird, 1972, who speak about principles governing the "cohesion of discourse"). In this regard, of course, the operators of the vernacular differ from their truth–functional namesakes of propositional logic which may connect any p with any q whatsoever in a complex formula. This point needs to be stressed because this difference is an important one in that it represents a significant divergence between the logical operators and the connectives of everyday speech and exhibits a crucial respect in which any account of the former is, by itself, insufficient as an account of the latter. The matter is important also because it poses an important question in the pragmatics of communication as to why there should be such a constraint of common topic, as well as semantic and pragmatic questions as to how a listener proceeds in trying to connect together the semantic contents of the constituent propositions to determine whether and, if so, in what ways, a particular complex proposition satisfies such a constraint. More parochially, the matter is of interest because psychologists in their experimental work have often proceeded as though any p and any q might be connected into a complex proposition by use of the appropriate operator of interest. To the extent that the topic constraint actually does generally obtain, one might anticipate considerable problems in generalizing from the findings of such research to properties of the sentence operators in their everyday use.

But is there evidence that subjects actually are sensitive to the

constraints of common topic? The answer is overwhelmingly "Yes."
We shall cite some data from sentences involving OR (Fillenbaum,
1974b) and from conditionals involving IF (Fillenbaum, 1975b).
Disjoint OR sentences, i.e., sentences such as "Will he wear sandals or
sell Cokes?" where there appears to be no simple or obvious connection between the disjuncts, were characterized as strange or weird on
the average 96% of the time. In a setting where subjects were
required to identify strange sentences and provide a justifying context, on the average 94% of the disjoint items were judged strange,
while in each case OR sentences satisfying the topic constraint
elicited only a small scattering of "strange" judgments. Disjoint
sentences took longer to memorize, and recall performance on both
intentional and incidental learning tasks was substantially worse than
performance on variously well-formed OR sentences, with many of
the recalls involving normalization of one sort or another—for details
of the findings see Fillenbaum (1974b).[5] Next consider whether
topically disjoint or unrelated sentences are differentiated from IF
sentences that respect the topic constraint. In some work fully
reported in Fillenbaum (1975b) it was found that on the average
92% of conditional sentences whose constituent propositions were
topically unrelated were judged to be extraordinary or strange, while
conditional sentences respecting the topic constraint were judged
strange on the average less than 5% of the time.[6] It does appear
as though subjects are in fact sensitive to constraints of common
topic in the use of the sentence operators, so sooner or later questions of the sort raised above as to why this should be so, and as to
how subjects can determine what sorts of relations hold between the

[5] It might be noted that OR sentences may be malformed also in that there may be a
topical connection between the two propositions involved, but that connection is somehow
perverse or opposite to the one that holds normally; consider, e.g., the perverse threat, "Get
out of my way or I won't hit you." Performance on such sentences was similar to that on
disjoint sentences and worse than that for topically normal sentences on a variety of tasks,
e.g., 89% of such perverse threats were judged strange, it again took substantially longer to
memorize such sentences, memorial performance on them was generally poor, etc. To
mention only one other set of findings, on a paraphrase task over half of the paraphrases of
perverse threats represented normalizations which turned these sentences into more conventional threats (Fillenbaum, 1974c).

[6] Further similar results for conditionals where the connection between the constituent
propositions is in some ways perverse or counter to expectation may also be found in
Fillenbaum (1976). Here we need only mention that perverse warnings phrased as AND and
OR sentences were overwhelmingly (84% and 95% of the time, respectively) judged to be
extraordinary sentences while conventional warnings phrased with AND and OR were rarely
(13% and 16% of the time) regarded as abnormal.

connected propositions such as to satisfy this constraint, will have to be faced. Here we need only note one point which will come up again and again during the course of this chapter on the basis of a variety of evidence: It seems essential to pay close heed to the contents of the elementary propositions that are related by the various sentence connectives; one must mind one's p's and q's.

We turn now directly to a consideration of some evidence on uses of AND, OR, and IF.

A. AND

Linguists have been clear that AND may be variously employed (see, e.g., Quirk, Greenbaum, Leech, & Svartvik, 1972; Schmerling, 1975). One of the major distinctions that has been made is that between symmetric and asymmetric conjunction (Lakoff, 1971). If one says "He ate some cake and drank some coffee" AND is used as an unordered operator and the order of the constituent propositions may be permuted without making any difference. On the other hand AND may be used as an ordered operator to signal some temporal or causal–temporal sequence such that "He died and was buried" communicates something very different from "He was buried and died." Generally something about the semantic properties of the verbs involved will select how AND is understood in a given case. Thus there may be temporal or temporal–causal relations contingent on our knowledge of the customary order of events, as in the example immediately above, or there may be entailment relations of a meaning sort between two verbs such that the action or state described by the one must always precede that described by the other, as in "He arrived in Washington Monday and stayed there for a week," where it is obvious that one cannot stay at some place until one has got there. Or, as in the ate–drank example above, the verbs may be such that neither their senses nor our knowledge of the world requires any particular order between them. (Indeed, in our example, the actions referred to very likely take place in an interleaved fashion.) To the extent that persons use or respond to AND in differential fashion, there is evidence of their sensitivity to the semantic properties that do or do not prescribe some temporal ordering between the conjoined verbs.

We shall be concerned with determining whether or not people are sensitive to the distinction between sentences involving an unordered use of AND and those that involve an ordered use (for details of this work, see Fillenbaum, 1971). Direct tests of understanding were employed as well as tests to see whether or not recognition memory for sentences of these two kinds is systematically different. In the case of unordered AND sentences, the order of the conjoined propositions is irrelevant, there is no compelling reason to mark the order at time of entry into memory, and at time of recall the subject might well falsely provide or recognize a sentence with order changed which is meaningfully equivalent to the original sentence. In the case of ordered AND sentences, on the other hand, the order of the conjoined propositions significantly affects the meaning of the sentence, and one might therefore expect an ordered entry into memory, and that subjects would be less likely to recall or falsely recognize a sentence where order has been changed since such a sentence is, in fact, a sentence of different meaning. The prediction is therefore that on a recognition task there should be far more false alarms for unordered AND sentences than for ordered ones.[7]

To assess understanding two tasks were employed: (a) *equivalence judgments,* where subjects were directly confronted with pairs of sentences with clause order permuted and required to indicate whether or not the two sentences in a pair were equivalent in meaning, and (b) *paraphrasing,* where subjects were required to paraphrase each of a series of sentences and, where, for each paraphrase one can determine whether or not order has been maintained. The latter task was employed so as not to force the subject to attend to clause order and the particular sort of AND involved, but rather to get him to focus on providing a meaning equivalent version for each sentence as a whole. The equivalence judgments revealed that over 90% of the pairs involving unordered uses of AND were judged equivalent in meaning while only about 10% of the pairs involving an ordered use of AND were rated as equivalent in meaning. The paraphrase task was run in a number of versions which all yielded basically the same result. For sentences involving an unordered use of AND the order of clauses was sometimes maintained and sometimes changed in the paraphrases, suggesting that preservation of order is not essential for preservation of meaning. For sentences involving an ordered use of AND and normal or conventional order there were hardly any order changes in the paraphrases. Such results indicate

---

[7] Obviously one must guard against the possibility that even ordered AND sentences might not be entered in memory in any ordered form, since the particular verbs employed could constrain a given order at time of (reconstructive) recall, given only knowledge of the way things generally work out in the world and the fact that the sentences are normal, conventional ones. Appropriate control foils, involving an ordered use of AND, but where the ordering of the conjuncts was reversed to make for extraordinary sentences, were employed to guard against such a possible artifact.

clearly that people are sensitive to differences between ordered and unordered uses of AND. However, for the case of ordered AND sentences where the order is reversed from the normal to be expected order, for every one of the three versions of the paraphrase task a majority of the paraphrases involved normalizing changes in order. We shall return to this last result, and more extensive similar results (Fillenbaum, 1974c) later, when we discuss the role of pragmatic knowledge of the ways of the world in the interpretation of messages, and indicate how work with sentence operators such as AND may give us some purchase on that sort of a problem.

The results on the recognition memory task were quite clear. Sentences that had actually appeared earlier, whether involving an unordered use of AND or an ordered use (and in the latter case whether in normal or reversed order) were overwhelmingly recognized as "old" sentences and there was little difference between these three sorts of sentences. The error rate was quite low, averaging around 6% misses. The particularly interesting results are those for false alarms or false recognitions. Here there were substantial and significant differences as a function of the sort of AND sentence involved, and the differences were of the sort expected. There were far more false alarms for sentences involving an unordered use of AND when the test items represented permutations in clause order (the error rate was almost 50%) than for permuted sentences involving an ordered use of AND, whether the original sentence represented conventional order changed into strange order on the test item, or whether the original sentence involved reversed, extraordinary order changed to normal order on the test item. Detailed examination of the results (Fillenbaum, 1971) indicated that these findings could not be explained in terms of procedural artifacts, or simply as a function of pragmatic reconstructive constraints at time of testing for memory. It suggested rather that ordered and unordered AND sentences were indeed differently entered in memory. Stating it more generally, the results both of the tests of direct understanding and of the memory test imply that subjects are sensitive to the semantic properties governing the relations between verbs or verb pairs, since it is principally in terms of such properties that the distinction between unordered and ordered AND sentences can be drawn.

B. OR

While the OR of logic is unordered, inclusive, and may connect any two propositions whatsoever with interpretation completely specifiable in terms of a truth table, the OR of ordinary usage may be unordered ("He will drive to Washington or fly to Philadelphia") or ordered ("Shut up or I'll fire you"), is generally exclusive, and can only connect propositions between which there is some constraint of common topic. (For some linguistic accounts of various ORs, see Culicover, 1972; Lakoff, 1971; Quirk et al., 1972; for a psychological analysis of the representation of OR involved in certain sorts of pseudoimperatives ["Flip the switch or the fan goes on"], see Springston & Clark, 1973.) Just as in the case of AND there appears to be a whole family of various if related uses, with a particular understanding selected as a function of some properties of the propositions connected. Our main concern here is to make some elementary distinctions with regard to some important different uses of OR, and to show, with reference to performance on a variety of tasks, that people are sensitive and appropriately responsive to such differences in use. Given well-formed topically coherent OR sentences one may distinguish between those involving an ordered use ("Get out of my way or I'll hit you") and those involving unordered or symmetric uses. As to the latter, one can distinguish between sentences that are exclusive and exhaustive (e.g., "He will stay here or go out"), sentences that are exclusive but not necessarily exhaustive, as our example above ("He will drive to Washington or fly to Philadelphia"), and sentences that are (possibly) inclusive (e.g., "He will write his father or call his mother"). The caution represented by "possibly" reflects the fact that in normal English it may, ordinarily, be quite difficult to interpret OR inclusively; this, as will be seen, is reflected in various ways in the results. Obviously the above by no means exhausts the various possible uses of OR, but at least it would seem to represent some of the common cases that might be of interest, and some common distinctions that might be made by the language user.

A variety of tasks was employed to determine whether or not subjects respond differently to the various kinds of OR sentences described. These tasks may perhaps be arranged on some sort of dimension of directness—indirectness ranging, at the direct end, from tasks where subjects were asked to make some judgment of strangeness/normalcy on sentences or to say whether or not a pair of sentences was equivalent in meaning to tasks, at the indirect end, involving memory (intentional and incidental) for sentences or time freely taken to commit various sorts of sentences to memory. Insofar as possible all tasks were posed as studies of the knowledge of English and of a feel for the language (for procedural details and full presentation of findings, see Fillenbaum, 1974b).

First, let us point out some ways in which the response to ordered or asymmetric OR sentences was different from that to sentences involving unordered uses. We shall then note some ways in which subjects responded differentially to various of the latter. About two-thirds of the threats involving an ordered use of OR were judged strange when clause order was permuted. If one looks at equivalence judgments on pairs of sentences one discovers that for 75% of ordinary threats the statements were judged to be different in meaning when the order of clauses in the second statement was permuted from that in the first. Compare these results with those involving unordered uses of OR, where the highest figure for "different" responses was only 4%. The paraphrase results were also revealing in a number of regards. While permutation of clause order around OR occurred in about 10% of the paraphrases of the various unordered uses, it essentially never occurred in the case of sentences involving an ordered use (threats). For well-formed threats more than 75% of the paraphrases were negative conditionals; thus "Get out of my way or I'll hit you" became "If you don't get out of my way I'll hit you." For the various sentence kinds involving unordered uses of OR such changes from *p or q* to *If not p, q* averaged about 10%. There are obviously some very striking differences between the paraphrases of ordered and unordered OR sentences.

Next consider some results that indicate differences in response to the three sorts of unordered uses of OR. On two of the three tasks requiring judgments of normalcy/strangeness inclusive OR sentences elicited distinctly more "strange" judgments than the two sorts of exclusive sentences. On the paraphrase task about 10% of the paraphrases of inclusive items involved a change from OR to AND; there were essentially no such changes for the exclusive items. About 40% of the paraphrases of inclusives explicitly changed these to exclusive by adding an "either" in the paraphrase, which provides some warrant for our calling such items "possible inclusive." Inclusives took substantially and significantly more time to memorize than did either kind of exclusive item in a task where subjects could take as much time as they needed to commit each item to memory. There were differences too in the responses to exclusive and exhaustive items as compared to simply exclusive ones. Subjects were asked to assess the informativeness of "yes" or "no" responses to questions. Given exclusive and exhaustive items (e.g., "Did he accept or reject the offer?"), both affirmative and negative answers were appropriately and overwhelmingly (about 90% of the time) judged to be uninformative. Given exclusive items (e.g., "Did you stay home or go to New York?"), affirmative answers were judged to be uninformative substantially more frequently than negative answers. This makes sense if one considers that an affirmative answer still leaves it completely open as to which of the two exclusive alternatives actually occurred, while a negative answer may be understood as ruling out both of these alternatives and as thus providing some real information. The paraphrasing data revealed that about 10% of the paraphrases of exclusive and exhaustive items involved fusion into a simple sentence which functions as a sort of superordinate (e.g., "He will accept or reject the offer" might become "He might accept the offer"); such paraphrases hardly ever occur for the simply exclusive items. Subjects took less time to memorize exclusive and exhaustive items than simply exclusive ones, and memorial performance on a variety of tasks was better for the former than the latter. Such results are intelligible if one considers that exclusive and exhaustive items are in a sense redundant, since the second part of such an item can be constructed given knowledge of the first part, something not possible for the simply exclusive items.

The results cited above and others to be found in Fillenbaum (1974b) strongly suggest that people are responsive to differences in the use of the OR connective. Such findings should lead to caution in generalizing from the results of work on concept learning where the disjuncts are quite arbitrary and ad hoc to the experimental situation. Results of such work cannot simply, or perhaps at all, be extrapolated toward an interpretation of the common uses of OR (or any other connective) in the vernacular. Also, the present results argue for caution in regard to any claim as to the specific natural language representation of OR, not so much because a particular representation offered is wrong as because it may be limited to and appropriate only for use in a particular context or contexts.

C. IF

While linguists have identified many different sorts of uses of IF (see, e.g., Heringer, 1971; Horn, 1972; Yamanashi, 1975, as cited earlier; or Fraser, 1971), perhaps the most characteristic use of the conditional by experimental psycholinguists is one in which the propositions involved are general and abstract, and the connection between them a completely arbitrary one. Such a strategy is illustrated in extreme form in Taplin and Staudenmayer (1973), where the problems were actually phrased using letters of the alphabet to represent the p and q propositions, so that a problem might be read "If there is a Z then there is an H." This sort of procedure may be found even in Wason on hypothesis testing, where a problem might be posed as "If a card has a D on one side, it has a 5 on the other side." In such uses of the conditional as a sort of contingent universal the connection between the two propositions is completely arbitrary. Merely making the task concrete and posing the rule as "If the letter is sealed then it has a 5^d stamp on it" led to enormous differences in performance. If switching from an abstract to a concrete or realistic embodiment of a rule in a contingent universal use of IF makes for large differences in performance, then there is warrant for caution in generalizing any results to conditionals of quite different sorts involving temporal, temporal–causal, or (implicitly) purposive or intentional relations between their constituent propositions. (For some data on differences in performance on conditionals used as contingent universals as against their use in causal contexts, see, e.g., O'Brien, Shapiro, & Reali, 1971.) Indeed, considering performance in a variety of reasoning tasks, Wason and Johnson-Laird (1972) assemble much evidence that "the meaning of component propositions may decisively influence the interpretation of everyday conditionals," and that content is crucial, suggesting "that any general theory of human reasoning must include an important semantic component." We need only add that such a theory must also include an important pragmatic component, sensitive to the sorts of things the speaker seeks to accomplish by saying what he does in the particular circumstances in which he says it (c f. Staudenmayer, 1975).

The present research is directed in part to the same issues as the work of Wason and Johnson-Laird. It constitutes an extension of their work (a) *methodologically* in the use of rather different procedures for obtaining data (see, e.g., the use of a paraphrase task to discover differences in the understanding of various sorts of conditional sentences), (b) *substantively* in the consideration of some uses of the conditional not treated by them (see, in particular, the purposive–causal use of inducements where a speaker seeks to control the behavior of an addressee by signaling his intentions with regard to the actions of the latter—this constitutes a case where explicitly there is a causal relation between the antecedent and consequent propositions but where, implicitly, the principal role of the conditional is purposive, i.e., its use is to get the addressee to do something or not to do something), and (c) *conceptually* insofar as a pragmatic analysis is offered for conditional promises and threats.

Paraphrase and inference techniques were employed to study the understanding of various sorts of conditional sentences. To the extent that the paraphrase of a sentence may be taken as indicative of the way in which it is understood, systematic *differences* in the paraphrases of sentences sharing some surface property, such as the conditional IF, may be taken as grounds for supposing that there must be systematic *differences* in the ways in which these sentences are understood, even if such findings do not go very far in revealing what these differences in understanding may involve. To know what a proposition means requires, among other things, a knowledge of what inferences may be drawn from it. To know what a connective means "is tantamount to knowing how to draw certain inferences on the basis of the formal patterns" in which it occurs (Johnson-Laird, 1975). If IF may be differently understood when occurring with different sorts of contents, it would seem reasonable to suppose that different sorts of inferences might be made in different cases. The matter of inferences is particularly of concern in the case of conditionals since such propositions are directly, overtly concerned with relations or contingencies among events or states and, in fact, provide a machinery by which inferences may be drawn. Therefore one needs to determine what inferences are actually, characteristically drawn from conditional assertions, whether or not they are legitimate by some criterion such as the stipulations of the propositional calculus, and whether, for a given conditional form, some inferences are more or less likely as a function of the conceptual properties of the propositions involved. We shall take as our problem the relation that is believed to obtain between a premise and its obverse, i.e., the relation between a statement of the general form *If p, q* and one of the form *If not p, not q* (where *p* and *q* might each itself be a negative statement thus permitting examination of the relation between e.g., *If not p, q* and *If p, not q*). To agree that a statement implies its obverse is to succumb to the fallacy of the denied antecedent. It has been argued by Geis and Zwicky (1971) that in a wide variety of circumstances a sentence of the form *If p, q* invites the inference that its obverse *If not p, not q* will hold. The fallacy of the denied antecedent constitutes a particularly interesting case since conditionals often serve as contingency statements or projections as to what holds or will hold if some condition is met, and a very natural question to ask is what holds or will happen if that condition is not met.

Subjects were required to paraphrase a variety of different sorts of conditional sentences (for details of procedure and findings, see Fillenbaum, 1975b). The IF sentences employed included (*a*) causal–purposive IF sentences involving conditional promises and threats,

(b) temporal or temporal–causal conditionals (e.g., "If he goes to Washington he will get drunk"), (c) noncausal conditionals functioning as contingent universals (e.g., "If the truck is red it belongs to the Exxon Company"), as well as a variety of other sorts of conditionals. In the inference task subjects were presented with pairs of sentences and asked to decide whether or not the second sentence was "a reasonable, natural sort of inference given the first sentence." It was stressed that they should consider the study as one concerned with their knowledge of English and feel for the language, with an "understanding of the relation between what is said explicitly and what is left implicit in normal speech." As in the paraphrase study there were purposive–causal statements involving conditional promises and threats, temporal–causal statements and conditionals that involved contingent universals, as well as some other sorts of items.

The results of the paraphrase studies are clear. Quite different patterns of paraphrase were obtained if a sentence was a promise as against being a threat, if it embodied a contingent universal rather than a temporal or temporal–causal connection, etc. Details may be found in full in Fillenbaum (1975b); we shall cite just a few illustrative findings. Threats elicited a substantial proportion of paraphrases in OR; this was particularly true for threats where the first clause was negative—over half the paraphrases of such threats were phrased as OR sentences. Paraphrases of conditionals in OR were otherwise quite uncommon (in the case of promises such paraphrases occurred less than 1% of the time). Paraphrases in AND were very common for promises, with 40% of the paraphrases for promises with a positive first clause and over 50% of the paraphrases for promises with a negatively phrased first clause involving AND. Except for threats with a positively phrased first clause, AND paraphrases were otherwise very rare. Temporal–causal conditionals, at least when the first clause was positively phrased, elicited a lot of paraphrases involving temporals. Conditionals which are really contingent universals were overwhelmingly paraphrased as "simple" propositions, i.e., as propositions where the sentence is collapsed into a single clause around the q proposition with the p proposition serving as a sort of modifier, thus "If the shoes are leather they will wear well" became "Leather shoes wear well," a more direct expression of the universal involved in the conditional. And so on! In terms of the above and other results that could be cited (recall that O'Brien and his associates, see e.g., O'Brien *et al.*, 1971, have consistently found differences in response to conditionals used in causal as against class inclusion [= our contingent universal] contexts), it seems clear that IF sentences may be rather differently paraphrased as a function of conceptual properties of the conditional which they embody. Insofar as the understanding of a sentence is revealed by the sentences which are produced as its equivalents or paraphrases, there is thus evidence that IF may have rather different uses in different contexts of the sort examined.

Examination of the data on invited inferences reveals that the obverse of a conditional was often accepted as following from it, the average value of such judgments ranging up to 90%, with even the lowest value over 50%. There seems to be very little difference between promises and threats with regard to the frequency of accepted inferences from an item to its obverse; perhaps the main thing to notice is how frequently such inferences were accepted (with values ranging from 81% to 90%). Such examination reveals that there are differences in the likelihood that these inferences will be accepted as a function of conceptual properties of the conditional involved. The obverse was characteristically less likely to be accepted as an inference from a proposition involving a contingent universal than for any other kind of item, and such judgments also took significantly longer to make. For temporal–causal conditionals, and particularly for purposive–causal conditionals embodied in inducements, what is actually phrased as a sufficient condition is very often also taken as a necessary one. For the case of conditional promises and threats we shall later provide an account for such findings, arguing that given some very simple and intuitively compelling assumptions about the logic of conversation the fallacy of the denied antecedent is no fallacy at all.

The principal lesson to be drawn from the data presented so far must be clear: If one is interested in the use of conditionals and in the everyday reasoning which employs them, it is essential to pay heed to the conceptual properties of the constituent propositions connected in these conditionals. This lesson holds obviously not only for sentences using IF, but equally, as we have seen already, for sentences using OR and AND.

D. SENSES OR SENSE TOGETHER WITH
    CONTEXTUALLY CONDITIONED USES

To this point we have exhibited only the brute fact that operators such as AND, OR, and IF may have different uses and that sentences employing them may be differently understood. Such facts obviously demand analysis with regard to such matters as the nature of the underlying representation or representations involved in each case, the nature of the topic constraint, and the nature of the conditions controlling the uses considered (and others that might be encountered). We have been careful to distinguish between the claim that a connective may have different uses and the claim that it must have different senses or different underlying logical representations. In principle, a connective might have a single unitary representation but different uses as a function of the appropriate application of relevant conversational principles, or the different uses, or at least some of them, might indeed depend on differences in underlying representations.

The first sort of position has been argued most strongly by Grice (1967) who suggests that each of the connectives may have a single underlying representation, indeed a truth–functional one, and that the various relations between the conjoined propositions in sentences employing the connectives might be suggested by the speaker and inferred by the addressee on the basis of general principles of communicative interaction falling under some basic cooperative principle. Consider an illustration with regard to the use of AND. In a sentence like "Harry had a shower and got dressed," clearly more is conveyed than that both conjuncts are true; in most normal circumstances the action described in the first clause will be understood to precede that described in the second clause; i.e., in this case at least a specific temporal order will be understood to obtain between the clauses (which is what would make a sentence reversing the clauses, as "Harry got dressed and had a shower," at least striking if not curious). In other cases, such as Morgan's (1975) example "Spiro told a joke and infuriated Paul," presumably some causal relation is understood to hold between the conjuncts. But do such examples require that there be some underlying distinct temporally and causally ordered AND's as well as an (only) truth–functional AND of the sort to be found in "John had some cake and drank some coffee"? Perhaps in the spirit of Grice, following Kempson (1975), one might argue that what is required is only a truth–functional sense together with the application of some principle of conversation (such as "Be brief, be relevant, give as much information as appropriate, do not say what you believe to be false, etc."). Thus the maxim of manner has the overall instruction "Be perspicuous" which Kempson interprets as "Be orderly" so as to "make the narration of events reflect their sequence." Presumably proper application of such a principle, where proper must involve a sensitivity to the semantics of the verbs related in the complex proposition, could handle many temporal and temporal–causal uses of AND without requiring separate senses for this connective. Analogous arguments calling as necessary on other conversational maxims could be offered to account for various uses of the other operators, and save us from being forced to postulate multiple senses or underlying representations. And recourse to a principle of relation or relevance (Grice, 1967) might perhaps be made to account for the topic constraint.

The issue is obviously a significant one, for one would like to avoid the multiplication of senses, and psychologically it would be very important if one could show that, indeed, each of the basic connectives had only a single representation, and then determine the properties of that representation, whether truth–functional or whatever; i.e., the important point is not that each representation be unique *and* truth–functional, but only that it be unique. Among other things, all sorts of interesting ontogenetic questions could then be raised with regard to the course of development of the underlying representation for each connective. All this of course requires that the relevant conversational principles which are assumed to interact with the unique representation of each connective are general principles which it would be necessary to postulate anyway. Obviously, there would be little gain if one had to postulate special ad hoc conversational principles to make a unitary underlying analysis work for the sentence connectives or, even worse, separate ad hoc principles for each of the connectives. And any analysis along such lines must be able to characterize in a reasonably specific way the nature of these general conversational principles and the manner of their interaction with the postulated underlying sense which could generate the various uses actually identifiable. Otherwise an analysis that requires the mysterious interaction of ill-specified conversational principles with a single underlying representation would hardly have much advantage, or be more economical than an analysis that requires different underlying senses, but dispenses with conversational principles entirely. While one might worry about the vagueness with which conversational principles have been phrased, see in particular the notion of "relevance," and about the psychological problems that will arise in trying to say how these articulate with a semantic analysis of sense, those who have argued for such an account have certainly stressed that the principles at issue are general ones of wide scope and application which are requried anyway to deal with a large variety of conversational facts. (See, e.g., their application to questions of conveyed meaning in Gordon & Lakoff, 1971; see also many of the papers in Cole & Morgan, 1975.)

The problem with the hypothesis of "unitary" underlying representation as offered by Grice (1967) and argued further by Kempson (1975) is simply that this hypothesis is a very debatable one, and that a variety of evidence has been offered by linguists and philosophers against the hypothesis. Thus, e.g., Schmerling (1975) disputes Grice's views, shows that asymmetric conjunction may be found in a great variety of sentences, and adduces much linguistic evidence to the point that conjunction in English may not be a unitary phenomenon, arguing "against the position that *all* instances of use of the English word AND can be considered instances of logical conjunction," even though she grants that there are important asymmetric or ordered uses of AND which can be treated as instances of logical conjunction that "owe their asymmetry to very general principles of human interaction [p. 229]." Or consider Morgan (1975) who shows that there are cases of conjunction which require either that one assume "two distinct logical structures" or a pragmatic analysis with a single underlying structure but where the rules of conversation will have to be stated so as to be sensitive to the operation of syntactic rules, and one is thus forced to give up "the assumption that rules of conversation are grammar free." This assumption is surely one not lightly to be sacrificed. More generally, Cohen (1971) has offered a variety of arguments against the adequacy of a conversationalist analysis of AND, OR, and IF. Walker (1975) in assessing these and other arguments suggests that while "the Conversational Hypothesis appears capable of overcoming these objections [this] does not show that it is right; nor does it show that anything is wrong with Cohen's Semantical Hypothesis [which holds that the sentence connectives are non truth–functional in sense, with context on occasion deleting some elements of the sense of an expression], or with the alternative theory which is prepared to multiply senses for the logical particles . . . because as yet we have no method of telling which of the elements of what is conveyed by an utterance are due to its sense, and which if any are conversational implicatures [p. 154]." In short, the conclusion is that no general conclusion is possible.

The issue of unitary sense plus contextually conditioned conversational uses versus multiple senses is unsettled and in dispute, given the sorts of evidence and arguments that can be marshalled by linguists and philosophers. It is not at all obvious that the psychologist controls any tools that might be used to settle the matter. At first thought, decision latency techniques might seem appropriate and powerful here. If there is a difference between sentences involving the literal meaning of a connective, where "literal" is construed

to refer to cases that involve the putative sense or underlying representation of a connective and only that, and cases that involve its
sense plus the application of relevant conversational principles, as say
in a temporal or temporal–causal use of AND, then perhaps decision
tasks involving the latter sorts of sentences should take longer than
those that involve the former sorts of sentences. Leaving aside the
question of proper controls for sentence content, the basic problem
is simply that such differences if they were obtained could probably
be handled equally well or badly on the hypothesis that different
senses of a connective, say different AND's, are of a different
complexity. Nor is it obvious that negative results, e.g., results
indicating no systematic differences in reaction time between sentences involving unordered uses of AND and those involving ordered
uses, could be taken as strong evidence against the conversationalist
hypothesis. In short, it is hard to see how experiments could be
designed so that their results might discriminate between the two
sorts of hypotheses. What work there is that might be considered
relevant is certainly not overly encouraging. There is a very little
evidence in Clark and Lucy (1975) which suggests that in the case of
conversationally conveyed requests the listener may construct the
literal meaning before the conveyed one, but the data to this point
are quite fragmentary. On the other hand, in a study of pseudo-
imperative OR sentences, Springston and Clark (1973) found no
systematic differences in decision latency, or in error rate, in favor of
genuine over "invited inferences" (where "invited inferences" might
perhaps be considered as requiring the intervention of conversational
principles to go beyond literal meaning). Finally, we know essentially
nothing about how conversational principles and the manner of their
operation should be represented in a psychological processing model.

  Whatever the eventual answer to the general question of unitary
sense versus multiple senses of the connectives, it does seem reasonable to suppose that in some ways one will have to have recourse to
conversational principles to account for at least certain aspects of the
understanding and use of complex sentences involving such terms as
AND, OR, and IF. Consider an example already cited with regard to
the use of OR. Someone who says p or q will generally be understood not to know which of p and q actually obtains. This implicature has a ready explanation on the basis of the cooperative principle
(see Grice, 1967; or for a quite compatible formulation, Ducrot,
1972). Since the speaker should make his contribution as informative
as he can (maxim of quantity) and since he should have proper
evidence for what he says (maxim of quality), a speaker who says p
or q must have evidence only for p or q and not sufficient evidence

to claim just p or just q, for if he did have sufficient evidence for the latter and nevertheless said only the former then he would be violating the quantity maxim. Hence by saying p or q he "is implicating that he does not know which of p or q is true [Kempson, 1975, p. 146]." Since such an implicature can be contradicted it cannot be taken as simply part of the representation of the meaning of the sentence. We shall see later that recourse to conversational notions makes it possible to provide a very plausible account of why people are so prone to succumb to the fallacy of the denied antecedent when IF is used in conditional promises and threats. That conversational notions should be relevant for the analysis of such inducement statements seems very reasonable, if we remember only that inducements represent an inportant use of the IF connective in a dialogic, interpersonal context.

The question of unitary sense versus multiple senses remains unsolved, and it is not clear how one might proceed as a psychologist in order to resolve it. But it must be stressed that whatever the answer to this question, the business of minding or having to mind one's p's and q's remains basically unaffected. Unless one minded one's p's and q's, one could not even have different uses of the various connectives. The two sorts of hypotheses simply provide different ways, in principle, of doing the minding. On the one account, the semantic interpretation of the connected clauses engages the appropriate conversational principle(s) to permit proper understanding of the complex proposition; on the other account, it selects the appropriate sense of the connective that makes such understanding possible. But on either hypothesis different uses of the connectives (or of sentences in which they figure) are recognized, and on either hypothesis the addressee must be able to recognize the actual use involved because he is responsive to the particular semantic properties of the p and q constituents of the complex proposition, in context. The above suggests that our inability to settle matters as between Grice and his critics need not be any barrier to attempts to provide analyses of the circumstances that control different uses of AND, OR, and IF. Indeed such analyses may constitute the best way to develop an account that might permit us to probe further and possibly adjudicate between these views.

E. A PRAGMATIC ANALYSIS EXEMPLIFIED: THE USE
     OF IF IN INDUCEMENTS

All that we can attempt here, by way of example and thus possibly as a model, is the beginnings of an analysis of one use of the conditional, its purposive–causal use in inducements (conditional promises and threats). This analysis will seek to account for the phenomena in terms of pragmatic factors involving consideration of the conversational context in which inducements are employed and of their communicative role as attempts to control the behavior of the addressee, a role which depends on certain assumptions held in common between the speaker and the addressee of the inducing communication. Some suggestions will be made as to the relations holding between inducements phrased as conditional sentences, conjunctive sentences, and disjunctive sentences, and with regard to some inferences that may be drawn from inducements phrased as conditionals. An analysis will be offered which exhibits some of the implicit rules that appear to govern the use of the purposive conditional in inducements. We will consider how expectation of consequences affects the form in which inducements may be phrased and the inferences that they engender.

Essentially we shall be looking at one class of clearly purposive–causal uses of the conditional. What is said explicitly involves a causal connection; thus given If p, q, p on your part will be the cause of q on my part. What is implicit or conveyed and in a sense primary is a purposive notion, for q on my part is being "offered" to get something done or not done with regard to p on your part. In important measure this purposive role is what defines an inducement as such.

We shall seek to show that the relations obtaining among propositions phrased in IF, AND, and OR are systematically affected as a function of whether a promise or a threat is involved. A conditional threat may be phrased more or less equivalently by use of IF, AND, or OR. Thus "If you do that I'll shoot you" may be paraphrased as "Do that and I'll shoot you" or as "Don't do that or I'll shoot you," where in the case of the disjunctive phrasing the antecedent proposition must be negated. A conditional promise must be treated rather differently. Thus "If you do that I'll give you $100" may indeed be paraphrased in AND in a way quite parallel to the paraphrase of a conditional threat ("Do that and I'll give you $100"), but it cannot very well be paraphrased as an OR sentence with negated first proposition. Thus "Don't do that or I'll give you $100" is strange, and certainly not an acceptable paraphrase for "If you do that I'll give you $100." If a conditional promise is to be paraphrased at all as a disjunction it will require the negation of the second or consequent proposition "Do that or I won't give you $100." While in general this paraphrase does appear to be an acceptable one, in at least one important respect it would appear to be rather different from its source sentence, in that the source sentence is a conditional promise while the disjunctive paraphrase is really a sort of conditional threat involving the conditional withholding of an incentive, as contrasted to its conditional offer in the IF phrasing. It will be shown that subjects are sensitive to these paraphrase relations between IF, AND, and OR sentences, and to differences in paraphrase relations as a function of whether a promise or a threat is involved. Given a very simple assumption to the effect that a person wants good outcomes and seeks to avoid bad ones and reference to the contrastive force of OR (as OTHERWISE), we shall see that such findings can readily be interpreted.

A classical fallacy in reasoning is the fallacy of the denied antecedent; thus given *If p, q* and *not p* people may conclude *not q*, a conclusion that is fallacious within the context of the truth–functional calculus.[8] We shall argue that given some very simple assumptions about the logic of conversation, this fallacy is not fallacy at all in the context of conditional promises and threats. If the speaker who utters such a promise or threat is believed to be sincere by the addressee, then it must be assumed that he is offering the inducement contingent on the actions of the addressee, and there would be no point in offering the inducement if he were going to give it regardless of the actions of the addressee, for in that case there is no reason why it should affect those actions one way or the other.

We shall now briefly report some relevant data on equivalence judgments, paraphrases, sentence descriptions, and inferences (for full procedural details and description of the findings, see Fillenbaum, 1976), and will then sketch a conceptual account for the results.

1. Equivalence Judgments

Subjects were presented with a series of pairs of sentences and for each pair asked to decide whether or not the two sentences had the same meaning. The first sentence in each pair was always an IF sentence and involved a threat, a promise, a warning, or a prediction of future good consequences. If the first sentence is symbolized by *If*

---

[8] The compellingness of the inference from a proposition to its obverse is paradoxically exhibited by a case where the inference must be *disinvited,* and where the temptation to such an inference must be strongly resisted. Consider a statement of the form *If no p, q* such as "If I don't see you before you leave, have a good trip" which could hardly seem curious or lead to the bantering reply "And if you do see me before then, I'm not to have a good trip?" unless there were a strong and generally justifiable tendency in many or most circumstances to infer *If p, not q* from *If not p, q.*

p, q, then the second sentence of a pair may be represented as either *p and q, not p or q,* or *p or not q,* i.e., as a conjunctive or a disjunctive with negation on either the first or second proposition. The results were quite straightforward: In all cases the conjunctive sentence was overwhelmingly (between 87% and 100% of the time) judged to be equivalent to the conditional. In other regards the response to threats and warnings was quite similar, and so was that to promises and predictions of future benefits. The main difference between these two classes, which represent respectively negative and positive consequences for the addressee, was in regard to the response to disjunctives. If a negative consequence is involved, then characteristically a paraphrase in OR which negates the first proposition was regarded as acceptable while one that negates the second was regarded as unacceptable; if a positive consequence is involved, a paraphrase in OR which negates the second proposition was regarded as acceptable while one that negates the first proposition was generally regarded as unacceptable. These results were very much as expected.

2. Paraphrases

The procedures and results for this task have been mentioned earlier. It need only be recalled that the most frequent paraphrases of promises and threats involve AND and OR statements, and that particularly with regard to paraphrases of conditionals as disjunctives there were some striking differences in the response to promises and threats. There were essentially no disjunctive paraphrases of promises while such paraphrases of threats, especially if these involved a negatively stated antecedent proposition, were very common. (Thus statements such as "If you don't do that I'll hit you" were rendered as something like "Do that or I'll hit you" over half the time.)

3. Descriptions

Subjects were given a series of sentences and asked to decide for each whether it constituted a threat, a warning, a promise, or none of these. The sentences used were phrased as IF sentences, as AND sentences, and as OR sentences with negation on either the first or second proposition, and involved threats, promises, warnings, and predictions of future good consequences. When phrased as conditionals or conjunctives, threats were characteristically described as threats, warnings as warnings, promises as promises, and predictions of future good outcomes were most commonly (around 60% of the time) described as promises, although they also were put into the N.O.T. (none of these) category about 20% of the time. Upon a disjunctive phrasing, the signing of the consequences comes to have some interesting and striking effects. When the first proposition of the disjunctive is negated, threats were described as threats, and warnings were called warnings. However, when the second proposition is negated, over half of the descriptions for threats and for warnings fall into the N.O.T. category. Next consider promises and predictions of future good outcomes phrased disjunctively. If the first proposition of the disjunction is negated, then items from each of these classes were assigned to the N.O.T. category over half the time. If the second proposition of the disjunction is negated, then items from these classes were characteristically regarded as threats or warnings, very seldom as promises. Thus a statement which urges a listener to do something and indicates that otherwise a good consequence will not follow is no longer regarded as a promise, but rather as a threat or warning. It seems difficult if not impossible to pose a promise as a disjunction; some possible reasons for this will be considered later.

4. Inferences

The inferences subjects draw from inducement statements may be considered as revealing of their understanding of such statements and of their appreciation of various consequences of different actions on their part. The procedure and results for the invited inferences task have been mentioned earlier. In short, with regard to conditional threats and promises, subjects very readily accepted the "fallacious" inference from a proposition to its obverse, with average value for acceptance ranging between 81% and 90%. It does not seem to make much difference whether a threat or promise is involved, or in which direction (e.g., from If p, q to If not p, not q, or from If not p, not q to If p, q) the relation goes—subjects are very prone to commit the fallacy of the negated antecedent for propositions involving inducements.

We shall now seek to account for the ways in which inducements may or may not be phrased, and to indicate why the fallacy of the denied or negated antecedent is so seductive in the context of inducements.

Let us make the very simple (perhaps tautological) assumption that a person wants to get good outcomes and wants to avoid bad outcomes. A conditional promise constitutes an effective inducement insofar as the person wants the good outcomes offered (and is willing to do something in exchange), and a conditional threat constitutes an effective inducement insofar as the person wants to avoid the bad outcomes threatened (and will do something or refrain from doing something in exchange). The logic of this is laid out quite starkly in our notation when we symbolize a conditional promise in IF as *If p, q+* and a conditional threat in IF as *If p, q−*. What happens when one goes to a conjunctive phrasing? The forms *p and q+* and *p and q−* are presumably understood with AND as an ordered or asymmetric causal or causal–temporal operator which exhibits the consequences of doing *p*, whether these be positive or negative, just as directly as does the conditional proper. So in the first case wanting *q+* you do *p*, in the second case wanting to avoid *q−* you refrain from doing *p*. What happens, finally, when one goes to a disjunctive phrasing using OR? Used in the context of inducements, the form *p or q* involves an ordered or asymmetric use of OR with the force of OTHERWISE. In the disjunctive phrasing of an inducement the first disjunct amounts to an imperative and the second disjunct is a statement of consequences for the addressee, whose role it is to enforce the first disjunct, i.e., to get the addressee to obey the order by choosing the first disjunct. Consider a threat *If p, q−* which is paraphrased as *Not p or q−*. You as addressee are being presented with two alternatives, only one of which will come about; it is up to you to choose. You will generally know that the speaker wants *Not p*, so if *Not p* occurs everything would be well. But if *Not p* does not occur, then *q−* will occur, which is something you want to avoid. Hence you know that you must bring about *Not p* so that *q−* should not come about, i.e., since you want to avoid *q−* there is some incentive to take the other alternative, viz. *Not p*. So this paraphrase in OR seems reasonable enough. Now consider a paraphrase for *If p, q−* in OR which negates the second proposition, namely *p or not q−*. Since you want to avoid *q−*, *not q−* constitutes a perfectly acceptable alternative, in fact the desirable alternative, and there is no reason to take the other alternative, *p*. Indeed, an inducement of the form *p or not q−* is additionally strange in that it offers or seeks to command *p* as an alternative, in circumstances where you as addressee will generally know that the speaker really wants and is trying to elicit *not p*. Since the whole point of a conditional threat is to get the addressee to choose the first disjunct desired by the speaker by offering as an alternative in the second disjunct consequences that are unacceptable to the addressee, a threat of the form *p or not q−* where the speaker commands an action he does not want and offers as alternative something that the addressee does want must appear incoherent and useless as an inducement.

The analysis for conditional promises phrased disjunctively follows parallel lines. Consider a promise of the form *If p, q+* which is paraphrased as *p or not q+*. Since you want *q+* you will not wish to lose it by taking the second alternative of *not q+*, so there is an incentive to take the other alternative, viz. *p*. Thus this paraphrase appears appropriate enough, subject only to the qualification that this paraphrase in OR is really a threat not to offer some good outcome, while the source conditional was a promise of that good outcome. However, insofar as both statements are compelling inducements to do *p* they may be regarded as equivalent as to their effects. Now consider a paraphrase for *If p, q+* in OR which negates the first proposition, namely *not p or q+*. Since you want *q+* this constitutes a desirable alternative and there is no reason to take the other alternative, *not p*. An inducement of the form *not p or q+* is additionally strange in that it appears to command *not p* in circumstances where you as addressee will generally know that the speaker really wants to elicit *p*. Again we have a case where the speaker is commanding an action he does not want and offering as alternative to enforce this command something that the addressee does want. Such a conditional promise is incoherent and useless as an inducement in a way exactly parallel to the way in which a conditional threat of the form *p or not q−* is incoherent and useless. An important aspect of the difficulty with threats and promises phrased as *p or not q−* and *not p or q+*, respectively may derive from the fact that the addressee is being asked explicitly to do something or not to do something that he understands is exactly opposite to the desires of the speaker. If a disjunctive inducement statement is to be appropriately phrased it must begin with a command which explicitly expresses what the speaker wants the addressee to do, and then must present as an alternative the relatively bad outcome which will result from not going along with that command (perhaps the conversational maxim to call upon here is that of *manner* which, among other things, requires that the speaker be clear and avoid obscurity).

The above analysis provides an account of why it is difficult if not impossible to phrase a conditional promise in disjunctive form. We have already seen that the only paraphrase of a conditional promise in OR that is coherent is *p or not q+* and that this paraphrase is regarded characteristically as a threat or warning, not as a promise. But why should this be? Why is there this difficulty of phrasing a conditional promise in OR? If a promise is to be phrased disjunc-tively then the second proposition in the OR sentence must have a positive force, i.e., it must be either $q+$ or *not q−*, but if the second proposition has such positive force then, as we have seen above, it loses any incentive value toward getting the person to take the first alternative and thus, because the person can always take the second and positive alternative, such statements cannot serve as sensible or plausible inducements. Only if the second proposition in the disjunc-tive has a negative force, being either $q−$ or *not q+,* will it serve to make the listener take the other alternative, and thus function adequately as an inducement.

We have seen that in the case of inducements people are very ready to accept the obverse of a proposition as following from it, such implications were accepted between 80% and 90% of the time, and that it did not seem to make any difference whether promises or threats were involved. Why, offered an inducement of the form *If p, q,* might the addressee of such a statement believe that *If not p, not q* follows? Consider that the inducement q is being offered to get the addressee to do or refrain from doing p. Now precisely insofar as the obtaining of q is contingent upon some action with regard to p, the inducement would lose all point or force if that contingency were eliminated. Thus, in the case of a promise if $q+$ were to come about whether or not the addressee refrained from doing p, the condi-tionality of the inducement which really defines it as an inducement rather than as a simple straightforward offer of a good or bad outcome would be lost, and the statement would have no point. If the speaker is going to give the addressee $100 regardless of what he does, or if he is going to attack him regardless of what he does, then there is no good reason for the addressee to modify his behavior, one way or the other. To the extent that the addressee believes the speaker to be sincere in his inducement statement, he must assume that the outcomes that will be offered to him will be differential and contingent upon his own action, which the speaker is seeking to control through the inducement he is offering. The "conversational implicature," to use Grice's (1967, 1975) term, follows quite directly if the addressee of the inducement statement assumes the speaker is conforming to the maxim of "quantity" in saying no more and no less than appropriate to the circumstances. The crucial point concerns the contingency between an action and its consequences. The ad-dressee need not assume that in the absence of his action he will certainly not receive the incentive or punishment being offered, only that his action will affect in some substantial or significant degree the likelihood of obtaining those consequences.

While the general analysis offered above applies equally to promises and threats, there is one respect in which these differ somewhat, and in which the analysis has a particularly direct bearing for threats. First consider a promise of the form *If p, q+* where the speaker is trying to get the addressee to do *p*. Here the addressee might employ a legitimate argument form (*modus ponens*) by affirming the antecedent: he wants *q+*, he knows that *If p, q+* holds, so he does *p* and *q+* will follow. But what of a threat of the form *If p, q−*, where the speaker is trying to get the addressee not to do *p*? This can only work if the addressee realizes, at least, that he must not do *p*, and infers (and presumably also hopes) that if he does *not p* then *q−* will not result, which amounts to assuming *If not p, not q−* given *If p, q−*. The point is simply this: that the very understanding of the force of a conditional threat depends in large measure upon the addressee making the invited inference from a proposition to its obverse, and that thus the "fallacy" of the denied antecedent is particularly intimately involved in the understanding of conditional threats.

The analysis of inducements, as sketched above, is clearly only a very partial analysis and needs to be developed further in a number of directions. Here we shall touch on one problem only. It must be obvious that for a threat or promise to be reasonable it is not sufficient that the *q* proposition be appropriately negatively or positively signed for the addressee, with the speaker asserting that he will bring about these negative or positive consequences. The sign or extremity of the sign of the *p* proposition and the relation between the values of the signs of the *p* and *q* propositions must also be considered. While "If you do that I'll give you $50" may be a commonplace promise with *p* as a sort of dummy proposition of unspecified or zero sign, matters become quite different if *p* is extremely negatively signed. Thus "If you break your mother's arm I'll give you $50" is ludicrous and presumably ineffective as a promise just because of the disproportion between the extreme negative value of the act being demanded of the addressee and the (moderate) positive value of the incentive being offered. If the speaker believes the addressee to be some sort of utilitarian who weighs the costs and values of various courses of action, then for a conditional promise to be effective the absolute positive value of *q* needs to be greater than the absolute negative value of *p*, and in the case of a conditional threat the absolute negative value of *q* needs to be greater than the absolute positive value of *p*. In fact, subjects are sensitive to "felicity" conditions on inducements, i.e., conditions that must be met if a conditional threat or promise is to be pragmatically appropriate or plausible. In some work reported in full in

Fillenbaum (in press) it was found not only that subjects could correctly identify the patterns of signing on various sorts of inducement statements, but further, and more directly to the issues raised above, that certain patterns of signing were considered to represent ordinary, normal promises or threats, whereas other patterns of signing were regarded as yielding strange or extraordinary inducements. Thus sentences of the form $p-q++$ and $p+q--$, which may be taken to represent fairly conventional sorts of promises and threats, were judged to be ordinary on the average 87% and 80% of the time, respectively, while sentences of the form $p--q+$ ("If you break your mother's arm I'll give you \$50") and $p++q-$ ("If you save the child's life I'll spit in your face") which seem perverse and presumably ought to be ineffective as inducements, since the reward offered in the promise is less than the cost involved and since the punishment offered in the threat is far less than the positive value of the act being forbidden, were judged to be extraordinary on the average 75% and 60% of the time respectively. Other results obtained were also consistent with such a general condition on the pragmatic plausibility of inducements in terms of the relation between the value/cost of the act being requested or forbidden and the value/cost of the incentive offered.

The preceding discussion constitutes an attempt to reveal some properties of a particular sort of purposive–causal use of IF in an interpersonal, dialogic situation, for a case where there is an explicit causal relation between the p and q propositions, but where implicitly the principal role of the conditional is purposive, i.e., the speaker reveals his intentions so as to get the addressee to do something or to refrain from doing something. We have tried to say something about relations holding among propositions phrased in IF, AND, and OR which involve such a use, and to indicate the role of at least one condition with regard to the sign of the consequences, i.e., whether a threat or promise is at stake, in governing these relations. This work may be regarded as illustrating the potential value of a pragmatic analysis in which attention is directed to the circumstances of use of a certain utterance type involving conditionals. In these terms one may begin to understand how the illocutionary point of a statement may affect its logical form, and how principles of conversation may license or even require inferences not legitimate given only a consideration of truth–function relations. Perhaps the above may be taken as something of a model as to how one might proceed in looking at other uses of IF, as well as various uses of the other connectives. (For some comments on similar lines with regard to UNLESS, and particularly with regard to why it is difficult to use UNLESS in promises, see Fillenbaum, 1976.)

III.   Some Uses to Which the Sentence Operators May Be Put

To this point we have been concerned mainly with describing some uses of each of the connectives, something of significance in its own right because of the ubiquity of their employment and their indispensability in permitting the construction of complex propositions whose understanding and use is in critical ways controlled by the particular connective involved. But there is yet another rather different reason to motivate interest, namely that work with these terms may provide us with a tool for the study of major substantive semantic and pragmatic problems that are of interest to cognitive psychology. In some ways the immediately preceding section which sought to provide the outline of a conceptual analysis of the uses of the conditional in inducements may be regarded as falling under this second rubric, in that it says something about "How to do things with words" (Austin, 1962) in the sense of a consideration of the relation between the illocutionary point or force of a statement and its logical form, and of an examination of the role played by a speech act in the context in which it occurs. Obviously there are many other general problems that could be approached by a judicious utilization of terms such as AND, OR, and IF. Here we shall just mention one such problem, and then look a bit more closely at two others. What all these cases involve is a going beyond what is *directly, literally given,* and surely the inferential capacities that permit passage beyond literal understanding are particularly characteristic and significant aspects of linguistic functioning, and indeed more generally of human cognitive functioning.

The problem only to be mentioned is that of memory for sense or gist, a problem that has again come to be important in recent years (Fillenbaum, 1973). Thus it may be pertinent to note that a recent study of sentence memory (Fillenbaum, 1975a) indicates considerable confusion among different phrasings of inducement statements. Subjects encountered warnings variously phrased as conditionals, conjunctives, and disjunctives with the first proposition negated, i.e., warnings phrased in ways known to be regarded as meaning equivalent (in terms of some of the work reviewed earlier in this chapter). Later their memory was tested in an incidental recognition task. There were many false recognitions of related sentences, i.e., sentences that represent alternative, meaning equivalent phrasings of the warnings using either of the other two sentence operators. While verbatim correct sentences were recognized as old sentences on the average 70% of the time, related sentences were recognized as old on the average 52% of the time (with control sentences falsely recognized only 17% of the time).

Two problems will be considered more fully. The first is that of how people attain information never explicitly provided, of their understanding of and memory for information never directly encountered in a linguistic message, but rather presupposed or inferable from what is said explicitly. (For quite diverse examples of consideration of these matters, see, e.g., Bransford, Barclay, & Franks, 1972, on a constructive approach to sentence memory; and see Gordon & Lakoff, 1971, on conversational postulates for indirect speech acts in the making of requests.) The second problem is that of the ways in which knowledge of the world and knowledge of language articulate—how preexisting knowledge of ways of the world may systematically effect or bias the interpretation of linguistic messages. (On the significance of the relation between world and linguistic knowledge, see many of the papers in Bobrow & Collins, 1975.)

A. AMPLIFICATION OF INFORMATION

Characteristically people do not remember the particular surface syntactic form of the sentences they have encountered, but rather propositional content that includes not only information explicitly specified but also information that in various ways is inferable from that provided directly. If in processing information one is responsive not only to what is directly and explicitly provided, but also to what must be assumed if the directly provided information is to be coherent and employed in a normally communicative way, then concern with the functions of presuppositional knowledge and conversational implicatures (Grice, 1967, 1975) becomes unavoidable. And here particularly intriguing questions will arise with regard to the possibility of information gain or amplification in memory as opposed to the more usual emphasis on abstraction and information loss.

The conceptual status and proper analysis of counterfactual conditionals have long vexed philosophers. Nevertheless counterfactual conditionals may provide valuable test material that is particularly useful for the study of memory for information implicit in sentences. A counterfactual conditional strictly presupposes the negation of its antecedent proposition, for one cannot coherently conceive of a counterfactual without assuming the falsehood of its first proposition (*pace* some curious and marginal counter examples offered by Wilson, 1975). A counterfactual conditional in most conversational contexts also strongly suggests or "invites" as inference the negation of its consequent proposition, but does not strictly require such an inference since the inference is cancellable in a way that presuppositions and entailments are not (Ducrot, 1972; Karttunen, 1971). Thus given "If he had caught the plane he would have arrived on time," it is presupposed that "He did not catch the plane," and in most contexts it is at least strongly suggested that "He did not arrive on time." A counterfactual conditional may also be seen as related to a causal in which the negation of the antecedent is given as the reason for the negation of the consequent, in our example "Because he did not catch the plane he did not arrive on time" or, more common stylistically, "He did not arrive on time because he did not catch the plane."

Given prior presentation of a counterfactual conditional, one may ask if the subject will later falsely recognize (*a*) the negation of the antecedent proposition, which is presupposed, or (*b*) the negation of the consequent proposition, which is strongly suggested if not entailed; and whether false recognition is more frequent for (*a*) or (*b*). Further, given a counterfactual conditional, one may ask if the subject will later falsely recognize its causal relative, which consists of the causal conjunction of (*a*) and (*b*) with the negation of (*a*) given as the reason for the negation of (*b*). This relation between counterfactual conditional and causal may be viewed as going in the other direction as well (i.e., from causal to counterfactual), since there would appear to be few, if any, occasions appropriate for the causal ("He did not arrive on time because he did not catch the plane") which would not also assume the counterfactual ("If he had caught the plane he would have arrived on time"). Two experiments in recognition memory will be presented (for details, see Fillenbaum, 1974a). The first experiment is concerned with memory for the simple offspring of counterfactual conditionals, and the second with memory for related complex sentences where the original sentences are either counterfactuals or causals and the recognition sentences include their causal and counterfactual relatives.

The basic format of the two experiments was the same. The subjects were told that they would hear a series of sentences on tape and were requested to listen carefully, since they would later be "asked questions about the sentences." After the original series was finished, they were told that they would hear another series of sentences and would have to decide for each sentence whether or not it had appeared in the first series.

In the first experiment both the original and the test series consisted of a mixture of counterfactual conditionals and simple propositions, and some physical or social nexus always held between the clauses of the counterfactuals, as in "If he had eaten the fish he would have become sick" or "If he had talked with the boss he would have got a raise." In the second experiment, which involved the same sort of sentence contents as the first, the original and test series consisted of a mixture of counterfactual conditionals, simple conditionals, and causals involving negation in both of their propositions (with simple conditionals included as a control so as to be able to determine whether any systematic recognition effects obtained were simply due to the prior occurrence of same or similar content).

The basic trend of the results is quite clear in each experiment, and consistent over the two experiments. Offspring or related sentences were more frequently falsely recognized as having occurred earlier than were their appropriate controls. Thus in the first experiment offspring negated sentences were judged to be old significantly more frequently than the control sentences, with this effect considerably stronger for offspring that negated the consequent proposition of the counterfactual than for offspring that negated the antecedent proposition. In the second experiment related sentences were falsely recognized as old significantly more frequently than their controls, with counterfactuals related to previously presented causals falsely recognized more frequently than causals related to previously presented counterfactuals (with both of these recognized significantly more frequently than causals corresponding to previously presented simple conditionals).

Even though the interpretation of some of the details of the results must be quite tentative with regard to the difference between offspring sentences which negate the antecedent and those which negate the consequent proposition of a previously encountered counterfactual (first experiment), and the difference between causals related to previously encountered counterfactuals and counterfactual conditionals related to previously encountered causals (second experiment)—(see Fillenbaum, 1974a, for a detailed discussion of those and other findings)—it seems clear that there are substantial and consistent effects such that both simple offspring sentences and complex related sentences involving the causal conjunction of simple offsprings are often falsely recognized as old sentences. Listeners appear to operate on the information directly provided them, amplifying and elaborating that information. Wittingly or, more likely, unwittingly, subjects seem to go beyond the givens, using information explicitly provided as the basis for determining what is implicit and what can be inferred given such information. If much of communication depends on the ability to go beyond what is said directly in order to understand what is implied by what is said, and what is revealed of the communicative purposes of the speaker who said it that way in that particular context, then the various processes of inference or natural logic involved in such elaboration of information become of great interest. To the extent that one can capitalize on properties of the English connectives in work directed to such problems, there is further warrant for interest in these terms.

B. PRAGMATIC NORMALIZATION

The tendency to normalize connected discourse or stories in memory has been well known for a long time (see, e.g., the classic work of Bartlett, 1932). It is possible that such normalization involves not so much or not only memorial processes, but may largely be a consequence of the way in which strange material is initially interpreted and stored, such that extraordinary descriptions are transmuted into more commonplace ones in a manner responsive to our knowledge of the ways things usually transpire, given a presumption of the sensibleness of the material actually encountered. Thus in some work presented earlier in this chapter (based on Fillenbaum, 1971) it was shown that verb order was often permuted for disordered conjunctive sentences, changing meaning, normalizing the sentences, and assimilating the order of events to conventional order. The work described immediately below (reported fully in Fillenbaum, 1974c) extends the earlier study in two ways: (a) in that a new kind of ordered conjunctive sentence is examined in addition to the kind considered before and in that a class of strange disjunctive sentences ("perverse" threats) is also studied, and more important (b) in that we also sought to determine whether the subject could detect meaning changes in his paraphrases by making him review each at the end, and having him say whether or not there was any difference in meaning between the original sentence and his paraphrase of it, and if he felt there was, to indicate what was involved. Thus this research capitalizes on some properties of AND and OR (with the latter really serving the role of a conditional) in order to study the interpretation of pragmatically extraordinary messages, i.e., sentences which are not syntactically or semantically malformed but rather strange or perverse given the subject's knowledge of the ways in which things characteristically happen.

The subjects were asked to paraphrase each of a series of sentences under instructions which stressed that they were not to improve the sentences or make them more sensible but rather that they were to reword them with maximum fidelity to the meaning as given. After completing the paraphrase task the subject was shown each original sentence and his paraphrase of it, asked if there was any difference in meaning between them and, if so, to indicate the nature of the difference or differences. The sentences presented included ordered conjunctive sentences in normal order (e.g., "John got off the bus and went into the store"), ordered conjunctive sentences with normal order reversed, these sentences being extraordinary but semantically coherent (e.g., "John dressed and had a bath"), ordered conjunctive sentences with normal order reversed which violated entailment relations between their main verbs (e.g., "John finished and wrote the article on the weekend"), disjunctive sentences involving commonplace threats (e.g., "Stop that noise or I'll call the police") and disjunctive sentences that were "perverse" in that the consequent clause indicated that the speaker would *not* bring about some undesirable event commonly to be expected in the circumstances (e.g., "Don't print that or I won't sue you").

Ordered conjunctive sentences in normal order and normal conditional threats phrased as disjunctives were essentially never perversely paraphrased, and in each case paraphrases that preserved meaning were overwhelmingly regarded as doing just that. Results for the two sorts of disordered conjunctive sentences and for the "perverse" conditional threats were quite different. For the disordered conjunctive sentences with contingent relation violated and with entailment relation violated 64% and 70% respectively, of the paraphrases involved normalization, while for the "perverse" conditional threats 54% of the paraphrases involved normalization. Turning next to judgments of whether or not the paraphrases changed the meaning of the various kinds of strange sentences, we find that for disordered conjunctive sentences where a contingent relation between verbs has been violated, normalizing paraphrases were detected almost twice as often as they were missed (the figures are 42% and 22%), while for disordered conjunctive sentences where an entailment relation between verbs has been violated normalizing paraphrases were detected less often than they were missed (the figures are 27% and 43%). Thus subjects were responsive to differences in the semantic properties of these two kinds of sentences, even though the actual percentages of normalizing paraphrases were quite similar (64% and 70%). For "perverse" threats we find that paraphrases that normalize the source sentences were detected less often than they were overlooked (the figures are 20% and 34%).

What do subjects say is involved when they do detect differences between the strange source sentences and their paraphrases of them? For disordered conjunctive sentences of the two kinds studied a great majority of the comments refer to order changes, changes in temporal sequence, and changes in causal sequence. These comments are quite realistic, for it is just these sorts of changes that were actually involved in the meaning normalizing paraphrases. When paraphrases of "perverse" threats are judged to be different the most common observation was that the paraphrase is a sentence opposite in meaning to its source sentence. Again such comments are quite realistic, for normalization of perverse threats characteristically involved just that, see e.g., the difference between "Clean up the mess or I won't report you" and a paraphrase such as "If you clean up the mess I won't report you."

Such results pose two questions: (a) If subjects can detect differences between their paraphrases and the source sentences with regard to such significant matters as changes in temporal and causal order and changes which result in opposite meaning, then why did they provide such misleading paraphrases, given strong instructions to conserve meaning and warnings against attempting to improve or make the sentences more sensible? (b) If subjects cannot detect such substantial differences between the source sentences and their paraphrases, then what might be responsible for such blindness?

It seems plausible that the same general answer holds for both questions. Even in the peculiar circumstances of the psychological laboratory subjects seem to be acting on the basic assumption that *what is described in discourse will be sensible,* that what is described will conform to the customary order of events and will satisfy normal qualitative and causal relations between events or actions. If a sentence is encountered which appears to violate this assumption one may consider it to be a clumsy, inadequate phrasing or description, and turn it into a more appropriate version in one's paraphrase. Thus what is taken as awry or extraordinary is not the world, but the linguistic account of it. As to why subjects should have provided normalizing paraphrases when they *could* detect significant differences between these and the source sentences, it may be that as far as subjects are concerned a difference detected is not so much one between descriptions of two different sorts of events, as one between two different descriptions of the same event, with the paraphrase expressing properly what is *intended and badly expressed* by the original sentence. Finally, why might subjects have failed to notice differences between the source sentences and their normalizing paraphrases? This may just constitute further testimony to the strength of the basic assumption, such that the original "malphrased" sentences and their own "improved" versions are really regarded as amounting to the same description of sensibly ordered and organized events. The above suggestions, while speculative, find support in the comments subjects made at the end by way of explanation and justification of the paraphrases (see Fillenbaum, 1974c, for details). For about 80% of the subjects who often changed meaning in their paraphrases there is evidence in terms of these comments for the operation of an assumption that what is described in discourse must be sensibly organized, the subjects' claim being that, in one way or another, their paraphrases somehow put more adequately what was badly phrased in the original sentences. It seemed as though it was somehow very important for subjects to adjust things to conventional order and sequence and to exhibit the normal relations among events, so as to say properly what the speaker of the source sentence must have intended or meant.

People may make the basic assumption that sentences are sensible just because they believe that the events of which such sentences purport to be accounts occur or are organized in characteristic ways, and that it is much more likely that the world that is being described is the commonplace one and that the description is burdened with the errors and malapropisms of the speaker than that extraordinary events are being accurately and faithfully presented. It is as though people focus not on linguistic messages per se, but on the information they embody or appear to convey, considering and assimilating this information in relation to their preexisting knowledge of the ways of the world.

The term AND in one class of uses functions as an ordering or asymmetric operator, specifying a temporal–causal relation between the propositions conjoined. The term OR when appearing in an inducement statement which serves as a conditional threat must govern as alternative or second disjunct a proposition that involves something that the addressee does not want or wants to avoid. One may violate such constraints on the normal relations between events, whether in regard to physical or social causality, and determine what happens. In terms of the results just presented what often happens is that such pragmatically wild sentences are tamed, and that people may not even recognize what they are doing when in interpreting and making sense of such sentences, they assimilate them to the conventional relations among events. Thus this work illustrates how by a systematic misuse of some of the connectives one may study the interaction between prior knowledge and current linguistic inputs, and may demonstrate the enormous effects of the former on the latter.

IV. Problems for the Present and Future

So far we have only presented one or two examples of how one may capitalize on properties of terms such as AND, OR, and IF in order to approach some general semantic and pragmatic problems of interest to psycholinguistics, and have presented evidence that these terms may be variously used and understood. Results of the latter sort tell against any attempt by psychologists to develop an account of *the* representation of each of the connectives, unless they are also willing to have recourse to a set of conversational principles which might articulate with such a representation in each case so as to yield the various uses and understandings actually encountered—and that is certainly something that psychological theorists seem not even to have dreamed of. A consideration of the uses of the connectives also may have important consequences for linguistic theory as can be seen in Lawler (1975) who, on the basis of an examination of what he calls "elliptical conditionals," which correspond very closely to what we have been calling inducement statements, is forced to the conclusion that "any theory of language that employs centrally the concept of 'derivation' is wrong [p. 371]," and that an account in "transderivational" terms will not do very well either. But obviously such observations only provide a starting point or point of departure. What is needed are conceptual analyses of and empirical research on the various uses of such terms, perhaps in the spirit of our comments and work on conditional promises and threats. Analysis is needed for all sorts of phenomena already touched on, as well as for others that have not even been mentioned. As to the latter, consider e.g., how "factoring" works when there is a conjunction of modals such that the AND of "You can have steak, and you can have chicken, and you can have fried fish" amounts to an underlying disjunction "You can have steak or chicken or fried fish" (see Horn, 1972, pp. 161–180, on factoring for modals, negated statements, and conditionals). Or, with regard to the constraint of common topic, note how a statement like "Robin is a bachelor and he is a man" is strange in a way that "Robin is a man and he is a bachelor" is not, as though it were a further condition on ordinary conjunction that the second conjunct not assert some content which already follows from the first conjunct, perhaps in the spirit of some Gricean principle of economy (Horn, 1972, p. 79). Or, to touch on only one more example, how is it that something like "The dress is not red and it is not orange" may characteristically be understood to suggest or bracket a color region, viz. somewhere in between the adjacent named colors, in a way very different from the understanding of "The dress is not red and it is not green," which does not appear to bracket any larger intermediate region, but may rather leave the auditor puzzled as to quite what the speaker was trying to communicate? Obviously conceptual analysis and empirical research is needed and one cannot very well predict or anticipate the outcomes of such work. What we can do is to offer some general considerations that appear relevant on the basis of what has been done already or touched on already, as well as to mention a few other problems obviously of significance that will need to be faced. What all this amounts to is a very partial catalogue of our ignorance, which reveals the great gap between what we know and what we need to know.

To start we shall elaborate here on some issues already considered, and in doing so will note first implicitly and then explicitly that much of the understanding and use of the connectives requires reference to an interpersonal or dialogic situation and that many of the phenomena can only be understood by reference to such a situation, something systematically ignored in much of the psychological work in this area. Then we shall mention some further issues that demand investigation, e.g., with regard to the understanding of propositions complex because they involve more than a single connective, particularly propositions that include negation as well as conjunction, disjunction, or implication.

A. NATURAL LOGIC

Following Johnson-Laird (1975) we have argued that, in large part, propositional reasoning depends on or even amounts to an understanding of the meaning of the basic sentence connectives. What we have here is a sort of fusion of the phenomena of lexical understanding and reasoning, and any adequate account of these phenomena should tell us much about natural logic, i.e., how people reason with or in natural language. This is so not only because of the crucial and indispensable role played by the sentence connectives themselves, but also because of their intimate relation to quantificational phenomena. Consider the suggestion made by a number of linguists (see, e.g., McCawley, 1972) that some of the connectives are very closely related to the quantifiers, that "The operators AND and OR are in important logical respects parallel to the quantifiers ALL and SOME respectively [Horn, 1972, p. 93]." And note that in the present chapter we have identified at least one use of the conditional, that as a sort of contingent universal ("If the coat is wool it will wear well"), which seems to relate IF rather closely to the universal quantifier ALL. Obviously the relation between the connectives and quantificational phenomena requires and merits much further exploration, and it may turn out that a study of the former can provide us with important insights into the understanding and use of the quantifiers. For a significant start on these issues see the work of the linguist Horn (1972), who has already shown that there is not only a syntactic and logical relation between AND and OR and ALL and SOME, respectively, but that there are also pragmatic correspondences in regard to what is conversationally suggested or "implicated." Insofar as the study of the connectives may provide us with information about propositional reasoning and about the working of quantificational phenomena, it necessarily will have bearing of large scope with regard to natural logic.

Certain "fallacies" in reasoning may be particularly interesting and revealing. In part this is so because they show, again, that a truth–functional account is inadequate as a description of propositional reasoning. Perhaps more important is the possibility that "The prescriptivist logician, by banishing specific forms of argument, reveals to us how people actually reason . . . [for] we are only warned against those sins we are considered susceptible of committing [Horn, 1973, p. 213]." Given, e.g., that people commit the fallacy of the denied antecedent in the context of conditional promises and threats, or that they believe that someone who says "Some chapters of this book are interesting" means to convey that some *only* (but not all) are interesting, then it becomes of great importance to determine the contextual factors and pragmatic conversational rules that not only permit but may even require such "fallacious" inferences. Thus such phenomena starkly exhibit the importance of pragmatic, contextual considerations and the ways in which knowledge of the world interacts with sentence content in determining message interpretation. Consider again the book example immediately above, now given knowledge of the fact that the speaker has only very recently obtained the book and at most had a chance to read three or four chapters. Under those circumstances the "some" of "some chapters of this book . . ." is much more likely to be interpreted as *at least some* than as *only some.* The basic point here, of course, is that knowledge and assumptions about the world are important in guiding interpretations and determining the inferences that are made, and that such knowledge depends on an understanding of p's and q's in context. The preceding raises difficult questions as to how one can characterize contexts and conversational principles or rules, and how one may conceive of the manner of their interaction. Perhaps even more basic and more difficult yet, it raises reasoning in natural logic, and how contextual information is to be assessed to determine validity or invalidity in particular cases. Only to raise this problem is enough to induce panic.

All the preceding makes sense only on the premise that people are concerned with communication in context, and that communication in context characteristically requires going, in various ways, beyond what is explicitly and directly said. We have shown earlier that knowledge of the ways of the world may systematically affect the interpretation of pragmatically strange messages, that people are sensitive to the presuppositions and "implicatures" of statements, that in the context of inducements people are very prone to make inferences that are logically "fallacious" but quite compelling given only some reasonable general assumptions about the logic of conversation. Our position is basically similar to that of Johnson-Laird (1975) who points out "that a listener is able to draw on general knowledge to allow a speaker to leave many things unsaid" and argues "that people exploit a communal base of knowledge . . . this knowledge will be automatically elicited by any utterance with a relevant topic, and it can be used by the inferential machinery in order to make good any gaps in the explicit discourse." The interesting and difficult problems arise when one tries to formulate the underlying contextually and conversationally sensitive rules necessary to account for the ways in which the often conveyed meanings may be attained. Both in such general terms and in terms of some of the particular examples considered here it seems unlikely that any account that focuses on or restricts itself to truth–functional considerations will prove sufficient to the phenomena. What is important is not only that a message be true, but that it have a point in context, and understanding the point of a message will often require that one go beyond what is said literally, and beyond truth–functional considerations.

B. THE LANGUAGE OF REGULATIONS

By way of a partial aside, one may refer to a class of rather extraordinary uses of language that by a contrasting attempt to stick to literal meaning highlights the more usual dependence on meanings conveyed via conversational principles. Consider legal language, in particular the language of regulations which in order to minimize misinterpretation, or rather multiple interpretations, is replete with qualifications usually largely carried by multiple, nested uses of the sentence connectives; thus one gets something like "No agency shall do . . . [X] . . ., except . . . [A] . . . or . . . [B] . . . unless . . . [C]," where C itself is an 11-way disjunction of conditions, almost every one of which is stuffed with further AND's, OR's, and IF's nested within each other (see Public Law 93-579, 93rd Congress, S. 3418, December 31, 1974). Such phrasing which seeks to eliminate ambiguity by spelling everything out explicitly can very readily defeat its own purposes, even on its own terms, by making it almost impossible to traverse and grasp the structural network of the regulation, even given a written text and a sophisticated reader equipped with aids to memory and calculation. Obviously as spoken language it is ludicrous and impossible because neither a speaker nor an addressee could keep track of all the nested relations and qualifications involved. Actually even as a written text it can work only if the sentence operators or connectives and their scopes as used in legal documents are completely and unambiguously specifiable (in context-free ways), in a manner different from their employment in everyday language. Given the amount of litigation involving the range of application of regulations and laws this seems unlikely. In any case the main point here is that it is at the very least very difficult, and certainly *qua* normal conversational use quite extraordinary, to restrict oneself only to literal understanding of what is said directly and explicitly (cf. Walker, 1975, pp. 171–173).

C. COMMON TOPIC

On numerous occasions we have referred to a constraint of common topic on most of the uses of the various connectives, without saying anything much as to what might be meant by "common topic" which "may be overtly present in the superficial structure of the sentence, or may be derivable by more or less complex combinations of presuppositions + deductions [Lakoff, 1971, p. 148]." One might look to conversational principles of the sort offered by Grice (1967, 1975) for help in this matter. When one does, one finds under the cooperative principle which specifies the conventions people should and normally do obey in conversation a maxim of relation which says "Be relevant." Presumably this may be understood not only as requiring that what is said be properly connected to what it is being said about, but also that the various things being said be appropriately connectible to each other. So here is a conversational principle that is pertinent to the matter of the topic constraint. The problem, of course, is that the maxim of relation is so broadly and vaguely phrased that, at best, it may be taken as a restatement of the constraint of common topic, not as an explication of what that constraint involves. It is not that an appropriate conversational principle is lacking, but rather that the one available is not worked out sufficiently to be useful. Perhaps another way to approach the problem is, as it were, to turn things upside down, by taking the topic constraint on the use of the sentence connectives as a given and then systematically varying properties of the connected p and q propositions to see how this affects the acceptability of the resulting complex sentences. Also, since we know that subjects can find justifying contexts for sentences judged to be strange because at first encounter the individual propositions appear to be unrelated (Fillenbaum, 1974b), we may look for useful information to the nature of the justifying context offered, and particularly to the difficulty they have in providing contexts as reflected by the amount of time it takes to do so for various cases.

D. THE INTERPERSONAL CONTEXT

At this point it may be well to reiterate explicitly something that has been implicit in much of the prior discussions, viz. that any account of the sentence connectives will need to consider their understanding and use in interpersonal at least dialogic situations, that the more common practice of examining these terms from a monologic, intrapersonal perspective is grossly inadequate. (Perhaps it is just because of the latter sort of emphasis that psychologists have so often focused on trying to develop a truth–functional account for these terms.) All the talk about conversational principles and conveyed meaning obviously presupposes an interpersonal or dialogic account in which one directs attention to the speech act in

which a complex proposition occurs and worries about the illocutionary force or role of the utterance, about what the speaker is
trying to do by saying just that, just then. In this sense any speech
act account is very intimately tied to an interpersonal situation. The
example that has been discussed most fully in the present chapter,
the use of the conditional in inducements, would be literally mean-
ingless and pointless except in an interpersonal context, and the
whole analysis of this use of the conditional depends absolutely on
certain assumptions about interpersonal communication. Many other
examples could be given and other cases we have presented could be
used in support of this general thesis, but here we shall limit ourselves to one further example only, the very important case of
negation. Perhaps the principal use of negation is to correct or falsify
some preconception (Wason, 1972), "to contradict or correct; to
cancel a suggestion [Strawson, 1952]." Obviously one cannot readily
correct or contradict unless there is already something there that
needs to be challenged or corrected. To say "The train was not late
today" seems rather pointless, unless the train is usually late or
unless someone thought it was late today. Thus while overtly there is
nothing dialogic about sentence negation, implicitly this is one of its
characteristic preconditions. We shall see a little later that for the
case of negation of propositions that are themselves complex because
they involve one of the sentence connectives such as AND, OR, or
IF, it is by no means always obvious quite what is being corrected or
cancelled, or what the governing conditions for cancellation may be
(which among other things will again raise difficulties for any simply
truth–functional analysis).

To summarize much of what has been said above, perhaps psychologists have been too much concerned with the logic of the
connectives, where "logic" is narrowly construed to emphasize
truth–functional considerations as the individual engages in propositional reasoning with stress on formal patterns, obliging one to
systematically ignore the particular p's and q's involved (and where
doing just that counts as a *virtue*), and have not been sufficiently
concerned with the rhetoric of the connectives, where "rhetoric"
broadly conceived draws attention to semantic content and pragmatic contextual considerations and the interpersonal uses of language in communicating and practical reasoning, forcing us to consider how the connectives function in complex sentences uttered to
some (specific) purpose. Only in such terms can one understand the
popularity of studies on rule learning (see, e.g., Bourne, 1970), and
of studies like that of Taplin and Staudenmayer (1973) cited earlier

where, in the service of control, the p and q propositions were realized by letters of the alphabet, and the relative scarcity of studies such as that of Naess (1962) which show how "*les structures conceptuelles impliquées dans les inférences utilizant 'ou' sont différentes et présentent des variations marquées en fonction du contenu de p et q et du contexte verbal* [p. 161]." As Naess states "la question de la frontière entre le formel et le contenu est encore une question ouverte [p. 164]"; some 15 years have elapsed, but that question is still open and, if anything, looks even more formidable.

E. PRESUPPOSITIONS

We turn now to a mention of some important problems that have not even been broached hitherto, on each of which there is little or no psychological work. Consider first the matter of the presuppositions of complex propositions involving the sentence connectives. In recent times linguists have become very interested in questions as to the nature of presupposition (see, e.g., some of the papers in Fillmore & Langendoen, 1971; Kempson, 1975; Wilson, 1975), and psychologists too have come to be concerned with these questions (see, e.g., Harris, 1974; Osgood, 1971). Indeed one of the studies discussed earlier in the present chapter dealt with memory, among other things, for the presuppositions of counterfactual conditionals, and it was shown that people often falsely remembered having directly encountered such presuppositions. But the concern there was with memory for presuppositions and other information implicit in the individual propositions entering into a counterfactual. A natural further question is to ask about the presuppositions of the complex propositions themselves, to ask for each connective what the function is that relates the presuppositions of the complex proposition to the presuppositions of its constituent propositions (in a way quite analogous to that in which one asks for each connective about the truth value of the complex proposition as a function of the truth values of its constituent propositions). In the context of a more general study of the presuppositions of compound sentences, Karttunen (1973a, 1973b) has addressed himself to this matter. The basic problem is that the presuppositions of a complex sentence (complex because it involves one of the sentence connectives AND, OR, or IF) sometimes include all the presuppositions of the constituent p and q sentences, sometimes not. If the p and q propositions are semantically unrelated then the complex proposition always includes all the presuppositions of the constituent clauses, but if they are semantically related this does not happen. Consider, for example, the difference between "If Jack has sisters then all of Jack's children are bald" and "If Jack has children then all of Jack's children are bald," where the first complex sentence maintains the presupposition of the consequent, that Jack has children, whereas in the second case the presupposition of the consequent is not kept in the complex sentence. The obvious problem is to formulate appropriately the conditions that filter presuppositions for complex sentences involving each of the connectives when the p and q propositions are semantically related. Karttunen (1973a) argues that a pragmatic account in which presupposition is treated as relative to context is necessary, that "the most important aspect of the filtering conditions is that the cancelling of presuppositions depends on the semantic relations between the sentences involved and not their truth values [p. 191]," and that there is an asymmetry between the behavior of the presuppositions of the first and second clauses of complex sentences such that presuppositions of the first clause are always maintained in the complex sentence while those of the second clause may become void. He then formulates filtering conditions for IF, AND, and OR, respectively. The filtering conditions for the first two terms turn out to be identical (basically that relative to context any presupposition of the first clause is always a presupposition of the complex sentence and that any presupposition of the second clause is also a presupposition of the complex sentence unless it is entailed by the first clause), and different from those for OR (in which case the presupposition of the second clause is filtered out only if it is entailed by the negation of the first clause). Karttunen (1973b) has extended and modified his analysis in a number of respects, but both the original analysis and the revised version have been severely challenged. Thus Katz and Langendoen (1976) argue that a contextual, pragmatic account of presupposition is unnecessary and that a purely semantic analysis of presupposition is all that is needed, and claim that in any case "AND and OR are never by themselves associated with the filtering or presuppositions." Wilson (1975) provides evidence against the correctness of the asymmetry condition (indicating that the presuppositions of the first clause may also be filtered out of the complex sentence), and both Wilson (1975) and Kempson (1975) develop arguments that favor an entailment based theory over a presuppositional account. Given the recency of this work and the disputes among linguists as to the most appropriate analysis of the phenomena, it is perhaps not surprising that psychologists have as yet done nothing with the problem. Regardless of the outcome of the disputes mentioned above, however, one basic point should be clear, namely that the properties of the p and q propositions connected in a complex proposition are important in that the complex proposition will be differently understood if the p and q propositions are semantically unrelated than if they are semantically related, and that therefore the listener will need to be responsive to such properties in order to be able to determine whether or not the p and q propositions are semantically related and, if so, how they are related. Again the lesson is the same as before: One must mind one's p's and q's, now with regard to matters of presuppositions or entailment.

It may perhaps be worthwhile to remind ourselves as to why presuppositional phenomena must be of interest to the cognitive psychologist concerned with problems of reasoning and communication. Someone who makes some statement implicitly imposes the presuppositions of that statement on his audience (and himself), and what is taken for granted may in important ways constrain and determine the conclusions that can be drawn and responses or replies that can be made. Now in this regard there may be some interesting and important similarities between presuppositional phenomena, where the listener is constrained and thus implicitly coerced into making certain assumptions, and suppositional phenomena, i.e., uses of the conditional, where the listener is overtly solicited to consider some assumption, which is explicitly presented as a hypothesis and which, *qua* hypothesis, is therefore open to challenge. Consider, e.g., the possible parallels between what happens when there is presupposition failure in the first case and what happens when the antecedent clause of a conditional is false in the second case. Thus it is quite possible that a general consideration of the phenomena of presupposition may have important implications for an understanding of conditionals and, in turn, that analyses of the uses of the conditional may have some bearing on our understanding of presuppositional phenomena. For some suggestive and intriguing comments on these lines, see Ducrot (1972), particularly chapter 6 which is titled "Supposition et présupposition" in which he argues that "l'hypothèse de la subordonnée conditionelle se comporte en beaucoup de points, lorsque la phrase conditionelle subit diverses modifications, selon les règles habituelles de la présupposition [p. 168]."

F.   MORE THAN ONE OPERATOR: NEGATION OF
   COMPLEX SENTENCES

The present work is limited in scope in that we have considered only three simplex sentence connectives, although these, AND, OR, and

IF, are surely particularly important terms. We have had nothing to say about the major negation operator(s), or about what might be called complex connectives, i.e., terms that on semantic or pragmatic grounds combine more than one function. (For some discussion of a term such as BUT, see e.g., Lakoff, 1971; Osgood & Richards, 1973; see also Fillenbaum & Rapoport, 1971; for some data and comments on UNLESS, in particular considering the role of this term in inducements, see Fillenbaum, 1976.) Further, to this point essentially nothing has been said about cases where a proposition involves more than one operator. Perhaps the most interesting and important class of these propositions is that where negation operates on a complex proposition involving one of the simplex connectives. Some data on the interpretation of such complex negated propositions in the characteristic context of an interpersonal, dialogic encounter may be cited here (Fillenbaum, unpublished study). Subjects were asked to indicate what they understood by the negation of various kinds of complex sentences, the task being posed in a dialogic context where they were to indicate what an overheard speaker most likely meant when he replied, "No, that's not so" to a given target sentence. Let us present some of the principal results.[9] In these circumstances the denial of propositions involving use of an un-ordered AND was interpreted as *not p and not q* over 60% of the time and as *p and not q* not quite 20% of the time, while the denial of propositions involving use of an AND that was ordered in a temporal or temporal–causal fashion was interpreted as *not p and not q* only about one-third of the time and as *p and not q* over 40% of the time.[10] The denial of propositions involving an unordered exclusive use of OR was interpreted as *not p and not q* 50% of the time, while the denial of propositions involving an ordered causal use

[9] These results are averages based on the coding of the interpretations given in a free response task. Results of a later study using a multiple-choice format with prespecified alternative interpretations were different in important respects. While this suggests caution in interpreting the results presented here, we believe nevertheless that such results are more likely to be valid than those based on a multiple-choice task where the subject is provided with alternatives that might never even have occurred to him on his own, something which might grossly affect the responses.

[10] These results are compatible with those obtained on a different task where for each of the sentences subjects were asked to indicate explicitly what they thought was being denied—the first clause, the second clause, or the entire sentence. For sentences involving an unordered use of AND 75% of the responses claimed that the entire sentence was being denied, while for sentences involving an ordered use of AND only a little over 50% of the choices were for sentence negation and 30% claimed that the second clause only was being denied.

of OR (e.g., "He will leave immediately or miss the plane") was interpreted as *not p implies not q*, or simply *not q* 50% of the time, and as something like *not necessarily the case that not p implies q* or *not p may or may not imply q* almost 40% of the time. The denial of a causal–temporal *If p, q* proposition was interpreted as *If p, not q* almost 60% of the time and as something like *If p, maybe q maybe not q* roughly 40% of the time. The results for negation of ordered OR propositions and negation of temporal–causal *If p, q* propositions are thus rather similar, which is not surprising if one recalls that the former, which function more or less as warnings, may readily be rephrased as (temporal–causal) conditionals with the first proposition negated. (Thus "He will leave immediately or miss the plane" can be paraphrased as "If he does not leave immediately he will miss the plane.") The denial of a contingent universal *If p, q* proposition was interpreted as *If p, not q* around 25% of the time and as something like *If p, maybe q maybe not q* a little over 60% of the time. Thus the results for temporal–causal and contingent universal conditionals are quite different under negation, which is again not too surprising given some of the differences between these reported earlier when negation was not involved. The last finding reported, on the interpretation of negation of contingent universal IF sentences, is of interest if one considers the relation between contingent universals phrased with IF, such as "If the coat is wool it is warm," and universally quantified statements of the form "All wool coats are warm," where the former sort of statement appears to presuppose the latter. We have noted above that negation of a contingent universal use of IF yielded an interpretation of something like *If p, maybe q maybe not q* about 60% of the time. But the negation of matched universally quantified sentences yielded the interpretation *Some p are q some are not q* between 98% and 99% of the time. Thus the sort of interpretation that is given essentially unanimously to the denial of the presupposed universally quantified statement is given only about 60% of the time to the denial of the entailed conditional. Obviously there will be problems in making sense of such data on the relation between conditionals and universally quantified statements under negation. More generally, data of the sort cited above indicate that indeed it is not always clear what is being cancelled when negation operates on a complex sentence involving one of the connectives AND, OR, and IF, and that different uses of a particular connective may systematically bias interpretation one way or another under negation. Such findings again argue against the adequacy of any simple truth–functionally based account, now for the case of the negation of sentences employing the basic simplex sentence connectives. While it would be very desirable to have an account of such results based on the application of conversational principles, it is not at all obvious how such an account is to be developed.[11]

G. INDIVIDUAL DIFFERENCES

In all the foregoing we have treated questions of the understanding and use of the sentence connectives as though these phenomena, whatever they might be, were pretty much the same for all people or subjects, i.e., we have completely ignored the possibility of consistent individual differences. But there is considerable evidence that there are systematic individual differences in coping with sentences involving such terms as AND, OR, and IF (see, e.g., Fillenbaum, 1971, 1974c; Shapiro and O'Brien, 1973; Staudenmayer, 1975; Taplin, 1971; Taplin & Staudenmayer, 1973). Such evidence on differences in the understanding of the connectives is disturbing because these are critical, indispensable terms used with very great frequency and one would expect communication often to falter in serious ways if different people understood and used these terms in different fashions. One might perhaps offer two general suggestions which if correct might mitigate matters, or at least provide a perspective on such results. First, demand characteristics may be of importance here with different subjects understanding task requirements differently, so that in the context of the experimental situation some subjects are moved toward logical and linguistic rigidity, what Tennessen (1962) has called "a logico-maniacal" attitude of "rigid pedantic hairsplitting," while others remain more flexible "latitudinarians" respecting everyday vernacular uses of the terms.[12] If this is so then in substantial measure interindividual differences in coping with the sentence connectives may be an artifact of and specific to the experimental situations in which

---

[11] For some discussion of difficulties in interpreting the denial of conditionals and an attempt to approach the problem via the notion of "implicature," see Grice (1967, Chap. 5) who notes "that it is by no means clear just what a speaker who says 'it is not the case that if p,q' *is* committing himself to or intending to convey"; also see Ducrot (1972, Chap. 6) who makes some attempt to comment on these problems in terms of the operation of a "composant rhétorique"; for some relevant comments on negation and falsity see Wilson (1975, pp. 149–151).

[12] Tennessen (1962) has shown that prior instruction can systematically bias subjects to the one or the other attitude.

subjects have been tested, and in normal extralaboratory circumstances such differences might be considerably reduced. The second suggestion has bearing on possible (remaining) interindividual differences in understanding in ordinary everyday situations, outside the laboratory. To the extent that such understanding is pragmatically based requiring the application of conversational principles and assumptions about knowledge of the world and states of the speaker, listeners may differ in their interpretations because they order the maxims of conversation differently or make different assumptions about the world or different attributions about speaker knowledge and intentions, etc. The point is simply that if contextual determinants are important, different listeners may assess or evaluate such contextual information differently, and thus come up with different interpretations. What has just been suggested is schematic in the extreme, but an account developed along these lines might perhaps make it possible to make sense of interindividual differences in everyday understanding and "practical" reasoning.

H. OMISSIONS

   The present chapter has addressed itself to problems where understanding constitutes a sort of interface between thinking and communication and, from a broader perspective, has dealt with questions of the relation between logic (or rhetoric) and language and of the cognitive representations that subserve these. Such matters fall into an interstitial area or sort of no-man's land between logic/philosophy, linguistics, and psychology. Work in this area has had a long and difficult, if not bedeviled history, yielding little in the way of large or well-established conclusions, so the limited progress made in the present enterprise should not be surprising. What is perhaps worth stressing is how much has been deliberately omitted or left aside, even of the work that is, in principle, fairly directly pertinent. Thus, in the area of philosophy we have not touched on work on the logic of entailment of the sort reviewed by Anderson and Belnap (1976) in their magisterial volume. In linguistics we have barely mentioned the sort of descriptive work to be found in Quirk *et al.* (1972), the analyses of phenomena of coordination to be found in Dik (1968), and the work on the semantics of the logical operators of English as presented in Horn (1972). And from psychology proper, too, there are large omissions. Nothing has been said about the work on rule learning (see, e.g., Bourne, 1970). In addition, and perhaps most importantly, developmental research on the relation between the "logical connectives in language and their cognitive correlates" has been ignored. (See Beilin, 1975, for a fine review of this work together with reports of some new, extensive experiments.[13]) The list of meae culpae could easily be extended.[14] About all that can be pleaded in extenuation is a lack of space, together with difficulties in assessing quite how, specifically, work of the sorts just cited bears on our present concerns. To take an example from psychology, it is not clear what implications work on the learning of conceptual rules defined in truth table terms that establishes, say, some consistent rank ordering of difficulty among these concepts (e.g., Bourne, 1970; Bourne & O'Banion, 1971) can have for an understanding of the uses of the sentence connectives in everyday speech, if it is the case, as we have sought to demonstrate throughout, that the use and understanding of these connectives falls beyond the scope of any simply truth–functional system.

I. CONCLUSION

What this chapter has attempted to do is show that there are various uses of the connectives and that such uses are *content* and *context* sensitive. It seems clear that a monologic account of propositional thinking in terms of truth–functional logic, which has been the favored approach of the psychologist, is insufficient if one considers the uses of the connectives in everyday speech, and that a dialogic, rhetorical approach which focuses on the speech act and which considers what the speaker is trying to do by saying what he does in the relevant interpersonal context will be necessary, and that such an

---

[13] With regard to Beilin (1975) it should be noted that this work whose purpose was to study "the empirical or psychological relations between the cognitive operations that underlie set union, intersection, complementation, and the comprehension of the theoretically related language connectives [p.187] " deliberately ignores what are called "alogical or colloquial language uses of these terms," the language tasks being set up so that "temporal order and other alogical functions which might otherwise interact with connective comprehension are precluded [p. 219]." Proceeding so may rule out of court, right at the start, some of the most significant phenomena that should be of concern. If one is interested in the cognitive correlates or antecedents of comprehension of the connectives, it may be theoretically suicidal to purge these terms of some of their most characteristic properties before one starts. Obviously such work cannot provide much in the way of information on "the formal relations between English idioms expressing conjunction, disjunction and negation and the set theoretical operations . . ." which Suppes and Feldman (1971) see as important for a deeper understanding of linguistic and semantic issues.

[14] For some work too recent to be taken into account here see, e.g., Braine (1976) and Rips and Marcus (in press).

account will somehow have to provide an analysis of how people manage to go beyond what is explicitly said so as to understand the communications addressed to them.

By stressing that the listener must go beyond what is said to him directly, we are drawing attention to the need for an account of the uses and understandings of complex AND, OR, and IF propositions in terms of a theory of indirect speech acts (Searle, 1975). Such a need has been implicit in much of the discussion throughout this chapter, and has been directly exemplified in our suggestions toward an analysis of the conditional as used in inducements. The problem of indirect speech acts is that of how a speaker can say something and mean that *and* something else (or even *only* something else), and of how an addressee can understand the indirect speech act when the actual sentence he encounters literally means something else. In indirect speech acts the speaker communicates to the addressee more than he actually says by relying on their mutually shared background information, both linguistic and nonlinguistic, together with general powers of rationality and inference on the part of the addressee. The conceptual apparatus for an account of indirect speech acts includes a theory of speech acts proper together with principles of cooperative conversation, mutually shared background information, and the ability of the addressee to make (appropriate) inferences. (See Searle, 1975, p. 63, which illustrates the steps that may be necessary to derive the "primary illocution" in a particular case; see also pp. 71–74.) Insofar as a conceptual apparatus for the understanding of indirect speech acts has already been developed in terms of relevant felicity conditions (see, e.g., Searle, 1969, 1975), it may be possible to apply this apparatus to the study of complex sentences involving such sentence connectives as AND, OR, and IF, and the study of such sentences from this point of view may serve to enrich and extend that conceptual apparatus. (For some preliminary observations in this vein, see Munro, in press, who comments on Fillenbaum's 1976 analysis of conditional threats from the perspective of what he calls "procedural" semantics.)

Just as the definition of concepts and categories solely in terms of arbitrary constellations of features may have been misleading (see, e.g., Rosch & Mervis, 1975, and work cited there), so the psychologist's propensity to look just for a truth–functional account of the sentence connectives may prove to have been overly constraining and misleading. The work presented in this chapter constitutes a study of lexical semantics that demonstrates the contextual control of word use and understanding, for the case of two or three *very* important words. There is little reason to believe that such contextual effects are unique to just these words, and therefore perhaps the present work, and in particular the sketch of an analysis of inducements, may be taken as at least suggestive with regard to the need for and possible yields of a psycholexicology that includes a pragmatic perspective.

To conclude: *that* one needs to mind one's *p*'s and *q*'s by considering content and context has hopefully been established; *how* this is done by people and *how* this may be represented and handled in any conceptual account is certainly still unclear, and all we have been able to do is to note some of the problems that will have to be confronted by any viable theory and some of the considerations that will likely prove to be relevant. Any model of semantic memory with pretense to realism will have to address itself to such matters insofar as it provides representations for the connectives and procedures for their use, and insofar as it fails to do so any pretense to realism will be pretense only.

REFERENCES

Anderson, A. R., & Belnap, N. D. *Entailment: The logic of relevance and necessity* (Vol. 1). Princeton: Princeton University Press, 1976.

Austin, J. L. *How to do things with words.* London & New York: Oxford University Press, 1962.

Bartlett, F. C. *Remembering.* Cambridge: Cambridge University Press, 1932.

Beilin, H. *Studies in the cognitive basis of language development.* New York: Academic Press, 1975.

Bobrow, D. G., & Collins, A. (Eds.). *Representation and understanding.* New York: Academic Press, 1975.

Bourne, L. E. Knowing and using concepts. *Psychological Review,* 1970, 77, 546–556.

Bourne, L. E., & O'Banion, K. Conceptual rule learning and chronological age. *Developmental Psychology,* 1971, 5, 525–534.

Braine, M. D. S. The natural logic of propositional reasoning: A proposal. Unpublished, 1976.

Bransford, J. D., Barclay, J. R., & Franks, J. J. Sentence memory: A constructive versus interpretive approach. *Cognitive Psychology,* 1972, 3, 193–209.

Clark, H. H., & Lucy, P. Understanding what is meant from what is said: A study in conversationally conveyed requests. *Journal of Verbal Learning and Verbal Behavior,* 1975, 14, 56–72.

Cohen, L. J. Some remarks on Grice's views about the logical particles of natural language. In Y. Bar-Hillel (Ed.), *Pragmatics of natural language.* Dordrecht: Reidel, 1971.

Cole, P., & Morgan, J. L. (Eds.). *Syntax and semantics* (Vol. 3). *Speech acts.* New York: Academic Press, 1975.

Culicover, P. W. OM-sentences. *Foundations of Language,* 1972, 8, 199–236.

Dik, S. C. *Coordination.* Amsterdam: North-Holland Publ., 1968.

Ducrot, O. *Dire et ne pas dire.* Paris: Hermann, 1972.

Fillenbaum, S. On coping with ordered and unordered conjunctive sentences. *Journal of Experimental Psychology,* 1971, **87,** 93–98.

Fillenbaum, S. *Syntactic factors in memory?* The Hague: Mouton, 1973.

Fillenbaum, S. Information amplified: Memory for counterfactual conditionals. *Journal of Experimental Psychology,* 1974, **102,** 44–49. (a)

Fillenbaum, S. OR: Some uses. *Journal of Experimental Psychology,* 1974, **103,** 913–921. (b)

Fillenbaum, S. Pragmatic normalization: Further results for some conjunctive and disjunctive sentences. *Journal of Experimental Psychology,* 1974, **102,** 574–578. (c)

Fillenbaum, S. A note on memory for sense: Incidental recognition of warnings phrased as conditionals, disjunctives, and conjunctives. *Bulletin of the Psychonomic Society,* 1975, **6,** 293–294. (a)

Fillenbaum, S. IF: Some uses. *Psychological Research,* 1975, **37,** 245–260. (b)

Fillenbaum, S. Inducements: On the phrasing and logic of conditional promises, threats, and warnings. *Psychological Research,* 1976, **38,** 231–250.

Fillenbaum, S. A condition on plausible inducements. *Language and Speech,* in press.

Fillenbaum, S., & Rapoport, A. *Structures in the subjective lexicon.* New York: Academic Press, 1971.

Fillmore, C. J., & Langendoen, D. T. (Eds.). *Studies in linguistic semantics.* New York: Holt, 1971.

Fraser, B. An analysis of "even" in English. In C. J. Fillmore & D. T. Langendoen (Eds.), *Studies in linguistic semantics.* New York: Holt, 1971.

Geis, M. L., & Zwicky, A. M. On invited inferences. *Linguistic Inquiry,* 1971, **2,** 560–566.

Gordon, D., & Lakoff, G. Conversational postulates. In *Papers from the seventh regional meeting of the Chicago Linguistic Society.* Chicago: University of Chicago Department of Linguistics, 1971.

Grice, H. P. *Logic and Conversation.* Unpublished lecture notes, William James Lectures, Harvard University, 1967.

Grice, H. P. Logic and conversation. In P. Cole & J. L. Morgan (Eds.), *Syntax and semantics* (Vol. 3). *Speech acts.* New York: Academic Press, 1975.

Grize, J. B., & Matalon, B. Introduction à une étude éxperimentale et formelle du raisonnement naturel. In E. W. Beth, J. B. Grize, R. Martin, B. Matalon, A. Naess, & J. Piaget, *Implication, formalisation et logique naturelle. Études d'épistémologie génétique* (Vol. 16). Paris: Presses Universitaires de France, 1962.

Harman, G. *If* and modus ponens. Unpublished manuscript, 1975.

Harris, R. J. Memory for presuppositions and implications: A case study of 12 verbs of motion and inception-termination. *Journal of Experimental Psychology,* 1974, **103,** 594–597.

Heringer, J. T. *Some grammatical correlates of felicity conditions and presuppositions.* Unpublished doctoral dissertation, Ohio State University, 1971.

Horn, L. R. *On the semantic properties of logical operators in English.* Unpublished doctoral dissertation, University of California, Los Angeles, 1972.

Horn, L. R. Greek Grice: A brief survey of proto-conversational rules in the history of logic. In *Papers from the ninth regional meeting of the Chicago Linguistic Society.* Chicago: Chicago Linguistic Society, 1973.

Johnson-Laird, P. N. Models of deduction. In R. J. Falmagne (Ed.), *Reasoning: Representation and process.* Hillsdale, N.J.: Lawrence Erlbaum Associates, 1975.

Karttunen, L. Counterfactual conditionals. *Linguistic Inquiry,* 1971, **2,** 566–569.

Karttunen, L. Presuppositions of compound sentences. *Linguistic Inquiry,* 1973, **4,** 169–193. (a)

Karttunen, L. *Remarks on presuppositions.* Paper presented at the Texas Conference on Performances, Conversational Implicature and Presuppositions, March 1973. (b)

Katz, J. J., & Langendoen, D. T. Pragmatics and presupposition. *Language,* 1976, **52,** 1–17.

Kempson, R. M. *Presupposition and the delimitation of semantics.* London & New York: Cambridge University Press, 1975.

Lakoff, R. If's and's and but's about conjunction. In C. J. Fillmore & D. T. Langendoen (Eds.), *Studies in linguistic semantics.* New York: Holt, 1971.

Lawler, J. M. Elliptical conditionals and/or hyperbolic imperatives: Some remarks on the inherent inadequacy of derivations. In *Papers from the eleventh regional meeting of the Chicago Linguistic Society.* Chicago: Chicago Linguistic Society, 1975.

McCawley, J. A programme for logic. In D. Davidson & G. Harman (Eds.), *Semantics of natural language.* Dordrecht: Reidel, 1972.

Morgan, J. L. Some interactions of syntax and pragmatics. In P. Cole & J. L. Morgan (Eds.), *Syntax and semantics* (Vol. 3). *Speech acts.* New York: Academic Press, 1975.

Munro, A. Comments on lexical semantics. In J. W. Cotton & R. L. Klatzky (Eds.), *Semantic factors in cognition.* Hillsdale, N. J.: Lawrence Erlbaum Associates, in press.

Naess, A. L'emploi de la disjonction chez les adolescents. In E. W. Beth, J. B. Grize, R. Martin, B. Matalon, A. Naess, & J. Piaget, *Implication, formalisation et logique naturelle. Études d'épistémologie génétique* (Vol. 16). Paris: Presses Universitaires de France, 1962.

O'Brien, T. C. Logical thinking in college students. *Educational Studies in Mathematics,* 1973, **5,** 71–79.

O'Brien, T. C., Shapiro, B. J., & Reali, N. C. Logical thinking, language and context. *Educational Studies in Mathematics,* 1971, **4,** 201–219.

Osgood, C. E. Where do sentences come from? In D. D. Steinberg & L. A. Jakobovits (Eds.), *Semantics.* London & New York: Cambridge University Press, 1971.

Osgood, C. E., & Richards, M. M. From yang and yin to *and* and *but.* Language, 1973, **49,** 380–412.

Quirk, R., Greenbaum, S., Leech, G., & Svartvik, J. *A grammar of contemporary English.* New York: Seminar Press, 1972.

Rips, L. J. & Marcus, S. L. Suppositions and the analysis of conditional sentences. In P. A. Carpenter & M. A. Just (Eds.), *Cognitive processes in comprehension.* Hillsdale, N. J.: Lawrence Erlbaum Associates, in press.

Rosch, E., & Mervis, C. Family resemblances: Studies in the internal structure of categories. *Cognitive Psychology,* 1975, **7,** 573–605.

Schmerling, S. Asymmetric conjunction and rules of conversation. In P. Cole & J. L. Morgan (Eds.), *Syntax and semantics* (Vol. 3). *Speech acts.* New York: Academic Press, 1975.

Searle, J. R. *Speech acts.* London & New York: Cambridge University Press, 1969.

Searle, J. R. Indirect speech acts. In P. Cole & J. L. Morgan (Eds.), *Syntax and semantics* (Vol. 3). *Speech acts.* New York: Academic Press, 1975.

Shapiro, B. J., & O'Brien, T. C. Quasi-child logics. *Educational Studies in Mathematics,* 1973, **5,** 181–184.

Springston, F. J., & Clark, H. H. *And* and *or,* or the comprehension of pseudoimperatives. *Journal of Verbal Learning and Verbal Behavior,* 1973, **12,** 258–272.

Staudenmayer, H. Understanding reasoning with meaningful propositions. In R. J. Falmagne (Ed.), *Reasoning: Representation and process.* Hillsdale, N. J.: Lawrence Erlbaum Associates, 1975.

Strawson, P. F. *Introduction to logical theory.* New York: Wiley, 1952.

Suppes, P., & Feldman, S. S. Young children's comprehension of logical connectives. *Journal of Experimental Child Psychology,* 1971, **12,** 304–317.

Taplin, J. E. Reasoning with conditional sentences. *Journal of Verbal Learning and Verbal Behavior,* 1971, **10**, 218–225.

Taplin, J. E., & Staudenmayer, H. Interpretation of abstract conditional sentences in deductive reasoning. *Journal of Verbal Learning and Verbal Behavior,* 1973, **12**, 530–542.

Tennessen, H. Permissible and impermissible locutions. In *Logic and language.* Dordrecht: Reidel, 1962.

Travis, C. *Saying and understanding: A generative theory of illocutions.* New York: New York University Press, 1975.

von Wright, G. H. On conditionals. In G. H. von Wright, *Logical studies.* London: Routledge & Kegan Paul, 1957.

Walker, R. C. S. Conversational implicatures In S. Blackburn (Ed.), *Meaning, reference and necessity.* London & New York: Cambridge University Press, 1975.

Wason, P. C. In real life negatives are false. *Logique et Analyse,* 1972, **15**, 17–38.

Wason, P. C., & Johnson-Laird, P. N. *Psychology of reasoning.* Cambridge, Mass.: Harvard University Press, 1972.

Wilson, D. *Presuppositions and non-truth-conditional semantics.* New York: Academic Press, 1975.

Yamanashi, M. Where do conditional expressions qualify?: Functional variability between logical and ordinary language conditionals. In R. W. Fasold & R. W. Shuy (Eds.), *Analyzing variation in language.* Washington, D.C.: Georgetown University Press, 1975.

ENCODING AND PROCESSING
OF SYMBOLIC INFORMATION
IN COMPARATIVE JUDGMENTS[1]

William P. Banks

POMONA COLLEGE, CLAREMONT, CALIFORNIA

I. Introduction

Memory rarely does justice to the perceptual experience it records. Out of the rich flux of available stimulus information we can select, encode, and store only a portion, and later, when we recall what we can, the remembered experience is generally more abstract and less compelling than the original experience. Few would disagree with these general statements about the relation between direct experi-

[1] The research reported in this chapter was supported by National Science Foundation grant BMS 75-20328, and some of the costs of producing the chapter were covered by a Pomona College Faculty Research grant. The assistance of Grayson Barber, Bill Lippincott, and Bill Prinzmetal in this research is gratefully appreciated.

ence and the memory of it. This chapter presents a particular theoretical interpretation of this relationship for one area of experience. The area of experience is that elicited by what are usually considered continuous attributes, such as brightness, size, and so forth, and the theoretical approach assumes that we remember and process these attributes in terms of discrete semantic codes.

The model presented in this chapter is designed to account for the experimental results pertaining to processing of attributes in comparative judgment tasks. It uses hypothetical processes of code manipulation to make the necessary predictions. The codes are called "semantic" because they are assumed to carry information in the same way as do other natural language codes, and they are considered to be discrete because linguistic codes are (cf. Leech, 1974). The processing mechanisms generate these codes from memory information and transform them until they match the previously coded and stored instructions.

This chapter has three major parts. The first part (Section II) describes the comparative judgment paradigm and the most important and robust effects obtained with it. The second part (Section III) describes and critically reviews the previous models of these results. Finally, the third part (Section IV) describes the semantic-coding approach and its application to data from comparative judgment experiments.

II. Symbolic Comparative Judgments: Paradigm and Data

A. THE EXPERIMENTAL PARADIGMS

Most of the data considered in this chapter comes from experiments on comparative judgment. In these experiments the subject is shown two items that differ in the amount of some attribute they possess. The subject must decide, while timed, which of the two has more (or sometimes less) of that attribute. The dependent variable is either the reaction time (RT) required for the decision, or the accuracy of the decision, and models have the task of predicting the pattern of RT's and errors over the experimental conditions. A related experimental paradigm, sentence verification, is also of interest. In the verification task the subject makes the comparative judgment by judging the truth or falsity of a sentence that asserts a comparative relation between two items. A verification experiment might, for example, present the subject with statements such as "A truck is smaller than a car" and require the subject to respond "true" or "false" while being timed. A comparative judgment experiment would obtain the same discrimination from the subject by presenting the words "truck" and "car" side by side in a tachistoscope and requiring the subject to indicate which is smaller by pressing one of two buttons placed side by side below the words. Polich and Potts (1977) seem to be the first to compare a sentence verification task with a comparative judgment task for the same material. Their results show apparent differences in the retrieval of symbolic information in the two cases, but many similarities in the results as well, and it seems that the memory representation is the same in both paradigms.

The "items" used as stimuli in these experiments are symbolic stimuli. That is, the stimulus items do not themselves possess the attribute in question; rather, they designate levels of the attribute or refer to objects that possess various levels of the attribute. The task is thus properly termed a symbolic comparative judgment task. Models of the task are most directly concerned with how we represent and process symbols, such processing being, of course, the main source of interest in the paradigm in the first place.

Experiments on symbolic comparative judgment can be classified in two ways, as is shown in Table I. This table shows a 2 X 2 cross-classification based on two ways of classifying the experiments. The first way of dividing them is based on the origin of the symbolic nature of the stimuli. The association between the symbolic stimuli and their referents can exist preexperimentally, or it can consist of arbitrary pairings set up by the experimenter and learned by the subjects to use in the experimental task. The preexperimental case investigates the use of information that is a matter of common knowledge, linguistic convention, or real-world knowledge. Such tasks tap what is generally termed semantic memory. The other class of experiments, in which the subjects are tested on an arbitrary ordering, would investigate how they use information about order in short-term or episodic memory. Much research with arbitrary experimenter-defined ordering (e.g., Potts, 1972) has been particularly concerned with the way we transform relations imbedded in continuous discourse into a "schema," and with the way we use the schema in answering questions about the ordering.

A second way to classify experiments on symbolic comparative judgments is in terms of how often (and in what way) they test the possible relations among the elements in the set. The simplest dichotomy along this line divides the experiments into a *repeated-set* category and an *infinite-set* category. An experiment using a re-

TABLE I

2 × 2 CLASSIFICATION OF SYMBOLIC COMPARATIVE JUDGMENT EXPERIMENTS

Origin of symbolic association	Functional size of set of experimental items	
	Finite (or repeated) set	Infinite set
Preexperimental	*Paradigm:* subjects are tested repeatedly on comparative relations among a set of items about whose ordering they already have an opinion.	*Paradigm:* subjects are tested only once on any given pair of stimulus items; experimental analysis based on normative (e.g., rated) position of items on the continuum.
	Representative studies: Moyer & Landauer (1967); Moyer (1973); Banks, Fujii, & Kayra-Stuart (1976)	*Representative studies:* Paivio (1975); Banks & Flora (in press)
Arbitrary	*Paradigm:* subjects learn an ordering in the experiment and are then tested on it.	*Paradigm:* subjects are tested only once on relations in an experimentally defined order; in most cases would seem to be insignificantly different from the case with repeated testing.
	Representative studies: DeSoto & Bosley (1962); Potts (1972); Moyer & Bayer (1976)	*Representative studies:* None

peated-set paradigm tests the relations among items in the set over and over, while an infinite-set experiment tests any given item in the set only once for a given subject. The designations come from the way the task appears to a subject. In the case of a repeated (or "finite") set, the subject is tested on the same items over and over and can usually recall with ease the entire list, ordered on the dimension under test. In the infinite case, the subject never sees the item twice, and so the items seem to be drawn from an infinite population.

I shall consider separately the four classifications in Table I created by the combination of the two dichotomies. First, the top row. It is possible to present a preexperimentally defined ordering to subjects either in a repeated set, with repeated testing of relations among the members, or in an infinite set, with only one test per item for any given subject. Moyer's (1973) experiment can serve as an example of the repeated case, with preexperimental definition of the ordering. He had subjects choose which of two animals was larger, with the animals tested organized into sets of seven, and the subjects saw the

42 different pairs created from members of the set four times each in testing sessions. Other experiments with a preexperimentally defined order and a repeated set include the experiments on digit inequality judgments (e.g., Banks, Fujii, & Kayra-Stuart, 1976; Buckley & Gillman, 1974; Moyer & Landauer, 1967; Parkman, 1971) where subjects make comparative judgments of the sizes of simultaneously presented digits.

On the right in the top row we have preexperimental orderings in an infinite-set design. Paivio's (1975) Experiment I seems to be the first such experiment. He performed this experiment in order, among other things, to make sure that Moyer's (1973) results were not an artifact of the repeated use of the set. Banks and Flora (in press, Experiment I) also conducted such an infinite-set experiment for a reason similar to Paivio's.

Continuing clockwise through the table, we come to a category that contains no experiments. When the order of elements is arbitrarily defined in the experiment it seems impossible to have a truly infinite set. The subjects would have to see the items at least once while learning them, and they would know which were the end terms and what the exact serial order was among the items when they were tested. It is precisely to avoid having subjects learn such properties of the set that experimenters perform infinite-set experiments.

Finally, the combination of a repeated, small set and an arbitrary order is a very frequently used paradigm. De Soto and Bosley (1962) may have been the first to use it. Their subjects learned men's names arbitrarily paired with the traditional four school class designations: freshman, sophomore, junior, and senior, and the dependent variables were learning rate and errors made in learning. Potts (1972, 1974a, 1974b) and Trabasso and Riley (1975) are among those who have used RT as a dependent variable in such a paradigm.

B. THE RESULTS OF THESE PARADIGMS

As mentioned above, the different versions of the symbolic comparative judgment paradigm seen in Table I were created for very different reasons. Those using preexperimentally defined orders were designed to investigate the form in which quantitative information is stored in semantic memory and the way it is used, while the arbitrary orderings were intended to investigate how we organize and draw logical inferences from information presented to us for the first time.

Despite the fact that these versions of the paradigm have been created for different reasons and have used many different kinds of

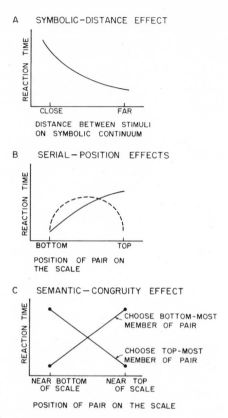

Fig. 1A–C. Schematic diagrams of the three most general effects on RT in comparative judgment. (B) The dashed line traces out the general form of the bowed "end-anchor" effect found consistently in some experiments, and the solid line shows the monotonic increasing (or only slightly bowed) function obtained in others.

material and many procedural variations, the data show some re-markable similarities. These similarities encourage us in the search for processes common to the various tasks. The important effects are the *symbolic-distance effect,* the *serial-position effect,* and the *semantic-congruity effect,* and they will be covered separately below. Figure 1 gives a schematic plot of all three effects.

1. Symbolic-Distance Effect

The symbolic distance effect (so named by Moyer & Bayer, 1976; we will sometimes call it simply the distance effect) seems to be universal. Performance, whether measured by accuracy or RT, improves as the distance between the quantities denoted by the stimuli increases. The schematic plot of this effect is seen in Fig. 1A. This effect holds for small, arbitrary orderings (De Soto & Bosley, 1962; De Soto, London, & Handel, 1965; Potts, 1972; Trabasso & Riley, 1975), and for preexperimentally defined orderings, whether tested in a fixed set (Moyer, 1973) or an infinite set (Paivio, 1975).

Different implications have been drawn from the different situations and materials that have yielded the effect. Moyer and Landauer (1967) originally discovered the distance effect for digits and concluded that the magnitudes of digits were processed as analog quantities. Moyer (1973) and Paivio (1975) found the effect for comparative judgments of the sizes of objects and suggested that processing was done by an "internal" psychophysical mechanism.

The distance effect in small, arbitrary sets has been used by Potts (1972) and Trabasso and Riley (1975) to investigate processes of inferential reasoning with a small universe of items. Potts (1972), for example, had his subjects learn arbitrary four-term orderings of the form A>B>C>D. He presented them only the adjacent pairs A>B, B>C, and C>D during learning, but in testing they were faster and more accurate in processing remote pairs (A>C, B>D, A>D) than the adjacent pairs, even though they had been presented the adjacent pairs and had to infer the information contained in the remote pairs.

The prevalence and robustness of the distance effect make it the first goal of modeling efforts. The distance effect is found in every paradigm in Table I and for every semantic attribute, including size, that has been used in comparative judgment (cf. Banks & Flora, in press; Friedman, 1976). And, as we shall see, the effect, to begin with, rules out a number of perhaps common-sense models of symbolic comparison.

2. Serial-Position Effects

Two different kinds of serial-position effect are commonly obtained. Both of these are shown in Fig. 1B. The dashed line traces out the general form of the bowed "end-anchor" effect found consistently in some experiments, and the solid line shows the monotonic increasing (or only slightly bowed) function obtained in others. The "monotonic" function may in some cases have an end-anchor effect at the top, but the bowing is strongly asymmetrical.

Repeated-set experiments, with arbitrary, experiment-specific orders (e.g., Potts, 1972; Trabasso & Riley, 1975) almost always shows a bowed serial-position curve. The only experiment using such a

paradigm I know of that did not obtain a bowed position curve is
Moyer and Bayer's (1976), in which subjects learned pairings of CVC
nonsense syllables and circles of various sizes and then had to select
the CVC corresponding to the larger circle. The RT for making the
selection among the CVC's declined monotonically as the circles they
represented increased in size. Figures 2 and 3 in this chapter each
report an attempted replication of the Moyer and Bayer experiment.
As can be seen, in only one case out of four is the position effect
monotonic, and even in that case, it is still not the linear function
Moyer and Bayer obtained. The difficulties I have encountered
replicating their effect are discussed later.

Preexperimental orderings, when the items so ordered are presented in a small, repeated set, will sometimes show the bowed
end-anchor, serial-position curve and sometimes the nearly monotonic curve. End-anchor effects in RT were found, for example, by
Friedman (1976) for comparative judgments of the "goodness" of a
set of words, where the relative goodness of the words was based on
the subjects' own ratings. An experiment that, in part, replicated
Moyer's (1973) comparative judgments of sizes of animals will be
reported later in this chapter. It gave very pronounced end-item
effects, and a bowed position curve. Figures 5 and 6 give plots of
these effects, and the experiment is described in the discussion
surrounding these figures.

The steadily increasing position curve has consistently been obtained for two kinds of stimuli in a repeated-set paradigm: digits and
letters. The serial-position effect for comparative judgments among
digits is such that pairs composed of small digits yield faster RT's
than pairs of large digits. The analogous effect for letters is one in
which subjects judge the alphabetic order of pairs of letters more
rapidly at the beginning than at the end of the alphabet (Lovelace &
Snodgrass, 1971). While it is definitely an increasing function, the
serial-position effect seems to be nonlinear for numbers (Moyer &
Landauer, 1973), and it may not even be monotonic (cf. Shepard,
Kilpatric, & Cunningham, 1975).

How can we distinguish the conditions that lead to the two kinds
of position effect? First, it would seem logically necessary to have a
repeated set rather than an infinite one in order to get a curve with
symmetrical end anchors. In an infinite-set paradigm the subject
could not know which were the end terms until the experiment was
over. There have been no experiments looking for end-anchor effects
in an infinite-set paradigm, but it seems unlikely they could occur.
The plots in Figs. 5 and 6 below show that the end effects still occur

even if the end items fall in the middle of the natural range. Thus it seems that end effects depend on ordinal position in a series rather than real-world size.

Second, within the repeated-set category (see Table I), we find that a bowed curve is always obtained—with the one exception of Moyer and Bayer (1976)—when the ordering is arbitrarily set up for the experiment. There is, then, just one problem cell in Table I in which the two different curves are reliably obtained for different kinds of material. This is the cell in which the ordering is defined preexperimentally but the items form a small, repeatedly tested set. Possibly the serial-position function depends on the salience of the preexperimental order. If it is a very strong and frequently used ordering, such as that for the numbers or letters, subjects do not develop a strategy of specially marking the end items, but treat the items almost as they would in an infinite-set task. Then, there would be little or no bowing at the ends. However, if the preexperimental ordering constitutes a very weak scale, then subjects may process the items just as they would in an arbitrary ordering and show end effects. One can certainly imagine preexperimental bases for ordering stimuli that are so obscure that subjects would treat them as invented for the occasion, and memorize the stimuli as if in an arbitrary order.

3. Semantic-Congruity Effect

The semantic-congruity effect is an interaction between the direction of judgment required by the instructions and the position of the stimuli on the continuum of judgment. It is called a congruity effect because of the form of the interaction: RT's are faster when the instructions "agree" with (are congruent with) the stimuli than when they "disagree" (are not congruent) with them. For example, given two small things subjects will be relatively faster at discriminating them under the instructions "choose smaller" than "choose larger"; given two large things they will be faster with "choose larger" than "choose smaller."

Figure 1C schematically illustrates the congruity effect with an interaction of the crossover type, but other forms of interaction qualify just as well as semantic-congruity effects (see Fig. 13 for more examples of the form a semantic-congruity effect can take). The definition is simply that the RT's are faster for instruction–stimulus congruity than incongruity, and this defining criterion translates into a statistical interaction of any form, as long as it is in the correct direction. Some forms of interaction are, however, more desirable as experimental outcomes than others, since they cannot be removed by any monotonic transformation of the RT data, and thus do not depend on assumptions about the scale of measurement of RT. Interactions of the crossover type fall in this category, as do all cases in which the RT functions for the two instructions have slopes of opposite sign.

The semantic-congruity effect is quite robust. It has been shown for experimental paradigms falling in every cell in Table I and for a wide variety of stimulus material. Banks and Flora (in press) found a congruity effect for an infinite-set paradigm like Paivio's (1975); Trabasso and Riley (1975) and Riley (1976) found semantic-congruity effects for small, arbitrary, repeated sets; and Banks et al. (1976) found a semantic-congruity effect for comparative judgments of magnitude of digits, a preexperimental ordering in a repeated set. In sheer number, there are now quite a lot of studies reporting a semantic-congruity effect for symbolic judgments and none, to my knowledge, looking for one but failing to obtain it. Banks, Clark, and Lucy (1975) studied the semantic-congruity effect in *perceptual* discriminations, not symbolic ones, but their paper reviews most of the previous findings in symbolic as well as perceptual paradigms. More recent studies reporting a congruity effect in symbolic comparisons include Jamieson and Petrusic (1975), Holyoak and Walker (1976), and Friedman (1976).

The Clark (1969, 1971) principle of congruence (or congruence effect) differs from the congruity effect. It refers to the relationship between the comparative in a question ("Who is better/worse: *a* or *b*?") and in a logical premise ("*a* is better/worse than *b*"), while the congruity effect refers to the relationship between the comparative in the question and the position of the compared items on an underlying scale. The difference lies in the fact that the position of an item on the scale may or may not correspond to the pole of the comparative used to place the item. For example, the proposition "*b* is *worse* than *a*" puts *a* at the *best* end of the continuum when combined with the propositions "*b* is better than *c*; *c* is better than *d*; *d* is better than *e*." The Potts and Scholz (1975) finding of no "congruence effect" in some three-term series problems does not, therefore, detract from the generality of the congruity effect, as defined in this chapter.

While the semantic-congruity effect is very robust in symbolic comparative judgments, it is quite variable in perceptual discriminations. The main intent of the Banks et al. (1975) paper was to show that the cases in which the congruity effect was and was not obtained could be distinguished on the basis of semantic-coding processes. If the subject codes the stimuli in such a way that they are in some conditions congruent with one of the instructions and in others, congruent with the other, then a semantic-congruity effect will be obtained in the interaction between conditions and instructions. If the subject does not code the stimuli in this way, or uses some other strategy altogether, then a semantic-congruity effect will not occur. Banks *et al.* (1975) reviewed the literature on the congruity effect to show that this was a plausible interpretation, and Experiment I in the paper supported this interpretation.

III. Models of Symbolic Comparison

Despite the relatively short history of research on symbolic comparisons, a large number of models have been proposed to account for the data. It would seem that the present sociology of the cognitive area favors a "rush to model," or else that a certain maturity has been attained in the field, in which scientific progress is measured more by construction and destruction of models than by accumulation of data (Platt, 1964). Whatever the reason, we are faced with a wealth of models and can affort to be very strict in evaluating them. I shall therefore hold them responsible for the paradigms of Table I and for explaining the three basic effects (seen in Fig. 1): namely, the distance effect, both types of serial-position effects, and the semantic congruity effect. In addition, the models should be at least loosely held to the unwritten laws of reasonableness and parsimony. In part as an aid to exposition, the model's assumptions about the *representation* of information in memory and the *process* that generates performance from this representation will be distinguished.

A. THREE MODELS THAT HAVE BEEN DISCONFIRMED

The weight of evidence is so heavy against three models that it seems unlikely that any version of them will be maintained in the future. These can be termed the inference, the serial scan, and the response bias models. We can briefly consider their assumptions and the critical data relevant to them.

1. Inference

The information relevant to the symbolic comparisons is, by this model, propositional. If a subject is given a list of relations of the form A>B, B>C, etc., then he stores these relations as A>B, B>C, etc. The subject might also derive these basic relations from a story or a situation of some kind, but in either case the ordering on which he is tested is represented by a set of propositions expressing the relations among adjacent elements in the ordering. The name of the model comes from the process at time of test of relations. The subject given, for example, the question "A<B?" must search his list for the proposition. If it is not found, he must infer from the set whether it is true or not.

As Potts (1972) and Trabasso and Riley (1975) have shown, the inference model fails to predict the distance effect, since it predicts that RT and errors will be lower for adjacent pairs than distant ones. It does not help the model to add the inferred relations (e.g., A>C), as Anderson and Bower (1973, pp. 408–409) suggest, to the representation. At best, such an addition only changes the model so that it predicts no distance effect at all, rather than one that goes in the wrong direction.

The failure of the inference model should not lead us to conclude that inference never takes place in comparative judgment. It is possible that processes of inference might still take place in some situations, most plausibly in paradigms using the infinite-set approach. The *availability principle,* introduced in a later section as a mechanism that may account for the distance effect in infinite-set paradigms, relies in part on processes of inference. This principle asserts that the need for inference will *decline* as the symbolic distance between items *increases,* in contrast to the simple propositional inference model.

2. Serial Scan

Parkman (1971) introduced the scanning model to account for the distance effect in comparative judgments of the numerical magnitudes of digits. The representation is simply a serial list of the digits in numerical order, and the process of computing the correct responses starts with a serial scan of the list when the subject is presented with a pair for judgment. The scan goes at a constant rate per digit, starting at the small end. When the subject reaches one of the digits he stops scanning and selects the *other* digit as the correct response. The distance effect comes about because, as the distance between two digits increases, the smaller of the two will, on the average, be smaller and less scanning will be required.

The problems for the model in just the realm of digit comparisons are very great. The model predicts linear increasing serial-position effects, which are simply not obtained (Banks *et al.*, 1976; Moyer & Landauer, 1973). Furthermore, the model predicts there will be no distance effect remaining if the effect of the smaller digit in the pair is partialed out. Parkman (1971) himself showed that this prediction did not hold up, and others since then have presented data in which it is clear that the prediction fails (Buckley & Gillman, 1974; Shepard *et al.*, 1975). Finally, Banks *et al.* (1976) showed that the scanning model, without a great number of ad hoc modifications, cannot handle the form of the semantic-congruity effect in digit comparisons.

At least two serious problems confront any attempt to use a serial scanning model for comparative judgment paradigms that do not use digits. The first is that the serial-position effect is often markedly nonlinear (Fig. 1B, dashed line). A scanning model could not begin at just one end, but would need to search sometimes from each end (or in parallel from both). The second is that both the distance effect and the semantic-congruity effect (Banks & Flora, in press; Paivio, 1975) are obtained with an infinite-set paradigm in which the subject does not know the list of items before the experiment and so cannot possibly scan through them.

3. Response Bias and End-Anchor Effects

These are explanations by artifact rather than models. They explain the data in terms that do not require the subject to process the information symbolized by the stimuli and they do not propose either a particular representation or a process model. A strategic explanation of the end-anchor effect (faster RT's for pairs containing end terms) would, for example, point to the fact that each end term in a series is invariably associated with one of the responses, and processing of the pair is not necessary when a pair contains an end term. The response bias argument would point to the same fact but suggest that habitual response tendencies rather than a consciously adopted strategy account for the effect. Both kinds of serial-position effects could be influenced by different sorts of end-item strategies, or by effects of response bias. An end-item strategy would lead to the congruity effect if the different instructions, coming before the stimuli, prepared the subject differently for the two end terms. The distance effect could come about because pairs spanning a wider distance are more likely to contain an end term, and end terms are more quickly processed.

Studies of end-anchor effects and response bias have generally shown that they cannot account for distance or congruity effects.

Moyer and Landauer (1967), Parkman (1971), and Banks *et al.* (1976) all tested the effect of expectancies and response bias by varying, in different conditions, the probability with which different pairs of digits were associated with each of the responses. The results do not show systematic effects of response bias on either the distance effect or the semantic-congruity effect. In addition, both the distance effect and the congruity effect exist for pairs that do not contain an end term (Holyoak & Walker, 1976, also showed this for other types of stimuli). Potts (1974b) also showed a distance effect for pairs that did not include an end term, in this case in totally arbitrary serial orders. One of the most convincing demonstrations of a distance effect without response bias or end-term effects was made by Sekuler, Rubin, and Armstrong (1971). They had subjects decide whether singly presented comparison digits were larger or smaller than a constant digit, which was always 5. Since there are four digits smaller and four larger than 5, and all were presented equally often, there was no way for the subject to predict the correct response without processing the comparison digit, but RT still declined with the numerical difference between the constant and comparison digits. Finally, Banks and Flora (in press) have shown both distance and semantic-congruity effects in an infinite-set paradigm in which neither response bias nor end-term strategies can explain the results as they might in a fixed, repeated set.

Even though differential end-term processing cannot account for the major effects in the paradigm, there is no question about the fact that end terms are processed differently from middle terms. It seems, on the basis of available data, that pairs containing end terms show less of a distance effect and more of a semantic congruity effect than pairs separated by the same distance but not containing an end item (cf. Holyoak & Walker, 1976; Riley & Trabasso, 1974; Trabasso, Riley, & Wilson, 1975). The various end effects may constitute an important difference between infinite- and repeated-set paradigms, and in any case should be accounted for by any model of the task.

B.   SEMANTIC MEMORY AND THE AVAILABILITY
     PRINCIPLE

1. Semantic-Memory Models

Models of semantic memory are quite diverse (cf. Anderson & Bower, 1973; Collins & Quillian, 1972; Meyer, 1970; Smith, Shoben, & Rips, 1974), and there has been a tremendous amount of activity devoted to them in recent years. However, these models have not devoted much attention to comparative judgments along unidimensional continua, and there is no way to know how well the various models will ultimately fare with comparative judgment data. Paivio (1975) attempted to show a limitation of a whole class of semantic-memory models. He compared RT's for size judgments among pairs of objects having the same mean ratio of rated size but either the same or different category membership, and he found that RT's did not depend on whether the pairs fell in the same or different categories: animals and objects. Such a pair of categories amounts to a dichotomy on the animate–inanimate feature, but other features or taxonomic splits among the items Paivio used may be more salient to the subjects. If so, then some of his between-category pairs would be functionally within-category, and vice versa, and he would show no RT difference even though category membership really did affect performance. At the least, we should withhold judgment on the point until experiments like Paivio's are performed with finer category divisions and with categories whose psychological salience is empirically determined.

Network models are an important variety of semantic-memory model, but seemingly the only network model explicitly directed at comparative judgments was put forth by Hayes-Roth and Hayes-Roth (1975). This model is very associationistic in flavor. The model is mainly concerned with the plasticity of network configurations, which are assumed to be created "entirely through individual experience [p. 508]." Their experiments test the effects of repeated testing of various relations among members of a set on RT in tests of other relations. Their data do show strong effects of the type they predict, but these effects seem to depend critically on large numbers of repeated tests of certain relations. In addition, they did not employ a unidimensional ordering but a fairly complex 12-term treelike structure. These two factors required for verification of the model, the large number of tests, and the nonlinear organization of items, seem to limit its generality. Furthermore, their model predicts that, without very special training procedures, performance will be worse on nonadjacent than adjacent members of a linear ordering, in contradiction of the distance effect. They suggest an end-anchor strategy (p. 521) to account for the distance effect, but as we have seen, end-anchor strategies cannot account for it.

2. The Availability Principle

What I have previously referred to as the *availability principle* may serve to explain the distance effect when the data base for the comparative judgment is semantic memory. The principle can be stated as follows: The more similar two items are on the dimension of comparison, the longer it will take to find the information that will give their relative positions on the continuum. The principle seems to apply to any of the current models of semantic memory except for Paivio's model for relative size judgments, which model postulates direct access of analog size information. In general, the principle follows from the consideration that the necessary information about the relative positions of the items on the continuum in question is encoded in propositions or linkages or elements of some sort, and these elements of information must be searched for in semantic memory. If the items are quite far apart on the continuum, almost any proposition connecting them and the continuum will contain the information needed to discriminate them, but if they are close together only a few of the facts known about them will provide the necessary information. The distance effect is predicted because the greater the proportion of the elements that will satisfy the search, the sooner one of these will be found.

As is stated, the availability principle applies to a wide variety of models of semantic memory. The exact way it predicts the distance effect will differ from case to case, however. Specific examples of mechanisms in which it operates will illustrate the principle better. Consider, as a first example, a model that proposes items in semantic memory are organized by categories. (See Section II, D, below, for discussion of category models.) If regions of the continuum being tested fall into different categories (e.g., "large," "medium," and "small" things), subjects may use the categorical information to make a rapid response. If such categorical information is not available, then a search for other distinguishing information would begin. This second search would add to the RT. Since items are more likely on the average to fall into different categorical regions if they are further apart on the continuum, the distance effect is predicted. The Smith *et al.* (1974) model would predict a distance effect by a similar application of the availability principle, since it allows a fast exit from processing to the response when items are quite far apart on the continuum and a slower search among semantic features when the fast response cannot be made.

Another strategy for determining the relative positions of two items on a continuum would be to search for a third item whose ordinal relation to both of the first two is known. Such a third item cannot, however, establish the relative positions of the first two unless it falls between them. (The relations A>C and B>C do not define the relation between A and B, but A>C and C>B do.) The further apart the two items to be compared are, the larger is the proportion of the population of possible "third items" falling between them, and the faster one of these will be found. The availability principle thus predicts a distance effect for this strategy.

I do not know if it can be proved that the availability principle will produce a distance effect in all semantic-memory models. I do think it is probably true for any memory model in which quantitative attribute information must be searched out from various sources of stored knowledge, but not if quantitative attribute information is directly accessible. I find the availability principle particularly appealing because it gives a way of predicting the distance effect in what seems to me to be a reasonable phenomenological account of the process of performing unexpected comparative judgments. My introspections typically reveal an idiosyncratic search for information relevant to the question, a search of the type generally reported by subjects performing difficult memory retrievals (cf. Bartlett, 1932; also chapters in Norman & Rumelhart, 1975). The "retrieval" is really a sort of problem-solving exercise, and all sorts of information in memory is searched for a clue to the solution of the problem. The distance effect seems to emerge naturally from such a process, because of the way the relative availability of clues will vary with symbolic distance.

C. ASSOCIATIVE MODELS

As Trabasso and Riley (1975) and others have argued, a simple associative chaining theory of serial list learning is disconfined because it predicts the opposite of the distance effect. Anderson and Bower's (1973, Fig. 13.5) neoassociational suggestion for explaining comparative judgments (by a sort of "propositional chaining") also has the problem that it predicts the opposite of the distance effect. Trabasso and Riley (1975) have shown that associative strength mechanisms can predict the major effects in comparative judgment paradigms with fixed, well-learned lists. Trabasso and Riley's models use associative strength, generalization between adjacent items, and the consequent discriminability functions to predict distance and serial-position effects.

Bower (1971) has shown, however, that associative models like Trabasso and Riley's fail a different, and crucial, test. This is that they cannot account for learning in cross-dimensional transfer or in within-dimension transpositions of the scale. Bower suggests that memory for serial orders is mediated by associations to abstract ordinal positions in a amodal cognitive "scaffold." This scaffold is a cognitive structure for representing serial orders. Results of the transfer experiments indicate that this structure is used quite flexibly to encode ordinal information about relative positions of symbolic stimuli along whatever continuum is used in a serial-order experiment, but information about the absolute value denoted by a symbolic stimulus is lost. Later it will be discussed how a schema like Bower's scaffold may also predict RT effects in comparative judgments among symbolic stimuli.

D. CATEGORICAL MODELS

Here the representation would be a category label stored with each symbolic element. The label would indicate the general region of the continuum in which the element falls. Jamieson and Petrusic (1975) and Holyoak and Walker (1976) have shown in different ways that a simple categorical model cannot account for comparative judgments. The intent of these studies was to test a semantic-coding model (Banks et al., 1975, 1976), but because the semantic-coding model is quite far from being a pure categorical model, they do not test it. The semantic-coding model does assume that the "working" codes used in processing are categorical, but these codes are generated from a memorial data base that has a very different form (see Section IV). Banks et al. (1976) assume an analog memory representation, and other sorts of memory representation are discussed in this chapter. On analysis, these supposed experimental tests of the semantic-coding model turn out to be tests of the assumption, not made by the model, that the memory representation is purely categorical.

One serious a priori argument against the pure categorical model is that it must assume that the appropriate categorical membership of every word in memory is designated, precoded, and ready to use for every possible attribute that might be tested. It seems very implausible to assume that every substantive concept is explicitly marked for membership in every category, but it must be if we always base our comparative judgment on category membership.

E. ANALOG MODELS

The term "analog" has two different meanings when applied to models of mental activity. The first meaning comes directly from the idea of an analogy. It indicates that the mental processes themselves model in some way the events or objects being thought about, and perceptual mechanisms may even be used internally. Analog models of this type are generally called image-processing models.

The other sense of "analog" implies only that mental processing operates on a continuous representation of some kind. This sense derives from the first, since a complete mental representation of perceptual events that mapped, one for one, every possible sensory level would have to be a continuous representation. A continuous representation is generally considered to be one in which any two points, arbitrarily close together, can still have a third point placed between them. However, a weaker form of the concept of a continuum that retains the idea of mapping could preserve the interval scale (or ratio scale) properties of the perceptual continuum but not have the accuracy that would be required to represent separately every possible level of it.

The following discussion will cover the two types of analog models separately. First, I will consider the more general sort of analog model that assumes a continuous representation of information. Following that, the discussion of imagery models can concentrate on their assumptions about internalized perceptual events.

1. Analog-Continuum Models

The mental representation in such a model is a continuum on which items are "placed" for processing. De Soto *et al.* (1965) used such a notion, which they termed "spatial paralogic," to explain subjects' performance on linear syllogisms. Others assuming a continuous, analog representation include those of Huttenlocher (1968), Marks (1972), and Jamieson and Petrusic (1975). The assumed process that mediates between the representation and performance has varied from model to model. De Soto *et al.* (1965) seem to assume something close to mental imagery, while Marks and Jamieson and Petrusic assume a much more abstract decision process. We will defer discussion of the decision process until another section and concentrate here on the representation.

Models have chosen an analog representation of information because it has seemed to be the best way to build either accuracy or interval-scale properties into the representation. The analog model is theoretically capable of any degree of precision of discrimination and of interval or even ratio-scale properties. The issues of accuracy and scale type are quite separate and will be given separate coverage below. A later section (IV, C, 3) will cover the predictions of the analog-continuum models for the semantic-congruity effect. As will be seen, at least four different types of evidence pertaining to the semantic-congruity effect are very difficult for the analog-continuum model to model. These findings require explanation of the mechanisms by which the analog models predict the semantic-congruity effect. Here we will concentrate on properties of the memorial data base assumed by the analog models and will postpone discussion of the mechanism behind the semantic-congruity effect until later.

a. *Accuracy of Memory for Absolute Quantities.* Moyer and Landauer (1967) suggest that subjects decide which of two simultaneously presented numerals is larger by converting them to analog magnitudes and comparing the analog quantities in "much the same way that comparisons are made between physical stimuli such as loudness or length of line [p. 1520]." Such an analog representation would need as many discriminable positions as there are numbers to be processed. Paivio's (1975) model also requires a very accurate analog representation, in this case of the real-world sizes of objects and animals, since the model assumes we use a precoded, stored analog measure of the size of things in symbolic comparative judgments of their size. Paivio (1975) and Banks and Flora (in press) have shown that subjects can discriminate fairly accurately the sizes of objects in a functionally unlimited set of objects. The accuracy required by an analog representation would have to be very fine indeed.

The rather large body of research on our ability to remember absolute quantities should, however, cause us to doubt that memory can give us the ability to discriminate more than a few steps on an analog continuum. The "magical number 7 ± 2" has not grown in size since Miller's (1956) review of absolute judgment. The ability of memory to capture absolute positions on perceptual continua is simply not very good. If analog memory for absolute size or position on a continuum were as good as Paivio, for example, has supposed, then absolute memory for continua would also be quite good, much better than the classic 7 ± 2 steps. It seems that the best way to model the semantic memory representation of quantitative information would be through some mechanism that does not rely on an analog representation.

b. *Ordinal or Interval Scale in the Memory Representation?* Absolute judgment experiments indicate that the memory representation does not mirror the interval scale properties of the sensory scale. Pollack (1952) and Gravetter and Lockhead (1973) have shown that the number of absolute stimulus levels people can remember and use accurately is not much affected by bunching the levels together on the continuum or spreading them out. Spreading out the stimulus levels denoted by each step in the scale will certainly make them perceptually more discriminable, but in some cases it can actually make memory performance worse. These findings imply that the memory representation is not an internalized version of the sensory scale. If it were, discriminability effects for memory information would have the same interval properties as sensory discrimination.

Experiments looking for interval properties of memorized scales in comparative judgment have obtained various results. Potts (1974a) looked for interval properties in a four-term series in which the distance between adjacent terms was varied. If more than ordinal information is preserved, performance will be better when subjects attempt to discriminate adjacent pairs that are far apart than when they attempt to discriminate pairs that are close together. Potts found no such difference, and it would therefore appear that only ordinal information was preserved in the memory structure. Griggs and Shea (in press) have shown, however, that far or near spacing of adjacent items in a serial order does affect performance. Their paradigm was very similar to that of Potts (1974a), but their dependent measure was RT while Potts' measure was accuracy, presumably less sensitive than RT. Griggs and Shea also made certain that the task motivated subjects to learn the interval scale information, but Potts' subjects could perform his task with only ordinal information.

Moyer and Bayer (1976) have devised a technique that also indicates that memorial representations have more than ordinal properties. They paired four CVC's uniquely with four circles of different sizes and then presented all pairs of the CVC's to the subjects. They then timed the subjects as they decided which CVC denoted the larger circle. There were two groups of subjects, both with four circles but one with circles close together in size (small range) and one with circles more widely spaced (large range). The small range circles were 11, 13, 15, and 17 mm in diameter and the large range, 11, 15, 19, and 23 mm in diameter. The RT's to the CVC's in the small range condition were 100 msec slower than the RT's to the CVC's in the large range. This result suggests that the memorial representation preserves interval scale information, since the two groups had exactly equivalent ordinal relations among the CVC's on which they were tested. The result does conflict with findings from absolute judgment paradigms (e.g., Gravetter & Lockhead, 1973), but it is not completely impossible that different memory representations are used for absolute and comparative judgment.

Moyer and Bayer proposed a model that combines an analog-search process and a comparison of imaged circles. They also suggested an explanation based on semantic coding. We will turn to these explanations at different points later. My own attempts to compare a semantic-coding model with Moyer and Bayer's have been hampered by my failure to replicate Moyer and Bayer's results. Figure 2 shows the result of an attempt that closely followed the procedure reported in Moyer and Bayer's article, using the same monetary incentives and the same double-blind procedure that prevented the experimenter in RT testing from knowing the group membership of the subjects. These subjects were given only five tests on each pair instead of the 14 Moyer and Bayer gave, but the results showed no systematic changes in any of the important variables over trials. Only five tests were made so that the remainder of the RT testing session could be used to determine the form of the semantic-congruity effect in this situation ("choose larger" vs. "choose smaller" instructions). A congruity effect was obtained and its form was not what the Moyer and Bayer model would predict, but neither is Fig. 2.

After I obtained the result in Fig. 2, I contacted Moyer, who supplied me with some details of procedure that seemed insignificant and had been omitted from the reported procedure, but that may have influenced the outcome. Figure 3 shows the results obtained

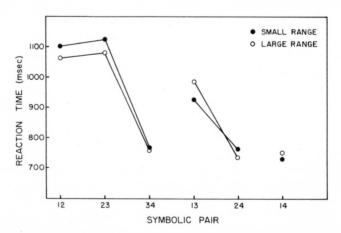

Fig. 2. RT to select the nonsense syllable symbolizing the larger circle for two groups; one with a small range of circles, and one with a large range. Both groups had four syllables, each syllable arbitrarily associated with a circle. Pairs of symbolic stimuli are designated in the figure by pairs of numbers in which 1 designates the syllable associated with the smallest circle, 2 the next smallest, 3 the next to largest, and 4 the largest.

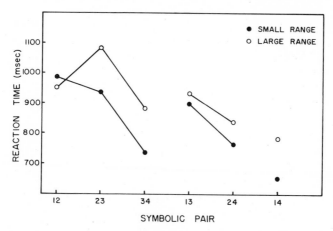

Fig. 3. Same as Fig. 2, but with eight subjects instead of four in each group, and matching of subjects in the groups with an RT test.

with 16 subjects (two groups of eight), for whom the procedure included the following added details: The RT for a simple right–left judgment was used to match subjects in the two groups, circles and CVC's during learning were seen in a 4.5 cm high × 5.5 cm wide frame (rather than in the middle of a 5 in. × 8 in. index card, on which they are very difficult to discriminate), and the distance from each subject's eye to the circles was adjusted for his or her comfort and maintained constant throughout the learning session (it ranged from 70 to 100 cm). Only five rather than 14 RT's were taken for each pair but, as in the earlier attempted replication, there were no systematic shifts of effects over the five trials.

The results of the second replication go 87 msec in the direction opposite to Moyer and Bayer's main effect of range (the first replication went 10 msec in the same direction as theirs). The only explanation for the difference I can offer is a weak one, that matching subjects with a simple discrimination task did not adequately control for their ability on the much more difficult symbolic comparison task. The data are consistent with this interpretation, since there is considerable overlap in the mean RT's for subjects in the two groups, and $F < 1.0$ for the main effect of group. It may seem strange that an 87-msec main effect in RT falls short of significance, but the standard error for the comparison was 40.5 msec, and it is a between-group comparison. The within-subject conditions had much more stable effects, with standard errors around 15 msec. Evidence for interval-scale properties of the memorial representation of small, arbitrary sets seems still to be lacking. Even if the conditions for replicating the Moyer-Bayer range effect are eventually isolated, it is clear that the effect does not have the robustness of the major effects in comparative judgment.

I have recently completed a different experimental test of interval properties in a well-learned list. (This experiment is my contribution to a collaborative research effort with Stephen M. Kosslyn.) This experiment used a set of animal names, whose relative positions on the size continuum subjects know preexperimentally, rather than the arbitrary pairings Moyer and Bayer used. The experiment began with a master list of 12 animals: *ant, fly, bat, rat, eel, cat, fox, dog, pig, ram, cow,* and *elk.* For convenience I will refer to these names by their ordinal numbers in the master list, with *ant* = 1 and *elk* = 12, and to pairs by hyphenated combinations of numbers; e.g., "1-12" stands for the pair consisting of *ant* and *elk.*

The experiment had three groups with eight subjects in each, and each group was tested with comparisons among a different subset of six of the animals. The small animals group had animals 1–6, the large animals group had animals 7–12, and full range group had animals 1, 3, 5, 8, 10, and 12. Each subject in each group was shown the list of the six animals appropriate to his or her group, agreed to the ordering given, and after about 20 practice RT trials, began RT testing. Each subject was tested on all pairs of animals in his or her group's list that differed by one or by two ordinal steps, plus one more pair that differed by 4 ordinal steps (the pair 1-5 for the small group, 8-12 for the large group, and 3-12 for the full group). The instructions, "choose larger" or "choose smaller," were presented before the stimuli and were randomly varied from trial to trial. The 40 different stimuli (10 pairs × 2 instructions × 2 orders) were presented four times each in separate blocks after practice trials.

The results show, overall, a greater effect of ordinal position in each group's sublist than of real-world size. Consider first the pairs shared by the full and small or full and large groups. These have the same preexperimental size ratio but different ordinal relationships in the different groups. The full and small groups share the pairs 1-3, 3-5, and 1-5. The mean for 1-3 and 3-5 was 920 msec in the small series, where they are 2 ordinal steps apart, but 954 msec in the full series, where they are only 1 step apart. The pair 1-5 took 791 msec in the small series (4 ordinal steps) and 829 msec in the full (2 ordinal steps). The analogous differences between large and full series are even greater. The pairs 8-10 and 10-12 took a mean of 778 msec in the large series but 906 msec in the full (ordinal steps of 2 and 1 in large and full, respectively). The pair 8-12 took 650 msec in the large series (4 steps) but 809 in the full (2 steps). Thus, the RT for discriminating *dog–elk*, for example, varies by over 150 msec as a function of the context in which it is tested, but *eel–ram* and *dog–ram*, which differ greatly in size ratio, have about the same RT when they are separated by the same ordinal difference in the ordering.

Figure 4 plots RT as a function of ordinal difference for all pairs used in each series, not just those in common to the different series. It seems clear from this plot that ordinal position difference in the series in question describes the RT function better than the interval-size ratio does.

Figure 5 shows the mean correct RT's for "choose larger" and "choose smaller" instructions for each pair separated by one ordinal step in the small, large, and full series. While the small series is slightly slower than the full series and the large slightly faster (as is seen in Fig. 4 as well), the overall RT functions seem roughly

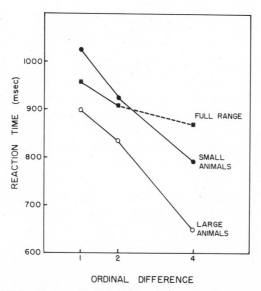

ORDINAL DIFFERENCE

Fig. 4. Mean RT for comparative judgments among pairs of animals drawn from sets of six that span the range from *ant* to *elk* (full range points), or from sets of six that span from *fox* to *elk* (large animals) or from *ant* to *cat* (small animals). Ordinal differences of 1, 2, or 4 steps in the full range data correspond roughly to real-world size differences of 2, 4, and 8 steps, respectively, for either the small or large animal series. The dashed line indicates that the data for 4 steps from the full range is not fully comparable with that from the small or large animal series.

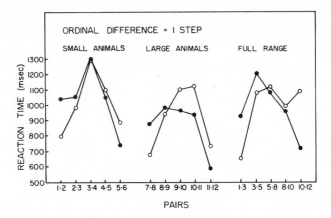

Fig. 5. Mean RT to pick the smaller (open circles) or larger (closed circles) animal from a simultaneously presented pair of animal names. The small and large animal groups and the full range group are the same as in Fig. 4, and the pairs are designated by numbers corresponding to the ordinal position of the animal in the master list, where *ant* is 1st and *elk* is 12th.

equivalent for the three series. All three show a nonmonotonic serial-position curve for both instructions, and a semantic-congruity effect that is strongest for end terms. These data show very clearly that the end-anchor effects depend upon the end points of the subscale of items used by a given group of subjects, not upon the real-world end points (if such end points can even be said to exist). This fact can be seen in RT's for the top of the small series (pair 5-6) and the bottom of the large series (pair 7-8). These pairs show the standard end-item effect, yet they fall right in the middle of the range spanned by the full series, which has a peak there.

Figure 6 plots the RT's for an ordinal difference of 2 steps analogously to Fig. 5. The plots in Fig. 6 show much the same pattern as those in Fig. 5 except that they are faster overall. If real-world size determined RT, the small and large series in Fig. 6 would have the same RT's as the full series in Fig. 5, but they do not.

The data from this experiment indicate very strongly that ordinal rather than interval properties of the series subjects learned determined their performance. Is it possible, then, that subjects simply ignored the interval-scale sizes of the animals denoted by the names and treated the names as ordered nonsense syllables? Two features of the data show an effect of the real-world sizes of the animals. First, the congruity effect for the full series was greater than for either the small or the large series. Considering end points only, the mean

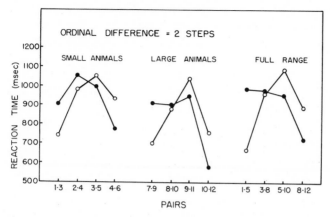

Fig. 6. Same as Fig. 5 except RT's are for ordinal differences of 2 steps rather than 1. Note the change of scale in the RT's.

congruity effect was 92.6 msec per point for the small and large series and 137 msec per point for the full series. Since the congruity effect typically declines as the range is narrowed (cf. Banks & Flora, in press; Banks et al., 1976; Jamieson & Petrusic, 1975), this difference between the full and the other ranges in the congruity effect indicates that the span of the ranges on the general size continuum affected the subjects' processing of the series. Second, a semantic-congruity effect was obtained for the small and large ranges as a whole. In this congruity effect the "choose larger" instructions were faster overall than the "choose smaller" instructions for the subset of large animals (854 vs. 889 msec), and the "choose smaller" instructions were faster than "choose larger" for the small subset (987 vs. 970 msec). This congruity effect is even stronger when pairs containing end items are excluded from the average: In the large range "choose larger" takes a mean of 951 msec to be processed, but "choose smaller" takes 1017 msec; for the small range the larger choice takes 1084 msec and the smaller, 1078 msec. These effects would not be found if the subjects ignored the real-world size of the animals and treated their names as nonsense syllables put in a serial order.

2. Imagery

Debates about the role of imagery in mental processes are as old as psychology itself. Mental imagery of one kind or another is probably a universal human experience, but introspection into the experience is not adequate for analysis of the process. There seems little question that imagery has some function in mental processes. However, the following discussion attempts to show that imagery is not frequently or importantly involved in symbolic comparative judgments.

To say that imagery is used in the task is to say that the choice process uses internalized perceptual (and sometimes motor) functions. For example, Shepard and Feng (1972) showed that "mental" (imaged) paper folding takes real time and appears to be performed in a spacelike medium. It is as though the subject performs an internalized version of the act of paper folding and keeps track of the results by watching with his "mind's eye." Paivio's (1975) or Moyer and Bayer's (1976) theories of mental size comparisons assume a similar sort of process. To decide whether the word "cow" or "dog" denotes the larger species of animal we call up an image of a cow and a dog, "look" at the two, and pick the larger one.

Two general problems with the hypothesis that perceptual imagery is used in comparative judgments strike me from the outset. The first is that if images are to be compared to compute the correct response in, say, a size judgment, it is necessary to make the images the right size to begin with. Kosslyn's (1975) research shows that mental images are quite flexible as to relative size, and it would seem necessary to retrieve size information along with shape information in constructing the images. (Our long-term memory for imageable things cannot be little snapshots that are all just the right size.) Thus, size information must be available, and used, before the image is constructed, and the imagery process itself hardly seems to be necessary. The second problem for the imagery theory is that we can perform comparative judgments perfectly well on semantic dimensions whose values we cannot image. People can, for example, decide which of two professions is more prestigious or which of two crimes is more heinous (Stevens, 1972) very consistently, but it seems unlikely that they must visualize the activities involved in either case every time they decide. Several researchers have shown distance effects and/or congruity effects for nonimageable as well as imageable continua (Banks & Flora, in press; Friedman, 1976; Holyoak & Walker, 1976; Riley, 1976).

In a recent study of the possible role of imagery in comparative size judgments, Holyoak (1977) has obtained results that indicate that subjects do not use imagery to make their decisions unless specifically instructed to do so. He used diagnostics of image processing derived from Kosslyn's (1975) research on imagery, and he found evidence for the use of imagery only in those experimental conditions that required that subjects use it in the comparison. The results do show that subjects *can* use imagery, but they do not *normally* use it.

A different sort of evidence on the imagery issue comes from an experiment performed at Pomona College by Jon Threlkeld. In this experiment subjects learned associations between CVC's and physical stimuli in a paradigm similar to that of Moyer and Bayer (1976). The stimuli were squares, not circles as in Moyer and Bayer, and there were five CVC–square pairs rather than the four pairs Moyer and Bayer used. The five squares measured 1, 4, 7, 10, or 13 mm on a side, and there was no small range vs. large range variable.

After learning the CVC–square pairings by a method similar to Moyer and Bayer's, subjects were first shown all the different pairs of the CVC's and timed while they decided which corresponded to the larger or smaller square. Then they were shown all the different pairs of the squares and timed on the comparative judgment of relative size among the squares. Finally, they had to compare the size of a physically present square with the square that was denoted by a CVC typed beside it.

If imagery or anything like a perceptual trace of the square associated with the CVC is used in the comparative judgment, then the CVC–square condition should be superior to the condition where CVC's had to be compared with CVC's, since in that condition only one mental image of a square, rather than two, would have to be retrieved. The results showed, however, that the CVC vs. CVC comparative judgment was about 90 msec *faster* than the CVC–square comparison. As a whole, the results showed a very different pattern for comparisons purely among squares than for comparisons purely among CVC's, and the CVC–square data showed about the same pattern as the CVC–CVC data. Figure 7 plots the distance effects separately for the three conditions.

The best interpretation of this experiment seems to be that in comparative judgments among CVC's the subject uses a code of some kind for each CVC, and this code is considerably more abstract than an image of the associated square. Processing of the CVC's uses this abstract representation, while processing in the square–square condition uses other strategies not involving such codes. The CVC–square condition is slower than the CVC–CVC condition because it takes longer to generate the necessary code from the square than from the CVC. In no condition is the CVC translated to an image to be compared perceptually with the square. The congruity effects corroborate this conclusion. Both the CVC–CVC and CVC–square data

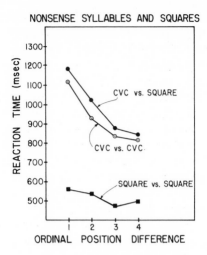

Fig. 7. Mean RT's for comparative judgments among pairs of CVC's (nonsense syllables), among pairs composed of one CVC and one square, or among pairs of squares. The subjects had learned an association between the CVC's and squares of the same size as those used in the RT task, and when they compared CVC's and squares in the RT task, they were instructed to compare the presented square with the one that had been associated with the CVC.

showed a strong congruity effect, but there was none for the square–square data.

As the following section shows, the best interpretation at present of the semantic-congruity effect is that it arises from code processing. The lack of a congruity effect in the square–square condition thus indicates that processing involved strategies that did not require size codes. The CVC–CVC and CVC–square conditions are not internal analogs of the square–square condition but, rather, do involve processing in terms of size codes.

IV. Semantic-Coding Model

This model was saved for last because it answers a number of questions about symbolic comparative judgments that the previous models could not answer. The model makes assumptions about three classes of hypothetical structure. These are the *data base,* the *processing codes,* and the *processing mechanisms.* The relationships among these three concepts can be summarized as follows: When stimuli are presented for comparative judgment, the *processing mech-*

anisms generate *processing codes* from the *data base* and manipulate them until they match the previously stored and coded instructions. The processing codes are assumed to be the discrete, componential semantic codes of natural language (cf. Leech, 1974; Miller & Johnson-Laird, 1976; Sapir, 1944). The data base is the memory representation that stores the symbolic information, and it may be organized in a number of different ways. The important distinction in modeling is between a short-term data base set up to organize repeatedly tested items on a continuum and the enduring data base used to process comparatives when a set of items cannot be specially organized for the task. Finally, the processing mechanisms are set in an information-processing model that assumes a series of separate functions to generate the codes and match them to the instructions.

A. THE PROCESSING MODEL

The two functions of processing treated here generate the codes and transform them to match the previously coded instructions. These two fairly global functions are separately embodied in two sequential processing stages that subsume a number of additional processing mechanisms. The two global processing stages will be termed the encoding and choice stages. These stages are, according to the model, sequential and contribute separate, additive components to the RT. Response processes constitute a third global stage that will not be covered here. It is assumed that the response stage waits for the outcome of the previous two stages before beginning its work and thus is separate and additive in the RT. Evidence supporting the additivity of processes in encoding and choice will be presented in a later section, but the additivity of the response processes simply stands as an untested assumption in this chapter. In the present section I will sketch out the processing model and describe, in general terms, how it accounts for each of the major effects in symbolic comparative judgment (cf. Fig. 1).

Figure 8 gives a schematic diagram of the model. Tracing through the hypothesized processes in a comparative judgment task, we start at the left with the presentation of the stimulus pair. The first processing step, labeled "perception and code generation," acts as a kind of analog-to-digital converter. It includes substages that handle primitive perceptual functions as well as those that connect perceptual events with memory. The box labeled "memory used in encoding" represents the knowledge about the stimuli and the continuum in question. It is the data base.

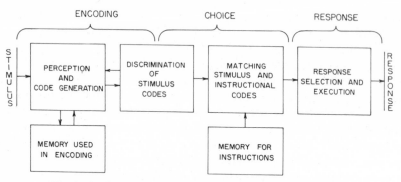

Fig. 8. Outline of processing functions in semantic-coding model.

The first stage may generate codes that do not discriminate the stimuli or that are irrelevant to the task. It is the job of the discrimination stage to send to the matching stage codes that are appropriate to the task and that distinguish the stimuli, and it will process the codes produced by the first stage until they distinguish the stimuli.

The process of discrimination is responsible for the distance effect (see Fig. 1A). The smaller the difference between two items on the continuum of judgment the more likely the codes are to be the same and thus the more likely is the discrimination process, which adds to the RT, to be required. The Banks et al. (1976) model, for example, had dichotomous codes coming from the first stage. A digit could be encoded as large (L+) or small (S+). Sometimes the two digits in the pair were coded differently (as L+/S+) and the discrimination stage could pass them, but when the digits are both given the same code (L+/L+ or S+/S+) a discrimination process has to accumulate more information about the digits in order to generate discriminable codes for the matching stage, and this adds to the RT. The smaller the difference between two digits, the more likely they are to be coded the same (L+/L+ or S+/S+). In an infinite-set experiment, on the other hand, the distance effect might arise because the generation of discriminable codes in the first place would take longer as the items were closer together. The processes assumed to take place in the discrimination stage might be very different in different experimental situations; in some cases it might be a passive buffer that checks codes, in others, an active problem-solving mechanism.

After the discrimination stage the codes are passed to the matching stage, which attempts to match one of them to the code for the instructions. It is here that the semantic-congruity effect (Fig. 1C) arises, through the process that must transform the codes that, while discriminable, may not be in the proper format to match the instructions. The instructions, as coded, are the same as the codes for the poles of the continuum. Thus, "choose larger" is interpreted as "pick the one nearer the large end," which we can symbolize as "pick L+." The code for "choose smaller" is, similarly, symbolized as "pick S+." The processing codes for the stimuli are cast in terms of the region of the continuum they occupy. Two large things are likely to end up coded as "large/larger" or L/L+, and two small things as S/S+. The congruity effect emerges quite naturally, then, because the instruction "pick L+" can find a match very easily for a stimulus pair coded as L/L+, but S/S+ must be transformed to L+/L, at the cost of some time, for the match to be made. Likewise, "pick S+" matches S/S+ codes more quickly than L/L+ codes, and the congruity effect is predicted.

The serial-position effects (Fig. 1B) can arise either from the structure of the data base used in encoding or from an end-item strategy in processing. The Banks et al. (1976) model predicted an asymmetrical, roughly monotonic function (cf. Fig. 1B, solid line) for the digits because large digits like 8 and 9 were closer together on the underlying continuum than small ones like 1 and 2. Thus, 8 and 9 were more likely to be given the same size code than 1 and 2 and were consequently more likely to require an extra discrimination step. This produced the increasing serial-position effect. In general, the similarity structure of the data base should affect the RT by varying the probability of use of discrimination processes. The digits have a monotonically compressive structure (cf. Banks & Hill, 1974), but other continua may not. I would guess that the sometimes oddly shaped position effects of Holyoak and Walker (1976) reflect irregular spacings of stimuli on the various semantic continua they used, and their subjective scales of these continua seem to verify this conjecture.

The processing strategy can influence the serial-position function if subjects are able to identify end terms and can quickly respond to pairs that contain them. Such a strategy would certainly result in the bowed serial-position curves. However, an end-term strategy may not be necessary at all to explain the faster RT's for discriminating pairs containing end terms. The end terms could simply have very discriminable codes in the data base and lead to fast RT's because they get through the discrimination stage quickly.

B. THE DATA BASE

1. Temporary Data Structures

When the subject is given repeated testing on a small set of items he can construct for them an organization that facilitates retrieval of symbolized information. Two kinds of model of such a special purpose data base have been suggested, an analog and a discrete one.

a. *Analog Model.* Banks *et al.* (1976) proposed that when digits are processed in a comparative judgment task the digits first elicit a quick intuitive "feel" for their magnitude and that this "feel" is the basis for generating the processing codes used in the task. This proposal, in the model, translates into an analog continuum on which the digits are "placed" when perceived. The analog continuum is convenient for modeling because it represents the subjective similarities among the magnitudes of the digits (the scale is monotonically compressed; see Banks & Hill, 1974; Shepard *et al.*, 1975) and because it gives a simple way to represent code generation. Codes are generated by a criterial process, in which the criterion varies stochastically over the continuum. If a digit falls above the criterion on the continuum it is coded L+, if below, S+. The distance effect follows easily from this code-generation process because the greater the distance between two digits, the more likely they are to fall on opposite sides of the criterion and thus to be given discriminable codes (S+/L+).

Quite a few models have used analog continua as either the data base or the processing medium (or both) for comparative judgments. (See Section III, E, 1, for a discussion of some of these uses.) Two strictures should, I think, be applied to analog modeling. The first is that no more than a small number of absolute quantities can be represented in an analog data base, as discussed in Section III, E, 1. The second is that, for the comparative judgment paradigm, the analog continuum is not itself the processing medium in which the choice of response is made. The semantic-congruity effect suggests that the processing medium is semantic codes and thus that the analog intuitions must be converted to processing codes before the match is made. More support for this point will be given later (cf. Section IV, C, 3, in particular).

b. *Ordinal Scaffold.* Bower (1971) very convincingly marshalled the evidence that the data base of memory for positions on unidimensional continua is a discrete, ordinal schema. He characterized this schema as a "generalized internal representation of linear ordering . . . a cognitive structure or scaffold" that is applied to whatever stimulus continuum is being tested. The structure expresses the "primitive relations of comparison, progression, and betweenness [p. 194]." Bower refers to the elements in the scaffold as "implicit conceptual representative[s] . . . such as 'first,' 'middle,' or 'last.' " Bower's evidence for an ordinal schema comes from the results of experiments on the transfer of symbolic relationships. These experiments show that the memorial data base for a symbolic relationship is unlikely to be a mental image of the referent or an analog quantity expressing the referent's position on a continuum. Bower's data follow quite naturally from the discrete, amodal, ordinal scaffold he discusses.

There are a number of ways that interval-scale information could be represented in an ordinal schema. One would be to have some steps in the ordering be wider than others or to allow adjacent stimuli sometimes to be two or more steps apart, leaving one or more "unfilled" steps in between. Moyer and Bayer (1976, p. 242) suggest a linguistically oriented data base that is ordinal but can express interval information to a first approximation through the use of adverbial modifiers (e.g., "small" vs. "very small"). They sketch out a process model to predict the RT effects and point out some problems the model has. Probably the simplest ordinal data base would be natural language comparatives applied to the dimensions in question and stored as paired associates with the symbolic stimuli. Trabasso et al. (1975) and Trabasso and Riley (1975) have proposed models that can predict the main features in RT with a data base like this.

Table II shows another sort of discrete data structure, one based on binary semantic features. For the sake of comparison, an analog version of the same data base is also shown in the table. Both memory structures can probably fit the data, but the structures have not been tested out in model fitting and are intended only to illustrate the points being made here. De Soto and Bosley (1962), whose results would be modeled with these data bases, had subjects learn school class designations as associates to men's names, and they reported the confusion matrix as well as the total errors for each stimulus and response during learning. Their data show the bowed serial-position curve, with faster learning and fewer confusion errors for end terms, and a symbolic distance effect in which confusions decline with distance. The analog schema in Table II gives approximate values on a unidimensional similarity continuum from which the "psychological distance" between the various classes can be

TABLE II

ANALOG AND DISCRETE MODELS OF THE DATA BASE FOR THE DE SOTO AND
BOSLEY (1962) EXPERIMENT

	Underlying representation				
	Discrete[a]				Analog
Class	Extreme	Upperclass	Beginning	Graduating	Distance from "freshman"
Freshman	1	0	1	0	0
Sophomore	0	0	0	0	5
Junior	0	1	0	0	7
Senior	1	1	0	1	10

[a]Features: 1 = positive, 0 = negative.

derived. De Soto and Bosley suggest that their results can be predicted from generalization gradients on the psychological similarity
continuum. The form of scale compression in the column of Table II
would model the similarity structure of the psychological continuum
De Soto and Bosley assume.

The discrete representation would have the subjects learning the
name–class associations by tagging each name with a "1" or "0" on
one or more of the features that describe the classes. The rate of
learning the terms and the pattern of confusion errors imply that
subjects learn the "beginning" feature first, then the "graduating"
feature, and finally the "upper-class" feature. Later still they may
begin to use an "extreme vs. middle" feature. RT's in a comparative
judgment task, with the men's names as the symbolic stimuli and
class designation as the criterion of judgment, could be predicted
from the discrete data base if subjects examine the features serially,
beginning with the most salient ones, which are presumably also the
ones acquired first in learning. The subjects would terminate their
search as soon as they came to a feature that discriminates the pair.

I do not think that, at present, there exist data to distinguish the
two underlying representations in Table II. Coupled with the appropriate processing assumptions they can probably account for any
effect obtained with a small series. A priori plausibility is probably as
much a matter of taste as anything else. It is true that the discrete
representation is redundant and inefficient in its use of features, but
this should not in itself be an objection to a model of human
memory. The featural representation gains plausibility in my mind
because of its similarity to the discrete, componential structure of
natural language concepts (cf. Leech, 1974, esp. chaps. 3 & 6). The

analog representation has some points in its favor, although it is less appealing to me than the discrete structure for this particular experiment. Its main advantage is in relating the similarity structure of the continuum to the RT's for comparative judgment. This is the role it had both for De Soto and Bosley (1962) and Banks *et al.* (1976).

2. The Data Base in Semantic Memory

Despite the interest in the retrieval and use of symbolic information from semantic memory (e.g., Holyoak & Walker, 1976; Moyer, 1973), there have been, to my knowledge, only two experiments (Banks & Flora, in press, Experiment I; Paivio, 1975, Experiment I) that have studied symbolic comparative judgments in a situation where subjects could not set up temporary data structures to mediate performance. Nevertheless, retrieval of comparative information from semantic memory is an important topic, and while it has not been thoroughly studied, we can be fairly certain that the symbolic-distance effect and the semantic-congruity effect are as robust when the subject must use semantic memory as when he can use a data base specially structured for the task.

How is quantitative attribute information stored in semantic memory? Some have suggested that for some continua, and particularly for physical size, every item has stored with it in semantic memory an analog quantity that encodes its value on the continuum. I have discussed in this chapter how such a suggestion is implausible for anything but a small set of items, given the limited capacity of human memory to capture absolute positions on a continuum. Furthermore, if relatively exact analog values are stored, it seems difficult to account for our flexibility and sensitivity to context in making quantitative assignments of attributes (Halff, Ortony, & Anderson, 1976; Walker, 1975).

My own answer to the question of storage is that quantitative attribute information, per se, is not in general stored at all in semantic memory. The process when semantic memory must be consulted for a comparative judgment seems to be one of searching for information in the data base that will give the correct answer, examining isolated facts about the items, constructing visual images, and generally going through what could be termed ad hoc heuristics for coming up with the correct choice. A few sets of items may have precoded attribute information, but retrieval of the precoded information in these cases would be just another heuristic, not an example of the general process of performing the comparative judgment.

The notion of a search using problem-solving heuristics rather than a search for precoded attribute information can still predict the distance and semantic-congruity effects. The distance effect comes about, as mentioned earlier, by the availability principle: The more distant from each other two items are on the dimensions of comparison, the sooner, on the average, will a piece of information be found that can discriminate them. The semantic-congruity effect results from the processing codes that are assigned to the items after they are discriminated. The processing codes will usually be in terms that reflect the position of the items on the continuum of comparison, since some information about the items will place them near one end or the other of the continuum. Two large things, for example, might initially be coded L+/L+, then as more information was found, be coded L/L+. The semantic-congruity effect thus comes about for the same reason as in the cases when the data base is temporary. Once the processing codes are generated their condition of match or mismatch with the instructional code creates the congruity effect. Effects at the matching stage do not depend on whether the stimulus codes were derived from a data base in semantic memory or from a temporary, experiment-specific organization of the relations among the items.

Figure 9 plots a distance effect that illustrates the availability principle in the network model proposed by the LNR group (Norman & Rumelhart, 1975). This figure is based on data presented in Linton's (1975) study of memory for events. In her paper she proposed a two-step process of determining the date of an event. First, an explicit temporal tag is searched for. If no explicit date is found, a search begins for other events whose relation to the event is known and thus that may help date the event in question. The second search predicts a distance effect by the availability principle, since a third event whose relation to the first two is known will immediately date them properly if it falls between them. Such third events form a larger proportion of the population, and are found sooner on the average, as the time interval between the first two increases. If relations involving third and fourth (or more) events are needed to place the first two in order, these additional events will also be found quicker as the time interval increases, and the need for using more events will also, of course, decline as the time interval increases.

As is seen in Fig. 9, the predicted distance effect is found, and it is quite strong. The points in this figure were derived from Linton's Fig. 14.3, which shows sequencing time as a function of the mean age of the pair being sequenced (only points for mean ages from 9 to

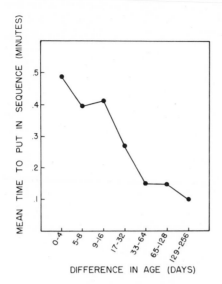

DIFFERENCE IN AGE (DAYS)

Fig. 9. Mean time to choose the correct sequence for a pair of remembered events, plotted as a function of the amount of time between them. (Derived from data in Linton, 1975.)

256 days were used for Fig. 9). The support for the hypothetical search process comes from introspection and subject's protocols, but the reports seem universally to support an ad hoc search process and a problem-solving strategy something like that which is proposed. Experimental tests of Linton's two-step search process and of the role of the availability principle in the search could be performed by giving subjects specially constructed data bases, although to prevent subjects from setting up special schemas for these data bases they might have to be very large. Potts (1972) used paragraph-length stories to give his subjects the data base for his task; tests of the availability principle in heuristic search processes might require full-length novels.

C. STUDIES OF PROCESSES IN THE MODEL

1. Separateness of Encoding Stage

The processes of perception and code generation in the model are assumed to be functionally separate from the later stages that discriminate the codes and match them to the instructions. The early stages generate the codes and the later stages use them. Since the distance and semantic-congruity effects come from the later stages, variables that affect encoding alone should simply slow down or speed up encoding and should not interact with variables that affect the later stages. The logic of using interactions in RT to discover separate stages of processing has been extensively discussed by Sternberg (1969). This section will present data that support a separate encoding process by showing that two different sorts of variables that affect the encoding process do not interact with variables affecting later processes.

   a.   Pictures vs. Words as Stimuli.   Pictures used as stimuli in a symbolic comparative judgment task lead to faster RT's than words (Paivio, 1975). Banks and Flora (in press) showed that the distance effect is almost perfectly additive with the picture–word difference. Figure 10 summarizes Banks and Flora's results for two different

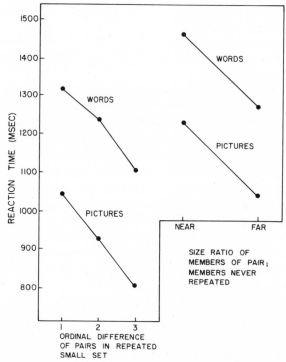

Fig. 10. RT for comparative judgment as a function of distance for pairs of objects represented by either words or pictures, replotted from Banks and Flora (in press). Left panel reports data from a repeated-set paradigm where the continuum of judgment was rated intelligence of animals; right panel is from an infinite-set paradigm where continuum was rated real-world size of objects.

experimental situations. The left panel shows the results for pictures and words for a small, repeated set of items, and the right for an infinite-set task.

The semantic-congruity effect (not shown here) was nearly the same for pictures and words in the repeated set, but in the infinite set there was somewhat less of a congruity effect for pictures than words when the discrimination was difficult. The reduced congruity effect for pictures in the infinite-set case turned out to be best explained by difficulties subjects had interpreting some of the pictures. When the instructions came *after* the same pictures in Banks and Flora's Experiment V, the subjects had plenty of time to identify them before making their choice, and the congruity effect was just as great for pictures as it was for words.

Banks and Flora concluded that the encoding stage is generally faster at putting out codes for pictures than words. Not only was the picture–word effect additive with the other effects, but it was approximately the same in absolute amount for two different attributes: size of objects and assumed intelligence of animals. Using a rather different semantic-processing task, Friedman and Bourne (1976) came to essentially the same conclusion about the picture–word difference. The explanation of the faster processing of pictures is yet to be found, however. We know it occurs for different reasons than the symbolic distance or semantic-congruity effect, but we do not know why it occurs. It may be that a given picture of an object suggests fewer semantic encodings than the word that describes it. The picture also might be processed faster because it avoids a phonemic recoding stage that words go through. It is possible, too, that pictures are processed faster than words in these experiments just because they are bigger and easier to see. The fact that pictures are faster than words for attributes that do and do not allow visual imagery (e.g., size judgments vs. intelligence judgments) indicates that the faster processing of pictures has nothing to do with the possibility that visual imagery is used in the task, as Paivio (1975), among others, has supposed.

b. Size Congruity. Paivio (1975) reported a Stroop-like interference effect when the symbolic stimuli for comparative judgments of size were pictures. One picture in each pair was large and one was small, and when the physically larger of the two pictures denoted the larger object the RT was faster than when it denoted the smaller. Banks and Flora (in press) termed this interference between the size of the symbol and the referent the *size-congruity* effect to distinguish it from the semantic-congruity effect. They speculated that the size-congruity effect resulted from operations in the encoding stage because pictures and not words show it. If the size-congruity effect came from a processing stage after code generation it should affect pictures and words equally, since there seems to be no difference in the processing of the two kinds of stimuli once the codes are generated.

Figure 11 presents the results of two experiments that combined a size-congruity variable with symbolic distance and semantic congruity in a comparative judgment task. Both of these experiments used the same stimuli: There was a set of four large and four small animals, pairs were always composed of animals within a large or small set, and subjects sometimes had to pick the larger and sometimes the smaller animal. The entire stimulus deck was made up in two versions, one with the relative sizes of the pictures the same as that of their referents (size congruent) and one with the relative sizes of the pictures the opposite of that of their referents (size incongruent).

Figure 11 shows that the size-congruity effect is approximately additive with the symbolic distance effect. In the left panel, which

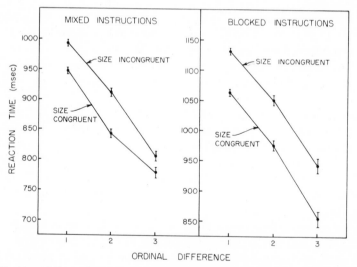

Fig. 11. Mean RT as a function of symbolic distance for comparative judgments of size. Symbolic stimuli were line drawings of the objects judged, and one drawing was always twice as big in both dimensions as the other. The size-congruent condition is that in which the larger drawing in the pair corresponded to the larger object, and the incongruent condition is that in which the larger corresponded to the smaller object. Bars indicate ± 1 standard error of the mean.

shows the result obtained with 16 subjects who had "choose larger" and "choose smaller" instructions randomly varied from trial to trial, there is some nonadditivity between the distance- and size-congruity effects, but it is neither large nor systematic. In the right panel, which shows data from a different group of eight subjects who had separate blocks of instructions, the additivity between the effects is quite good. These experiments taken together suggest strongly that size-congruity and the distance effects result from different stages of processing, but I would withhold final judgment on the point until an experiment is performed showing additivity with a size-congruity variable that had a greater mean effect on RT.

The semantic-congruity effect turned out not to be additive with size congruity. There was less of a semantic-congruity effect for the size-incongruent pairs than for size-congruent ones. For mixed instructions the semantic-congruity interaction declined from 46 msec to 32 msec from size-congruent to size-incongruent pairs, and for blocked instructions it declined from 52 msec to 21 msec. My interpretation of this decline is that the stimulus codes were less often cast in polar terms for size-incongruent than size-congruent conditions, but the point is clearly not settled.

2. Code Generation

The model of Banks *et al.* (1976) assumed that the code for each digit in a pair presented for comparative judgment is generated without reference to the other digit. Banks and Flora (in press), in using the general principles of this model to account for other comparative judgment data, let this assumption stand. The experiment discussed in this section was intended to test the assumption.

In the usual comparative judgment paradigm the stimuli are presented simultaneously, and if one is coded relative to the other, it is impossible to tell which is coded relative to which. No model of code generation that assumes relative coding can be adequately tested unless the order of processing and encoding the stimuli is known. This experiment therefore controlled the order of presentation of stimuli. One condition presented stimuli in the usual side-by-side simultaneous fashion while the other presented them one at a time. In the latter, successive condition the first stimulus was read to the subject and then, after a 1-sec delay, the second stimulus was presented visually. The visual stimulus in the successive condition has just one member of the pair, always typed on the right side of the fixation point. If the subject chose the second stimulus, he was to press the microswitch held in his right hand. If he chose the first stimulus, he pressed the microswitch on his left, on the same side as the "empty" space on the tachistoscope card. This procedure confounds hand of response with stimulus chosen, but it was employed because it made it easy for subjects to perform in the task.

The continuum of judgment was size of objects. The 16 pairs used by Banks and Flora (in press, Experiment I) were augmented by 16 more drawn from Paivio's (1975) norms. An infinite-set design was used to prevent subjects from guessing the correct response in the successive condition. In addition to the simultaneous vs. successive variable, there were two instructions ("choose larger/smaller," randomly varied from trial to trial and always presented before the stimuli), pairs of large and of small objects, and near and far ratios within the pairs. The design therefore allowed examination of the distance effect (near vs. far size ratio), the semantic-congruity effect, and their interaction, for both simultaneous and successive presentation of stimuli. The experiment had 16 subjects, eight of whom performed in the successive condition first and eight in the simultaneous condition first.

The results showed some striking differences between the simultaneous and successive conditions. First, the distance effect was considerably less in the simultaneous condition than the successive one (66 msec vs. 161 msec). Second, the congruity effect for the cases when the first stimulus was chosen in the successive condition was very different from those when the second stimulus was chosen. Figure 12 shows the congruity effect for the simultaneous condition and for the two stimuli separately in the successive condition. (This experiment is, incidentally, the third I know of that shows a distance effect and a congruity effect in an infinite-set paradigm.) None of the interactions involving simultaneous vs. successive presentation was reliable.

The pattern of results suggests some sort of relative encoding process in at least the successive condition, but it is difficult to narrow the set of possible models with just the data at hand, and all the models I can think of have trouble with at least some aspect of the results. Interestingly, Wallis and Audley (1964), in an experiment on comparative judgment of highness or lowness of pitches, also found a semantic-congruity effect when the second of two successively presented pitches was the correct choice but did not get a semantic-congruity effect when the first was the correct choice. They also had some difficulty explaining this difference in the congruity effect; it does not seem to disconfirm the model they proposed for the task, but it is not expected, either.

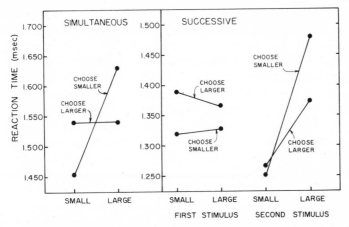

Fig. 12. Mean RT for deciding which is the larger or smaller object denoted by a word in a pair. Left panel shows results with simultaneously presented pair. Right panel shows results separately when the first and second words in a successively presented pair are chosen.

My present guess as to the possible causes of the pattern of congruity effects in the successive condition is that the subject tentatively matches the code for the first stimulus to the instructions while waiting for the second one. If the second stimulus confirms the initial choice, the subject responds, but if not, he must transform the second to match the instructions. A semantic-congruity effect therefore results only for the second stimulus. This explanation has several defects: The process of "checking" the second stimulus is not defined (it would have to be a relative encoding rather than a matching to the instructions), the increased distance effect in the successive condition is not explained, and the roughly equal RT's for the first and second stimuli do not seem to be predicted (a weak explanation is that subjects respond faster with their right than their left hands and thus eliminate the RT superiority of the first stimulus). I can say with confidence only that the successive case is an important condition to understand, if only because it is so difficult to understand.

3. The Choice Process

The semantic-coding model can predict the major effects in comparative judgment, but it is the semantic-congruity effect that gives the model its strongest intuitive support. This effect seems to necessitate the assumption that linguistic codes are used in processing. There are, however, some alternate explanations of the congruity effect, and this section shows some problems they have. The first alternative explanation, an expectancy principle, is quite general, and its disconfirmation leaves a large number of models without an explanation of the congruity effect. The second is an explanation that applies only to an analog-continuum model, but this is a fairly broad class of model.

a. *Expectancy.* In the typical comparative judgment experiment the instructions (e.g. "choose larger/smaller") are given prior to the stimuli to be judged. It is possible, therefore, that the semantic-congruity effect could arise from some sort of expectancy set up by the instructions. In an imagery model like Paivio's (1975), for example, "choose larger," could prepare subjects to process large objects by, say, scaling subjects' image space (cf. Kosslyn, 1975) appropriately for large things, and they would process large things faster than small things under "choose larger" instructions. "Choose smaller" would similarly prepare them better for small than large things, and the semantic-congruity interaction would result. Moyer and Bayer (1976) suggested a different expectancy-based explanation of the congruity effect. Retrieval of symbolic information requires a serial search process in their model, and the instructions could cause the subject to begin searching at one end or the other of the continuum to find the information. The congruity effect would emerge because the search would come to items near the end of the continuum specified by the instructions faster than to items near the opposite end. Holyoak and Walker (1976, pp. 297–298) propose still another expectancy mechanism to allow an analog model to predict the congruity effect. According to this model, analog quantitative information is retrieved in a form congruent with the question. If, for example, the questions used in an experiment are "choose larger" and "choose smaller," analog magnitude information about both the largeness and the smallness of objects will be stored, and "choose larger" will cause the subject to retrieve analog largeness values, while "choose smaller" will cause him to retrieve analog smallness values. (I do not see how purely analog magnitudes can separately and uniquely denote smallness and largeness without propositional information to specify which scale is intended, but this is a separate issue.) The congruity effect is predicted because smallness information is retrieved faster than largeness information for small objects and largeness faster than smallness for large objects. This explanation cannot predict a congruity effect when the instructions are given after the stimuli have been in view for a while. By the time the instructions are presented the magnitude information, whether in terms of largeness or smallness, will have already been retrieved, and differential retrieval times for the two kinds of information cannot account for the congruity effect.

Banks and Flora (in press) reported three experiments that tested the expectancy explanation of the congruity effect by presenting the instructions after the stimuli. In all three cases a reliable congruity effect was obtained. Two of Banks and Flora's experiments left the stimuli in view for 2 full sec before presenting the instructions. This amount of time should have been adequate for the subjects to identify the stimuli before the instructions. They must have done some processing during the 2 sec because their RT's were considerably faster when the instructions were given after than before the stimuli. (The RT was measured from the time at which the instructions were presented and so did not include the 2 sec.) Yet in both of these experiments the congruity effect was robust and in one it was actually greater with instructions after the stimuli than before.

The finding of a congruity effect with instructions after the stimuli shows that expectancies set up by the instructions are not necessary for obtaining a congruity effect. In the imagery theory the images of the objects should have been retrieved and set up in an optimally sized image space by the time the instructions were presented. In Moyer and Bayer's (1976) model the search for the symbolized information should have been concluded by the time the instructions were presented and thus have been uninfluenced by them. These models, then, would have to resort to a different explanation for a semantic-congruity effect for before and after instructions. The semantic-coding model, on the other hand, has the same explanation for the congruity effect whenever the instructions are given. This is so because the processing codes for the stimuli are determined by the position of the stimuli on the continuum, not by the instructions.

According to the semantic-coding model the distance effect should decline when instructions come after the subject has had a chance to process the stimuli. The model predicts this decline because the distance effect itself arises from the time required by the discrimination stage to generate codes that distinguish the stimuli. The discrimination process is not contingent on the instructions and can operate before they are given. When the instructions come after the stimuli, the discrimination stage can usually have its work done before the clock starts on the RT measurement, but when the instructions come before the stimuli, all of the time consumed by discrimination falls within the period of time measured as the RT.

   b. *Analog-Continuum Models of the Congruity Effect.* Analog-continuum models are distinguished from other types of analog

models in Section III, E, and some theoretical and empirical problems for this type of model are also discussed in that section. In this
section we will focus on the way in which these models predict the
semantic-congruity effect. It will be seen that a class of commonly
obtained patterns of RT in the semantic-congruity effect pose a
serious problem for analog-continuum models, and the variances of
the RT's in the congruity effect do not, as Jamieson and Petrusic
(1975) suppose, support the analog model but, rather, disconfirm it.

Two very similar analog-continuum models have been proposed,
the first by Marks (1972) and a later one by Jamieson and Petrusic
(1975). The mechanism Marks devised to account for the congruity
effect is quite ingenious. It assumes that stimuli in a comparative
judgment task are represented mentally on an analog continuum, and
each stimulus has a mean and a variance, or discriminal dispersion, on
the continuum. The RT for a comparative judgment between two
stimuli declines as either the distance between them increases or their
variance on the continuum (their discriminal dispersion) decreases.
The model assumes that discriminal dispersions increase along a
continuum as distance from an end point or anchor point increases.
The instructions given for comparative judgment set the anchor point
against which the stimuli are measured on any given trial. Thus, if the
comparative judgment is made after the instructions "choose larger"
or "choose smaller," for example, the stimuli are judged against the
larger or smaller end, respectively, of the continuum. Two small
objects will be further from the end anchor under "choose larger"
instructions than under "choose smaller" instructions, and their
discriminal dispersions will be greater in the former case than in the
latter. Therefore the RT to discriminate them will be greater in the
former than the latter case. Two large objects will show the opposite
pattern of RT's, and the semantic-congruity effect is predicted.

Jamieson and Petrusic's (1975) analog-continuum model is very
similar to Marks'. The main difference is that no assumptions are
made about discriminal dispersions. Instead of computing a difference between stimuli on the memorial continuum, subjects base their
response on the ratio, R, between the quantities on the continuum.
The distance effect is predicted because RT is assumed to decline
monotonically as R increases. The semantic-congruity effect comes
about because R is computed as a ratio of the quantities measured
from the pole specified by the instructions. Two small things, for
example, will be measured against the small pole under "choose
smaller" instructions and against the large pole under "choose
larger." The analog quantities associated with them will thus be

smaller under smaller than larger instructions, but since the absolute difference will be the same in both cases, the ratio between them will be more extreme under smaller than larger instructions. Consequently, the RT will be faster for small things under "choose smaller" than under "choose larger" instructions. In like manner, the RT for pairs of large things will be faster under "choose larger" than "choose smaller" instructions, and the overall semantic-congruity interaction is predicted.

A third, logically different, type of analog-continuum model uses the concept of scale compression, rather than discriminal dispersions or a ratio response rule, to predict distance effects and the serial-position effect. Two examples of this model are the Shepard *et al.* (1975) and the Banks *et al.* (1976) models of the data base for digit inequality judgments. However, no one has attempted to use this sort of analog model to predict the semantic-congruity effect. Banks *et al.* predicted the semantic-congruity effect from processes that operate on information derived from the data base, and Shepard *et al.* did not attempt to predict the semantic-congruity effect at all. A purely scale-comparison model of the semantic-congruity effect would probably assume that the different instructions (e.g., choose larger vs. choose smaller) each induced a different scale-compression function. While this model has some attractive features, it seems to me to give an account of the semantic-congruity effect that is, at the least, terribly imparsimonious. Since a scale-compression model has never been presented as an explanation of the semantic-congruity effect, I will not discuss it here.

There are four findings that seem to disconfirm one or the other or both of the analog-continuum models, or at least reduce their plausibility. These are the Banks and Flora (1977) congruity effect found with poststimulus instructions, the Schneider and Lane (1963) finding that variability of perceptual magnitude judgments varies with position on the judgmental scale, the bowed serial-position function, and the form of the semantic-congruity effect in a great number of experiments. I will cover each of the findings below and discuss in places how the analog-continuum models might handle them.

The Banks and Flora (1977) finding that a congruity effect is obtained with instructions presented after the stimulus shows that the anchor point for the judgment does not need to be set before memory information about the stimuli is retrieved. The results show that the stimuli are discriminated to some extent before the instructions are given because there is much less distance effect with poststimulus instructions than with prestimulus instructions.

The fact that the semantic-congruity effect can be found in undiminished form with poststimulus instructions, while the distance effect does decline, indicates that the semantic-congruity effect is not caused by the same mechanisms that create the distance effect. The Marks or the Jamieson and Petrusic models may therefore be acceptable models of the discrimination stage of the semantic-coding model, but they do not model the processes responsible for the congruity effect.

Schneider and Lane (1963) obtained magnitude judgments and category productions of both the loudness and the softness of an auditory stimulus. In the terms of Marks's model, the physical continuum was sound intensity, and the anchor point was at the loud end of the continuum for loudness judgments (and productions) and at the soft (quiet) end for softness judgments (and productions). The analog-continuum model predicts an increase in variability (discriminal dispersion) as stimuli further from the anchor point in either case are judged or produced. However, for both judgments and productions the variability increased with stimulus intensity. The subjective anchoring on the continuum (softness vs. loudness instructions) appeared to have no effect on the discriminal dispersions. There is no evidence at all for the change in variability Marks' model requires.

I can think of two objections that might be maintained against the relevance of the Schneider and Lane experiment. First, it could be held that the discriminal dispersions are different for RT and judgment or production. Of course, this is possible, but we need *some* measure of dispersion independent of RT to avoid circular reasoning, and judgment and production do seem to be somewhat different tasks that are appropriate for converging on a single underlying concept of discriminal dispersion. Second, experiments such as Schneider and Lane's have not been performed on any of the continua (perceptual or memorial) for which semantic-congruity effects have been shown. I can only comment that I see no reason to think that a semantic-congruity effect would not be found for judgments of loudness and softness, but the experiment has not yet been performed as far as I know. Only one case in which discriminal dispersions do not vary with instructions but in which a congruity effect is nevertheless obtained is needed to show that the two are not causally related. An experiment looking for a semantic-congruity effect for loudness and softness judgments might turn out to be a very important one.

The bowed serial-position curve (see Fig. 1) is frequently obtained in comparative judgments, and it is not predicted by either the Marks or the Jamieson and Petrusic models. Both models require a monotonic serial-position curve for either direction of judgment on the continuum. Marks' model predicts a monotonic increasing position curve because the discriminal dispersion is assumed to increase monotonically with distance from the anchor point. Jamieson and Petrusic's model predicts a monotonic increasing function because the ratio, R, between two items spaced a constant distance apart will decline monotonically as they are moved further from the end anchor against which they are measured. Marks' model might be saved with the additional assumption that the discriminal dispersion is not always a monotonically increasing function of distance from the anchor, but Jamieson and Petrusic's model cannot benefit from this assumption. One possible approach to saving the analog model from disconfirmation by the bowed serial-position curve would be to limit its applicability to just those cases in which monotonic serial-position curves are obtained. However, to avoid circularity we must specify those cases in advance, and it is difficult to find a principle to specify them that includes very many cases. If the breakdown of Table I is used to categorize studies, only studies that have a preexperimental basis for ordering and nonrepeated items qualify, since bowed serial-position curves are found in the other cells. However, there is only one serial-position effect (Paivio, 1975) reported in this category, and future research may find bowed serial-position curves here also. One might think that preexperimental orderings that rely on magnitude information would be perfect candidates for analog modeling, but the digits—which form an almost prototypical scale of this type—actually give a slightly bowed serial-position effect (cf. Banks et al., 1976, Experiment 2; Shepard et al., 1975) and other magnitude scales sometimes give very peculiar, nonmonotonic serial-position effects (cf. Holyoak & Walker, 1976).

The final problem I see for the analog-continuum model is a failure to predict a fairly commonly obtained form of the semantic-congruity interaction. This form of interaction is one in which the RT functions for the two instructions have different slopes, but slopes of the same sign. Examples of such interactions are seen if Fig. 13. Figure 1 shows an ideal, symmetrical congruity effect that looks like a perfect "x," but forms such as those in Fig. 13 are obtained about as often as the one in Fig. 1. Semantic-congruity effects in which the functions for the two instructions had slopes of the same sign were obtained by Banks et al. (1975), Banks et al. (1976), Friend (1973), Marks (1972), Ellis (1972), and Audley and Wallis (1964).

The problem these functions create for both Marks' and Jamieson and Petrusic's versions of the analog-continuum model is that both generate the semantic-congruity effect from the different serial-posi-

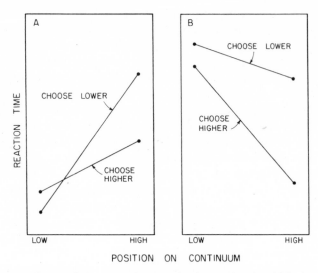

Fig. 13. Two forms of the semantic-congruity interaction in which the serial-position functions for the two instructions have slopes of the same sign.

tion effects obtained with the two versions of the instructions. Since the two serial-position effects have slopes of opposite sign, the semantic-congruity effect must be made up of two functions of opposite slope. The added assumptions that would allow Marks' model to predict a bowed serial-position effect would also allow it to predict semantic-congruity effects made up of functions with slopes of the same sign, but these assumptions will not help the Jamieson and Petrusic model.

A final point on the semantic-congruity effect concerns the prediction of the variance of the mean RT. Jamieson and Petrusic (1975) have attempted to use variances of the RT to demonstrate the superiority of their analog approach over a semantic-coding approach in modeling comparative judgment experiments. There are two major problems with their attempt, however. The first is that they do not break down the variance data in a way that allows a test of the semantic-coding model. There is no way of knowing from their report what the variances are that correspond to the congruity or the distance effects; they present only the variances for the serial-position effect for items separated by one ordinal step. The data they did not report might have allowed a test of the model, but one cannot know what was not reported.

The second problem is that they nowhere report the mean RT's that correspond to the variances. It is therefore impossible to know how to go about fitting the semantic-coding model to the data they do report. The variances they say the semantic-coding model would predict for the position effect depend upon the bowed pattern of RT's (cf. Fig. 1B), but we cannot be sure this pattern was found. Even if it was, the model might still be able to predict the RT's. The lack of reported RT's also makes it impossible to know how well Jamieson and Petrusic's own model would fit the data. They do not present a fit of the model to the variances either, and I am not at all sure it would fit them. Below, we will consider some data that do allow a test between the models.

Some data collected for a different purpose were reanalyzed in order to obtain the RT's and variances necessary to make a test of the Jamieson and Petrusic model. These data were obtained from a total of 30 subjects who performed in two related experiments. In both experiments they learned an association between nonsense syllables (CVC's) and physical stimuli, such as in Moyer and Bayer's (1976) experiment. Both experiments used the same four CVC's, but in the first (with 12 subjects) they were associated with four different pitches, and in the second (with 18 subjects), with four sizes of circle. The RT task required the subjects to process the CVC's on the basis of the associated physical stimulus. On every trial of RT testing subjects saw a pair of CVC's and had to pick sometimes the one associated with the higher pitch (or larger circle) and sometimes the one associated with the lower pitch (or smaller circle). Instructions, always presented before the stimuli, were varied randomly from trial to trial. All six different combinations of the four CVC's were presented under both instructions and with the correct response on the left and right equally often, making a total of 24 (6 × 2 × 2) stimuli, which were presented in random order once each in four separate blocks of 24. When a subject made an error the card that led to the error was repeated later in the block to keep the same n in all cells.

The results of the two experiments were combined to give greater reliability to the variance measure. Combination seemed justified since the mean RT's were extremely close in absolute terms. The means of the 24 conditions in the two experiments were within ± 20 msec of each other, without any correction for overall group differences in RT. It seems that subjects processed the series of four CVC's in the same way whether they were associated with pitches or circles.

The mean RT's and variances are seen in Table III. The variance measure was obtained by first computing the variance of each subject for the four RT's he had in each of the 24 conditions and then averaging over the 30 subjects to get a mean variance for each

TABLE III

VARIANCE AND MEAN OF RT TO PROCESS EACH PAIR IN A FOUR-TERM
ORDER UNDER BOTH INSTRUCTIONS

Instruction	Measure	Pair					
		12	23	34	13	24	14
Choose smaller	Variance (1,000 msec^2)	54	105	77	63	47	32
or lower	RT (msec)	663	1,124	1,020	688	927	659
Choose larger	Variance (1,000 msec^2)	60	84	53	50	53	45
or higher	RT (msec)	935	1,090	716	932	730	706

condition. (Table III shows only 12 conditions because a mean was taken over left and right responses.) The "pair" heading in the table designates the six possible combinations of the CVC's, where 1 = the smallest (lowest) CVC and 4 = the largest (highest) one. Pairs 12, 23, and 34 designate a symbolic distance of 1 ordinal step, 13 and 24 designate a distance of 2, and 14 a distance of 3.

The RT's show a strong distance and congruity effect, as well as the bowed serial-position effect. Below I will sketch out the way that the semantic-coding model predicts the variances and later discuss the problems the variances pose for the analog model.

There are two different sources of variance in the semantic model. The first is the variance associated with each stage. This would be a parameter estimated for each stage. The second is the variance created by the probabilistic mixture of latencies within a condition. Both discriminability of codes and semantic congruity vary the mean RT by varying the probability with which different stages are entered. Thus, the variance of the latency distribution should increase as the probabilistic mixture of different stages with different mean latencies becomes more diverse. The semantic model would, in general, predict an increase in variance (and RT) as discrimination between codes becomes more difficult. It would also predict a decrease in variance as semantic congruity between stimulus and instructional codes becomes either very good or very bad. Highest variance from this source would be associated with the conditions in which the probability of entering the congruity-ensuring loop was .50 and lowest when it was either 0 or 1.0.

The data in Table III support the qualitative predictions of the model for the variances. (The number of free parameters in the model makes quantitative prediction an uninteresting exercise for this set of data.) The variances declined with RT's in accord with the distance effect. For ordinal differences of 1, 2, and 3 steps, the mean variances are 72, 53, and 38 msec^2 ($\times$ 1000), respectively, and the mean RT's are 925, 819, and 682 msec. The variances associated with the conditions of semantic congruity also generally followed the model. The prediction is that stimuli that are always congruent or are never congruent with the instructions will have less variable RT's than intermediate ones whose codes sometimes do and sometimes do not require a congruity-ensuring transformation. As can be seen in Table III these predictions hold up fairly well.

Jamieson and Petrusic's analog model predicts both the distance effect and semantic-congruity effect through the single function RT $= f_{mon}$ (R). The congruity effect arises, as discussed above, because the instructions determine the pole against which the items to be compared are measured, and for this reason the semantic-congruity effect becomes, quite literally, a form of the discriminability effect. Since the variance will be given by f^2_{mon} (R), the analog model must predict the same relation between RT and variance, whether the cause of variation in RT is semantic congruity or symbolic distance. The analog model predicts the decline in variance and mean as symbolic distance increases, but it does not predict the variance for the different conditions of semantic congruity. The mean RT for the conditions in which stimuli and instructions were congruent was 699 msec, and it was 954 msec for the incongruent conditions. The variances, despite the 255 msec difference in mean RT, were very nearly the same, 56,000 and 58,000 $msec^2$, respectively.

The RT varied over a range of 240 msec with discriminability, and the variance in the least discriminable condition was almost twice that in the most discriminable condition. Jamieson and Petrusic's model must predict an equivalent change in variance due to the 255 msec variation in RT caused by the semantic-congruity effect. There is no such variation, and the model is disconfirmed. Marks' (1972) model was not explicitly formulated to predict variances, but it would, I think, have to make the same prediction as Jamieson and Petrusic's. The simplest version of the semantic coding would have the same variance for congruity and noncongruity paths in processing and would predict the same variance for each despite the difference in mean RT.

V. Concluding Remarks

Three unsolved problems touched on in this chapter strike me as particularly important. The first concerns the general question of the data base. We know very little about how quantitative attribute information is generated from semantic memory, and there are very few experiments that we can look to for information on this matter. The complete picture of the short-term data base and its relation to semantic memory also needs to be worked out. The second problem is a fairly specific one, but it may turn out to have general consequences. This is the explanation of the pattern of data when the stimuli for comparative judgment are presented successively (Fig. 12). Wallis and Audley (1964) found the same pattern of results for perceptual comparative judgments, and this pattern, if we can understand it, may tell us something very fundamental about encoding and decision processes. The third problem is the faster processing of pictures than words. We know a few things that are definitely not related to the superiority of pictures, but we have yet to come up with a mechanism to explain it. It would be very interesting if the faster processing of pictures turned out to be related in some way to the superiority of pictures over words in memory, but we are a long way from knowing it is.

I may be a victim of self-hypnosis, but I have come to think of the semantic-coding model as being relatively simple. At least, the broad outline of the model is easy to state: Processing functions generate processing codes for the stimuli and operate on the codes until one (and only one) matches the instructions. It is true in the model that the data base in memory for generating the processing codes can have several forms and that processing codes have the structure of linguistic concepts, but these seem natural assumptions to make and do not overly burden the model in my mind. I do hope that the model will continue to be simple as we learn more about comparative judgment.

REFERENCES

Anderson, J. R., & Bower, G. M. *Human associative memory*. Washington, D.C.: Winston, 1973.

Audley, R. J., & Wallis, C. P. Response instructions and the speed of relative judgments. I. Some experiments on brightness discrimination. *British Journal of Psychology*, 1964, 55, 59–73.

Banks, W. P., Clark, H. H., & Lucy, P. The locus of the semantic congruity effect in comparative judgments. *Journal of Experimental Psychology: Human Perception and Performance*, 1975, 1, 35–47.

Banks, W. P., & Flora, J. Semantic and perceptual processes in symbolic comparisons. *Journal of Experimental Psychology: Human Perception and Performance*, in press.

Banks, W. P., Fujii, M., & Kayra-Stuart, F. Semantic congruity effects in comparative judgments of magnitude of digits. *Journal of Experimental Psychology: Human Perception and Performance*, 1976, 2, 435–447.

Banks, W. P., & Hill, D. K. The apparent magnitude of number scaled by random production. *Journal of Experimental Psychology*, 1974, 102, 353–376. (Monograph)

Bartlett, F. C. *Remembering*. Cambridge, Eng.: University Press, 1932.

Bower, G. Adaptation-level coding of stimuli and serial position effects. In M. H. Appley (Ed.), *Adaptation-level theory*. New York: Academic Press, 1971.

Buckley, P. B., & Gillman, C. B. Comparison of digits and dot patterns. *Journal of Experimental Psychology*, 1974, **103**, 1131–1136.

Clark, H. H. Linguistic processes in deductive reasoning. *Psychological Review*, 1969, **76**, 387–404.

Clark, H. H. More about "adjectives, comparatives, and syllogisms:" A reply to Huttenlocher and Higgins. *Psychological Review*, 1971, **78**, 505–514.

Collins, A. M., & Quillian, M. R. How to make a language user. In E. Tulving & D. Donaldson (Eds.), *Organization of memory*. New York: Academic Press, 1972.

De Soto, C. B., & Bosley, J. J. The cognitive structure of a social structure. *Journal of Abnormal and Social Psychology*, 1962, **64**, 303–307.

De Soto, C. B., London, M., & Handel, S. Social reasoning and spatial paralogic. *Journal of Personality and Social Psychology*, 1965, **4**, 513–521.

Ellis, S. H. Interaction of encoding and retrieval in relative age judgments. *Journal of Experimental Psychology*, 1972, **94**, 291–294.

Friedman, A. *Comparing words: An "internal psychophysics" for a non-physical dimension*. Paper presented at the 21st International Congress of Psychology, Paris, July 1976.

Friedman, A., & Bourne, L. E. Encoding the levels of information in pictures and words. *Journal of Experimental Psychology: General*, 1976, **105**, 169–190.

Friend, K. E. Perceptual encoding in comparative judgments of race. *Memory & Cognition*, 1973, **1**, 80–84.

Gravetter, F., & Lockhead, G. R. Criterial range as a frame of reference for stimulus judgment. *Psychological Review*, 1973, **80**, 203–216.

Griggs, R. A., & Shea, S. L. Integrating verbal quantitative information in linear orderings. *Memory & Cognition*, in press.

Halff, H. M., Ortony, A., & Anderson, R. C. A context-sensitive representation of word meanings. *Memory & Cognition*, 1976, **4**, 378–383.

Hayes-Roth, B., & Hayes-Roth, F. Plasticity in memorial networks. *Journal of Verbal Learning and Verbal Behavior*, 1975, **14**, 506–522.

Holyoak, K. J. The form of analog size information in memory. *Cognitive Psychology*, 1977, **9**, 31–51.

Holyoak, K. J., & Walker, J. H. Subjective magnitude information in semantic orderings. *Journal of Verbal Learning and Verbal Behavior*, 1976, **15**, 287–299.

Huttenlocher, J. Constructing spatial images: A strategy in reasoning. *Psychological Review*, 1968, **75**, 550–560.

Jamieson, D. G., & Petrusic, W. M. Relational judgments with remembered stimuli. *Perception & Psychophysics*, 1975, **18**, 373–378.

Kosslyn, S. M. Information representation in visual images. *Cognitive Psychology*, 1975, **7**, 341–370.

Leech, G. *Semantics*. Baltimore: Penguin Books, 1974.

Linton, M. Memory for real-world events. In D. H. Normal & D. E. Rumelhart (Eds.), *Explorations in cognition*. San Francisco: Freeman, 1975.

Lovelace, E. A., & Snodgrass, R. D. Decision times for alphabetic order of digit pairs. *Journal of Experimental Psychology*, 1971, **88**, 258–264.

Marks, D. F. Relative judgment: A phenomenon and a theory. *Perception & Psychophysics*, 1972, **11**, 156–160.

Meyer, D. E. On the representation and retrieval of stored semantic information. *Cognitive Psychology*, 1970, **1**, 242–299.

Miller, G. A. The magical number seven, plus or minus two: Some limits on our capacity for processing information. *Psychological Review*, 1956, **63**, 81–97.

Miller, G. A., & Johnson-Laird, P. N. *Language and perception*. Cambridge, Mass: Harvard University Press, 1976.

Moyer, R. S. Comparing objects in memory: Evidence suggesting an internal psychophysics. *Perception & Psychophysics*, 1973, **13**, 180–184.

Moyer, R. S., & Bayer, R. H. Mental comparison and the symbolic distance effect. *Cognitive Psychology*, 1976, **8**, 228–246.

Moyer, R. S., & Landauer, T. K. The time required for judgments of numerical inequality. *Nature (London)*, 1967, **215**, 1519–1520.

Moyer, R. S., & Landauer, T. K. Determinants of reaction time for digit inequality judgments. *Bulletin of the Psychonomic Society*, 1973, **1**(3), 167–168.

Norman, D. H., & Rumelhart, D. E. *Explorations in cognition*. San Francisco: Freeman, 1975.

Paivio, A. Perceptual comparisons through the mind's eye. *Memory & Cognition*, 1975, **3**, 635–647.

Parkman, J. M. Temporal aspects of digit and letter inequality judgments. *Journal of Experimental Psychology*, 1971, **91**, 191–205.

Platt, J. R. Strong inference. *Science*, 1964, **146**, 347–353.

Polich, J. M., & Potts, G. R. Retrieval strategies for linearly ordered information. *Journal of Experimental Psychology: Human Learning and Memory*, 1977, **3**, 10–17.

Pollack, I. The information of elementary auditory displays. *Journal of the Acoustical Society of America*, 1952, **24**, 745–749.

Potts, G. R. Information processing strategies used in the encoding of linear orderings. *Journal of Verbal Learning and Verbal Behavior*, 1972, **11**, 727–740.

Potts, G. R. Incorporating quantitative information into a linear ordering. *Memory & Cognition*, 1974, **3**, 553–538. (a)

Potts, G. R. Storing and retrieving information about ordered relationships. *Journal of Experimental Psychology*, 1974, **3**, 431–439. (b)

Potts, G. R., & Scholz, K. W. The internal representation of a three-term series problem. *Journal of Verbal Learning and Verbal Behavior*, 1975, **14**, 439–452.

Riley, C. A. The representation of comparative relations and the transitive inference task. *Journal of Experimental Child Psychology*, 1976, **22**, 1–22.

Riley, C. A., & Trabasso, T. Comparatives, logical structures, and encoding in a transitive inference task. *Journal of Experimental Child Psychology*, 1974, **17**, 187–203.

Sapir, E. Grading: A study in semantics. *Philosophy of Science*, 1944, **11**, 83–116.

Schneider, R., & Lane, H. Ratio scales, category scales, and variability in the production of loudness and softness. *Journal of the Acoustical Society of America*, 1963, **35**, 1953–1961.

Sekuler, R., Rubin, E., & Armstrong, R. Processing numerical information: A choice time analysis. *Journal of Experimental Psychology*, 1971, **90**, 75–80.

Shepard, R. N., & Feng, C. A chronometric study of mental paper folding. *Cognitive Psychology*, 1972, **3**, 228–243.

Shepard, R. N., Kilpatric, D. W., & Cunningham, J. P. The internal representation of numbers. *Cognitive Psychology*, 1975, **7**, 82–138.

Smith, E. E., Shoben, E. J., & Rips, L. J. Structure and process in semantic memory: A feature model for semantic decisions. *Psychological Review*, 1974, **81**, 214–241.

Sternberg, S. The discovery of processing stages: extensions of Donder's method. In W. G. Koster (Ed. and trans.), *Attention and performance II*. Amsterdam: North-Holland Publ., 1969. (Reprinted from *Acta Psychologica*, 1969, **30**, 276–315.)

Stevens, S. S. *Psychophysics and social scaling*. Morristown, N.J.: General Learning Press, 1972.

Trabasso, T., & Riley, C. A. On the construction and use of representations involving linear order. In R. L. Solso (Ed.), *Information processing and cognition: The Loyola Symposium*. Hillsdale, N.J.: Lawrence Erlbaum Associates, 1975.

Trabasso, T., Riley, C. A., & Wilson, E. G. The representation of linear order and spatial strategies in reasoning: A developmental study. In R. Falmagne (Ed.), *Psychological studies of logic and its development*. Hillsdale, N.J.: Lawrence Erlbaum Associates, 1975.

Walker, J. H. Real-world variability, reasonableness judgments, and memory representations for concepts. *Journal of Verbal Learning and Verbal Behavior*, 1975, 14, 241–252.

Wallis, C. P., & Audley, R. J. Response instructions and the speed of relative judgments: II. Pitch discrimination. *British Journal of Psychology*, 1964, 55, 121–132.

MEMORY FOR PROBLEM SOLUTIONS

Stephen K. Reed and Jeffrey A. Johnsen

CASE WESTERN RESERVE UNIVERSITY, CLEVELAND, OHIO

I. Introduction

One of the major trends in memory research over the past several years has been an increasing emphasis on memory for meaningful material with paragraphs replacing nonsense syllables as stimulus materials (see Dooling & Christiaansen, this volume). The experiments reported in this chapter are consistent with this trend, but explore a relatively neglected area in the memory literature, memory for problem solutions. We consider different procedures for discovering what a person has learned after solving a problem that would result in an improved performance when he or she solves the problem for a second time. As a part of this study, we will examine whether traditional research on paired-associate learning and serial learning is sufficient for understanding problem solving or whether we will need new concepts to theorize about what a person remembers after solving a problem.

It is likely that our ability as problem solvers depends to a great extent on our memory for how we solved previous problems. After emphasizing that plans are important for guiding complex behavior, Miller, Galanter, and Pribram (1960, pp. 177–178) argued that the major source of new plans is old plans. According to their argument, plans are usually remembered and not created. It is still not clear, however, exactly what is remembered after having solved a problem or under what circumstances the prior solution of a problem will facilitate solving a similar problem. As was pointed out by Greeno (1973), prior experience can even hinder problem solving if people use a previous solution when a different or easier solution is required. Greeno refers to Luchins' (1942) water jar problem as a case in which subjects would have done better if they had not used their previous solution. In other cases, the use of an analogous solution can facilitate problem solving although the extent of facilitation depends on what is remembered about the analogous solution and knowledge of how the problems are related (Reed, Ernst, & Banerji, 1974).

The three experiments reported here make use of a variety of paradigms in an attempt to determine what is remembered after solving a problem. The problem in all three experiments is a version of the missionary–cannibal (MC) problem in which there are five missionaries (5M), five cannibals (5C), and a boat which can hold three people. The task requires the transportation of all people across a river under the constraint that the missionaries are never outnumbered by cannibals on any side of the river or in the boat. The first experiment investigated whether subjects would improve when solving the problem for the second time. Half of the subjects were given a recognition memory task between the two solutions. They saw a series of problem states and were asked to indicate which states occurred during their first solution. The purpose of the recognition memory task was to provide data on recognition memory and study the effect of an intervening task on memory for their first solution. The second experiment studied how well subjects could recall the moves they made at different problem states. In addition, they were asked questions about the strategies they used to solve the problem. After subjects solved the problem in the third experiment, they were shown different problem states and were required to generate all the legal moves at each problem state. Once again, the experimenter asked subjects about strategies they had used to solve the problem.

The issue of intentional vs. incidental learning provided an independent variable for all three experiments. The intentional learning group was told that they would have to solve the problem twice so they should try to remember their solution. The incidental learning group was merely asked to solve the problem. The incidental–intentional learning distinction seems relevant to problem solving since a solution to a problem may often be one's only objective, resulting in no conscious effort to learn the solution. At other times, such as studying for a mathematics exam, considerable effort can be devoted to learning solutions to different kinds of problems. This distinction is also emphasized in the levels of processing approach to memory (Craik & Lockhart, 1972), since incidental learning can be equivalent to intentional learning when the level of processing is the same for both groups (Hyde & Jenkins, 1969). We are therefore interested in learning whether the intentional (Int) group is superior to the incidental (Incid) group when resolving the problem and what is the cause of group differences, if found.

Before presenting the experiments, we will review other research on the role of memory in problem solving. The review is fairly short because of the lack of research on this topic, but there are two areas which have received some attention—the role of working memory in solving problems and the role of experience on memory for board positions. Neither area of research corresponds exactly to the issues investigated in our experiments, but the previous findings provide a useful context for our study.

II. Previous Research

A. WORKING MEMORY

When constructing theories of problem solving, it is essential to consider the characteristics of the human information-processing system. Simon and Newell (1971) summarized this system as follows:

> The basic characteristics of the human information-processing system that shape its problem-solving efforts are easily stated: The system operates essentially serially, one-process-at-a-time, not in parallel fashion. Its elementary processes take tens or hundreds of milliseconds. The inputs and outputs of these processes are held in a small short-term memory with a capacity of only a few symbols. The system has access to an essentially infinite long-term memory, but the time required to store a symbol in that memory is of the order of seconds or tens of seconds. (p. 149)

Simon and Newell point out that these properties impose strong constraints on the ability of people to solve problems. One of these constraints is the limited capacity of working memory, which is usually equated with short-term memory. A limited-capacity working memory restricts the number of alternative moves that can be considered at each point in solving a problem which in turn restricts the strategies that can be used. When evaluating strategies that might be used to solve a problem, it is important to consider the demands each strategy would make on a limited-capacity working memory. Detailed analyses of alternative strategies have recently been formulated by Greeno and Simon (1974) for sequence production and Simon (1975) for the Tower of Hanoi. A central issue in both papers is the different demands alternative strategies place on short-term memory.

Although most theorists would agree that the limited capacity of working memory places a major constraint on our ability to solve problems, there is still some debate regarding whether working memory has the same characteristics as the short-term memory studied in memory-span experiments. A dissenting opinion is expressed by Greeno (1973) who considered working memory to be an intermediate memory between short-term and long-term memory. The working memory in his system has greater capacity and longer holding time than short-term memory but is not permanent storage. The most extensive analysis of the relation between working memory and short-term memory is contained in volume 8 of this series (Baddely & Hitch, 1974). These investigators report a series of 10 experiments, designed to study the relation between the short-term memory and working memory in tasks requiring reasoning, language comprehension, and learning. Their procedure required subjects to hold various kinds of additional information in short-term memory while they were working on another task. The general pattern of results was that the additional memory load disrupted processing on the primary task, but the degree of disruption was not extensive. The results suggest that, although the digit span and working memory overlap, there appears to be a considerable component of working memory which is not taken up by the digit-span task.

One of the most detailed models of the role of memory in problem solving was developed by Atwood and Polson (1976). The task in their experiments was the water jar problem consisting of three jugs (A, B, C) of varying sizes; for example, 8 gallons, 5 gallons, and 3 gallons. Initially the largest jug was full and the subject's task was to divide the contents of the largest jug evenly between the largest jug and the middle-sized jug. Figure 1A and B shows the problem space of legal moves for the (8, 5, 3) (A) and (24, 21, 3) (B) problems. The three numbers inside the parentheses show the content of each jug.

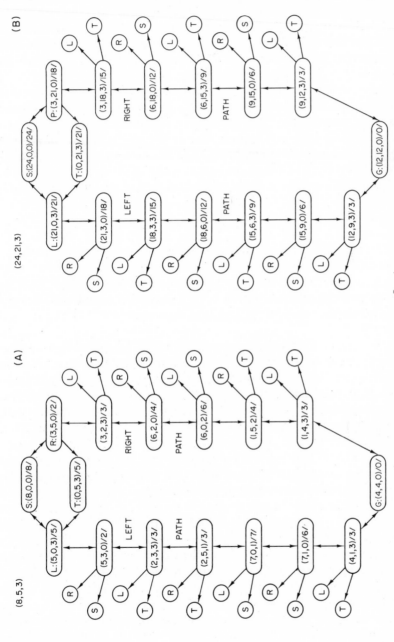

Fig. 1. Problem space of legal moves for the (8, 5, 3) (A) and (24, 21, 3) (B) water jar problems. See text for further explanation. (From Atwood & Polson, 1976.)

For the (8, 5, 3) problem (Fig. 1A), the starting state (S) is (8, 0, 0) and the goal state (G) is (4, 4, 0). The arrows connecting each state show successor states which result from legal moves. There are usually four legal moves at each state, causing either a return to the previous state, a return to one of the initial states (S, L, T, or R), or an advance to a state closer to the goal.

Atwood and Polson proposed a three-stage model that was quite successful in predicting the moves subjects would make at each point in solving the problem. The model was based on a means-end heuristic, combined with assumptions about the utilization of short- and long-term memory. The means-end heuristic was used to compute an evaluation, e, of the differences between the content of jugs A and B, $C(A)$ and $C(B)$, and the content specified by the goal state, $G(A)$ and $G(B)$:

$$e = |\, C(A) - G(A) \,| + |\, C(B) - G(B) \,|. \qquad (1)$$

Small values of the evaluation function would indicate the content is similar to the desired content. The evaluation of each problem state is given by the fourth number in each problem state (e.g., 5 for state L since the content of jug A is 1 gallon more than the desired content and the content of jug B is 4 gallons less than the desired content).

Figure 2 summarizes the three-stage model. The model first decides whether a move is acceptable by determining whether its evaluation satisfies a criterion of acceptability. An acceptable move leading to a "new" (unrecognized) state is taken with probability α; an acceptable move leading to an "old" (recognized) state is taken with probability β. If the move is not taken, the move, the resulting state, and the value of the evaluation function are stored in short-term memory (STM). The Stage I process continues until a move is taken or all moves are evaluated. Move selection during Stage II is based on information retrieved from long-term memory (LTM) which is used to search for a move that leads to a "new" state. If there are no new states, subjects may use the information in STM to select the best move, having the lowest value of the evaluation function (Stage III). If the number of legal moves is less than the capacity of STM (r), the best move is selected with probability α and a legal move is selected at random with probability $1-\alpha$. If the number of legal moves is greater than the capacity of STM, there is no guarantee that the best move will be selected so a subject always selects a move at random.

The model has four parameters which were estimated to predict subjects' moves in a number of water jar problems, differentiated by

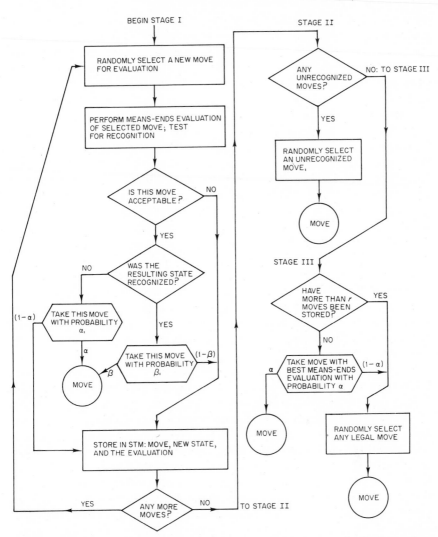

Fig. 2. Atwood and Polson's model for water jar problems. See text for further explanation. (From Atwood & Polson, 1976.)

different contents of the three jars. As you may recall, α is the probability of taking an acceptable move that leads to a "new" state in Stage I and the probability of taking an optimal move in Stage III; β is the probability of taking an acceptable move to an "old" state, s is the probability of storing a representation of a state in LTM; and r is the number of successors for which information can be perfectly retained in STM. Best-fitting values for the parameters were $\alpha = .60$, $\beta = .20$, $s = .90$, and $r = 3$. The estimate that only three successor states can be stored in STM seems reasonable since subjects must store not only the successor, but the corresponding move and evaluation. Atwood and Polson argue that the limited capacity of STM prevents subjects from always selecting the best move, as determined by the evaluation function. Hence, good moves but not necessarily the best move are selected during Stage I (a satisfying search) and the best move is selected during Stage III only when the number of successors does not exceed the capacity of STM. The primary role of LTM in the model is to enable the subject to distinguish between old and new states. The parameter estimates indicate a preference for new states since $\alpha = .60$ and $\beta = .20$. A preference for new states usually facilitates problem solving, but distinguishing between old and new states depends on storing visited states in LTM. The estimated probability of storing a state in LTM (.90) suggests that subjects could usually remember where they had been. The Atwood–Polson model is an important one showing explicitly how complex behavior can depend on memory. We will return to this model later in the chapter.

B. EXPERIENCE AND LONG-TERM MEMORY

Another area of research that has attracted attention is the role of memory in chess. This research was stimulated by the classical work of deGroot on the ability of master chess players. According to deGroot (1966), the ability of the master chess player depends to a great extent on his ability to code board configurations. The process of selecting a good move begins with perception, giving the master an immediate advantage over the weaker player. deGroot demonstrated this superior coding ability by showing players a chessboard from an actual game that had progressed 20 moves. The players viewed the board for 5 sec and were then required to replace the pieces on the board to reproduce what they had just seen. The experimenter then removed the pieces which were wrongly placed and asked the subject to try again. This procedure continued until the subject correctly reproduced the board or until 12 trials had elapsed. The master players performed remarkably better than the weaker players, correctly reproducing 90% of the pieces on the first trial, compared to about 40% for the weaker players. The superiority of the master players was not the result of guessing, since they were not much better than the weaker players in reproducing an unseen board, nor was it the result of a superior memory, since they were not superior in reproducing a board of randomly placed pieces. deGroot attributed the difference to a superior coding of the chess pieces based on game experience.

Chase and Simon (1973a, 1973b) extended deGroot's paradigm in order to isolate the groups of pieces (chunks) which presumably produced the superior coding ability of master chess players. The experimenters hypothesized that (a) everyone has about the same memory span for chunks, (b) this limit is about the same as the traditional limit of STM, 7 ± 2 chunks, and (c) the superior recall of skilled players is associated with larger chunks. A master chess player, a Class A player, and beginner were tested on deGroot's reproduction task. Chunks were determined by measuring how quickly the subject placed each piece on the board since pauses (greater than 2 sec) would likely indicate chunk boundaries. The results supported two of the three hypotheses. The latencies suggested that, for middle-game positions, the average chunks per trial was 7.7 for the master player, 5.7 for the Class A player, and 5.3 for the beginner with the number of pieces per chunk averaging 2.5, 2.1, and 1.9, respectively. There was some tendency for more skilled players to use more chunks, particularly for end-game positions in which the average number of chunks per trial was 7.6, 6.4, and 4.2, respectively.

A simulation program (Memory-Aided Pattern Perceiver or MAPP) of the chess reproduction task was developed by Simon and Gilmartin (1973) to gain further insight into the kinds of chunks stored in LTM. The memory structure was based on an EPAM discrimination net containing either 447 or 572 terminal nodes with two to seven chess pieces composing each pattern. The model used salient pieces located on the chessboard to access the nodes at the top of the discrimination net. Using the larger net on five middle-game positions, MAPP was able to reproduce an average of 4.4 patterns containing an average of 2.45 pieces per pattern. MAPP did slightly better on nine tactical middle-game positions, reproducing an average of 4.5 patterns containing 2.78 pieces per pattern. Overall, the simulation model was somewhat more effective than the Class A player, but less effective than the master player. There was, however, a substantial correlation between which pieces were remembered by MAPP and the master player even though the discrimination net was developed independently of a detailed knowledge of the master's performance. Extrapolating from the performance of the simulation model, Simon and Gilmartin estimated that the master players have between 10,000 and 100,000 patterns stored in LTM.

Although previous research on reproducing board configurations was limited to the game of chess, Reitman (1976) has recently applied the reproduction paradigm to the game of GO. The objective of GO is to surround maximum territory by placing pieces on a 19 X 19 grid. Reitman's study replicated the basic pattern of results found for chess. On Trial 1, the beginner and master recalled about the same number of random patterns; 25% and 30% of the pieces. But the master recalled 66% of the pieces for meaningful patterns compared to 39% for the beginner, a significant difference. Although this difference was likely caused by the master's use of chunks of information, the interresponse time measure used by Chase and Simon was unable to divide the pieces into consistent chunks for either player. A more direct measure revealed the kinds of chunks used in GO. When the master player was given diagrams of board positions and asked to circle subpatterns, his responses indicated overlapping clusters of pieces, which would reduce the effectiveness of the interresponse time measure.

C. IMMEDIATE MEMORY FOR PROBLEM SOLUTIONS

The research discussed in Section II, A and B emphasized two different aspects of memory. Section II, A reviewed experimental and theoretical approaches to working memory, a storage system for holding information while making evaluations at each problem state. Section II, B emphasized the role of experience in building pattern chunks in LTM. These chunks were constructed from many hours of practice on chess or GO. The research reported in this section falls in between these two areas. We are interested in learning about what a problem solver has learned when he or she has finished solving a novel problem.

The objective of discovering what a problem solver learns is a difficult one because of the many possibilities. Egan and Greeno (1974) refer to three kinds of information that could be learned. One alternative is a series of moves in which each move is a stimulus for the succeeding move. Egan and Greeno refer to this as "problem solving in the past" since it requires keeping track of previously executed moves. A second alternative is a large paired-associates list in which each problem state is associated with an appropriate move. This alternative is analogous to "problem solving in the present" since a move would be selected on the basis of the current problem state. A third alternative, and the one favored by Egan and Greeno, is a goal tree specifying a series of subgoals. Solving a problem by using a goal structure corresponds to "problem solving in the future" since moves are selected in order to reach subgoals on the solution path.

Subjects' performance on the Tower of Hanoi task indicated that subgoals were a major determinant of their performance (Egan & Greeno, 1974). The Tower of Hanoi problem requires that subjects move different-size disks from one peg (A) to another peg (C) under the constraint that a larger disk cannot be placed on a smaller disk. The problem is easy to represent as a goal structure; for example, the first subgoal might be to transfer the largest disk from peg A to peg C. Several kinds of evidence indicate that the goal structure influenced subjects' performance. First, the probability of making an error (a move not on the minimal solution path) declined as subjects approached important subgoals. Second, subjects' performance on a subsequent recognition memory test was closely related to the goal structure. The probability of "recognizing" a problem state as a part of one's solution depended on how the problem state related to the goal structure of the task. Third, there was little evidence to suggest that subjects had learned a series of moves or associations between a move and problem state. For example, although there is a repeated series of moves (moving the smallest disk in a circular pattern on every other move) that will solve the problem, few subjects noticed this regularity.

Why are subgoals effective? Simon and Reed attempted to answer this question for a particular case by proposing a strategy-shift model. Data collected by Reed and Abramson (1976) indicated that giving subjects the subgoal—3C across the river by themselves and without the boat—significantly decreased the number of moves required to solve the 5M–5C problem. Figure 3 shows the space of legal moves. The first number in each problem state is the number of M on the left bank, the second number is the number of C on the left bank, the third number is the number of M on the right bank, and the fourth number is the number of C on the right bank. The asterisk shows the location of the boat. State A is the initial state, since L is the subgoal state, and State Z is the goal state.

The strategy-shift model is based on two alternative strategies—a balance strategy that attempts to equalize the number of M and C across the river and a means-end strategy that transports as many people across the river as possible and brings back as few as possible. The model assumes that subjects start with the balance strategy but

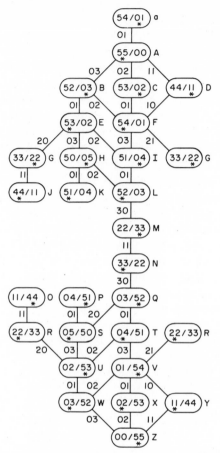

Fig. 3. Problem space of legal moves for the five missionary–five cannibal problem. See text for further explanation. (From Simon & Reed, 1976.)

shift with probability p to the means-end strategy before making each move. Since a balance strategy tends to direct subjects toward a blind alley (state J), shifting to the means-end strategy improves performance. The model accounts for the superior performance of the subgoal group by postulating that the subgoal (an unbalanced problem state) resulted in a faster shift from the balance strategy. The strategy-shift model was very successful in predicting the average number of moves between problem states (see Simon & Reed, 1976; or see Reed, 1977, for a more complete description of the model). The correlation between predicted moves and actual moves was .95 for the control group and .94 for the subgoal group.

To evaluate the generality of the model, Simon and Reed tested how well it could account for performance during the learning experiment discussed in the next section (the intentional [Int] –no recognition [No Rec] group of Experiment I). This group knew they would have to solve the problem twice and did not have an intervening task between their two solution attempts. They required an average of 21.2 legal moves to solve the problem the first time and 16.0 legal moves to solve the problem the second time, a significant reduction. The strategy-shift model proposes that improved performance results from a more rapid shift to the more efficient, means-ends strategy. The correlation between predicted and actual moves was .86 for performances on Trial 1 and .89 for performances on Trial 2. The correlations are high, but not as high as found for the subgoal experiment, suggesting partial support for the model's ability to account for learning. The following three experiments attempt to provide more direct evidence regarding what is learned after solving a problem.

III. Experiments

The first experiment measured the effect of two variables on learning and memory for problem solutions. One variable was intentional vs. incidental learning. The second variable was the presence or absence of an intervening task between the two solution attempts. The intervening task was a recognition memory task and was used to provide data on how well subjects could remember having visited the different problem states. Subjects solved the problem only once in the second and third experiments, but received various tests and questions following their solution to measure what they had learned. The test in Experiment II required that subjects recall the move they made at various problem states and indicate what they considered to be the best move. In addition, they were asked to indicate what strategies they used in solving the problem and what strategies they would use if they were to solve the problem again. Subjects in Experiment III were shown problem states and were asked to generate all the legal moves for each problem state, indicating which move they thought was the best move. They were then asked questions about their strategies. In addition to the Incid and Int learning groups, a group which had not solved the problem was tested on their ability to generate legal moves and select the best move.

A. EXPERIMENT I: TRANSFER AND RECOGNITION

1. Method

a. Subjects. The subjects were 100 undergraduate students from introductory psychology and child psychology courses. Each student received course credit for participation in the experiment.

b. Design. Subjects were randomly assigned to one of four experimental groups. These four groups were created by the combination of two factors. Subjects were either informed that they would be required to solve the MC problem again (intentional learning) or were naive (incidental learning). After solving the problem the first time, subjects were either required to complete a recognition task before resolving (recognition), or a 1-min rest period filled this interval (no recognition).

The stimuli for the recognition task consisted of all legal combinations of M, C, and position of the boat. Some of these combinations could not actually occur (e.g., all M and C on one side and the boat on the other side of the river), some had to occur (e.g., state M), and the rest were optional (e.g., state C). The stimuli were presented in either a forward or backward random order.

c. Procedure. Each subject was given written instructions explaining the rules of the MC problem. The Int Learning group's instructions contained the additional information that they would be asked to resolve the problem and should therefore try to remember what they had done. Before beginning the task the subject's questions were answered and a brief review of the rules was given by the experimenter. Pennies and dimes were used to represent the C and M, respectively (both in the problem-solving sessions and recognition memory task). A cardboard boat was used to convey the passengers. The subject was also told that if he did make a move that violated the rules of the problem, the experimenter would point out why the move was not permitted. The subject would then have to return the pieces to the previous state.

In the course of solving the problem, the subjects of all groups were given some additional help. Whenever a subject returned to a problem state the second time and each subsequent time, he was told that there existed a move that would help him toward the solution, and he was encouraged to try a different move than was made previously.

All moves were recorded by the experimenter as they were made. The incidence of an illegal move was also noted, although the specific combination of M and C which the subject tried was not recorded. The time, in seconds, required to solve the problem was also recorded. Subjects did not know that their solution time was being measured.

Following the first solution of the task, subjects in the No Rec groups were asked to relax while the experimenter totaled the results. After a 1-min interval the second trial was started.

The students in the Rec groups were given a set of written instructions for the recognition task. These subjects were asked to decide whether each of the situations which the experimenter set up had actually been encountered at some point in their first solution of the problem. They were to respond orally with a positive number from 1 for least confident to 3 for most confident if they felt that the state had occurred. Likewise, a response from −1 to −3 indicated that the problem state had not occurred. The experimenter played a tape recording which contained cues for setting up each of the situations. These cues were recorded at a rate of 15 sec per state. The responses were made within this interval. The entire recognition task took 8 min. At the completion of the task the second trial was started.

2. Results

a. Solution Times. A 2 × 2 × 2 analysis of variance was calculated with Rec–No Rec, and Int–Incid as between factors and trials as a within factor. Solution time in seconds, the number of legal moves, and the number of illegal moves provided three separate dependent variables for analysis.

These initial analyses revealed highly significant trials effects for solution time, F (1, 96) = 70.34, $p < .001$; the number of legal moves, F (1, 96) = 12.55, $p < .001$; and the number of illegal moves, F (1, 96) = 46.69, $p < .001$. A Tukey's HSD test (cited in Kirk, 1968) showed that the Int–No Rec, Incid–No Rec, Int–Rec, and Incid–Rec groups all significantly reduced their solution times from Trial 1 to Trial 2, d (2, 96) = 448.24, 198.00, 235.80; 185.68, respectively, $p < .01$. Likewise, these groups also made significantly fewer illegal moves on their second trials, d (2, 96) = 2.56, 1.76, 1.64, 1.44, respectively, $p < .01$. Only the Int–No Rec group, however, made fewer legal moves over trials, d (2, 96) = 5.20, $p < .01$. These results are shown in Table I.

The main effects of intentional learning and the intervening recognition task were best reflected in the solution time data since differences in the number of moves made by subjects were not

TABLE I

AVERAGE PERFORMANCE OF EACH GROUP IN THE THREE EXPERIMENTS

Group	Legal moves		Illegal moves		Solution time	
	Trial 1	Trial 2	Trial 1	Trial 2	Trial 1	Trial 2
Experiment I						
Int–No Rec	21.2	16.0	3.4	0.8	718	270
Int–Rec	18.4	16.6	2.8	1.1	550	315
Incid–No Rec	20.8	19.1	3.0	1.2	609	411
Incid–Rec	20.1	19.2	3.3	1.9	565	380
Experiment II						
Int	20.8	–	2.5	–	679	–
Incid	19.0	–	2.9	–	608	–
Experiment III						
Int	18.7	–	2.9	–	585	–
Incid	19.8	–	2.8	–	625	–

significant. The absolute solution times for trials, however, provided somewhat masked results. In particular, subjects in the Int groups took longer to solve the problem on the first trial than the Incid groups by a mean of 46 sec. This increased solution time would tend to negate any differential improvement made by the Int groups when the results of both trials were averaged. Therefore, the reductions in solution time over trials were computed and analyzed.

Using these difference scores, an analysis of variance showed the Int–Incid factor to be significant, F (1, 96) = 6.11, $p < .025$. The Rec–No Rec factor also approached significance, F (1, 96) = 3.54, $p < .10$. Dunn's procedure (cited in Kirk, 1968) was used to make a priori comparisons among individual groups. These results revealed that the Int–No Rec group improved more than the Incid–No Rec, Int–Rec, and the Incid–Rec groups, d (6, 96) = 250.25, 212.74, 262.56, respectively, $p < .05$. All other group comparisons were not statistically significant. Figure 4 illustrates this finding, not only for solution time, but also for legal moves and illegal moves. The differences between the Int–No Rec group and all other groups for these two measures approached significance, $.05 < p < .10$, in all cases.

In order to determine where in the solution of the problem subjects in the Int–No Rec group were improving in relation to the other groups, the times required to reach state L, the first mandatory state in the problem, and state Q, the next critical point, were

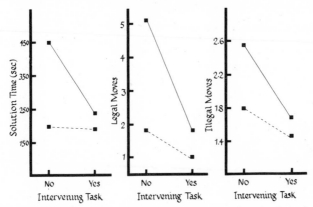

Fig. 4. Degree of improvement (Trial 1 minus Trial 2) for the intentional (——) and incidental (- - -) learning groups.

recorded for the last 10 subjects in each group. A test among means showed that these subjects in the Int–No Rec group improved significantly more than the other groups in getting to state L, t (36) = 2.20, $p < .025$. From state L to state Q, however, this group did not differ from the other three groups. Therefore, the comparative improvement of the Int–No Rec group was made in the initial portion of the problem.

   b. Recognition Task.   Analysis of the recognition task data indicated that subjects in the Int group were no better than the Incid group at correctly identifying problem states with correct judgments of 68% for both groups. This score includes a 63% hit rate and a 73% correct rejection rate for both groups. Subjects were more accurate at judging those states in which the boat was situated on the initial side of the river, 71% correct compared to 66% correct, $z = 2.04$, $p < .05$. Table II shows the recognition scores for 15 problem states that were included in Experiments II and III.

   To determine whether subjects were better able to recognize states the more often they were encountered, the data were partitioned according to the number of times each state was encountered. Since the initial and final states were almost always correctly identified, and would artificially inflate the correct proportions for states which were encountered only once, these instances were deleted from the results. The only significant difference among these proportions was that those states which were encountered four or more times were correctly recognized a greater percentage of the time than those which were encountered only once, $z = 1.96$, $p < .05$. Although only

TABLE II

PERCENT CORRECT RECOGNITION, RECALL, AND SELECTION OF
THE BEST MOVE FOR EACH PROBLEM STATE

	Recognition				Recall^a		Best move^a				
	Experiment I		Experiment II		Experiment II		Experiment II		Experiment III		
State	Int	Incid	Int	Incid	Int	Incid	Int	Incid	Int	Incid	None
A	100	100	100	100	68	62	100	100	100	100	100
B	68	60	52	48	25	19	100	88	86	60	8
D	80	72	80	68	64	23	44	28	82	73	47
E	64	64	76	76	48	36	−20	−28	−21	−47	−56
F	52	64	76	68	40	25	5	−15	7	−19	13
G	60	84	88	80	6	18	−44	−56	−69	−43	−43
H	76	64	76	64	−50	−37	10	28	2	−17	−23
I	20	28	32	44	−35	−40	40	4	67	28	34
L	28	36	36	40	− 8	10	40	58	67	28	34
M	60	40	60	64	− 4	20	36	36	73	39	65
N	96	92	92	96	44	20	76	92	21	21	−39
Q	72	52	76	48	64	− 2	100	64	47	−17	−82
R	32	60	52	40	−	−	76	52	47	−30	47
T	32	48	40	44	4	6	88	88	100	86	100
V	56	68	84	56	77	27	100	90	89	89	− 8

^{a}Corrected for guessing.

the extreme points differed significantly, Fig. 5 shows the linear relationship between the number of times a state was encountered and the proportion of correct recognitions. These results are consistent with Atwood and Polson's (1976) suggestion that the frequency of visiting a problem state influences one's recognition memory for that state.

3. Discussion

All four groups significantly reduced their solution time and number of illegal moves when solving the problem for the second time. Some degree of learning therefore occurred even when subjects were not informed they would have to solve the problem twice and when they were given an intervening recognition task before solving the problem for the second time. However, as we might expect, the greatest improvement in performance occurred for the Int learning group which did not receive an intervening task. This was the only group in which subjects significantly reduced their average number of

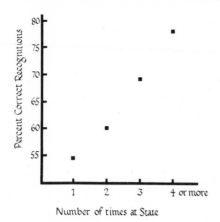

Fig. 5. Percent correct recognitions of a problem state as a function of the number of visits to that state.

legal moves during the second solution attempt and the reduction in solution time was significantly greater for this group.

But the advantage of intentional learning over incidental learning is nearly eliminated if there is an intervening recognition task. Figure 4 shows that the Int–No Rec group improved more than the other three groups, which did not differ statistically from each other. The combined results suggest that all groups learn some information about how to solve the problem, but intentional learning is superior to incidental learning only if there is no intervening task. The effectiveness of the intervening task in reducing the superiority of intentional learning suggests that the additional knowledge gained in intentional learning is difficult to retain, perhaps because it is more specific and detailed than the general knowledge learned by all groups.

Although the difference scores shown in Fig. 4 suggest that the intervening task caused considerable forgetting for the Int group, a word of caution is necessary regarding this interpretation. A large part of the reduction in solution time for the Int–No Rec group can be attributed to the fact that this group took longer to solve the problem on Trial 1, perhaps because they were trying to learn the solution (see Table I). Their superior performance on reducing legal and illegal moves relative to the Int–No Rec group could then be attributed to their learning more during Trial 1 rather than to differences in forgetting caused by the intervening task. It is therefore not clear whether the difference between the two int groups on Trial 2 was caused by differential amounts of learning or by differen-

tial amounts of forgetting. We will return to this issue after attempting to discover what is learned by subjects in the Int group that
distinguishes them from subjects in the Incid group.

The results of the recognition memory test indicate that intentional learning does not result in a superior ability to recognize
previously encountered problem states. Experiment II was designed
to measure more specifically what is learned by the two groups.
Subjects in the Int group were given the same instructions as in
Experiment I. They were told they would have to solve the problem
twice so they should try to learn the solution. Subjects in the Incid
group were only asked to solve the problem. After solving the
problem, subjects in both groups were asked a variety of questions
about their solution of the problem and were required to recall their
moves at various problem states.

B. EXPERIMENT II: MOVE RECALL AND STRATEGIES

1. Method

a. Subjects. The subjects were 50 undergraduate introductory
psychology students who received course credit for their participation.

b. Procedure. The students in this experiment were given the
same instructions that were used in the previous experiment. They
were randomly assigned to either an Int or Incid learning group. The
Int group was told thay they would be asked to resolve the problem
and therefore instructed to try to remember their initial solutions.
The Incid group did not receive this information. While solving the
problem, both groups of subjects received the same assistance from
the experimenter that was used in Experiment I. Moves and total
solution time were recorded.

Following the solution of the problem, all subjects were presented
a memory task. The experimenter showed each subject 15 of the
most frequently encountered problem states at which there existed
more than one possible legal move. The problem states were set up
using the same materials (pennies and dimes) used in solving the
problem. They were presented in a random order to one-half of the
subjects in each group and a reverse order to the other half.

The subjects were asked to first recall whether the particular
problem state had been encountered at any time during their solutions of the problem and to record the number of times that it had
been reached. For those instances in which subjects reported that the

state had been encountered, they were required to select the move that had been made from that state the first time that they arrived at it. A list of all possible legal moves at each state was provided. When problem states were reported as having been encountered more than once, subjects were also asked to determine which move had been made from their last encounter. For all states, subjects were asked to record what they believed to be the best possible move from that state.

As much time as was necessary was provided for the completion of this memory task. This portion of the experiment typically required about 10–15 min.

After completing the memory task, subjects were given a questionnaire. The questionnaire contained verbal descriptions of 12 possible strategies which might have been used to try to solve the problem. The subjects were instructed to answer *true* to each strategy which they had used at any point during their solution of the problem. An additional question asked whether primarily M, C, or about an equal number of M and C had been moved in each third of the problem. The subjects were also asked to respond to these same items according to what they would do if required to resolve the problem as opposed to what they had actually done during their solutions (see Table IV for a list of the items). Once again completion of this part of the experiment was self-paced and usually took about 10 min.

2. Results

a. Memory for Problem States and Moves. The Int learning group correctly recognized a mean of 10.16 problem states and the Incid group a mean of 9.40; this difference was not significant, t (48) = 1.58, $p > .10$. Recognition of having encountered a state more than once, however, was significantly better for the Int group, t (48) = 2.40, $p < .05$. The Int group recognized 1.72 of these states as compared to .92 for the Incid group. To avoid a possible artifact introduced by the superior recognition of states by the Int group, the analysis of the recall of moves included only those instances where the state was correctly recognized. Table II shows the probability of recognizing a state, and the probability of selecting a best move at each state. The Int group recalled a significantly greater percentage of its first moves, t (48) = 2.16, $p < .05$. Recall of the last moves was equal for both groups, t (48) = .04.

As can be seen in Fig 6, the recall of first moves showed a serial-position effect. In this figure, states which are the same number

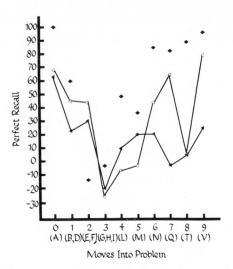

Fig. 6. Percent of first moves correctly recalled by the intentional (△) and incidental (▲) learning groups, and percent of best moves (♦) correctly chosen, both groups combined. Scores are corrected for guessing.

of steps into the problem are combined. The standard correction for guessing was used, where the probability of guessing correctly is a function of the number of possible moves at a given state. A negative score indicates performance was worse than chance. The Int group performed better than the Incid group on the first and last portions of the problem, although this difference was significant only over States 6–9, z = 3.36, p < .001. Both groups were statistically equivalent on the middle section of the problem, z = .84.

A best move was defined as being any legal move which would result in the subject being the minimum number of moves from the problem solution. Thus, most states have more than one move which are functionally equivalent with respect to the solution of the problem, and would all be classified as best moves. Both groups were equally able to determine the best move at a problem state, t (48) = 1.13. No significant differences between groups were found for any of the individual states. Therefore, the results from both groups were combined and are shown in Fig. 6. These results were also corrected for guessing, with the probability of guessing correctly being a function of the proportion of possible legal moves which were defined as best moves at each state. Once again, subjects' performance shows evidence of a serial-position effect.

b. Strategy Questionnaire. To obtain an adequate sample size upon which to base results, the same questionnaire was also given to subjects in the Int and Incid learning groups of Experiment III. These results are discussed later in conjunction with the next experiment.

3. Discussion

The recognition memory data replicate the results found in Experiment I—there was no significant difference between the two groups in their ability to recognize problem states. The Int group showed a superior ability to identify states which they visited more than once but this occurred relatively infrequently (an average of 1.72 states for the Int group and 0.92 states for the Incid group over the 15 problem states) and would likely have little effect on problem—solving performance.

Of more fundamental importance than recognition is the ability to recall one's move at a problem state and identify the best move. But here too there do not seem to be any fundamental differences between the two groups. The Int learning group was superior in recalling moves at the end of the problem for problem states N, Q, and V (see Fig. 6). However, the results from Experiment I revealed that the superiority of the Int—No Rec group in resolving the problem occurred in reaching state L. From state L to state Q, this group did not differ from the other three groups. It is therefore likely that the superior recall of moves at the end of the problem would have little effect on problem-solving efficiency. The most important determinant of performance should be one's ability to select a best move at each problem state. The data revealed no difference between the two groups in their ability to select the best move.

One reason why the results may have failed to differentiate between intentional and incidental learning is that, as Egan and Greeno (1974) have suggested, learning does not involve the kind of detailed knowledge studied in the recognition and recall experiments. As is indicated in Fig. 6, the overall level of recall is not very good, particularly for the intermediate problem states. What is remembered might be something less detailed such as a more general strategy or a few important subgoals. The superior performance of the Int group found in Experiment I could then be explained by a superior ability to formulate effective strategies or subgoals. There was some support for this view in Experiment II but a larger sample seemed necessary to adequately test this hypothesis.

Experiment III had several purposes. One objective was to collect more data about the strategies used by subjects to investigate whether they differed for the Int and Incid groups. A second objective was to determine how quickly subjects in the two groups could generate the legal moves at each problem state. Since a reduction in solution time is often the most sensitive measure of improvement in problem solving (e.g., Reed & Abramson, 1976; Reed *et al.*, 1974), a reduction in move generation latencies might be one measure which would distinguish between the two groups. A third objective was to include a control group which had not solved the problem. This group was included to determine the extent to which the ability to generate legal moves and select the best move depended on previous experience in solving the problem.

C. EXPERIMENT III: MOVE GENERATION AND
   STRATEGIES

1. Method

   a. Subjects. The subjects were 69 undergraduate introductory and cognitive psychology students who had not participated in either of the previous experiments. The students received course credit for their participation.
   b. Design. Subjects were randomly assigned to one of three conditions. There were 23 subjects in each group. In addition to the Int and Incid learning groups, which were distinguished by instructing the Int group to try to remember their solutions, a third group of subjects never actually solved the problem.
   c. Procedure. Subjects in the Int and Incid learning groups solved the problem in the same manner as the previous experiments. They received the same instructions and the same assistance that were used in Experiments I and II. Solution times and moves were recorded for these groups.
   The no solution (No Sol) group was given the same instructions as the Incid learning group. Thus, the rules of the problem were explained. They were. not asked to solve the problem, however. Instead, the 15 problem states used in Experiment II were presented to these subjects in either a random forward or backward order. Their task was to generate as many moves as possible in a 1-min time period. They were instructed to generate only those moves which were permissible, given the rules of the problem. The subjects were informed that they were being timed, and that they should try to generate moves as quickly as possible. They were permitted to try moves for 1 min, but were stopped if all permissible moves were generated before the end of this interval. The same materials as in the previous experiments were used. An example problem state not used

in the experiment was presented to each subject. Examples of permissible and illegal moves were explained by the experimenter prior to beginning the task.

After solving the problem, the Int and Incid groups were also presented with this same move generation task. As with the No Sol group, the time required to generate each move was recorded in seconds, using a stop watch. Illegal moves were also noted as to the number made for each problem state by each subject.

Following the completion of this task, each group was presented with a list of all possible legal moves for each problem state. The problem states were again set up by the experimenter, and the subjects were asked to select what they considered to be the best move.

Finally, the Int and Incid learning groups were presented the strategy questionnaire used in Experiment II and asked to answer each item (see Table IV) as in the previous experiment, first according to what they had actually done during their solution of the problem, and then according to what they would do if asked to resolve the problem. These results were combined with those of Experiment II.

2. Results

a. Generation of Moves. Analyses of variance were computed for the number of illegal moves and the number of legal moves which subjects failed to generate. As expected, the No Sol group made significantly more illegal moves than the Int group, F (1, 66) = 9.36, $p < .001$. Likewise, the Incid group generated more illegal moves than the Int group, F (1, 66) = 4.70, $p < .05$. There was no significant difference between the No Sol and Incid learning groups. The mean number of illegal moves was 4.39 for the Int group, 7.87 for the Incid group, and 9.30 for the No Sol group.

The No Sol group also failed to generate more of the legal moves than either the Int or Incid learning groups, F (1, 66) = 6.51 and 4.26, $p < .05$, respectively. There was no difference between the Int and Incid groups. The mean number of moves not generated were 1.00, 1.35, and 2.83 for the Int, Incid, and No Sol groups. Since there was a total of 48 legal moves for the 15 problem states, the number of undiscovered moves was quite small.

The times required to generate each move were difficult to interpret. Moves were usually not generated in a consistent order which resulted in considerable between-subject variance. To make the data more interpretable, the mean time to generate a particular move was calculated across subjects within a group. These results were then divided by the number of moves actually generated for each problem state so times across problem states could be compared more readily. Table III shows the results. The footnote a indicates moves that differed significantly from other legal moves for a given problem state. For states G, L, M, and N, the footnoted moves were generated significantly faster than the other possible moves, F (1, 136) = 16.70, 18.98, and F (1, 68) = 12.11, 24.20, $p < .001$ for all cases. It appears that, for some problem states, certain moves were more salient than others. It is interesting to note that for those states for which the most salient move was not the best move (G and N), the percent of best moves correctly chosen was relatively low (see Table II). When these moves were the best (L and M), best moves were correctly identified more often. A significant correlation ($r = -.49, p < .001$) between the mean time to generate the best moves and the percent of best moves identified correctly suggests that the choice of a best move is influenced by its obviousness.

Move generation times across the three groups were compared by using the Kruskal-Wallis one-way analysis of variance by ranks. The analysis revealed a significant difference between the groups ($H = 17.22, p < .001$). An analysis on pairs of groups revealed that subjects in the Incid group were faster than subjects in the Int group ($H = 12.25, p < .01$) who in turn were faster than subjects in the No Sol group ($H = 10.63, p < .01$). Overall, subjects in the Int group and Incid group did better than subjects who did not solve the problem. For the two groups who did solve the problem, subjects in the Incid group were quicker in generating moves but tended to generate more illegal moves.

b. Best Moves. After the move generation task, subjects in each group were shown the legal moves at each state and were asked to identify the best move. Figure 7 shows the performance of the three groups as a function of moves into the problem. The results are corrected for guessing and negative scores indicate performances worse than chance. The results for the individual problem states are shown in Table II.

Subjects in the No Sol group did significantly worse than the Int group at states B and O. They did significantly worse than subjects in both the Int and Incid groups at states N and V. The Incid group did significantly worse than the other two groups at state F. The general lack of a significant difference between subjects in the Int and Incid groups confirms the results found in Experiment II. The superiority

TABLE III

MEAN TIME TO GENERATE MOVE FOR THE INTENTIONAL, INCIDENTAL, AND NO SOLUTION GROUPS

State	1 C Int	1 C Incid	1 C No Sol	2 C Int	2 C Incid	2 C No Sol	3 C Int	3 C Incid	3 C No Sol	1 M Int	1 M Incid	1 M No Sol	2 M Int	2 M Incid	2 M No Sol	3 M Int	3 M Incid	3 M No Sol	1 M 1 C Int	1 M 1 C Incid	1 M 1 C No Sol	2 M 1 C Int	2 M 1 C Incid	2 M 1 C No Sol
A	3.3	2.8	4.5	3.2	2.9	4.0	2.5	2.9	3.6										3.2	2.3	2.6			
B	1.8	1.4	1.7	2.1	1.7	2.0	2.0	2.1	2.1															
D										2.8	2.5	2.9							3.5	2.8	3.4			
E	4.2	3.3	4.2	4.2	3.3	4.8	2.9	3.6	4.6				3.4	2.9	4.6									
F	3.6	2.1	4.8	3.7	3.3	4.1	3.9	2.6	4.6	3.3	3.5	3.7										2.9	2.4	3.2
G													4.1	4.8	4.3				2.4	2.4	3.6^a	4.6	5.2	3.0
H	2.8	1.9	3.5	2.8	2.0	3.3	2.3	2.2	2.8															
I	2.4	1.6	3.2	2.3	1.9	3.7	2.6	2.3	3.3															
L	5.1	2.7	5.1	4.2	3.3	5.0										3.1	3.4	2.4^a						
M																7.8	8.0	6.3	4.9	2.9	5.9^a			
N																12.8	9.6	11.5	3.8	5.2	5.0^a			
Q	3.5	3.1	4.8	3.4	3.3	3.9										3.0	3.1	3.1						
R													4.4	4.2	3.9									
T	1.5	1.3	2.3	1.8	1.6	2.3	2.1	1.8	2.5	3.5	3.3	3.8							3.0	2.6	2.8	6.2	5.2	7.7
V	3.4	2.7	4.6	3.6	2.8	4.5	3.8	2.9	5.2										3.0	2.3	2.6	3.0	2.3	2.6

^{a}Moves generated significantly faster than alternative moves at that state.

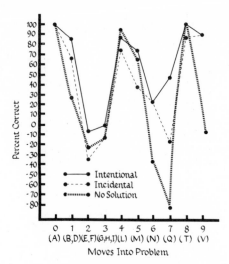

Fig. 7. Percent of best moves correctly chosen by the intentional (●——●), incidental (●- - ●), and no solution (●••••○) groups. Scores are corrected for guessing.

of the Int group found in Experiment I does not seem explainable either by differences in move generation or ability to select the best move.

c. Strategies and Subgoals. After generating legal moves and selecting the best move, subjects who had solved the problem were asked about the strategies they had used during their solution (previous solution) and strategies they would use if asked to resolve the problem (future solution). These responses were combined with the responses from Experiment II, giving a total of 48 subjects in both the Int and Incid groups. Table IV shows their replies. It can be seen that subjects in both groups reported using about the same strategies during the initial solution. The only significant difference was that the Int group indicated that they changed strategies during the course of solution more often than the Incid group, $z = 2.15$, $p <$ .05.

The most striking result shown in Table IV is that subjects report that their strategies would be quite different when solving the problem for the second time. Subjects responded to most questions differently, depending on whether they were asked about their previous solution or a future solution. The overall pattern of results indicates that subjects feel their solution attempts would be much more planned after having solved the problem. Almost all subjects reported they would use a single plan during a second attempt

TABLE IV

NUMBER OF TRUE RESPONSES (MAXIMUM = 48) TO THE STRATEGY QUESTIONNAIRE
FOR THE INTENTIONAL AND INCIDENTAL LEARNING GROUPS

Question	Previous solution		Future solution	
	Intentional	Incidental	Intentional	Incidental
1. I tried to move as many people as possible over and as few as possible back.	36	36	23	19
2. I tried to keep approximately equal numbers of missionaries and cannibals across the river.	35	32	16	21
3. I tried to get all of the cannibals across the river first and then all of the missionaries	10	9	6	8
4. I tried to get all of the missionaries across the river first and then all of the cannibals.	22	18	24	24
5. I tried to find a series of moves which could be repeated at regular cycles.	26	28	27	26
6. I tried to choose from the permissible moves at each point in the problem, remembering what hadn't worked in the past, but with no overall plan.	38	42	25	25
7. I merely experimented with different moves at each point in the problem.	33	34	13	11
8. I tended to formulate my moves in pairs, that is, a move over and a move back.	30	31	41	34
9. I tended to consider my moves over and back individually rather than in pairs.	17	15	6	10
10. I tried to plan a sequence of three or more moves before making the moves.	12	19	32	38
11. I formed subgoals or intermediate goals that I tried to reach while solving the problem.	3	1	35	24
12. I kept the same basic plan throughout the course of the problem.	7	16	45	45

whereas most subjects reported changing plans during their first attempt. More subjects indicated they would plan further ahead (three or more moves) and use subgoals during their second solution. Although nearly two-thirds of the subjects reported using a means-end (Question 1) and a balance strategy (Question 2) during their first solution, there is a significant reduction in the number of subjects who reported they would use these strategies during their second solution. This finding is consistent with the results that subjects would plan further ahead during their second solution, since both the means-ends and balance strategies do not require forward planning beyond a single move.

The greater reliance on subgoals during a second solution attempt is very apparent. Only four subjects reported using subgoals during their first solution whereas 59 subjects reported they would use subgoals during their second solution. A question raised during the discussion of the Experiment II results was whether the better performance of the Int learning group found in Experiment I was due to the more effective use of subgoals and plans. We now have empirical support for this hypothesis. About two-thirds of the subjects in the Int group reported they would use subgoals when resolving the problem compared to half of the subjects in the Incid group. This difference is significant; $z = 3.24$, $p < .01$. In addition, subjects who reported they would use subgoals were asked to indicate which problem state they considered to be the best intermediate subgoal. These results are shown in Table V. Previous research (Reed & Abramson, 1976) has shown that state L is an effective subgoal, since subjects given this subgoal did significantly better in solving the problem. It is likely that subgoals prior to state L would be less useful in helping subjects exit from the first third of the problem space, within which most of the difficulties are encountered. Likewise, subgoals which are too far into the problem lose their effectiveness (Reed & Abramson, 1976). Table V shows that all but two of the subjects in the Int group picked either state L, M, N, or Q as a subgoal. These states are not only in the middle of the problem, but are states which must be reached to solve the problem (see Fig. 3). In contrast, the subgoals selected by subjects in the Incid group were more evenly distributed throughout the problem. This result suggests that the subjects in the Int group not only were more likely to use subgoals in resolving the problem, but the subgoals they chose were better subgoals than those chosen by the Incid group.

There is also empirical support for the hypothesis that subjects in the Int group are able to formulate better plans for resolving the

TABLE V

PROBLEM STATES INDICATED AS GOOD SUBGOALS BY THE
INTENTIONAL AND INCIDENTAL LEARNING GROUPS

State	Group	
	Intentional	Incidental
D	0	1
G	0	1
H	0	2
L	6	1
M	10	4
N	8	7
Q	9	4
S	1	0
T	1	3
V	0	1

problem. An examination of the problem space of legal moves (Fig. 3) reveals that the best plan would be to first move C across (states A–J), then M (states L–N), then the remaining C (states Q–Z). Question 13 asked subjects to "Think of the problem as being divided into three equal parts, each requiring the same number of moves. During each part, did you primarily move missionaries (M), cannibals (C), or an equal number of missionaries and cannibals (MC)."

Table VI shows their answers to this problem. The data indicate for each third of the problem, the number of subjects who reported moving primarily M, C, or an equal number of M and C. The most interesting aspects of the results is that subjects in the Int group were more likely than subjects in the Incid group to pick for future solutions the correct strategy of moving C during the first third of the problem, $z = 2.14, p < .05$, and M during the second third of the problem, $z = 3.19, p < .01$. In contrast, subjects in the Incid group showed a clear preference for moving an equal number of M and C during future solutions, a plan which is consistent with the inefficient balance strategy. This finding provides the strongest support for the strategy-shift model (Simon & Reed, 1976) as a means of accounting for different levels of performance. Along with the subgoal results, the differential emphasis on strategies suggest that the advantage of Int over Incid learning is due more to differences in specifying strategies and subgoals than to memory for more detailed information such as recognition and recall of moves at different problem states.

TABLE VI

NUMBER OF SUBJECTS WHO REPORTED MOVING PRIMARILY MISSIONARIES,
CANNIBALS, OR BOTH DURING PREVIOUS (ROWS) AND
FUTURE (COLUMNS) SOLUTIONS

Intentional—First third of problem

	Missionaries	Cannibals	Both	Total (previous)
Missionaries	4	1	1	6
Cannibals	1	14	1	16^a
Both	0	7	19	26
Total (future)	6	22^a	21	48

Intentional—Middle third of problem

	Missionaries	Cannibals	Both	Total (previous)
Missionaries	22	1	1	24^a
Cannibals	2	1	0	3
Both	6	0	15	21
Total (future)	30^a	2	16	48

Intentional—Final third of problem

	Missionaries	Cannibals	Both	Total (previous)
Missionaries	5	4	1	10
Cannibals	1	28	5	34^a
Both	1	1	2	4
Total (future)	7	33^a	8	48

Incidental—First third of problem

	Missionaries	Cannibals	Both	Total (previous)
Missionaries	1	2	2	5
Cannibals	1	10	4	15^a
Both	4	3	21	28
Total (future)	6	15^a	27	48

Incidental—Middle Third of problem

	Missionaries	Cannibals	Both	Total (previous)
Missionaries	10	1	2	13^a
Cannibals	1	2	4	7
Both	8	2	18	28
Total (future)	19^a	5	24	48

Incidental—Final third of problem

	Missionaries	Cannibals	Both	Total (previous)
Missionaries	10	4	0	14
Cannibals	0	25	3	28^a
Both	1	1	4	6
Total (future)	11	30^a	7	48

^{a}Correct answer.

IV. General Discussion

The results of Experiment I revealed that although all four groups showed a significant improvement in reducing solution time and illegal moves when solving the 5 MC problem for the second time, only the Int group without an intervening task (Int–No Rec group) significantly reduced the number of legal moves required to solve the problem. The reduction in solution time was also significantly greater for this group than for the other three groups. Experiments II and III were designed to study what this group had learned that resulted in a better second-trial performance.

Experiment II confirmed the recognition memory results found in Experiment I, indicating that there was no difference between the Int and Incid groups in their ability to recognize problem states encountered during the course of solution. Subjects in the Int group did show a superior ability to recall what move they made at a problem state, but this finding was significant only for problem states at the end of the problem. In contrast, the superiority of the Int–No Rec group found in Experiment I was the result of their better performance during the first half of the problem. These findings, along with the finding that the Incid and Int groups did not differ in their ability to select the best move at a problem state, suggest that the two groups did not differ in their memory for details.

What distinguishes intentional from incidental learning in these experiments seems to be information that allows for more efficient planning. A significantly greater percentage of subjects in the Int group reported they would use subgoals during a second solution attempt and the subgoals they selected appear to be better than the subgoals selected by subjects in the Incid group. A significantly greater percentage of subjects in the Int group picked the optimal strategy of moving C during the first third of the problem and M during the second third of the problem. Subjects in the Incid group preferred the less efficient balance strategy of moving equal numbers of M and C. The importance of subgoals and strategies raises the issue of how subgoals and strategies are related. How does knowledge of a subgoal influence one's strategy in solving the problem? This question is examined in Section IV, A. Section IV, B considers the implications of these results for formal models of problem solving (Atwood & Polson, 1976; Simon & Reed, 1976), and Section IV, C discusses some methodological issues encountered during the course of this research.

A. RELATIONSHIP BETWEEN SUBGOALS AND
    STRATEGIES

The results of the three experiments are consistent with Egan and
Greeno's (1974) emphasis on subgoal formation, with the qualification that subgoals can only be effectively utilized in the MC problem
after it has been solved. Unlike the Tower of Hanoi, there are not
obvious problem states that must be reached to solve the problem.
Useful subgoals must therefore be learned.

The advantage of remembering important subgoals or general strategies is that they do not require the memory capacity that a detailed
solution would require. Subjects revealed only a limited ability in
these experiments to recognize problem states or recall moves. Even
the solution of the simpler 3M–3C problem is most likely too
difficult to remember exactly. When subjects were asked about their
memory for a previous solution in an analogy problem, no subjects
reported remembering an exact sequence of moves, seven subjects
reported remembering most of the moves, 32 subjects reported an
occasional use of memory, and 17 subjects said they did not use their
memory for the first solution at all (Reed et al., 1974).

The emphasis on strategies and subgoals as an explanation of the
Int group's superiority in resolving the problem raises the question of
how subgoals influence strategies. One answer would be that subgoals
enable the subject to plan further ahead. For example, if four moves
are required to reach a subgoal state, it may be possible for subjects
to explore different four-move sequences to find a sequence that
would reach the subgoal. A second answer would be that subgoals
change the evaluation function used to select the next move. Consider the evaluation function used by Atwood and Polson (1976)
which compares the content of jugs A and B with their desired
content (Eq. [1], Section II, A). Rather than using the goal state as
the desired content, subjects could use the subgoal state until they
reached the subgoal. In this case, subjects would not plan further
ahead but their use of a different evaluation function would influence their selection of the next move.

If a subgoal modifies the evaluation function, an important determinant of the effectiveness of a subgoal should be whether the
resulting evaluation function assists subjects in reaching the subgoal.
A subgoal such as state L in the MC problem (3C and 0M across the
river) should encourage subjects to move C, an appropriate strategy
for reaching this subgoal. A subgoal such as state M (3C and 3M
across the river) may suggest an inappropriate strategy of moving an
equal number of M and C (cf. Reed, 1977) rather than C across first

followed by M. Subjects who improve their performance by using this subgoal may have to either plan ahead or remember a strategy which is not suggested by the subgoal.

To examine the relation between subgoals and strategies, we looked at the initial strategy selected by subjects who picked either states L, M, or N as a subgoal. All seven subjects who picked state L as a subgoal indicated they would move C during the first third of the problem. This finding provides direct support for the strategy-shift model which proposes that the effectiveness of state L as a subgoal was caused by subjects shifting from the balance to the means-ends strategy (Simon & Reed, 1976). The means-end strategy is consistent with moving C prior to state L. Of the 14 subjects who selected state M as a subgoal, nine indicated they would move C during the first third of the problem and five indicated they move an equal number of M and C. As expected on the basis of different evaluation functions, this subgoal state was not as effective in producing the correct strategy. However, nine subjects did select the correct strategy, perhaps because they remembered the correct move sequence in addition to the subgoal. The worst selection of strategies occurred for subjects who selected state N (2M and 2C across the river without the boat) as a subgoal. Ten subjects indicated they would initially move an equal number of M and C, four subjects indicated they would move C, and one subject indicated he would move M.

The difference between states M and N was not anticipated since both are balanced states with an equal number of M and C across the river. A post hoc explanation of this difference is that state N is further into the problem and it is therefore more difficult to use forward planning or remember a sequence of moves (see Reed & Abramson, 1976). It may also appear to be more easily reached than state M since only four people are across the river, making a balance strategy seem like a quick solution to reaching the subgoal.

These results are based on a small sample size and are only suggestive. They indicate, however, how strategies and subgoals might be related. Additional research directed specifically at this issue should be carried out in view of the importance of subgoals and strategies in leading to improved performance.

B. FORMAL MODELS OF PROBLEM SOLVING

The relationship between strategies and subgoals gives us an opportunity to reconsider the strategy-shift model proposed by Simon and Reed (1976) to account for improvement on the 5 MC problem. As mentioned in Section III, B, this model proposes that subjects improved their performance by switching sooner from the balance strategy to the more effective means-ends strategy. The model was very successful in predicting the performances of subjects tested by Reed and Abramson (1976). The correlation between predicted moves and actual moves (for all possible legal moves) was .94 for the subgoal group and .95 for the control group. The subgoal group was given state L as a subgoal whereas the control group did not receive a subgoal. The strategy-shift model was less successful in predicting the performance of subjects in the Int–No Rec group of Experiment I (the only group that significantly reduced the number of legal moves on Trial 2). The correlations were .86 for Trial 1 performances and .89 for Trial 2 performances. However, the correlations are respectable and suggest partial support for the model when applied to learning.

The relationship between strategies and subgoals provides some insight as to why the strategy shift model was more successful in accounting for performances in the subgoal experiment. All seven subjects who stated they would use state L as a subgoal indicated they would begin resolving the problem by using the optimal strategy of moving C. Subjects who reported they would use other subgoals were less likely to begin with the optimal strategy. The subgoal provided by Reed and Abramson (1976) was therefore a good subgoal for causing a change in strategies, whereas the alternative subgoals learned by subjects were less effective in causing a strategy shift. We feel that the strategy-shift model provides a partial account of learning, but the variety of information which can be learned makes it unlikely that any single explanation can give a complete account.

The other formal model discussed in Section II was the Atwood–Polson model (Atwood & Polson, 1976), originally developed to account for performances on the water jar problem. There is one aspect of our data which we feel may require a distinction between an intermediate-term memory and a LTM. The probability of storing information in LTM is·quite high (.90) in their model. This information is used during the course of solving the problem, but Atwood and Polson did not test what subjects remembered at delayed intervals. Our experiments suggest that subjects have only a very limited memory for details when tested after solving the problem. For example, the recognition memory test given in Experiment I resulted in a 63% hit rate and a 27% false alarm rate ($d' = .94$). These results, along with a limited ability to recall moves at specified problem states, suggest that few details are stored in LTM, at least for the 5 MC problem.

Our solution to this dilemma is that what Atwood and Polson call LTM is really an intermediate, working memory that enables the problem solver to find new moves and problem states during the course of working on a problem. Bower (1975) describes an intermediate memory that has exactly these characteristics. The intermediate memory described by Bower provides an immediate context or frame of reference for making decisions. Information stored in this memory does not take up space in a limited-capacity STM, but has not been entered into a more permanent LTM. An intermediate memory is also consistent with the ideas proposed by Greeno (1973) and Baddeley and Hitch (1974). It would allow for the temporary preservation of detailed information that could be used during the solution attempt. Information retained after solution, in LTM, would more likely be in the form of important subgoals or general strategies.

As discussed by Jeffries, Atwood, Polson, and Hooke (1976), the similarities between the Atwood–Polson and Simon–Reed models are more apparent than their differences. Both models are based on a means-ends analysis that does not require extensive memory capacity since forward planning is limited to a single move. The memory assumptions are an important and explicit part of the Atwood–Polson model, whereas the Simon–Reed model emphasizes strategy changes rather than memory characteristics. A more detailed comparison of the strategy assumptions can be found in the paper by Jeffries *et al.* (1976) which applies the Atwood–Polson model to various versions of the 3M–3C problem. Moves across the river are determined by a fixed noticing order which evaluates moves in the following order: (*a*) 1M and 1C, (*b*) 2M, (*c*) 2C, (*d*) 1M, and (*e*) 1C. The probability of making a move is greater for moves higher in the order. Moves back to the original side are evaluated in the reverse order. This general strategy is modified for different versions of the problem by differentially weighting moving M across, C across, or pairs across. The strategy assumptions made by Jeffries *et al.* (1976) are more general than those preposed by Simon and Reed (1976). Their model should therefore have wider application, but requires more parameters such as the weights of the evaluation function.

The models proposed by Atwood and Polson, Simon and Reed, and Jeffries *et al.* represent recent attempts to formulate stochastic models that can account for problem-solving behavior at each point in solving a problem by predicting the probability of selecting different moves. The development of detailed models has resulted in a number of insights that would not have been discovered from a more global analysis of the data. Although further testing of the models is necessary, we believe that their success in predicting performances across a number of experiments is a promising beginning.

C. METHODOLOGICAL COMMENTS

We will conclude with several comments on the methodology used in this research. An investigator starting to plan experiments on memory for problem solutions is first confronted with the enormous complexity of the task. All the variables which can be more precisely controlled in traditional studies of learning suddenly gain their freedom. The problem solver, rather than the experimenter, determines which states he will visit, how often he will return to a state, and how long he will spend there. The structure of the task environment determines how many legal moves one has to consider at each state. Almost any variable one wishes to study is impossible to isolate, without covarying other variables.

In some cases, we were able to introduce reasonable controls which we would recommend to others. For example, in studying recall of moves, it is desirable to have some idea of how easy it is to generate the best move. Subjects may show a superior performance at some problem states, not because of selective memory but because it is easier to generate the correct move at those states. In other cases, our methodological controls should be improved.

In spite of the complexities of controlling variables in problem-solving tasks, we are quite pleased with the consistency of our findings, many of which were replicated both across groups and experiments. The significant differences we did find fit in well with previous work on strategies and subgoals (Egan & Greeno, 1974; Simon & Reed, 1976). These differences were found by asking the question: Why does one group of problem solvers perform better than another group? Intentional learning was used in these experiments to produce a superior performance, but subgoals (Reed and Abramson, 1976) and analogy (Reed et al., 1974) have also been used. The general approach of contrasting groups has two advantages. First, from a practical viewpoint, it enables us to look at what kind of information can be used to improve problem solving (Reed, 1977). Second, we can then try to discover why one group did better than another.

Our emphasis on subgoals and strategies in this chapter resulted from our finding differences between the groups at this more general level and our failure to find differences between the groups in memory for details. If we had tested only a single group, we might have argued that strategies and subgoals must be important because memory for details is poor. But this raises the question of what level of performance qualifies as "poor" and experimenters may differ on their criteria. We therefore conclude with the recommendation that comparing groups who differ in their level of performance is a useful approach to avoiding some of the complexities of this research area.

V. Summary

Three experiments were conducted in an attempt to learn what a problem solver has learned after solving the 5M–5C problem. The first experiment compared an Int learning group, who knew they would have to solve the problem twice with an Incid learning group. Half of the subjects in each group were given a recognition memory test between their two solution attempts. Although all four groups improved their performances when resolving the problem, the extent of improvement was significantly greater for subjects in the Int group who did not receive the intervening recognition task.

The two subsequent experiments were directed at discovering what information might have been learned by the Int group that resulted in a more dramatic improvement when resolving the problem. The results suggested that subjects in the Int group were better at learning general information such as appropriate strategies or subgoals. They were superior in identifying useful subgoals and in selecting the appropriate sequence of moving C during the first third and M during the middle third of the problem. There was no significant difference between the two groups in their ability to recognize problem states, recall moves at problem states (with the exception of the last few moves), or select the best move at a problem state.

The emphasis on strategies and subgoals raised the question of whether subgoals are differentially effective in producing good strategies and whether subgoals result in more forward planning or merely change the evaluation function used to select the next move. Support was found for the differential effectiveness of subgoals but the data were not sufficient to reveal exactly how a subgoal exerts its effect. The Section IV, B examined the implications of the findings for formal models of problem solving. It was argued that the data provide some support for the strategy-shift model proposed by Simon and Reed (1976) and for a possible distinction between an intermediate-term memory and a LTM in the Atwood–Polson (1976) model. Section IV, C discussed some of the methodological difficulties encountered in designing the experiments.

REFERENCES

Atwood, M. E., & Polson, P. G. A process model for water jar problems. *Cognitive Psychology*, 1976, 8, 191–216.

Baddeley, A. D., & Hitch, G. Working memory. In G. H. Bower (Ed.), *The psychology of learning and motivation* (Vol. 8). New York: Academic Press, 1974.

Bower, G. H. Cognitive psychology: An introduction. In W. K. Estes (Ed.), *Handbook of learning and cognitive processes* (Vol. 1). Hillsdale, N.J.: Lawrence Erlbaum Associates, 1975.

Chase, W. G., & Simon, H. A. The mind's eye in chess. In W. G. Chase (Ed.), *Visual information processing*. New York: Academic Press, 1973. (a)

Chase, W. G., & Simon, H. A. Perception in chess. *Cognitive Psychology*, 1973, 4, 55–81. (b)

Craik, F. I. M., & Lockhart, R. S. Levels of processing: A framework for memory research. *Journal of Verbal Learning and Verbal Behavior*, 1972, 11, 671–684.

deGroot, A. D. Perception and memory versus thought: Some old ideas and recent findings. In B. Kleinmuntz (Ed.), *Problem solving: Research, method, and theory*. New York: Wiley, 1966.

Egan, E. E., & Greeno, J. G. Theory of rule induction: Knowledge acquired in concept learning, serial pattern learning, and problem solving. In L. Gregg (Ed.), *Knowledge and cognition*. Potomac, Md.: Lawrence Erlbaum Associates, 1974.

Greeno, J. G. The structure of memory and the process of solving problems. In R. Solso (Ed.), *Contemporary issues in cognitive psychology: The Loyola Symposium*. Washington, D.C.: Winston, 1973.

Greeno, J. G., & Simon, H. A. Processes for sequence production. *Psychological Review*, 1974, 81, 187–198.

Hyde, T. S., & Jenkins, J. J. The differential effects of incidental tasks on the organization of recall of a list of highly associated words. *Journal of Experimental Psychology*, 1969, 82, 472–481.

Jeffries, R., Atwood, M. E., Polson, P. G., & Hooke, L. R. *A process model for hobbits-orcs and other river crossing problems* (Program on Cognitive Factors in Human Learning and Memory, Report No. 54). Boulder: University of Colorado, 1976.

Kirk, R. E. *Experimental design: Procedures for the behavioral sciences*. Belmont, Calif.: Brooks/Cole, 1968.

Luchins, A. S. Mechanization in problem solving. *Psychological Monographs*, 1942, 54 (Whole No. 248).

Miller, G., Galanter, E., & Pribram, K. *Plans and the structure of behavior*. New York: Holt, 1960.

Reed, S. K. Facilitation of problem solving. In N. J. Castellan, D. B. Pisoni, & G. R. Potts (Eds.), *Cognitive theory* (Vol. 2). Hillsdale, N.J.: Lawrence Erlbaum Associates, 1977.

Reed, S. K., & Abramson, A. Effect of the problem space on subgoal facilitation. *Journal of Educational Psychology*, 1976, **68**, 243–246.

Reed, S. K., Ernst, G. W., & Banerji, R. The role of analogy in transfer between similar problem states. *Cognitive Psychology*, 1974, **6**, 436–450.

Reitman, J. S. Skilled perception in GO: Deducing memory structures from inter-response times. *Cognitive Psychology*, 1976, **8**, 336–356.

Simon, H. A. The functional equivalence of problem solving skills. *Cognitive Psychology*, 1975, **7**, 268–288.

Simon, H. A., & Gilmartin, K. A simulation of memory for chess positions. *Cognitive Psychology*, 1973, **5**, 29–46.

Simon, H. A., & Newell, A. Human problem solving: The state of the theory in 1970. *American Psychologist*, 1971, **26**, 145–159.

Simon, H. A., & Reed, S. K. Modeling strategy shifts in a problem-solving task. *Cognitive Psychology*, 1976, **8**, 86–97.

HYBRID THEORY
OF CLASSICAL CONDITIONING

Frank A. Logan

UNIVERSITY OF NEW MEXICO, ALBUQUERQUE, NEW MEXICO

I. Introduction

The purpose of this chapter is to present the substance of a reductive theory[1] of behavior incorporating both S-S and S-R conceptualizations along with related notions developed by a variety of theorists. This theory draws most heavily on the ideas of Hull and

---

[1] Logan and Ferraro (1978) have recommended that the term "theory" be reserved for systems that involve the introduction of hypothetical constructs which are not directly reducible to empirical operations but are anchored to them on both the antecedent and consequent sides. A theory is thus reductive, although other uses of the term are commonplace.

Spence on the S-R side (e.g., Hull, 1943, 1952; Spence, 1951, 1956; as summarized in Logan, 1959) and Tolman (1932) on the S-S side. The empirical base is largely that of Pavlov (1927, 1928), although in some cases I have also drawn upon notions developed with respect to incentive motivation which I assume to be a conditioning phenomenon. This particular chapter deals specifically with some of the basic phenomena of classical conditioning, which is viewed as not necessarily the simplest form of learning, but perhaps the only procedure for establishing learned associations de novo.

Because of other connotations of the terms, I prefer not to call this theory a "two-factor," "two-process," or "two-kind" theory. It does assume that there are two types of learning processes which differ in their fundamental natures and obey somewhat different principles. But I wish specifically to distinguish it from issues concerning the necessity of reinforcement, because I assume contiguity to be sufficient for both S-S and S-R learning processes. It is, in part, cognitive, mentalistic, and associationistic; it is also behavioristic, deterministic, and peripheralistic. Because of its unabashed debt to so many influences, I prefer to call it a hybrid theory.[2]

There are several theories which assume more than one learning process (e.g., Bindra, 1974; Birch & Bitterman, 1949; Bower & Trabasso, 1968; Deutsch, 1960; Konorski & Miller, 1937; Mowrer, 1947, 1960; Rescorla & Solomon, 1967; Skinner, 1935; Solomon, 1964; Spence, 1956; Sutherland & Mackintosh, 1971; Tolman, 1949; Trapold & Overmier, 1972; Williams, 1965). Such theories have been based variously on distinctions as to the types of learning paradigms, natures of the responses, sources of drives or nervous systems involved, and some are two-process or two-stage theories of extinction, punishment, avoidance conditioning, or discrimination learning. A detailed comparison of the present theory with each of these, and their several variants, would be prohibitive. I assume that all learning phenomena can be encompassed by a single theory, but various components may be more relevant to some experimental operations than to others. Indeed, although this chapter concentrates on S-S associations, S-R associations may also be involved in some forms of classical conditioning.[3]

---

[2] Such a designation may also encourage its being infused with mutants It has always seemed inefficient to me for theorists to feel compelled to introduce new terminology where a perfectly useful one already exists, or to deny the value of other approaches while promulgating their own.

[3] There may develop some differences between appetitive conditioning and defense conditioning, to say nothing of avoidance conditioning and related procedures. There are also

II. Development of Terminology and Theory

My intermediate-range interests are clearly focused on discrimination learning and choice behavior. My hope is to develop an integrated theory of the phenomena in those areas with the belief that it will lead on to the so-called higher mental processes. It quickly became apparent that this endeavor requires an analysis of both the stimulus and the response viewed as hypothetical constructs (theoretical rather than empirical terms). This subgoal, however, requires a theory of instrumental conditioning, and yet antedating that, a theory of operant conditioning. These latter theories, however, require a theory of classical conditioning, or presumably so if one accepts the typical assumption that incentive motivation is somehow based on the principles of classical conditioning. And so I am now attempting to begin at this beginning (although perhaps still more fundamental processes such as reaction time would be appropriate).

This orientation is important because this is a theory of classical conditioning only in the presumptive sense. i.e., on the assumption that incentive learning is basically classical conditioning. Operating on that assumption, I have leaned heavily on phenomena observed in Pavlovian types of situations but the goal is a theory of incentive learning which, hopefully, will subsume classical conditioning. Accordingly, much of the difficult-to-define basis for the type of theory that I am proposing results from its anticipated role in later developments of the entire theory leading to discrimination learning and choice behavior.

Let me illustrate the way this type of thinking has influenced my decisions along the way. It may be recalled that both Hull (1952) and Spence (1956) retreated from a reinforcement theory of learning in favor of a contiguity-plus-incentive theory largely because of the results of the classic latent learning studies and related researches involving changes in the conditions of reinforcement (e.g., Crespi, 1942, 1944; Tolman & Honzik, 1930; Zeaman, 1949). The critical feature of those data was that performance changed very rapidly as a result of changes in the conditions; an important but subsidiary feature was that performance changes were sometimes excessive (then the elation and depression effects, now the positive and negative successive contrast effects). These facts appeared to imply more of a motivational than an associative role of reinforcement in the determination of behavior.

---

differences among the various response systems and their methods of measurement. Hopefully, any such differences will evaporate in the detailed application of the entire theory.

However, particularly according to Spence, incentive motivation is learned according to the principles of classical conditioning which, because his was a uniprocess theory, also reflects S-R associations. The basic problem is therefore not really resolved because a change in the conditions of reinforcement now requires new learning of incentive motivation, and that learning process is of the same nature as operant/instrumental learning. If it is gradual for one, it must be gradual for the other; if it is irreversible for one, it must be irreversible for the other. This reasoning forced me to the conclusion that the associative process in incentive learning *has* to be fundamentally different from that with respect to the operant/instrumental response itself, and if incentive learning is a form of classical conditioning, then this further implies a distinction between the fundamental natures of the associative processes in classical and operant/instrumental conditioning.

For this reason, I am now formally and explicitly postulating a cognitive (S-S) theory of classical conditioning and a behavioristic (S-R) theory of operant/instrumental conditioning. (One could, presumably as well on just this basis, have proposed the reverse set of alternatives.) This means that I am taking a cognitive view of classical conditioning not so much because the data demand it (although there are strong suggestions to this effect) as because that is the way it has to be in keeping with my larger theoretical conceptualizations. At least, I contend that to be true of incentive learning which, as I have indicated, is only presumptively a form of classical conditioning.

Let me give one more illustration of the way in which my larger objectives have affected the particular assumptions which I have made. If we recognize an ultimate need for cognitive processes in the context of concept formation, thinking, and problem solving, it seems reasonable to begin now to propose features which appear to have potential value in these later contexts. For example, I shall be assuming that the cognitive associative process in classical conditioning is established completely in one trial and then immediately begins to decay over time. I am actually drawing upon the notions of short- and long-term memory as the conceptual basis for this approach. In this same spirit, some of the complexities that I have introduced might not appear to be really required for basic phenomena of classical conditioning, but the goal is to make them fit the phenomena in that context and concurrently have the potential for extrapolation into larger domains.

Given this overall orientation, I was still missing a conceptual key which I believe to be largely terminological. That key was to change the word "conditioned" to "conditional" as a modifier of the words stimulus and response.[4] An unconditional response (for which the complete symbol is UC^1R, but which for simplicity I shall abbreviate to UR) is one whose occurrence is *not* dependent on *subsequent* stimulus events. It is not immune to modification as a result of such events but it is built into the organism's system. The UR in Pavlovian classical conditioning is reflexive, being elicited by an unconditional stimulus (UC^1S, abbreviated US). The US is unconditional because its occurrence is *not* dependent on any *antecedent* response. It is programmed for delivery regardless of the behavior of the organism. Following this same line of reasoning, the conditional response (C^1R, abbreviated CR) is one whose occurrence *is* dependent on *subsequent* stimulus events, namely the US.[5] If a US occurs, the likelihood of the CR increases; conversely, if no US occurs, the likelihood of the CR decreases. Hence, acquisition, maintenance, and extinction of the CR in classical conditioning are terminologically related to the US and UR.

At least at first glance, the development of this language system appears to break down with what is conventionally termed the conditioned stimulus. This is because I shall later want to use the term "conditional stimulus" for an event which is dependent on an antecedent response, whereas the CS in classical conditioning has no such dependency involved. But this may be a blessing in disguise because we can use the simple, unmodified symbol "S" to identify the stimulus event that occupies a position antedating some stimulus or response event.[6] It may be referred to verbally as the antecedent stimulus and thought of as the first component of an S-S or S-R association.

So now let me review the terminology. There are two types of stimuli and responses, conditional and unconditional. US events are ones whose occurrence are not dependent on prior responses; UR events are ones whose occurrence are not dependent on subsequent

---

[4] Gantt, in a footnote to his 1928 translation of Pavlov's *Lectures on Conditioned Reflexs* (see Pavlov, 1928), says, "Conditional and not conditioned is Prof. Pavlov's term, but as conditioned reflex has become fixed in English usage instead of conditional reflex, we adhere to the term conditioned" (p. 79). Even so, the meaning appears to be somewhat different from that intended here (see Gantt, 1966). It might also be speculated that the term "conditioned" predisposed behaviorists toward an S-R theory of learning.

[5] It should be noted that this terminology avoids the necessity to use the term "reinforcement." This will equally apply to CR's in operant and instrumental conditioning, although for convenience, and consistency with existing literature, I shall frequently use the term.

[6] I have never liked the term "conditioned stimulus" because it implies a past tense and would make sense only after conditioning has taken place. Further, the stimulus is not conditioned; the response is (or better, the association is).

stimuli. A CS is one whose occurrence is dependent on a prior response and a CR is one whose occurrence is dependent on a subsequent stimulus. There are thus two kinds of CR's; those that are dependent on subsequent US's and those that are dependent on subsequent CS's. The former are classical CR's for which I am assuming a cognitive (S-S) associative process; the latter are operant/instrumental CR's for which I shall assume a behavioristic (S-R) associative process. Further, the antecedent stimulus in classical conditioning may itself be a conditional stimulus or US. Typically in explicit classical conditioning, the stimulus is unconditional; the environment is simply arranged to insure that the CS precedes the US. Typically in operant/instrumental conditioning, the stimuli for the classical conditioning component are largely conditional, i.e., dependent on the emission of an overt response (response-produced feedback). We thus have a terminological system that makes all of the critical distinctions involved in conditioning, and in this language system, the sequence of observable events in classical conditioning is as follows: $S-C^1 R-UC^1 S-UC^1 R$.

The proposed cognitive learning process relates back to early associationism, and is most explicitly stated within behaviorism in the works of Tolman. In verbal form, the assumption is that, whenever an S more or less regularly precedes in time a US, these stimuli will become associated with each other, the S tending to call forth a representation of the US and the US also tending to call forth a representation of the S[7] We shall subsequently have occasion to identify some of the parameters that determine the strength of such associations.

At this point, we have arrived at the apparent impasse attributed to Tolman by Guthrie (1952) that the organism is left "buried in thought." A behaviorist must still provoke a response, and not just any response in the organism's repertoire. Tolman (1955) attempted to rectify this deficiency pretty much along the lines taken by MacCorquodale and·Meehl (1954). I believe that there is a much simpler solution to this problem. Let us call the hypothetical anticipatory representation of the US the us' (more fully, $uc^1 s'$ where the prime distinguishes it from the $uc^1 s$ provoked by the actual occur-

---

[7] This is, of course, a backward association for which there is no simple test with nonverbal animals. This is because, even if the US produces a representation of the S, the latter does not elicit a response other than the manifestation of the ur'. Of course, unconditional orienting and observing, or perceptual or attending responses might be ascribed to any stimulus. This process might also be studied in the context of sensory preconditioning.

rence of the US), and ascribe to it the property of eliciting a ur' (more fully, uc^1r', as distinct from the uc^1r which conceptually instigates the UR). In effect, then, the overt CR is the manifestation of this ur'.[8]

This theory of cognitive associative learning must be expanded a bit further because it is logically necessary for the hypothetical association to be formed within the organism. Specifically, the S must be translated into the theory, and although we may ultimately want to introduce various perceptual and coding processes (e.g., Lawrence, 1963), I shall stay for the present with Hull's concept of the stimulus trace (s). The hypothetical learning process in Pavlovian classical conditioning can thus be symbolized $sHus'$.[9] It is now, however, necessary to admit that the UR (and accordingly, the ur') is not unconditional in a sense different from that previously defined. It is true that the UR is not dependent on the occurrence of subsequent events, but in keeping with both the Tolmanian and Hullian approaches, associations must be activated by motivation (M). In the present case, there are two sources of M—dynamism (sD) based on the intensity of the relevant stimuli, and drive (Dr) based on deprivation and conceived of as a disposition to respond. Let me comment briefly on the latter and then somewhat more extensively on the former.

Pavlov recognized that for successful salivary conditioning, the dog must be hungry. He attached relatively little importance to this fact, but Hull introduced the familiar symbol D (or Tolman's early "demand") for the motivational state resulting from stimulation or deprivation. In the dynamic theory that I am proposing, Dr does not have the surplus goading properties ascribed to drive by Hull. Rather, it is a disposition to make a response given an opportunity or appropriate occasion to do so. [This is consistent with the position taken by Cofer and Appley (1964) and similar to Estes' (1969b) postulation of amplifier elements.] And since Dr must be present to

[8] Note that this approach gets around the difficulty encountered by some S-R theories from the fact that the overt CR is typically somewhat different from the overt UR. The present approach assumes that the CR bears some family resemblance to but is not necessarily identical with the UR.

[9] Hull used subscripts in the construct sH_R: I have elsewhere made the point that the association is a hypothetical internal one which should be symbolized sHr. Perhaps Hull's choice was related to the fact that he verbalized habit strength as H-SR, rather than SHR, the latter leading more obviously to sHr. It might also be noted that Spence (1956) pointed out that Hull's equations could equally well be used for sHs as for sHr, and that it was the verbal description that identified Hull and Spence as S-R theorists.

insure that a US evokes a UR, so too must Dr be present for a us' to evoke a ur'.

Dynamism is conceptually more complex, but also more exciting because it is assumed to have two aspects of its own, sD and $us'D$. I am adopting the general approach stated by Miller and Dollard (1941; also Dollard & Miller, 1950) that all stimuli have motivating or dynamogenic properties. For my purposes here, I shall concentrate on stimulus intensity dynamism, which Hull and Spence symbolized V and I shall symbolize sD. It has two components, that associated with the S (sD) and that associated with the US ($us'D$). The former is based directly on the intensity of the antecedent stimulus which combines with any sHs resulting from prior pairings of the S with a US and thereby leads to a recruitment of $us'D$ which is limited by the strength of $sHus'$ and the intensity of the US itself.

Let me now put these together in symbolic form. Motivation in Pavlovian classical conditioning is composed of sD and Dr. Dr represents the disposition to make the designated response based on deprivation, and sD is the behavioral summation (A + B = A + B − AB) of sD and $us'D$, the former based on the intensity of the S and the latter on the intensity of the US as recruiting rapidly over time depending on the $sHus'$ thus far accumulated. The entire sequence is therefore:

$$S \searrow \atop sHus' \times (sD + us'D) = sEus' \times Dr = ur' \nearrow \qquad CR\ US \searrow \atop us \times Dr = ur \nearrow \qquad UR.$$

In verbal form, I am proposing first that a stimulus does two things: it provides some level of motivation as a result of its own dynamism, and its cue properties call forth a representation of any stimuli with which it has been associated. As this anticipatory representation comes into being, its dynamism contributes further motivation which, combined with a prevailing disposition to make the response in question, produces the unlearned UR appropriate to that representation. This is manifested overtly in a CR which is maintained by the subsequent occurrence of an US itself. The occurrence of UR is superfluous except that the anticipatory response should bear some family resemblance to it.[10]

---

[10] This approach does not actually require that the UR occur because the learned association is not with that response itself. Hence, the results of experiments involving response prevention by drugs such as curare (e.g., Solomon & Turner, 1962) are not critical. Similarly the Loucks and Gantt (1938) results involving faradic stimulation are here interpreted as supportive of the cognitive interpretation of classical conditioning, rather than relevant to the issue of the necessity of reinforcement, as proposed by Spence (1951).

The preceding symbolic sequence adequately characterizes the present theory of classical conditioning in terms of the conceptual question, "What is learned?" However, it does not give a dynamic flavor to the learning process whereby conditioning occurs over repeated trials. It is the purpose of the next section to provide the rudiments of such an analysis. These descriptions are somewhat tentative and informal; however, a quasi-mathematical formulation of the theory for illustrative purposes is presented. My goal is to describe the hypothetical processes that take place during simple acquisition of a classical CR. I will then treat with extinction in some detail and subsequently selected empirical phenomena in rather cursory fashion.

III. Theoretical Analysis of Classical Conditioning

Before describing the postulates in relation to a quasi-mathematical formulation of the theory, it may be helpful at least for the benefit of some degree of redundancy first to describe the essential features of the theory backward from the behavior of interest. The general goal is to attempt to answer the question: Why does that dog salivate when that bell rings? My answer to that question is this: The bell makes the dog think that he is about to get some food and that thought naturally makes him salivate because he is hungry. The answer to the next question of why the bell makes him think that he is going to get some food is that historically the bell has signalled the impending occurrence of food. But then comes the question: Why does the fact that the bell has signaled food in the past make the dog think that he is going to get food this time? It is *that* question that the theory purports to answer. Unfortunately, the answer is not as simple as saying only that the dog "figures" that if that's the way it's been in the past, that's the way it ought to be this time.

As I have already indicated, my assumption is that the observed CR is an overt manifestation of a hypothetical UR (ur') that is directly elicited by the hypothetical anticipatory US (us'). This us' may be thought of as an *active* expectancy of the impending occurrence of the US. When the us' is active, the dog in Pavlovian conditioning is thinking about food, but although such thoughts have an unlearned tendency to elicit salivation, they will do so only if the dog also has a disposition to salivate. The word "disposition" should not be read to imply that the dog has freedom of choice with respect to its behavior; there could be competing dispositions based on additional antecedent conditions. Barring such, however, conditions of food deprivation are sufficient to establish the drive necessary to convert an active expectancy into an excitatory potential for ur' and its concomitant overt manifestation.

My notion is that an expectancy becomes active when its expectancy potential exceeds a variable threshold. It is important to recognize that both thoughts and actions are taking place continuously over time and it is essential for a theory to capture this dynamic feature of behavior. This means that time becomes a very pervasive aspect of the theory. For purposes of analysis, we may reduce the basically continuous nature of time to very small discrete intervals which I have called the behavioral unit of time (BUT or h in Estes' 1950 theory). My image is that expectancy potentials are changing on a moment-to-moment basis in relation to the ongoing pattern of environmental events, that the threshold is also varying (perhaps as a result of a multitude of other possible expectancy potentials), and that an active expectancy occurs when the momentary expectancy potential exceeds the momentary threshold.

It should be noted at this juncture that I shall adopt a micromolecular view of the stimuli being associated. I have elsewhere (Logan, 1956, 1960) attempted to deal with the various kinds of definitions of a response. In that terminology, a microtheory assumes that quantitative properties of responses are part of what gets learned, in contrast to a macrotheory which assumes that quantitative properties of responses serve as measures of strength. A molecular theory assumes that fine-grain topographical features of the response are part of what gets learned; a molar theory defines a response by its consequences without regard to such details. In similar fashion then, a micromolecular view of the stimulus treats all quantitative and qualitative properties of the stimulus as defining properties of what gets associated with what in S-S learning. A weak US leads to an expectation of a weak US even though the cognitive association may be of maximal strength.

The micromolecular approach to the definition of both stimuli and responses is itself a dynamic notion. It refers to the *momentary* properties of expectancies and responses, and the theory attempts to predict momentary probability conceived in this fine-grain detail. I am not contending that in classical conditioning the amplitude of the CR is part of what gets learned. (That would be the corresponding S-R assumption.) What gets learned are the micromolecular properties of the US, such as its intensity, and insofar as the UR is related to such properties, the micromolecular features of the CR are indirectly part of what gets learned. Other-than-momentary descriptions of a response, such as latency, are to be derived from the dynamic changes in probability.

In the proposed theory, the dynamic feature of expectancy potential is provided by stimulus-intensity dynamism. I assume that all stimuli including us' have some dynamogenic properties in the sense of activating cognitive associations. That is to say, even while the expectancy potential is below threshold, dynamism is being recruited cybernetically in relation to the intensity of the anticipatory representation of the US. Another way of expressing this assumption is that cognitive associations have intrinsic dynamic, dynamogenic properties which affect their potential for becoming active expectancies, or thoughts.

Thus we have worked our way back to the associative process itself, and I have previously stated one essence of this postulate: Cognitive associations are established at their limit (unity) upon a single more or less contiguous occurrence of two stimuli and thereupon begins to decay.[11] Such cognitions contain not only the information that something is likely to occur, but also when it is likely to occur. The dynamic feature of the latter aspect of an expectancy is presumably related to hypothetical internal processes that change over time, such as the stimulus trace. But whatever the underlying basis of this effect, organisms learn about the momentary micromolecular features of the US and its impending occurrence at some time in the continuous flux of the environmental stream. My assumption that such cognitions decay over time appears to be a straightforward theory of forgetting, but it is actually not quite so simple. Long-term memory results from the assumption that there is a nonzero limit to this decay process. An association may ultimately fall below even the lower limit of the threshold distribution, but it nevertheless approaches a nonzero value asymptotically. This decay, it should be recognized, refers to the hypothetical associative process itself; "one-trial learning" could occur if the dynamism of the stimuli is sufficient to arouse even a weakened association above the momentary threshold.

Within this general orientation, the cumulative effect of the number of trials arises from the somewhat unique memories of prior occasions on which the stimuli were paired. That is to say, the

---

[11] This is not the assumption made by Tolman, who contended that cognitive associations typically developed gradually, although he also favored insightful learning in some situations. One-trial learning was the hallmark of Guthrie, although he was proposing S-R associations. [It is interesting to note that his illustrations (e.g., Guthrie, 1959) frequently were what are here considered to be cognitive associations, e.g., human verbal learning.] The significance of one-trial learning has been discussed by Restle (1965).

cognitive association established on each preceding trial (Trial x) decays toward a nonzero limit, and these separately generalize to the target trial (Trial n). They aggregate into a net, or effective associative strength, each contributing in relation to the similarity of the antecedent stimuli on those prior trials to that on Trial n. In effect then, all trials save the first are generalization test trials. This means that we need to identify, at least in terms of general categories, the sources of potential generalization decrement which attenuates recall.

There is also a generalizationlike process on the consequent side of a cognitive association. This arises when several different associations have been formed during previous trials. If the US has varied, either in its micromolecular features or its temporal location with respect to a stimulus, the resulting separate associations will compete and, insofar as possible, lead to a compromise expectancy. It is especially important to recognize that organisms can learn that the conditions have been changed and particularly that events that have occurred in the past will no longer occur. Experimental extinction results in part from the development of just such an expectancy.

This may appear to be a very complicated way to conceptualize the associative processes involved in the presumably simplest form of learning, namely classical conditioning. My contention is that the process is simply not simple. It is conceptually no less complex than a free-recall task in humans. Its apparent simplicity derives only from the fact that we can observe the formation of new associations and we can arrange the experimental environment in such a way as to minimize various distracting influences. And we can build in progressively more complex features of the experimental environment and thereby develop some understanding of the combination and permutation rules involved. My eventual contention will be that there is nothing more complex about the so-called higher mental processes than appears at least in rudimentary form in classical conditioning.[12]

Briefly to summarize the theory working backward from the CR, it is viewed as an overt manifestation of UR to the expectancy of US given a disposition to respond based on setting operations such as

---

[12] This is, of course, precisely the proposition set forth by Watson in proclaiming the behaviorist manifesto. Watson, however, was not a theorist in the contemporary sense of the term, and insofar as one imposes theoretical interpretations on his position, his would be classified as a uniprocess S-R approach. Accordingly, I am agreeing with his most fundamental thesis but disagreeing as to the conceptual nature of the associative process involved in classical conditioning.

deprivation. An expectancy arises when the expectancy potential exceeds a variable threshold, expectancy potential changing dynamically over time as a result of a cognitive association and the stimulus-intensity dynamism of the stimuli involved in that association. The cognitive association is brought to bear on the basis of the generalization of associations formed on all previous occurrences of similar stimulus events. Those, in turn, have decayed to some extent as a result of the passage of time. Let us now begin again and describe the postulates of the theory in somewhat greater detail. (A mathematical statement of these postulates is given in the Appendix, and I shall indicate the relevant equations, but I am here more concerned with the logic of the theory than any particular mathematical realization of it.)

A. PROPERTIES OF STIMULI

I assume that any stimulus has four somewhat independent but interrelated properties. These are stimulus value, drive value, incentive value, and response value. All of these terms are hypothetical constructs inferred functionally from appropriate kinds of behavior indices. Stimulus value is the primary, defining property of a stimulus and it refers to the fact that the stimulus event either already controls the occurrence of some responses or can gain control over behavior as a result of appropriate conditioning procedures. Stimulus value refers to its distinctiveness, its perspicuity, its salience. This includes various qualitative features of the stimulus as well as its quantitative measure of intensity. Conceptually, stimulus value is a function of the amount of change in the total stimulus environment occasioned by a stimulus event. Stimulus value is thus a relative construct.

The dynamogenic property of a stimulus, its dynamism, or what I have here called its drive value, is monotonically related to its intensity in both absolute and relative senses. But quite frankly, I do not yet have a clear understanding of the asymmetries involved with respect to the drive value of stimuli. Clearly an imaginary stimulus with zero intensity could have neither drive value nor any other property, but a decrease in stimulus intensity to zero must have some drive value within the theory. As but one further complication, the change in the color of a visual stimulus accomplished without a concomitant change in brightness must also have drive value. The theory requires that any stimulus event that can be categorized as such because of its demonstrated stimulus value must be conceived of as having some drive value bearing some interacting relationship between the absolute intensity of the ongoing stimulus event and the amount of change from preceding sensory inputs. Probably it would be better to refer to stimulus-change dynamism rather than stimulus-intensity dynamism, but certainly my current postulates concerning the direct relationship between stimulus intensity and drive value are gross oversimplifications and desperately require a more sophisticated conceptual analysis than I have provided here.

Incentive value refers to the emotional significance of the stimulus event to the organism. Other terms suggestive of this feature of a stimulus are reinforcing, nonreinforcing, punishing, pleasant, neutral, unpleasant, desirable, undesirable, beneceptive, nociceptive, rewarding, aversive, and in still older lingos, hedonic value. I agree with Premack (1971) to the effect that incentive value does not reside in the stimulus but rather relates to the organism in commerce with the stimulus. Incentive value is not directly involved in classical conditioning as typically conceived although the stimuli in that conditioning paradigm may have incentive value.

The final property, namely response value, categorizes stimuli in terms of their unlearned tendencies to elicit some response. For my immediate purposes, this is the important feature of what I have called the US. The actual occurrence of the overt UR is not really important; what is important is that the US has the potential to elicit UR under appropriate circumstances. Otherwise, its anticipatory representation would not elicit a response and the hypothetical association could not be directly assessed in nonverbal organisms.

B. PROPERTIES OF COGNITIVE ASSOCIATIONS

My learning postulate is essentially that of redintegration. I assume that whenever two (or more) stimuli occur in reasonably close temporal contiguity they become associated with each other (a cognitive habit, sHs) and that the association decays over time (Equation [1.0]).[13] This means that each stimulus will tend to call forth a cognitive representation (thought, feeling, image) of the other stimulus and, in the process, bring with it some representation of the stimulus, drive, incentive, and response values of the associated

---

[13] In keeping with the Hullian tradition, I have chosen to use analytic equations but the postulate could equally well be stated in terms of difference equations such as used by Estes (1959) and described by Bush and Mosteller (1955): $p_n = 1 - (1 - \theta)^{n-1}$. In rate parameter terms, θ in the difference equation can be translated into its counterpart in the negative exponential equation by $\log 1/(1-\theta)$. I anticipate making this transformation because stimulus sampling theory has proven to be mathematically more tractable. However, doing

stimulus. It is the last of these that is most directly involved in the production of a classical CR. The second is known in the context of secondary motivation, the third in the context of secondary reinforcement and incentive motivation, and the first is employed as a mediating mechanism related to generalization, discrimination, and the integration of behavior chains. I am not adverse to thinking of this as a form of perceptual learning except that I am not interested in the notion of a total Gestalt so much as in the transference of the properties of one stimulus to another stimulus. This is the theoretical basis for what has been referred to as stimulus substitution.

I am obviously postulating a backward conditioning process, and this concept has very low regard in the context of classical conditioning. But in a larger context, human paired-associate learning may be thought of as a form of classical conditioning, and backward associations are readily observed in that setting. These are called forth by giving an appropriate disposition to respond by means of instructions. I would contend that the reason backward classical conditioning is not easy to demonstrate is that there is an overwhelming generalization decrement involved. Historically, the to-be-associated stimulus has occurred in the context of a preceding US and it is a markedly different stimulus when tested in isolation. Furthermore, since the organism learns to expect when the US will occur, it is already past in the typical classical conditioning paradigm.

C. PROPERTIES OF GENERALIZATION

According to this approach, "learning" is cumulative memory. Depending on the time since its occurrence, each prior Trial x leaves

---

so will require several assumptions that are quite different in that context. Specifically, Eqs. (1.0) and (2.4) combined suggest that although all stimulus elements sampled on any trial become associated at that moment, they are replaced over time with only a portion of them in the associated state. Further, elements not yet replaced are inaccessible, an assumption quite the opposite of that made by Estes (1959). Furthermore, I shall require the conceptualization of elements that are not associated with anything, be they stimuli or responses. Although this is antithetical to the original Guthrian notions, it seems to me to be quite reasonable that at least some elements of novel stimuli must begin without any extant associations. Given such a class of elements, I shall propose the concept of disociation, particularly in the context of what we currently call attention. (Such an assumption is similar to that made by Restle, 1955.) But what will most reduce the elegant simplicity of such theories is the proposal that a stimulus element can have more than one association and, which is more, such associations are not all-or-none in character. Specifically, stimulus patterning requires that several elements must combine to make a whole association. Finally, probability must be derived, perhaps along the lines taken by Luce (1959) or Restle (1961). Obviously a great deal is required to formulate such a mathematical realization of the conceptual principles described in this chapter.

some decaying memory trace of the events that transpired on that
trial, but only some of this memory is accessed on an upcoming Trial
n. The portion that is accessed depends upon the similarity of the
antecedent stimuli in Trial n to those on Trial x. The most obvious
source of a possible generalization decrement would be a change in
the physical stimulus itself (Equation [2.3]). There may also be
changes in the state of the organism (state-dependent learning, Equation [2.1]) and/or the physical context (Equation [2.2]). However,
even if these are rigorously controlled experimentally, there remain
three unavoidable sources of a generalization decrement generated by
the very context of acquisition and extinction. These are the time
between trials, trial number, and the aftereffects of trials preceding
Trials n and x.

My assumption is that the same stimulus can never be presented
twice and my further assumption is that the second occurrence is
more similar to the first occurrence the longer the time that has
elapsed between them. It would not be unreasonable that this recovery of similarity follows the same course as the decay of habit.
(Toward this end, I have chosen the same function form in Equation
[2.4], although I have left the parameters independent.) One way to
think about this assumption is that there is a prolonged refractory
period although I assume that recovery is never complete. The
important point is that the passage of time increases the extent to
which one can reinstate the same stimulus a second time.

The most complicated factor for our immediate purposes involves
trial number. I assume that the second presentation of a stimulus is
different from the first simply by virtue of being second even though
its similarity is greater the longer the interval of time separating the
presentations. I assume further that the third presentation is different from both the first and the second, and so on, with the size of
the difference depending on the relative trial numbers. That is to say,
the same absolute difference in trials numbers has a smaller effect the
larger the numbers themselves. (One way of capturing this idea
mathematically is given in the first portion of Equation [2.5].)

A complication arises when experimental sessions occur on different days. Specifically, the early trials of a day are different from
later trials of that day, and the 100th trial given as the tenth trial of
the tenth day is different from the 100th trial given as the first trial
of the 100th day. Accordingly, some formulation (such as that
presented in the second portion of Equation [2.5]) is necessary to
generalize both backward and forward according to trial numbers of
preceding days as well as generalization according to trial number
within day.

The final component here identified as being important in determining the similarity between trial stimulus events is based on the assumption that the aftereffects of what were the consequent events of preceding trials become a part of the antecedent stimuli for subsequent trials. This aftereffects approach was used by Hull (see, e.g., Sheffield, 1949) and also by Guthrie (see, e.g., Estes, 1959) and it has been systematically analyzed extensively by Capaldi (e.g., 1966). The substance of this assumption is that a generalization decrement is assumed to occur if the immediate history of reinforcement is different, diminishing in effect the further removed from the trials of interest. One way to capture this idea (Equation [1.6]) involves a rather unique use of the difference equations familiar in stimulus sampling theory (see Levine & Burke, 1972). This equation uses the successive increments in the familiar approach to determine the successive decrements depending on how many trials back from the trials of interest different reinforcement conditions were encountered. I have also made the formulation somewhat more general by including a parameter to represent the size of the differences in the intensities of the US in varied reinforcement conditions. The reader can anticipate that this aspect of the analysis will enter importantly in my theory of extinction, partial reinforcement, and repeated acquisitions and extinctions.

Because of the critical role played in this theory by the similarity of the stimulus events on an upcoming trial to those that obtained on preceding trials, let me review the essential ideas. The conceptualization that needs to be captured is this: Each preceding trial established some cognitive association involving a certain complex of antecedent stimulus events and how much generalization of this process there will be to an upcoming trial depends on the overall similarity between the stimulus complexes. The most basic factor is the similarity of the physical stimulus itself, but even if that is identical, there will inevitably be some differences in the contextual cues in which it is embedded. I have placed these contextual cues into five general classes, those related to the organism and the physical context, and those related to time, trial number (both within and between sessions), and aftereffects of the subsequent events on preceding trials. There may, of course, be other factors that I have overlooked and there may be reason to break the ones here identified down into finer analytic units. But all of these potential sources of generalization decrement must be computed for each and every preceding trial to determine the extent to which the extant associative processes will converge upon an upcoming trial.

Although the mathematics appears to be somewhat complex, the conceptualization is straightforward enough. Each trial establishes an associative process that will be in some state of decay at the time of a subsequent trial. A portion of this residual strength will generalize to the upcoming trial depending on the similarity of their antecedent stimulus complexes. The attenuation resulting from any generalization decrement needs to be determined (Equation [3.0]) and these then need to be combined (Equation [4.0]). The result is the net, or effective cognitive habit strength prevailing on the upcoming trial as generalized from previous trials. This provides the associative component (sHs) of an expectancy potential (sEs).

D. PROPERTIES OF EXPECTANCY POTENTIALS

A cognitive habit automatically becomes an expectancy potential because of intrinsic sources of motivation. The antecedent stimulus itself has some drive value (sD) which alone is sufficient to give rise to some expectancy potential ($sEs = sHs \times sD$) at the moment of its occurrence. This initiates a feedback loop and calls forth the dynamism of the US (usD) through its anticipatory representation ($us'D$). As this latter aspect is recruited over time, the expectancy potential builds to a limit jointly determined by the values of sHs, sD, and $us'D$. (Equations [2.0]−[2.5] accomplish this mission as a feedback loop in the mathematical formulation.)

Although I wish to avoid any semblance of reification of these hypothetical processes, a physical analogy may help give a feel for this feature of the theory. Consider igniting combustible material, such as a lighted match touched to a pile of crumpled paper. The heat of the match is sufficient to ignite the fire which then not only generates more heat but feeds back upon that heat to spread the flame. How vigorously the fire ultimately burns will depend primarily on the size of the pile of paper. In analogous but obviously only an analogous fashion, the dynamism of the antecedent stimulus initiates an expectancy potential which feeds upon itself in relation to the dynamism of the US.

An expectancy potential is only that, however, and remains to become active provided it exceeds a variable threshold.[14] To pursue

---

[14] Variability could be put on the input side, at various steps in the intermediate processes, or on the output side. It is quite likely that variability occurs at each of these points, and indeed I shall subsequently posit some variability inherent in the response. However, the elegance of the variable threshold model (Grice, 1972) is convincing to me although I am placing it in the cognitive domain. It is tempting at this juncture to introduce terms such as

the physical analogy, we need only insert a heat detector into the system with the provision that the sensitivity of the detector varies randomly on a moment-to-moment basis over some reasonable range of values. The mean sensitivity of such a variable detector would be set in such a way as to minimize false alarms while certainly reacting to a potentially serious fire. But again the dangers of reification must be underscored. I consider the threshold to be largely a mathematical device for accommodating to a large number of unknown (unknowable) determinants of behavior. For example one could contend that organisms are always thinking about something, that something being the expectancy with the highest momentary potential. The threshold for an expectancy of interest to an experimenter would therefore be the aggregate of a constantly changing flux of competing expectancy potentials.

Whatever its molecular basis, a variable threshold stands between an expectancy potential and an active expectancy, and the probability of the latter therefore changes dynamically over time (Equation [7.0]). Finally, but with one further complication, an active expectancy of the US gives rise to its UR (and its corresponding overt behavioral manifestation) depending on the strength of the organism's disposition to respond.[15] The complication is that, if several expectancies concurrently exceed the threshold, they result in a compromise (Equation [8.0]).

E. SUMMARY

Although there are many complicated facets to this theory which are necessary to accommodate to the multitude of fine-grain details of classical conditioning, the fundamental logic of the approach is relatively simple. Let us return to the question of why food having followed a bell in the past makes a dog expect food to follow the bell

---

consciousness or awareness, and I suspect that these will ultimately be appropriate. This would make many points of contact ranging from the difference between recall memory and recognition memory, to the remarkable memories recovered by reinstating cues under hypnosis. However, this would be running very far ahead of the present development of the theory.

[15] The requisite setting operations for various responses of various organisms will need to be specified more completely. It should be noted, for example, that instructions to human subjects constitute a setting operation in the sense I have in mind here. I should add further that some response systems may be assumed to have an effective Dr of unity without any particular intervention. This would arise, for example, in the case of fear, which is here assumed to be the ur' to the anticipatory us' resulting from prior painful experiences.

this time. Each time the bell and food occurred together in the past, they became cognitively associated with each other. These memories decay over time, but not completely; each trial leaves a residual which cumulates with those from other trials to determine the likelihood of their being recovered on some later trial. A later trial can never be precisely identical to any earlier trial and how similar it is will also affect the likelihood of a memory being recovered. When two stimuli regularly occur in temporal order, we may say that the organism comes to anticipate or expect the occurrence of the consequent stimulus and if it has varied or been changed, corresponding expectancies develop. Hence, the more frequently and consistently food has followed the bell, and the more similar this occasion is to previous occasions, the greater the likelihood that the dog will expect food. It is when the dog both expects food and is hungry that salivation appears as an overt manifestation of the UR to this expectancy.

IV. Experimental Extinction,
Spontaneous Recovery, and Relearning

My theory of experimental extinction involves two processes which are more-or-less generated by the fundamental nature of the present approach. Interestingly enough, they are substantially the processes which have sometimes been considered antitheses of each other: a decrease in the originally learned association, and the acquisition of a new, competing association. The distinction can be stated in everyday terms provided the nuances of the language are attended to carefully. On the one hand, the organism learns not to expect that the US will happen; on the other hand, the organism learns to expect that the US will not happen.

The symbol for this second process is $sH_{\overline{us}}'$ based on the failure of the US to occur ($\overline{US}$). The expectation that a US will not occur has a long history of a unique conceptual difficulty: If an organism can learn that a US of interest to an experimenter is not going to occur, would it not equally learn that neither is any other US going to occur? This would appear to lead to an indefinitely large quandary, because the organism would be running around preoccupied with a multitude of expectancies of useless information about what is not associated with what.

Within the present theory, the solution to this dilemma is relatively straightforward. I shall assume that $sH_{\overline{s}}$ develops only in the context of an sHs. This is somewhat analogous to the assumption made by Spence (1956) and more extensively by Amsel (1958) that frustration is occasioned by nonreinforcement only after some incentive motivation has accrued as a result of prior reinforcement. In this case, the constraint is simply that the limit of $s\bar{H}s$ is equal to sHs. That is to say, one only learns not to expect something when that something has occurred in the past, and then only to the extent that its happening is still expected.

This process would be sufficient for extinction were the assumption that $s\bar{H}s$ is analogous to conditioned inhibition (in this case, sIs) and subtracted directly from sHs to determine a net value. But such an assumption would not satisfy the overall objectives of this theory. If one comes to expect that something will not happen, but is left with the residual expectation that it will happen, these two expectancies give rise to a compromise expectancy. (The necessity for this is more apparent with partial reinforcement, where the organism is assumed to develop both sHs and $s\bar{H}s$ to their potential limits leading to an intermediate expectancy potential.)

Accordingly, for normal experimental extinction, it is also necessary to eliminate the sHs itself. This will never happen simply as a result of time because sHs from the previous acquisition trials have permanence to the extent of the limit of their decay. The solution is essentially that suggested by Guthrie and developed by Estes (1959), namely that acquisition took place in the context of the aftereffects of reinforcement, whereas extinction takes place in the context of the aftereffects of nonreinforcement. Accordingly, one does not actually lose sHs during extinction; rather, the amount of sHs generalized to the stimulus situation during extinction decreases as the immediate history of nonreinforcement increases.

The analysis is complicated by the need to convert sHs and $s\bar{H}s$ into sEs and $s\bar{E}s$, respectively. My equations, of course, will do this given the reasonable assumption that usD is the same for both processes. (The intensity of not getting something expected should be equivalent to the intensity of getting it.)[16] However, both of these expectancy potentials must yet exceed the variable threshold to be activated, and if they are unequal, then three states of affairs are logically possible: (*a*) neither may exceed the momentary thresh-

---

[16] It would not be unreasonable to introduce at this juncture motivational constructs related to the nonoccurrence of expected emotionally significant events, i.e., frustration (Amsel, 1958) and relief (Mowrer, 1960). I am inclined however to reserve these for the nonoccurrence of CS's rather than US's.

old; (b) only the stronger may exceed the momentary threshold; or (c) both may exceed the momentary threshold. And it is only in this last case that the compromise rule (Equation [8.0] rigorously applies. That is to say, the compromise is on the output side of the cognitive process. Accordingly, we shall have some probability of us' and some probability of the compromise between us' and $\overline{us}'$ (which I shall symbolize us'').[17]

Turning now to the assumption concerning aftereffects from preceding trials, I must employ a straightforward but somewhat cumbersome notational system. Let us list the preceding trials, reading backward, by a plus sign if a US occurred and a minus sign if no US occurred. For example, $+++{}^-s_n$ would represent the second trial of extinction if we only go back four trials in our notation. In computing the generalized sHs from acquisition, which took place entirely in the context of $++++s_x$, we note that there is a difference on Trial n-1 compared with Trial x-1. My approach is to attenuate the generalization factor as a result (Equation [2.6]). Of course, still further attenuation will be evident on the third extinction trial $(++--{}^-s_n)$ and so on progressively. In this way, sHs is being eroded at the same time $s\overline{Hs}$ is being developed.

It should be noted that I am assuming that $s\overline{Hs}$ follows the same principles that I have previously described with respect to sHs. The only constraint is that $s\overline{Hs}$ has a limit equal to sHs rather than unity. This means that the expectancy that the US will not occur is just as transitory and just as permanent as the original expectancy that it will occur. Nevertheless, there are several ways in which spontaneous recovery might be expected. The most obvious is that all decay processes with respect to sHs will typically have been completed before the end of extinction while the $s\overline{Hs}$ from the later extinction trials is still undergoing decay. Tests for spontaneous recovery also frequently entail a closer approximation to the contextual cues of acquisition than of extinction, resulting in differential generalization decrements with respect to sHs and $s\overline{Hs}$. Spontaneous recovery is thus a logically possible implication of the theory but it depends on the distribution of trials and the recovery interval involved.

---

[17] This is actually a simplification of the dynamics of the theory. It will be assumed that $s\overline{Es}$ reverts to zero upon its occurrence and begins again according to the feedback loop. This means that, at least momentarily, $s\overline{Es}$ is stronger and could occur in isolation during a later period of time. Indeed, in a truly dynamic theory, the compromise rule might not be necessary, the overall outcome being simply a result of the temporal integration of us' and $\overline{us}'$.

The partial permanence of both sHs and $sH\bar{s}$ also has immediate implications with respect to reacquisition and reextinction but these will similarly depend on procedural details related primarily to the number of original acquisition and extincting trials given. Were it possible to develop both sHs and $sH\bar{s}$ to their conceptual limits, then the only basis for changes in performance would relate to the aftereffects of preceding trials. Given a sufficiently large number of transitions between reasonably prolonged periods of reinforcement and nonreinforcement, these transition cues would gain sufficient associative strength with the appropriate expectancy to mediate very abrupt adjustments in performance.

Short of that, however, we can anticipate the changes in associations that should occur. Specifically, the first reacquisition phase should be relatively rapid because it reinstates the aftereffects of reinforcement to which sHs was initially developed, but it also contains progressively diminishing aftereffects of nonreinforcement to which new associations vis-à-vis the occurrence of the US must be developed. Predictions about the second extinction are somewhat more complicated in part because the development of $sH\bar{s}$ during the first extinction phase was rather markedly limited by the decreasing strength of generalized sHs. Furthermore, there is now a history of reinforcement following nonreinforcement (the first reacquisition phase) and hence those expectancies will be brought into play at that time.

It is this type of situation that I hope will convince the reader of the importance of my assumption that each and every trial results in the development of associations and all of these generalize to any subsequent trial in relation to the similarity of the relevant antecedent stimuli. It is admittedly more cumbersome in the context of simple acquisition to conceptualize each trial as leading to an associative process which combines with those from other trials to produce the effective associative strength on another acquisition trial. But that is the type of analysis that is required in order to handle predictions in situations in which there have been significant differences in the history of the consequent events. The fundamental thesis is that *all* cues that could conceivably lead to differential performance, were they selectively reinforced, must *always* be conceptualized as distinctive elements of the total stimulus complex. If they are not differentially reinforced, they may not develop different associations or any initial differences may be neutralized (Spence, 1936). But these facts are to be derived from the theory on the basis of the reinforcement history of such stimuli and are not to be presumed or tacitly ignored. In the last analysis, it is an empirical question whether hypothesized cues actually do gain control over behavior, but the better part of good judgment is to assume that they may do so and refine the theory to predict the extent of such control.

V. Random Partial Reinforcement

Conceptually, partial reinforcement involves the combination of the processes already described with respect to acquisition and extinction. Insofar as the occurrence and nonoccurrence of the US is random[18] with respect to any of the cues that have been identified, i.e., time, trial number, and aftereffects, partial reinforcement will eventually lead to high and equal values of sHs and $sH\bar{s}$ to all combinations of such cues. And my assumption is that two such expectancies compromise into some intermediate value (Equation [8.0]).

There is, however, one fine-grain feature of this prediction based on the assumption that the limit of $sH\bar{s}$ is sHs. Within the conceptual limits of both processes, sHs must always run ahead of $sH\bar{s}$, the latter continually catching up with the former. It will do so only after sHs has essentially reached its limit. The direct implication of this analysis is that acquisition with partial reinforcement should proceed more slowly than continuous reinforcement, peak below the level of continuous reinforcement, and then decrease somewhat with extended training. (These last two predictions must be considered in relation to possible limitations of the behavioral measures used.)

I have elsewhere (e.g., Logan, 1960) emphasized that partial reinforcement is only a very special case of varied reinforcement. It is the intent of this theory to encompass all possible variations in the conditions employed in classical conditioning, and most particularly varied US intensity and varied interstimulus interval (ISI). Such conditions lead to the development of different expectancies which,

---

[18] I am not referring here to the "truly random" control procedure described by Rescorla (1967) in which the occurrence of the US is equally likely in the presence and absence of the antecedent stimulus. Rather, I am presuming that the US occurs only in the presence of the antecedent stimulus and hence that stimulus is perfectly valid as a cue. However, it is not perfectly reliable in conditions of partial reinforcement provided no features of the antecedent stimulus receive inadvertent differential reinforcement.

depending on their relative frequence of occurrence, compromise at the time of the onset of the stimulus. In the case of varied ISI, there is the further dynamic complication that if the US did not occur at the shorter interval, then the expectancy is shifted entirely to that appropriate to the longer interval.

My analysis of resistance to extinction following partial reinforcement is essentially that developed by Capaldi (1966). Specifically, partial reinforcement established an expectancy of the US in the context of the aftereffects of prior nonreinforced trials and hence the generalization decrement occasioned by extinction conditions is not so severe as obtains after continuous reinforcement. Although that is probably the major aspect of the analysis, it should be recalled that my theory of extinction following continuous reinforcement involves two distinct processes, a loss of generalized sHs as well as the development of $sH\bar{s}$. Since the latter feature will have largely been developed during acquisition with partial reinforcement, it will not contribute greatly to a decrease in performance. It, too, will begin to come into play only after a run of nonreinforced trials during extinction that exceeds the length of such runs encountered during acquisition.[19]

VI. Blocking

My interpretation of the blocking phenomenon, in which an added cue gains little or no control after initial training with another cue with which it is subsequently compounded, borrows heavily from the modified continuity approach proposed by Wagner (1971) and Rescorla (1972). At least I assume that new cognitive associations are formed only to the extent that the entire stimulus complex has a combined effective habit strength of less than unity. Insofar as this has been achieved as a result of initial training with a single cue, further increments can be achieved only to the extent that an added cue changes the stimulus complex sufficiently to lead to a generalization decrement. Under typical conditions in which little or no decrement is observed upon the addition of a second cue, control by that cue would be blocked by the previously trained cue.

[19] This approach would suggest that the expression "partial nonreinforcement" is equally applicable. It would further suggest that there would be as much resistance to a change from partial nonreinforcement to continuous reinforcement as from partial reinforcement to continuous nonreinforcement.

However, according to my analysis, there is only one limit of associative strength and that is unity regardless of the intensity of the US. The reason that unblocking (e.g., Kamin, 1969) occurs if the intensity of the US is changed concurrently with the addition of a cue is that new associations must now be formed. The organism must learn not to expect the original intensity and to expect the new intensity and the added cue will participate in the development of these new associative processes. This means, then, that an added cue will gain affirmative control over behavior if the intensity of the US is increased *or* decreased (Feldman, 1971). Any change in either direction will lead to the formation of cognitive associations in which all elements of the stimulus complex are involved.

According to this line of reasoning, the only way short of punishment that an added cue can gain what might be called conditioned inhibitory properties is if the conditions are changed to those of extinction at the time the cue is introduced. In that special case of what would be, in effect, differential conditioning, the new learning is that the US will not occur and the added cue correspondingly acquires such associations.

VII. Differential Conditioning

My analysis of differential conditioning provides an interesting example of how the nature of the most primitive postulates directs the approach that best enables incorporating additional phenomena into the theory. This is because the empirical evidence on differential classical conditioning simply can not be fully accommodated by a direct combination of the basic principles of acquisition and extinction as proposed here. Something must be added which is new to the development of the theory at this juncture, but which is by no means new to the classic literature.

When the US is presented only on trials containing one antecedent stimulus and is omitted from trials containing a different but somewhat similar antecedent stimulus, it is well known that performance at first increases with respect to both stimuli and then gradually decreases to what is commonly called S−. Given sufficient training, this latter reduction is virtually to zero provided that S− is reasonably different from S+. When we set about to account for this phenomenon within the present framework, we have no difficulty in conceptualizing $s+Hus'$ and $s-H\overline{us}'$ being developed. The latter arises because of the generalization of the former from S+ to S− and the nonoccurrence of the US in that context. Similarly, there is no problem in granting that $s-H\overline{us}'$ also generalizes and one might think that we have only translated the familiar excitation–inhibition analysis into cognitive terms.

But that is not the case because $sH\overline{us}'$ does not subtract from $sHus'$ but rather compromises with it. Such an assumption was necessary to deal with partial reinforcement and for this reason, the analysis of experimental extinction required further recognition of a generalization decrement in $sHus'$ based on the aftereffects of preceding trials. Only by thus reducing $sHus'$ to zero could predicted performance correspondingly be reduced to zero. And assuming a random sequence of trials with S+ and S−, no such process is inherent in differential conditioning.

Accordingly, I must assume that differential reinforcement of somewhat similar stimuli increases their distinctiveness and directly reduces the amount of generalization between them. There is a substantial body of evidence that differential conditioning leads to a steepening of the generalization gradient (e.g., Hearst, 1969) and there are additional phenomena that fall under the rubric of acquired distinctiveness of cues (e.g., Lawrence, 1949). Debate has centered around the conceptual basis of these phenomena, usually anchoring either to Lashley's (Lashley & Wade, 1946) approach which contends that the stimuli become functionally more different, or to Hull's (1952) approach which contends that the results reflect a combination of excitatory and inhibitory processes. I am driven in Lashley's direction.

It would be premature to speculate very extensively on the underlying basis for these effects but a few preliminary remarks may be appropriate. Let us conceptualize a stimulus as a population of potential stimulus elements and we may presume with Guthrie that an organism initially samples from these at random on any trial. Following that approach, the degree of generalization to a second stimulus will depend on the proportion of overlapping elements. Now during differential conditioning, those overlapping elements receive 50% reinforcement while the nonoverlapping elements receive 100% reinforcement in the case of S+ and 100% nonreinforcement in the case of S−. What I am saying is that behavior progressively comes under control of the nonoverlapping elements.

Fortunately, there is empirical evidence supporting this contention (Wagner, Logan, Haberlandt, & Price, 1968). In those studies, one explicit cue (a light) occurred on all trials while a second cue (high or low tones) received differential reinforcement. Following such compound training, the light showed little or no control over behavior even though, viewed independently, it had received 50% reinforcement. I am simply applying those empirical facts to the conceptualization of single stimuli as compounds of elements. But this still leaves the phenomenon itself for theoretical explanation.

Clearly this theory can not contend that less reliable cues (elements) become "neutralized" by partial reinforcement as is the case in theories such as those of Spence (1936) and Hull (1952). Neutralization might be adequate for choice behavior since unreliable cues would not contribute to the differential excitatory potentials, but it is not adequate for differential conditioning because the net excitatory potential for S− must be reduced to zero. A more appealing approach would involve notions of attention (e.g., Bower & Trabasso, 1968; Sutherland & Mackintosh, 1971), but it could not be a two-stage model as conventionally conceived. Such models view the organism as first learning to which cues to attend, and then developing appropriate associations with respect to those cues. Were I to adopt an attention mechanism, I would propose that the organism first develops associations with all cues and then attention becomes increasingly focused on the most reliable ones. That is to say, the associations with unreliable cues are either decreased in strength or are made ineffective because of selective attention to more reliable cues.

But this is not the only molecular analysis that might be proposed and accordingly, I prefer to hold the issue in abeyance. As but one alternative, it may be preferable to anticipate the need for compound, relational, and configurational elements and view differential conditioning as actually taking place with respect to the configuration (Gestalt). The presentation of the elements separately would thus comprise tests for stimulus generalization. This approach might also encompass other phenomena such as the sharpening of the generalization gradient with extended training to a single stimulus. In any event, this remains a major deficiency of the theory but, whatever the molecular basis, I am postulating that behavior comes under selective control of reliable elements of a compound stimulus, that any stimulus is conceptually a compound of potential elements, and that the reliable elements are those that are nonoverlapping as between S+ and S− in differential conditioning. In this way, not only is $s-H\overline{us}'$ initially developed but concurrently there is a progressive decrease in the $s-Hus'$ generalized from S+.

VII. Deficiencies in the Theory

The deficiency which has just been described is one aspect of the more general need for a conceptual analysis of the stimulus as a hypothetical construct. Such an analysis must be both static, in the sense of describing the nature of the stimulus complex prevailing at any moment in time, and dynamic in the sense of describing the continuous-over-time changes in the nature of the stimulus complex. Without such an analysis, the theory is not yet ready to cope with some of the more interesting phenomena in the area of classical conditioning.

For example, I have stated that organisms learn to expect a US to occur at some particular point in time, presumably on the basis of a decaying stimulus trace. This is only suggestive of the way in which I anticipate handling one of the most important variables in classical conditioning, namely the ISI. To say that an organism expects the US to occur at some particular point in time also means that the organism does not expect it to occur at some earlier point in time. Accordingly, once the stimulus trace is formally introduced and its dynamic properties described, the theory will be in a position to cope with delayed conditioning. The derivations presented here deal only with the immediate recruitment of an expectancy potential, and has no process corresponding to what Pavlov called inhibition of delay.

A conceptual analysis of the stimulus will also need to include the notion of salience or perspicuity to handle phenomena such as overshadowing, but at the same time, there are phenomena such as compounding which appear to imply stimulus interaction and patterning. The use of meaningful words (Grant, 1972) as stimuli for humans does suggest a cognitive type of associative process, but bears most directly on the conceptual nature of a stimulus including whatever coding or transformation processes may be involved. For that matter, I have only indicated a few of the features of a stimulus complex that affect generalization, and I shall certainly want a more molecular view of the stimulus formalized in terms of stimulus elements. Some of these complications may not appear to be critical for an understanding of simple classical conditioning, their importance only becoming manifest in an analysis of discrimination learning. In fact, one reason for postponing an attempt at a conceptual analysis of the stimulus is that it involves other learning paradigms.

I would like to presume that, whatever the nature of a stimulus, that nature is substantially the same regardless of the behavioral context in which a stimulus is embedded. It is true that classical conditioning phenomena provide some very important leads toward a useful analysis, but some features are not immediately apparent in just that context. For example, the stimuli in instrumental conditioning typically are changing as the organism runs through the requisite behavior chain and this aspect of complex environments needs to be captured in a complete analysis of the stimulus. The orienting or investigatory reflex gives way to receptor-orienting acts and vicarious trial and error. These illustrate some of the ideas that will need somehow to be integrated into a really useful conceptual analysis of the stimulus.

There is yet another reason for separating such an analysis from the theory presented in this chapter. It is by no means necessary for an analysis of the stimulus to be tied uniquely to a particular theoretical approach. A stimulus occurs on the antecedent side of both S-S and S-R associative processes and an analysis of the stimulus can be quite indifferent as to what is on the consequent side of such hypothetical processes. It is equally indifferent as to the conditions which are assumed to be necessary and sufficient for the formation of such associations. The very antithesis of the present theory, namely Hull's 1943 pure S-R reinforcement theory, could use the same conceptual analysis of the stimulus while contending that responses are learned on the basis of drive reduction.

By no means do I wish to imply that I have such an analysis of the stimulus clearly formulated and am simply reserving it until a more propitious time for its debut. I am only contending that someone will need to make such an analysis and that, without it, a theory such as this one is deficient. And although this deficiency may be especially conspicuous, a conceptual analysis of the response is only slightly less urgent. As with the stimulus, I have provided only a few suggestions of some aspects of such an analysis, such as the micromolecular definition of a response, and the theory requires a more complete treatment. As one obvious example, I have proposed that, whenever possible, competing expectancies lead to a compromise output but this proposition should be derivable from a truly dynamic conceptualization of behavior. Which is more, many competing expectancies give rise to behaviors which simply cannot be compromised and some rule for selection or choice is then necessary.

There are more subtle reasons for requiring a conceptual analysis of the response in classical conditioning. I proposed a cognitive associative construct in that context because the conditional response is presumed to be dependent on US rather than a CS as obtains in operant/instrumental conditioning. But consider omission training in which the occurrence of the US is precluded by the occurrence of the CR. In such a paradigm, the US is in some sense not really a US because it *is* dependent on the *non*occurrence of the CR. If not responding is classified as a response, then the consequent stimulus is technically a CS in which case I would want to presume an S-R associative process to be involved. Perhaps the solution to this dilemma is analogous to my approach to handling the notion of an expectation that a US will not occur: Not responding is a response only in the context of an explicit tendency to make that response. In such an analysis, omission training would involve both S-S and S-R associative processes which converge upon the same CR.

Which quite naturally leads to a few preliminary remarks about the nature of S-R associative processes.[20] I shall contend at the outset that most systematic analyses of operant and instrumental conditioning are not so much theories of learning as they are theories of asymptotic performance. That is to say, they describe the steady-state behavior generated by particular schedules and conditions of reinforcement, nonreinforcement, and punishment. In such systems, the associative processes are of relatively minor importance. I shall want a theory that explicitly deals with transition processes, i.e., acquisition, extinction, and the dynamics of behavioral change when the conditions are changed.

I do not contend that all of the principles involving S-R associations are necessarily different from those involving S-S associations. On the contrary; both processes result from the contiguous occurrence of the events being associated, and both show generalization phenomena. I do believe that S-R associations are developed gradually, and that they are permanent. Because of my micromolecular definition of responses, they are not so much energized by motivation as they are selected by the relative incentive motivation associated with each response. However, since incentive motivation is

---

[20] It would be possible to conceptualize at least some forms of operant/instrumental learning in cognitive terms. Whenever a response occurs in the presence of a stimulus, the conditions for S-S as well as S-R associations are satisfied. Responses produce feedback stimuli which could become associated with the antecedent stimuli, and overt responses viewed as manifestations of anticipatory representations of the "feel" of the response. Such an approach would have obvious advantages in dealing with phenomena such as observational learning and, more importantly, would make the contention that response differentiation is basically a form of discrimination learning based on feedback stimuli a more meaningful proposition. Interestingly enough, it would also favor Skinner's term "emission" of an operant response as being more suitable than "elicitation" of such a response, although the present theory would also contend that classically conditional responses are also emitted as overt manifestations of a cognitive expectancy.

derived from the present theory of classical conditioning, it contains stimulus dynamism (including the parameters of reinforcement) as a part of the expectancy and drive motivation as a disposition to respond.

I anticipate the need for several and different types of inhibitory processes with respect to both S-S and S-R associations. But the greatest conceptual challenge will be to grapple with the mutual interdependence among all of these processes. I am personally convinced that the most serious deficiency of this theory (and virtually all other behavior theories) is that it is essentially linear in conceptualization. Stimuli go in and responses come out. I believe that the organization into direct causal chains involving independent and dependent variables is a grossly oversimplified model. But perhaps we cannot do better at the present time.

IX. Conclusion

I have referred to my approach toward a systematic analysis of behavior as a "hybrid" theory to underscore from the outset that many of the features of the system have been derived from a variety of conceptual lineages. Insofar as possible, I have attempted to identify the major figures in these lines of descent but I have, without doubt, failed to acknowledge some important influences. Nothing has been quite so convincing to me of the power of unconscious processes as to rediscover an article or book in which I had made clear underlines and marginal notes which, although ostensibly forgotten, have reappeared as "insights." It may well be that the only original contribution of this approach is the attempt to integrate a wide variety of useful ideas into a single formulation.

In that spirit, the theory at its present stage of development falls far short of being all-inclusive. Specifically, for example, the most closely related theoretical approach is that of Estes (1969a) who has also incorporated both S-S and S-R notions in his recent developments of stimulus sampling theory. It is at least interesting that Estes, whose lineage traces most directly to the pure S-R contiguity theory of Guthrie in which there were no explicit motivational constructs, and I, whose lineage traces most directly to the pure S-R reinforcement theory of Hull in which the conditions of reinforcement were assumed to affect associative strength, converge on what I call incentive motivation and Estes calls amplifier elements and independently arrive at the inclusion of both S-S and S-R associative processes in attempting to cope with these constructs in the context of instrumental conditioning.

Many of the differences between our approaches are probably more apparent than real but this is difficult to determine unless the verbal statements are translated into comparable mathematical formulations. Rather than the continuous decay process that I have posited with respect to cognitive associations, Estes favors a two-stage model of forgetting in which immediate memories are transferred to a long-term store with certain probabilities. The consolidation of memories thereby has a more active flavor, but it is also more difficult to formalize. He continues to think of additional trials as sampling from the original population of potential stimulus elements, and although I would also favor such a conceptualization, I have attempted to focus on stimulus elements that are uniquely introduced by additional trials, some of which can never be sampled again. It will be necessary to compare mathematical-model representations of the various theoretical propositions in these regards to determine their similarities and differences.

At the risk of appearing to protest too much, I would disavow the inclusion of this theory as a part of what may be thought of as a cognitive revolution or renaissance (e.g., Dember, 1974). At least insofar as that self-proclaimed zeitgeist is correctly interpreted as redefining psychology as the science of the mind in which cognitive processes are endowed with properties that defy deterministic, mechanistic principles, then I would rather be viewed as launching a counterattack. But should such debates ultimately reduce to controversies involving reification of hypothetical constructs, then I would side with Skinner (1950) that theories are not only unnecessary but actually counterproductive.

This point needs to be doubly emphasized. The only real parsimony of proposing that S-S associations are mediated by some response mechanism would arise if the laws governing such hypothetical responses were the same as those governing instrumental responses. I have assumed this not to be the case even though I contend that S-S laws are equally deterministic and mechanistic. I have no brief with those who prefer to think of representations, images, and thoughts as some form of responses, but I would eschew arguments over the "true" nature of a cognitive representation of US. It is neither more nor less than a hypothetical construct, anchored on the one side to contiguous occurrences of a stimulus with a US, and anchored on the other side to an overt manifestation of its UR. It has precisely the properties ascribed to it by the theory. It makes no difference what it is called because it is not presumed to have any existential reality.

Appendix
Quasi-Mathematical Formulation of the Theory

It is the purpose of this appendix to set forth the postulates of the theory in a relatively formal, quasi-mathematical form. I refer to it in that manner because this is only one of several possible mathematical realizations of the theory and somewhat different equations could be used to express the content of the postulates. Furthermore, the derivation given is only illustrative and assumes completely hypothetical values for the requisite constants and parameters. However, this is an extremely important aspect because a really useful behavior theory must be statable in sufficiently rigorous terms to preclude any debate about its implications. The present formulation can be programmed on a very limited computer.

1. The stimulus trace (s) of the antecedent stimulus (S) of each preceding trial (x) becomes associated (H) with a representation (us') of the unconditional stimulus (US), which representation is established at unity by the contiguous occurrence of the S and the US and thereupon decays over time at a rate (i) dependent on age and individual differences toward a nonzero limit (L_H):

$$s_x Hus' = L_H + (1 - L_H)[10^{-i(t_n - t_x)}].\qquad(1.0)$$

2. The residual $s_x Hus'$ resulting from each preceding trial generalizes to an upcoming trial (n) according to the similarity between the antecedent stimuli of Trials x and n. There are six sources of a potential generalization decrement each of which subtracts behaviorally $(A \doteq B = A - AB)$ from unity to determine the net generalization (G) factor:

$$s_n Gs_x = 1 \doteq s_n G_{Ox} \doteq s_n G_{Cx} \doteq s_n G_{Sx} \doteq s_n G_{tx} \doteq s_n G_{Tx} \doteq s_n G_{Rx}.\qquad(2.0)$$

2.1. Cues related to the momentary state of the organism (O) such as deprivation, health, diurnal cycle, and extraneous conditions of fatigue and excitation are a part of the total stimulus complex.

$$s_n G_{Ox} = \text{unit function of change in the state of organism.}\qquad(2.1)$$

2.2. Cues related to the physical context (C) in which the stimulus is embedded such as the apparatus, level of illumination, and the presence or absence of irrelevant stimuli are a part of the total stimulus complex.

$$s_n G_{Cx} = \text{unit function of any change in context.}\qquad(2.2)$$

2.3. The physical features of the stimulus including its location as well as its qualitative and quantitative properties are a part of the total stimulus complex provided that the stimulus energy impinges upon a suitable sensory receptor.

$$s_n G_{Sx} = \text{unit function of any change in the stimulus.}\qquad(2.3)$$

2.4. Each occurrence of a stimulus is inherently different from each other occurrence, but similarity recovers over time (t) at a rate (j) depending on age and individual differences toward a limit (L_t) less than unity:

$$s_n G_{tx} = L_t + (1 - L_t)[10^{-j(t_n - t_x)}].\qquad(2.4)$$

2.5. The similarity between occurrences of a stimulus depends in part upon the trial number within day (T'), there being a limit to this similarity (L_T) depending on relative trial numbers. There is also a similarity based on trial numbers between days (d) which has a comparable function form. These sources of similarity based on trial number combine to determine a joint generalization factor:

$$s_n G_{Tx} = L_T[1 - 10^{-k|\log T'_n - \log T'_x|}] \doteq L_T[1 - 10^{-k(\log d_n - \log d_x)}].\qquad(2.5)$$

2.6. If the US (including its nonoccurrence) differed on trials preceding Trials x and n according to some amount (g), there is a generalization decrement which is a decreasing function of the number of trials back such a difference occurred:

$$s_n G_{Rx} = g\Sigma(h^{nx-nx'-1} - h^{nx-nx'}).$$ (2.6)

3. The associative strength $(s_{nx}Hus')$ contributed by each preceding Trial x to an upcoming Trial n is the residual strength of $s_x Hus'$ attenuated by the net generalization factor:

$$s_{nx}Hus' = s_x Hus' \times s_n Gs_x.$$ (3.0)

4. The associative strengths resulting from all preceding trials combine behaviorally (A $\dotplus$ B = A + B − AB) to determine the net associative strength on Trial n:

$$s_n Hus' = \overset{.}{\Sigma} s_{nx}Hus'.$$ (4.0)

5. The net associative strength is activated by the momentary stimulus intensity dynamism $(s\dot{D})$ into a momentary expectancy potential:

$$s_n \dot{E}us' = s_n Hus' \times s\dot{D}.$$ (5.0)

5.1. The momentary value of $s\dot{D}$ is the combination of the dynamism of the antecedent stimulus (sD) and the momentary dynamism of the anticipatory representation $(us'\dot{D})$ of the US:

$$s\dot{D} = sD \dotplus us'\dot{D}.$$ (5.1)

5.2. The dynamism of the antecedent stimulus is a function of its intensity or intensity aspects of the change in stimulus energy.

$$sD = \text{unit function of S intensity}.$$ (5.2)

5.3. The momentary value of $us'\dot{D}$ is zero at the time of the occurrence of the antecedent stimulus and recruits cybernetically in relation to the dynamism of the US (usD) and the momentary expectancy potential:

$$us'\dot{D} = usD \times s_n \dot{E}us'.$$ (5.3)

5.4. The dynamism of the US is a function of its intensity or intensity aspects of the change in stimulus energy.

$$usD = \text{unit function of US intensity}.$$ (5.4)

5.5. According to the preceding equations, momentary expectancy potential approaches a limit with negative acceleration over time:

$$L\, s_n \dot{E}us' = \frac{s_n Hus' \times sD}{1 - [s_n Hus' \times usD(1-sD)]}$$ (5.5)

6. The increment in associative strength on each trial to the cues prevailing on that trial is the difference between unity and that available at the onset of the antecedent stimulus, i.e.,

$$\Delta s_n Hus' = 1 - s_n Hus'.$$ (6.0)

7. The momentary probability that an expectancy will become active is the probability $(\dot{p}us')$ that momentary expectancy potential exceeds a variable threshold (sT) which is normally distributed on a momentary basis over time:

$$\dot{P}us' = \int_{-\infty}^{s_n \dot{E}us'} sT, \quad \text{where} \quad sT \sim N(\mu,\sigma).$$ (7.0)

8. An active expectancy becomes an excitatory potential $(s_n\dot{E}ur')$ in relation to the strength of the organism's disposition to respond (Dr). Insofar as possible, several active expectancies compromise:

$$B = C\dot{R} = s_n\dot{E}ur' = f\sqrt{\frac{us_1'f + us_2'f + \cdots + us_n'f}{n}} \times Dr.$$

(8.0)

8.1. The disposition to respond depends upon setting operations such as deprivation, stimulation, and instructions to humans:

$$Dr = \text{unit function of requisite setting operations.}$$

(8.1)

Illustrative Quantitative Solution

In order to better illustrate the dynamics of the theory, Table I contains the complete analysis of the first five trials of classical conditioning and the terminal result for selected trials thereafter. The hypothetical values used for the necessary constants and parameters of the equations are listed there, and the first four columns contain the necessary information with respect to trial numbers and times of occurrence. If for the purposes of illustration, we assume that one BUT is equal to 100 msec, then this derivation would apply to conditioning with a 400-msec ISI and a 10-sec intertrial interval (ITI).

Since the same parameters were used for Eqs (1.0) and (2.4), the solutions are the same for sHs and sG_t, and these are shown in columns 5 and 6. The latter of these is combined with the computed values of sG_T as shown in column 7, the result appearing in column 8. The product of columns 5 and 8 yields the generalized value of sHs from each preceding trial; these are shown in column 9 and their behavioral summation is given in column 10. This is the net sHs available at the beginning of each trial.

In the next three columns are shown the results of the dynamic processes resulting from combining sHs with sD in order to determine the momentary values of $s\dot{E}s$ at each successive BUT in the ISI. (It is assumed that the irreducible minimum latency is one BUT and the indicated intervals of time are from their lower limits.) For each trial, the momentary values of $s\dot{E}s$ are converted into a cumulative probability of us' becoming active and if, for simplicity, we assume Dr to be unity, these are also the probabilities of the occurrence of a CR. From these latter values, one can determine the predicted distribution of the latencies of such responses. Specifically, the most likely latency during the early trials is in the third interval of time, and shifts to the second interval with further conditioning.

The penultimate column shows the limit of expectancy potential given sufficient time for the complete recruitment of dynamism $(us'D)$. Clearly, short ISI simply do not provide sufficient time for this full potential to be realized, although it should be detectable from test trials omitting the US. The final column shows the increment in associative strength occasioned by a reinforced trial.

Glossary of Symbols

The following symbols follow as closely as possible ones that are reasonably common in the literature. However, their referents are not always identical to other usages, and care must therefore be taken in their use here. (Because of the contemporary trend toward identifying by name those who developed and quantified a construct, I have in some cases included parenthetically some suggestions with the expectation that others who develop more refined measures could be added.)

TABLE I

QUASI-MATHEMATICAL THEORETICAL ANALYSIS OF ACQUISITION OF A CLASSICALLY CONDITIONED RESPONSE, WITH

$$L_H = .1,\ i = .001,\ L_t = .1,\ j = .001,\ L_T = .5,\ k = 1.0,\ L_T = .5,\ sD = .2,\ usD = .8,$$
$$\mu = .3,\ \sigma = .1,\ ITI = 100,\ \text{and}\ ISI = 4\ \text{BUT's.}$$

T_n	T_x	t_n	t_x	s_xHus'	s_nG_{tx}	s_nGTx	s_nGs_x	$s_{nx}Hus'$	s_nHus'	$s_{n1}\dot{E}s'$	$s_{n2}\dot{E}us'$	$s_{n3}\dot{E}us'$	$Ls_n\dot{E}us'$	$\Delta s_nHus'$
2	1	100	0	.815	.815	.250	.138	.113	.113	.023	.024	.024	.024	.887
									Cum $p(us')$ =.003		.006	.009		
3	2	200	100	.815	.815	.167	.154	.102	.235	.047	.054	.055	.055	.765
3	1	200	0	.668	.668	.333	.221	.148	Cum $p(us')$ =.006		.013	.020		
4	3	300	200	.815	.815	.125	.162	.132	.388	.078	.097	.102	.103	.612
4	2	300	100	.668	.668	.250	.249	.166			.035	.058		
4	1	300	0	.551	.551	.375	.281	.155	Cum $p(us')$ =.014					
5	4	400	300	.815	.815	.100	.167	.136	.500	.100	.132	.142	.147	.500
5	3	400	200	.668	.668	.200	.266	.177			.069	.122		
5	2	400	100	.551	.551	.300	.314	.173	Cum $p(us')$ =.023		.237	.277		
5	1	400	0	.458	.458	.400	.325	.149			.377	.632		
10	1	900	0	.213	.213	.450	.433	.092	.788	.158	.474	.333	.318	.212
									Cum $p(us')$ =.078			.805		
15	1	1400	0	.136	.136	.467	.461	.063	.884	.177	.296	.361	.407	.116
									Cum $p(us')$ =.111					
20	1	1900	0	.111	.111	.475	.467	.052	.928	.186	.550	.879	.457	.072
									Cum $p(us')$ =.127					

B. B is the generic symbol for behavior, and in principle subsumes all objective indices of behavior that might be employed in any particular experimental setting. The only explicitly derived systematic dependent variable in this theory is momentary response probability. (If Behaviorism is J. B. Watson's middle name, Behavior is B. F. Skinner's first name. Although both of these would eschew the type of hypothetical intermediating constructs involved in this theory, their constant focus on observable behavior has been a strong influence.)

D, sD, Dr. D is a generic symbol for drive, dynamism, and dispositional states of the organism; *sD* refers to drive resulting from stimulation; *Dr* is the disposition to make some relevant UR, and is based on the requisite setting operations such as deprivation, stimulation (including instructions), or some combination of these. (Darwin's vital influence on this theory stems from his thesis of the compelling power of survival of the individual and the species.)

E, sEs, sEr. E is the generic symbol for expectancy potential (*sEs*) or excitatory potential (*sEr*) based on the combination of learning and motivation. (E. C. Tolman emphasized the importance of this distinction for the theoretical analysis of performance.)

G, sG, Gr, sG$_S$, sG$_O$, sG$_C$, sG$_t$, sG$_T$, sG$_R$. G is the generic symbol for generalization processes, *sG* referring to stimulus generalization and *Gr* to response generalization of associative processes. *sG$_S$, sG$_O$, sG$_C$, sG$_t$, sG$_T$*, and *sG$_R$* refer to potential sources of a generalization decrement based, respectively, on the objective stimulus, the organism, the objective context, time between *S* presentations, ordinal number of *S* presentations, and aftereffects of previous trials (E. R. Guthrie was uniquely adept at the use of the principle of generalization in accounting for basic acquisition and extinction phenomena, although his usage is somewhat different from that employed here.)

H, sHs, sHr. H is the generic symbol for learned (habit) associations, sHs referring to S-S associations and sHr to S-R associations. *rHs* and *rHr* associations may also be mediated by response-produced cues. (C. L. Hull formally introduced habit strength as related to the number of trials.)

I, sI, Ir, sIs, sIr. I is the generic symbol for inhibitory processes of either a conditioned or unconditioned nature. *sI* refers to such effects when based on stimulus properties and *Ir* refers to inhibition resulting from responding. *sIs* and *sIr* refer to associative inhibition. (I. P. Pavlov was most influential in introducing the notion of inhibitory processes with respect to conditioning phenomena.)

K, Kr, sKr. K is the generic symbol for incentive motivation based on the prior occurrence of emotionally significant events following a response. *Kr* is the incentive to respond in a context without specific informative or enabling stimuli; *sKr* is the incentive to respond in the presence of an identifiable stimulus event. (K. W. Spence significantly influenced the formalization of this construct in a behavior theory of the type being developed here.)

M. M is a generic symbol for the combination of all sources of motivation relevant to the activation of some associative habit. (N. E. Miller has been highly influential in developing both primary and secondary motivation at the construct level and also relating these to their biological bases.)

R, C^{1}R, UC^{1}R, CR, UR, ur, ur'. R is the generic symbol for any response of interest, as measured in the manner appropriate to the situation. C^{1}R is a conditional response, and UC^{1}R is an unconditional response (often abbreviated to CR and UR). *ur* is the hypothetical unconditional response to a *us*, and *ur'* is the hypothetical anticipatory response to *us'*.

S, (S1, S2 . . . SX . . . SN), S1S2, (S$_1$, S$_2$, . . . S$_x$, . . . S$_n$), (S1$_1$, S1$_2$, S2$_1$, S2$_2$, iterated), $\bar{S}$, s, $\bar{s}$, UC^{1}S, C^{1}S, US, CS, uc^{1}s, c^{1}s. S is the generic symbol for an objective stimulus event and $\bar{S}$ refers to the context in the absence of S. The generic symbol for the hypothetical internal representation of an *S* is s, with $\bar{s}$ being its counterpart. Numbers on-line identify different stimuli in an array, with *X* used as a utility index; subscript numbers refer to successive occurrences of a stimulus event. UC^1S stands for a stimulus whose occurrence is not conditional upon any prior response and C^1S stands for a stimulus whose occurrence is conditional upon a prior response (US and CS are frequently used as abbreviations.) uc^1s and c^1s (abbreviated us and cs) are the hypothetical internal referents of the actual stimuli. Compound stimuli are identified by compound symbols, e.g., S1S2.

T, sT, Tr. T is the generic term for the threshold, sT when a threshold is applied to a stimulus dimension, and Tr when applied to a response dimension. (Although not directly involved with this type of theory, L. L. Thurstone developed many of the quantitative analyses involved in probability distributions of the type employed here.)

ACKNOWLEDGMENTS

I am indebted to the National Science Foundation and the National Institute of Mental Health for 25 years of continuous financial support during which time most of these ideas have germinated, and to Yale University and the University of New Mexico for the time to indulge these ideas. I am also indebted to G. R. Grice for helpful comments on preliminary drafts.

REFERENCES

Amsel, A. The role of frustrative nonreward in noncontinuous reward situations. *Psychological Bulletin*, 1958, **55**, 102–119.

Bindra, D. Motivational view of learning. *Psychological Review*, 1974, **81**, 199–213.

Birch, H. G., & Bitterman, M. E. Sensory integration and cognitive theory. *Psychological Review*, 1949, **56**, 292–308.

Bower, G. H., & Trabasso, T. R. *Attention and learning.* New York: Wiley, 1968.

Bush, R. R., & Mosteller, F. *Stochastic models for learning.* New York: Wiley, 1955.

Capaldi, E. J. Partial reinforcement: An hypothesis of sequential effects. *Psychological Review*, 1966, **73**, 459–477.

Cofer, C. N., & Appley, M. H. *Motivation: Theory and research.* New York: Wiley, 1964.

Crespi, L. P. Quantitative variation of incentive and performance in the white rat. *American Journal of Psychology*, 1942, **55**, 467–517.

Crespi, L. P. Amount of reinforcement and the level of performance. *Psychological Review*, 1944, **51**, 341–357.

Dember, W. R. Motivation and the cognitive revolution. *American Psychologist*, 974, **29**, 161–168.

Deutsch, J. A. *The structural basis of behavior.* London and New York: Cambridge University Press, 1960.

Dollard, J., & Miller, N. E. *Personality and psychotherapy.* New York: McGraw-Hill, 1950.

Estes, W. K. The statistical approach to learning theory. In S. Koch (Ed.), *Psychology: A study of a science* (Vol. 2). New York: McGraw-Hill, 1959.

Estes, W. K. New perspectives on some old issues in association theory. In N. J. Mackintosh & W. K. Honig (Eds.), *Fundamental issues in associative learning.* Halifax: Dalhousie University Press, 1969. (a)

Estes, W. K. Outline of a theory of punishment. In B. A. Campbell & R. M. Church (Eds.), *Punishment and aversive behavior.* New York: Appleton, 1969. (b)

Feldman, J. M. Added cue control as a function of reinforcement predictability. *Journal of Experimental Psychology,* 1971, **91**, 318–325.

Gantt, W. H. Conditional or conditioned, reflex or response? *Conditional Reflex,* 1966, **1**, 69–73.

Grant, D. A. A preliminary model for processing information conveyed by verbal conditioned stimuli in classical conditioning. In A. H. Black & W. F. Prokasy (Eds.), *Classical conditioning II: Current research and theory.* New York: Appleton, 1972.

Grice, G. R. Conditioning and a decision theory of response evocation. In G. H. Bower (Ed.), *The psychology of learning and motivation* (Vol. 5). New York: Academic Press, 1972.

Guthrie, E. R. *The psychology of learning.* New York: Harper, 1952.

Guthrie, E. R. Association by contiguity. In S. Koch (Ed.), *Psychology: A study of science* (Vol. 2). New York: McGraw-Hill, 1959.

Hearst, E. Excitation, inhibition, and discrimination learning. In N. J. Mackintosh & W. K. Honig (Eds.), *Fundamental issues in associative learning.* Halifax: Dalhousie University Press, 1969.

Hull, C. L. *Principles of behavior.* New York: Appleton, 1943.

Hull, C. L. *A behavior system.* New Haven: Yale University Press, 1952.

Kamin, L. J. Predictability, surprise, attention, and conditioning. In B. A. Campbell & R. M. Church (Eds.), *Punishment and aversive behavior.* New York: Appleton, 1969.

Konorski, J., & Miller, S. On two types of conditioned reflex. *Journal of General Psychology,* 1937, **16**, 264–272.

Lashley, K. S., & Wade, M. The Pavlovian theory of generalization. *Psychological Review,* 1946, **53**, 72–87.

Lawrence, D. H. Acquired distinctiveness of cues: I. Transfer between discriminations on the basis of familiarity with the stimuli. *Journal of Experimental Psychology,* 1949, **39**, 770–784.

Lawrence, D. H. The nature of a stimulus: Some relationships between learning and perception. In S. Koch (Ed.), *Psychology: A study of a science* (Vol. 5). New York: McGraw-Hill, 1963.

Levine, G., & Burke, C. J. *Mathematical model techniques for learning theories.* New York: Academic Press, 1972.

Logan, F. A. A micromolar approach to behavior theory. *Psychological Review,* 1956, **63**, 63–73.

Logan, F. A. The Hull-Spence approach. In S. Koch (Ed.), *Psychology: A study of a science* (Vol. 2). New York: McGraw-Hill, 1959.

Logan, F. A. *Incentive.* New Haven: Yale University Press, 1960.

Logan, F. A., & Ferraro, D. P. *Systematic analyses of behavior: Basic learning and motivational processes.* Hillsdale, N.J.: Lawrence Erlbaum Associates, 1978.

Loucks, R. B., & Gantt, W. H. The conditioning of striped muscle responses based upon faradic stimulation of dorsal roots and dorsal columns of the spinal cord. *Journal of Comparative Psychology,* 1938, **25**, 415–426.

Luce, R. D. *Individual choice behavior.* New York: Wiley, 1959.

MacCorquodale, K., & Meehl, P. E. Edward C. Tolman. In W. K. Estes, S. Koch, K. MacCorquodale, P. E. Meehl, C. G. Mueller, W. N. Schoenfeld, & W. S. Verplanck (Eds.), *Modern learning theory.* New York: Appleton, 1954.

Miller, N. E., & Dollard, J. *Social learning and imitation.* New Haven: Yale University Press, 1941.

Mowrer, O. H. On the dual nature of learning: A reinterpretation of "conditioning" and "problem solving." *Harvard Educational Review,* 1947, **17**, 102–148.

Mowrer, O. H. *Learning theory and behavior.* New York: Wiley, 1960.

Pavlov, I. P. [*Conditioned reflexes*] (G. V. Anrep, trans.). Oxford: Clarendon Press, 1927.

Pavlov, I. P. [*Lectures on conditioned reflexes*] (W. H. Gantt, trans.). New York: International Publishers, 1928.

Premack, D. Catching up with common sense or two sides of a generalization. In R. Glaser (Ed.), *The nature of reinforcement.* New York: Academic Press, 1971.

Rescorla, R. A. Pavlovian conditioning and its proper control procedures. *Psychological Review*, 1967, 74, 71–80.

Rescorla, R. A. Informational variables in Pavlovian conditioning. In G. H. Bower (Ed.), *The psychology of learning and motivation* (Vol. 5). New York: Academic Press, 1972.

Rescorla, R. A., & Solomon, R. L. Two-process learning theory: Relationships between Pavlovian conditioning and instrumental learning. *Psychological Review*, 1967, 74, 151–182.

Restle, F. A theory of discrimination learning. *Psychological Review*, 1955, 62, 11–19.

Restle, F. *Psychology of judgment and choice.* New York: Wiley, 1961.

Restle, F. Significance in all-or-none learning. *Psychological Bulletin*, 1965, 64, 313–325.

Sheffield, V. F. Extinction as a function of partial reinforcement and distribution of practice. *Journal of Experimental Psychology*, 1949, 39, 511–526.

Skinner, B. F. Two types of conditioned reflex. *Journal of General Psychology*, 1935, 12, 66–77.

Skinner, B. F. Are theories of learning necessary? *Psychological Review*, 1950, 57, 193–216.

Solomon, R. L. Punishment. *American Psychologiat*, 1964, 19, 239–253.

Solomon, R. L., & Turner, L. H. Discriminative classical conditioning in dogs paralyzed by curare can later control discriminative avoidance responses in the normal state. *Psychological Review*, 1962, 69, 202–219.

Spence, K. W. The nature of discrimination learning in animals. *Psychological Review*, 1936, 43, 427–449.

Spence, K. W. Theoretical interpretations of learning. In S. S. Stevens (Ed.), *Handbook of experimental psychology.* New York: Wiley, 1951.

Spence, K. W. *Behavior theory and conditioning.* New Haven: Yale University Press, 1956.

Sutherland, N. S., & Mackintosh, N. J. *Mechanisms of animal discrimination learning.* New York: Academic Press, 1971.

Tolman, E. C. *Purposive behavior in animals and men.* New York: Appleton, 1932.

Tolman, E. C. There is more than one kind of learning. *Psychological Review*, 1949, 56, 144–155.

Tolman, E. C. Principles of performance. *Psychological Review*, 1955, 62, 315–326.

Tolman, E. C., & Honzik, C. H. Introduction and removal of reward on maze performance of rats. *University of California Publications in Psychology*, 1930, 4, 257–275.

Trapold, M. A., & Overmier, J. B. The second learning process in instrumental learning. In A. H. Black & W. F. Prokasy (Eds.), *Classical conditioning II: Current research and theory.* New York: Appleton, 1972.

Wagner, A. R. Elementary associations. In H. H. Kendler & J. T. Spence (Eds.), *Essays in neobehaviorism.* New York: Appleton, 1971.

Wagner, A. R., Logan, F. A., Haberlandt, K., & Price, T. Stimulus selection in animal discrimination learning. *Journal of Experimental Psychology*, 1968, 76, 171–180.

Williams, D. R. Classical conditioning and incentive motivation. In W. F. Prokasy (Ed.), *Classical conditioning: A symposium.* New York: Appleton, 1965.

Zeaman, D. Response latency as a function of the amount of reinforcement. *Journal of Experimental Psychology*, 1949, 39, 466–483.

THE INTERNAL CONSTRUCTION
OF SPATIAL PATTERNS[1]

Lloyd R. Peterson, Leslie Rawlings,
and Carolyn Cohen

INDIANA UNIVERSITY, BLOOMINGTON, INDIANA

I. Introduction

This chapter is a systematic attempt to examine the characteristics of active visual–spatial memory. From another point of view it is an objective study of constructive imagery. A technique will be de-

[1] The authors are indebted to Jack Holsten for the execution of Experiment I, and Peter Spevak for the execution of part of Experiment IV. Judy Kiechle assisted with Experiment VI.

scribed which examines mental imagery at a microlevel. All of the experiments (save one) utilize a binary matrix technique in which auditory signals are presented to a human subject, and the latter applies spatial rules to the sequence of sounds. As a result, two-dimensional patterns are constructed in the imagination. The rationale for the use of the technique is that, first, it elicits a strong degree of confidence that imagery is what is being studied. Second, it affords more precise control of that imagery than is afforded by most other methods. Third, the technique can be extended to a wide variety of problems involving the nature of imagery, the relation of imagery to short- and long-term retention, as well as to information processing in general. The current chapter will describe a series of studies exploring various aspects of imagery, and the theoretical implications of the findings for views of imagery and memory will be discussed.

One can obtain precision on the stimulus side by presenting a drawing to the subject and requiring recognition at some later time. However, in the present case the objective was to study constructive imagery rather than memory for pictures, so a cross-modal approach was indicated. In bypassing the normal sensory mode, the contribution of central processing is better assessed.

The cross-modal approach has been used to study auditory–verbal processing after visual presentation of words. Confusions arise under these conditions which are related to the way verbal items sound, which suggests phonemic coding during verbal processing (Conrad, 1967). Since the coding follows a visual input, it must have been done by the central verbal system converting the input into a phonemic code. A variety of related findings have resulted in a tendency for short-term retention to be considered primarily if not wholly a product of a verbal short-term store.

In the last few years there has been greater recognition of the role of nonverbal factors in short-term retention. Kroll (1975) and his associates have obtained substantial evidence for the persistence of visual effects for many seconds following visual stimulation, in spite of shadowing carried on concurrently. In addition, the cross-modal approach has been used to search for visual characteristics of short-term retention after an aural input. M. J. Peterson (1975) has found memory for digits positioned in an imaginary matrix after aural presentation to be best for corner cells of the matrix. A similar superiority is found after equivalent visual presentation of a matrix.

In addition to facilitating memory, imagery is involved in a variety of information-processing operations. Instead of tests of memory, questions requiring judgments based on visual or spatial attributes can be asked about the imagery constructed by the subject. One can imagine a letter and count the number of corners (Brooks, 1968). Or, one can imagine two animals and judge their relative size (Moyer, 1973; Paivio, 1975). Experimentation of this kind indicates that information of a visual or spatial kind is somehow stored in long-term memory, and that it can be activated in an imaginal form to support answers to questions that have never been considered before. In all of these cases imagery is constructed from information learned some time in the past outside the laboratory. It seems plausible that visual information was stored during these earlier experiences, but it remains a problem to isolate the visual information from the verbal content that has been intermingled with the visual. The direction in which this line of research may go would involve experimental storage of information, rather than uncontrolled storage outside the laboratory.

Bower (1972) has described a technique devised by Brooks which seems promising. The experimenter guides subjects as they draw by giving continuing instructions about the direction and extent of lines. Subjects cannot see the designs that they draw, although they can imagine them. From the mental image subjects answer questions such as "How many times do the lines cross?" The experimenter knows that any visual information must be inferred from the constructed image due to the cross-modal input. There is no way the subject can answer on the basis of previously stored verbal information. In terms of its basic components this technique is similar to the imaginary matrix technique to be described in the next section. The latter differs chiefly in the kinds of procedures utilized, and in the types of images constructed. The two techniques were developed independently, and no attempt will be made to evaluate their relative merits.

II. Imaginary Binary Matrices

The construction of imaginary binary matrices has something in common with perception of certain visual displays. By laying out a grid and filling some positions while leaving others empty, visual patterns can be produced. The similarity of the pattern to anything likely to be seen outside the laboratory depends on the grain of the display, the density of the positions. Since subjects are required to hold such a grid or matrix of positions in memory and maintain information in it after a single presentation, it is not feasible to use fine-grain representations. A 3 X 3 matrix of binary positions is the smallest one that would permit a reasonable number of different patterns. Garner and Clement (1963) have used matrix patterns of this size in studying visual perception, and others have used larger arrays.

A sequence of three groups of three binary signals in any sensory mode could furnish the information necessary for construction of an imaginal 3 X 3 matrix. The signals that have been used in our experiments have been auditory. Words such as "black" or "white," "on" or "off," tones that were long or short—these have been used most frequently.

The technique can be easily demonstrated. Show someone a 3 X 3 matrix of dots and explain that they represent an array of lights. Then give information as to which lights are on and which are off, beginning with the first row and reading from left to right. Continue with the second and third rows in like manner. Illustrate with something easy, such as "OFF, ON, OFF; OFF, ON, OFF; OFF, ON, OFF." The lights that are on should resemble a pattern, in this case the letter I. Identify it for the subject if he fails to respond, and try again. Only a few persons fail after a couple of practice tests. Not all who respond appropriately acknowledge that they formed an image. Some say that they just know how the letter is supposed to look. Most claim to have constructed an image and then recognized the pattern.

In the initial experiments that have been reported (L. R. Peterson, Holsten, & Spevak, 1975) dots and dashes represented lights that were off or on, respectively. Subjects were able to identify letters from sequences of signals that they had never heard before with 79% accuracy, even though nothing had been said about what subset of the alphabet could be represented by the binary auditory sequence. Subjects went on to identify letters that were rotated 90°, 180° or 270°.

From a mnemonic point of view the technique was a device for combining sets of nine signals into a single chunk. The matrix coding facilitated retention of strings as long as 45 signals, with subjects attempting to recall the auditory signals at the termination of presentation by pressing keys to reproduce the sequence. Control subjects responded little better than chance beyond nine signals.

A point of interest lies in the multiple levels of information that must be retained concurrently in a multiple matrix task. First of all the auditory signals must be held long enough to permit entry of the appropriate signal in its position in the matrix. Then the imagined positive positions must be accumulated in the matrix until a recognizable patterm emerges. Finally, the symbols for previous matrices must be held while a new matrix is being described. That subjects can perform at a reasonable level is at once a tribute to human capacities and a challenge to the memory theorist to explain how the performance can be derived from theory. It should be noted that of the three levels of information storage, only one involves raw sensory stimulation. The other two levels involve secondary codes.

The multilevel storage in the present case is remindful of that postulated by Anderson and Bower (1973) in their analysis of memory requirements in processing a sentence. They found it necessary to include three independent storage devices. Considerations of what is required for these kinds of information processing should sharpen one's skepticism of any theory that holds to a single, unitary short-term store.

III. Experiment I:
Familiarity and Size of Patterns

The success of students in coding nine auditory signals into an imaginary 3 X 3 matrix led to investigations of the limits on such capacity. Larger matrices, 4 X 4 and 5 X 5, were investigated along with familiarity of the patterns which could result from matrix coding. It seemed plausible that limits on capacity would relate to familiarity of the patterns, if findings from verbal short-term retention experiments could serve as a guide.

A. METHOD

Thirty-six students from introductory psychology courses served as subjects. They were divided into two random groups, each receiving the same binary input and each recording their responses on paper having the appropriate number of blank squares arranged in a single row across a sheet of paper. The instructions emphasized that they were not to pick up their pencils until a given message had ended, yet, two subjects had to be eliminated for failing to obey this instruction.

The difference between the two groups lay in the type of instructions and practice given them. The experimental group was told to imagine a matrix, and three practice tests with blank spaces in the form of a matrix were given them. The recorded voice of the experimenter asked them at the end of a pause for writing the answer if they had seen the letter (I,D,V). They were told to write down the letter identifying a pattern before they recorded the dots and dashes that constituted the input sequence.

Subjects in the control group were urged to look for a way to code the sequence of dots and dashes. Their three practice tests utilized answer sheets in which the sequence of blank spaces went across the page in a row instead of in matrix form. Control subjects as well as experimental subjects were instructed to mark only the blanks representing a dash (long tone) to reduce time for responding to a minimum.

Following the practice tests, all subjects received eight tests on sequences nine units in length. Half of the sequences (in random order) formed a letter when organized in matrix form, while the remainder resulted in an unfamiliar pattern. The number of positive elements in a sequence was either four or five, and there was a random sequence of an equal number of dashes for each letter sequence. Two different sequences of tests were used in each group, but the first test in each case involved a letter pattern, and there were never more than two tests of letters in succession. Subjects were run in individual booths, never more than four at a time.

Following the 9-element presentations, each subject received eight tests on 16-element sequences. The letters T, L, X, and Y had been used in the 3 X 3 matrices; the letters N, H, Z, and U were among the patterns presented in the 4 X 4 matrices. Number of positive elements ranged from 8 to 10, and again there was a random sequence for each letter sequence.

Finally, eight tests on 25-element sequences were given each subject, in four of which the letters F, J, E, and M could be identified. Note that the progression from 9-element messages to 16–25 held for all subjects, so that size of matrix was confounded with stage of practice. Assuming that improvement occurs with practice, and evidence is later presented that it does, then differences due to length of sequence are underestimated by this procedure. The reason for the confounding was the desire to proceed step by step from easy to difficult tasks and maximize the possibility that the long sequences could be processed successfully.

B. RESULTS

A summary of data based on proportions of completely correct sequences is displayed in Fig. 1. There were two strong main effects.

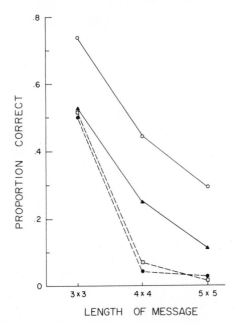

Fig. 1. Proportions of binary sequences correctly recalled in Experiment I. ○, Matrix letter; ▲, control letter; □, matrix random; ●, control random.

Recall varied inversely as the length of the sequence, and familiarity of patterns showed a marked superiority for letter patterns. In an analysis of variance of arcsin transformed proportions correct for individual subjects, length was significant, $F(2,68) = 102.54, p < .01$. Familiarity was also significant, $F(1,34) = 49.15, p < .01$. Note that not only did imagery-instructed subjects perform better with letter patterns, but so did the control subjects. Purely as sequences of sounds the letter sequences were easier than the random sequences.

The effect of instructions reached only borderline significance, $F(1,34) = 4.59, .01 < p < .05$. The interaction of instructions with familiarity was significant, $F(1,34) = 10.63, p < .01$. The interpretation seems to be that instructions made a difference only when letter patterns were involved. The limits on capacity for spatial positions and sequences of binary sounds were equal in the case of random sequences.

In a replication of this experiment under equivalent conditions, but with different subjects, length of sequence and familiarity of pattern were again significant and robust main effects. However, instructions were not significantly different, nor were any of the interactions involving instructions. This was true even though consistent differences favoring imagery instructions were found. The control subjects had their own ways of coding the auditory inputs, and they were not markedly inferior to the imagery subjects in this respect. The imagery subjects *were* forming images, for they accurately identified the letters to be found in almost every letter sequence which they successfully reproduced. However, to identify a pattern they had to hold the spatial positions in their frame for several seconds. This was obviously not easy in the case of eight or more positive elements, in a framework consisting of 16 or 25 positions.

The finding of some degree of retention after presentation of 25 binary signals is intriguing. Of course, one has only to remember the positive elements (8–10) and infer the remainder. But there is the problem of correctly positioning the positive elements. The imagery subjects can presumably group the positive signals into higher order units which are less than the complete pattern. One can notice a line forming and remember it as a unitary component, a chunk. In the case of the control subjects groupings can also be assumed to facilitate coding, in this case perhaps some kind of verbal description. When subjects are instructed to use verbal descriptions of binary sequences, it is known that the length of the necessary description is related to retention (Glanzer & Clark, 1963).

IV. Experiment II: Variable Readout

It could be said of subjects in the previous experiments that they were performing an operation which is sometimes referred to as reading an image. There are many who object to such language as based on a metaphor which has no scientific status. Pylyshyn (1973) notes that imagery is closer to the output stage of perception than the input stage, and hence the metaphor of a mind's eye reading an image is confusing if not worse. Kosslyn (1975) suggests a metaphor which uses more contemporary language. He suggests that imagery is like a pattern appearing on a cathode-ray tube attached to a digital computer. Information for producing the patterns on the visual display is stored in the computer. Of course, the computer itself does not read its own display, so the analogy is not perfect. But a machine could be built which would read that display and feed back information into the computer, something akin to the machines that read numbers on checks. At any rate, Kosslyn is attempting to point to a sense in which imagery can be interpreted in ways analogous to reading. What is read? Structures active in perception are interpreted. What does the reading? Mechanisms which are active in visual perception do the interpretation. When one asks a subject to construct an image and then describe it, operations are performed which are also involved in perception.

The previous experiments on internal construction of binary matrices suggest reading an image by identifying a letter pattern and by description of the elements that make up the pattern. In this section an experiment is described which manipulated type of readout. Instead of requiring a binary description that reproduced the input sequence, in some conditions transformations of the input were required. These transformations were accomplished by following rules related to the starting point and spatial direction of the interpretation of the image. Thus, the output was related to the input by the mediation of a spatial grammar. It was hypothesized that transformations of this kind would be learned readily by subjects instructed to construct binary matrices, while equivalent transformations of binary serial order would be accomplished infrequently and with difficulty by control subjects.

Figure 2 displays one of the four classes of transformation required of subjects in Experiment II. The four kinds of readout that were used are as follows. In the *forward* readout the order of normal reading in our culture was followed. Beginning with the top row of a 3 × 3 matrix, one read across the row from left to right, and then continued in like manner with the middle and the bottom row in that order. Correct performance reproduced the input order of the

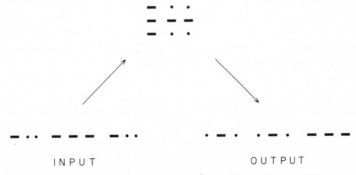

INPUT   OUTPUT

Fig. 2. Illustration of a sequence of binary signals transformed into a different sequence by means of an imaginary two-dimensional matrix. In this case the letter T lies on its side in the imaginary array. It is interpreted by reading up the columns starting with the column on the right, as in the bottom–top readout.

signals. The *backward* readout involved reading from right to left across rows, starting with the bottom row and continuing with the middle and upper rows. In this way the input order of signals was reversed. *Top–bottom* readout required reading down the columns of the matrix beginning with the left column and continuing with the middle and right columns. The *bottom–top* readout required reading up the columns beginning on the right and continuing with the middle and left columns.

A. METHOD

A total of 28 subjects from introductory courses was randomly divided into imagery and control groups. Subjects in the imagery group were instructed in binary matrix construction followed by practice in the four types of readout that might be required on a given test. Four practice tests accompanied each of the types of readout instruction to insure understanding of the procedure. Control subjects were told to use some form of grouping as an aid to performance. They were required to produce transformations of the input order that would lead to the same responses as the imagery subjects, but they were told to go about it in a different way. Instructions were straightforward in the *forward* and *backward* conditions; subjects were told to recall the auditory signals in a forward or backward order. The control equivalent of the *top–bottom* condition instructed subjects to *skip forward*. After reporting the first signal, the next two signals were to be skipped and the signal in the fourth position reported next, and so on through the sequence. Subjects were then to recycle back to the beginning and skip forward starting with the second signal. Finally, on the third cycle they would start with the third signal and again skip forward. This procedure produced the same order as the *top–bottom* readout. *Skip backward* instructions were the counterpart of the *bottom–top* instructions, and they were essentially a reversal of the *skip forward* instructions.

In this experiment subjects responded by pressing keys on a teletypewriter connected to a PDP-8L computer. The dots and dashes were controlled by the same computer and were heard over earphones by the subject in one of two small rooms adjacent to the computer. At the start of a test, the teletypewriter typed out the label for the kind of response order required in that particular test, i.e., *top–bottom* for the imagery group or *skip forward* for the control condition. After listening to the signals the subject would attempt to type out the appropriate sequence of dots and dashes. Both groups of subjects were told to close their eyes while listening to the auditory signals as an aid to concentration. Practice tests utilized the letters I, H, X, and U.

During the experiment proper two blocks of 20 tests were given with sequences which imagery subjects could organize to produce the letters T, L, U, Y, and J. The experimenter at no time indicated what subset of the alphabet was in use during the experimental session, and no knowledge of results was given save in four early practice tests with the practice letters. Four orientations of the letters were possible, an upright or 0° rotation and counterclockwise rotations of 90°, 180°, or 270°. Imagery subjects identified each letter aloud before typing in the early practice tests, but during the experiment they were told to imagine the letter and type its description as rapidly as possible without speaking.

Since there were five letters that were used with four orientations of each, no pattern was repeated within a block of 20 tests. The first encounter with a specific sequence of sounds occurred during the first block of 20 tests, and the second occurrence was at some random test in the second block. Response times were measured from the end of the ninth signal to the beginning of the ninth key press. Failure to complete a response within 24 sec after the end of stimulus presentation was counted as an incorrect response. Total time from the end of one sequence to the beginning of the next test was 26 sec.

B. RESULTS

The differential instructions to the two groups produced significant differences in performance. Imagery instructions led to superior accuracy in performance, as can be seen in Table I. Presentation order and instructions were between subject factors, and type of readout and block were within subject comparisons. The main effect of instruction was found to be significant, $F(1,24) = 10.15, p < .01$, as was type of readout, $F(3,72) = 39.21, p < .01$. Relatively few errors occurred in the *forward* condition for either group. There was a consistent superiority of the imagery instructions over the control instructions for all comparisons in both blocks of tests. The interaction of instructions with readout type was not significant, so not too much can be made of the finding that instructional differences were largest with the *top–bottom* and *bottom–top* readouts. The improvement from first to second block is noteworthy, $F(1,24) =$

TABLE I

PROPORTIONS OF CORRECT SEQUENCES
WITH SEVERAL READOUTS, EXPERIMENT II

Block	Group	Readout			
		Forward	Backward	Top–bottom	Bottom–top
First	Imagery	.76	.39	.44	.44
	Control	.67	.31	.26	.17
Second	Imagery	.87	.57	.66	.50
	Control	.69	.39	.23	.24

12.31, $p < .01$. All conditions showed improvement from first to second half of the tests save the *top–bottom* condition of the control group.

Response times were analyzed as mean times for nine key presses for each subject within a given condition over all sequences, right or wrong. An analysis of variance of these mean times converted to log ($X + 1$) scores indicated that type of readout was significant, $F(3,72) = 134.23$, $p < .01$. The readout by instruction interaction was likewise significant, $F(3,72) = 20.28$, $p < .01$. The means of the raw times are listed in Table II. Forward readout, reproduction of the input order, was the fastest mode of responding, as might be expected. Auditory memory could be assumed to effectively aid any strategy that might be attempted in reproduction of the original order. Of greater interest is the finding that nonimagery instructions resulted in faster responding than imagery instructions in both the *forward* and *backward* condition, while the differences were reversed

TABLE II

MEAN RESPONSE TIME (SEC) FOR SEVERAL READOUTS

Block	Group	Readout			
		Forward	Backward	Top–bottom	Bottom–top
First	Imagery	8.62	11.25	12.00	12.71
	Control	6.52	8.16	12.84	13.83
Second	Imagery	7.12	9.90	10.98	11.55
	Control	5.74	7.37	12.56	12.36

in the remaining two conditions. Response times decreased in the second block, $F(1,24) = 24.97, p < .01$.

When times for correct sequences were analyzed separately, the above findings based on all responses were supported. The analysis collapsed over order and block so that enough correct responses were available to permit each subject to be represented by a mean time score in every condition. The log $(X + 1)$ values again showed a significant interaction of readout type and instruction, as did the main effect of readout type.

C. DISCUSSION

The students who were instructed to construct imaginary matrices clearly performed the required transformations more often than the control subjects. However, control subjects responded faster than the imagery subjects in the *forward* and *backward* conditions. What can be inferred from this pattern of response times?

The imagery subjects were learning to construct a mediating representation that was new to them, so it is not surprising that they should be relatively slow compared to the controls, at least in that condition in which usual techniques were effective, namely, reproduction of the order of the input. Control subjects should be slow and inaccurate in those conditions in which the usual strategies were inadequate. On the other hand, the imagery subjects could then use the same basic representation with its associated interpretive system for all conditions, and therefore response times for different readout conditions should not differ greatly. Of course, as mentioned before, the *forward* readout did have the advantage of available auditory cues and their normal reproduction. But differences among the other three types of readout should be minimal. The mean response times mask a combination of the auditory store and the spatial store.

Experimentation on the Binet letter square is related to the current experiment in some respects (Fernald, 1912). Nine letters were presented visually in the form of a 3 X 3 array. Subjects read the letters in the normal way and memorized them during several such reading trials. Later, recall was tested in four different ways similar to the differential readout of the present experiment. Even subjects who were considered to be "visual" learners were found to be slower in recall when orders other than that of the original reading were required. The conclusion reached by the investigator was that even those learners who utilized visual imagery to the greatest extent could not hold all nine letters in an image at once.

Simon (1969) reported results supporting a similar conclusion in experiments using a digit square and measures of reaction times to probes for single positions. He suggests that the image of the square is stored as an hierarchical list structure, each row stored as a list which is subordinate to a list of the lists. He notes that a list-processing theory would predict that a subject should take twice as long to learn up–down relationships in addition to left–right relations as to learn the latter only.

The current experiment indicates that students could generally store the entire matrix of binary alternatives in a single presentation. More trials were required for letter and digit matrices, but assuming that a 9-letter square exceeds the limited capacity of imagery representation in the working memory, it need not be the case that arrays representing lesser amounts of information (binary digits) would also exceed that capacity. Indeed, the current experiments present evidence to the contrary. Of course, a binary matrix is a special case, since only the positive positions need be maintained, while the negative positions are available by inference. In any event, the 3 × 3 matrix seems to be well within the capacity of the imaginal memory. The letter or decimal square may exceed the limits.

For letter combinations the capacity to gain access in parallel may be more limited. Weber and Harnish (1974) provide evidence that three-letter words can be apprehended in parallel. It is reasonable to expect visual–spatial memory to have differential limits of capacity related to the kinds of symbols that are visualized. The same generalization could be made about verbal short-term storage. The discovery of a limited capacity for imaginal representation does not rule out a spatial interpretation of imagery, one not aptly described in terms of hierarchies of lists. In reading a page of print, a single fixation between eye movements permits intake of a limited amount of information. It may be that an imaginal "fixation" is even more limited in scope, and that the grain of imaginal representations is markedly gross in comparison to perception. Nevertheless it remains plausible that spatial representations correspond in some degree to spatial perceptual experience.

An explanation in terms of hierarchical list structure is more plausible for the control subjects in the present experiment. They were told to use grouping, and there were pauses between groups of three signals to make grouping easy. The representations of the signals could have taken the form of three lists of three signals each. On the other hand there are other interesting possibilities, one of which arises in connection with the performance of the backward transformation. Anders and Lillyquist (1971) report that in backward recall of digits subjects tend to group in two's or three's. Subjects report that in backward recall a group becomes available to which they have direct access. Objective evidence for the grouping was found in reaction time data showing longer pauses between groups than within groups of digits. Now, an introspective report of direct access to a group of digits hints at a visual image, but by itself is not to be taken very seriously. However, other evidence such as the Weber and Harnish (1974) probe data also suggests parallel access to a limited number of alphanumeric characters. It may be that in the present experiment each group of three digits may have been represented by the control subjects as a spatial image. If the experimental subjects were able to construct two-dimensional arrays in the imagination after appropriate instructions, they must also be able to construct a spatial representation of a group of three. Such a spatial representation could readily have been formed by the control subjects without explicit instructions, and this might have been the basis for backward report for the control subjects. The method or strategy would not be particularly helpful for the columnar readouts without appropriate instruction. The hierarchical explanation of the control performance would take the form of a group of three signals united by an image, with a list of images ordering the images at a higher level. Such a model is compatible with some contemporary structural analyses of serial verbal learning (Johnson, 1972). The data from the present experiment cannot be taken as strong evidence for such a model, since the explanation was conceived after the fact. Nevertheless, such an explanation seems to account for the response time data of the control subjects. It could also account for backward recall in other experimental situations.

V. Experiment III: Readout after Rotation

The previous experiment required subjects in the imagery group to keep track of the pattern as well as its orientation while applying one of four types of interpretation to the imaginal representation. A modification of this process was studied by introducing a stage of processing in which rotation of the representation was required, following which a standard interpretation of the representation was applied. Students were instructed to rotate the matrix representation into a standard orientation and then describe this imaginary array in a left-to-right order, from top row to bottom row. Even though the set of transformations was objectively the same as in Experiment II, the difficulty of the interpretation was eased by the addition of the rotational stage.

A. METHOD

A single group of 24 naive subjects from the population previously described was given imagery instructions and practice similar to that of the previous experiment. Then the letters Y, V, L, and T were used in three blocks of experimental tests. In the first block 16 tests in four orientations of the four letters were presented by means of binary auditory signals, and subjects attempted to type a description of the matrix representation as though the letter were in an upright orientation, no matter what the actual orientation had been after presentation. Thus, the output by the subject involved a transformation of 0°, 90°, 180°, or 270° from the matrix that was presented.

In a second block of 16 tests, the same patterns appeared in a different order, and subjects were instructed to type the binary description of the pattern in an inverted orientation. New input–output relationships were required, since a different response pattern was related to each of the previously presented sequences. In the third block, eight tests in length, the response was again a description of an upright letter.

There were a few changes from the method of Experiment II. The tests were self-paced, in contrast to the experimenter pacing of the earlier experiment. Knowledge of results in the form of the letter in an upright matrix representation was printed on the teletype after the ninth key press and the ready signal for a new test occurred 5 sec later. Two different orders of presentation were used in each block over the group of subjects.

B. RESULTS

The main finding was a robust improvement in proportions of sequences correctly transformed from block to block. Figure 3 indicates that performance in Block 2 improved over Block 1 even though different rotations of the representation were required. There was further improvement in Block 3. In an analysis of variance of the arcsin proportions correct, block produced the only significant result, $F(2,44) = 7.20, p < .01$. Inspection of Fig. 3 suggests that a 90° rotation of input to output resulted in lower performance in each of the blocks. However, rotation was not significant at the level of the

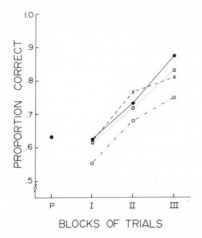

Fig. 3. Proportions correct in Experiment III. Performance in practice (*P*) was followed by three blocks of tests. •, 0°; ○, 90°; X, 180°; □, 270°.

criterion which was in use, though it did meet a lesser level of significance, $F(3,66) = 3.09$, $.01 < p < .05$.

Examination of the data showed that six subjects contributed most of the errors. Their overall performance in Block 1 ranged from 0% correct to 25%, while the other subjects were correct on 50–60% of the tests. Two of the six showed improvement in later blocks, but the others did not. Analysis of the data with these six subjects removed produced higher means, but the analysis of variance did not require a different interpretation from that for the whole group.

A high level of performance for the 18 subjects who did learn the imagery task can be seen in their proportions of correct sequences in Block 3; the 0°, 90°, 180°, and 270° rotations being .97, .94, .97, and .94, respectively. The corresponding mean response times for correct sequences over the last eight tests were 5.79, 6.05, 6.27, and 5.73 sec, respectively. The latter did not differ significantly from each other, $F(3,16) < 1$. It may be asked why rotation did not take differing lengths of time, since other studies have found a linear relationship between time and amount of rotation (Shepard, 1975). The answer is probably that rotation was inserted into a complex task in the present study, and therefore the time required was masked by other components of information processing. The time required to standardize the orientation of a two-dimensional, familiar pattern is relatively small compared with the time taken by the whole task.

VI. Experiment IV: Three-Dimensional Frames

Experiment IV involved two independent studies which examined the concept of capacity from a different point of view. Imaginary spatial construction was extended to a third dimension, depth. Subjects were instructed to imagine three matrices, one behind the other, so that a 3 X 3 X 3 cube resulted. A pattern resembling a letter might be found in any of several planes, for instance at a 45° angle to the line of regard, or in other cases parallel to it. In the former case no part of a letter was obscured by any other, so the condition was known to the experimenter as the *open* condition. When the pattern was in a plane parallel to the line of regard, parts of the letter hid other parts, if one were looking head on at the cube, and instances of this made up the *hidden* condition. In viewing a cube with the eyes, it was assumed that identification of a pattern would be easier with an open view than with a hidden view. Therefore, to the extent that imagery shared characteristics with visual perception, a corresponding difference in difficulty should be expected with an imaginary cube.

A. FIRST STUDY

Nine subjects who had performed well in Experiment III were persuaded to come back for a second session after an interval of several days. A three-dimensional marble game was used to demonstrate how they were to line up three matrices in the imagination to form a cube. Two arrangements of the letter I were shown in appropriate positions in the cube. Subjects were told to construct an imaginary cube from auditory signals and then identify a letter by typing out a two-dimensional description in dots and dashes as in the earlier experiment. Thus, the input consisted of 27 signals, while the subjects responded with nine on the teletype, collapsing the three-dimensional array into two dimensions. Ten practice tests were given with the letters I and X appearing in different orientations. The letters T, L, U, and Y were presented once each upright in the frontal plane.

The experiment was then run using T, L, U, and Y in two blocks of 24 tests each. In each block there were eight tests in each of three conditions, a *hidden* condition, an *open* condition, and a *control* condition in which the letter was in the last matrix only, i.e., in a plane at a 90° angle to the line of regard.

Identification of letters which were distributed over three matrices was only slightly poorer than that for letters confined to a single matrix. The mean proportions correct for *hidden, open,* and *control* conditions were .82, .82, and .94 for the first block, and .82, .93, and .96 for the second block of tests. For these experienced subjects, at least, there was no difficulty in identifying letter patterns at any angle in a three-dimensional imaginary cube. Neither of the main effects, plane or block, was significant in an analysis of variance of the arcsin proportions correct. Even though the *open* condition appeared to show the only improvement from first to second block, there is no evidence from the statistical analysis that this was other than a chance finding. In any event it is clear that interposition did not produce any marked deterioration in identification of the pattern, since accuracy was high in all conditions. Lack of an effect from interposition is in agreement with findings of Neisser and Kerr (1973) in a more traditional experimental approach. Imagery and visual perception appear to differ in the effect of interposition.

B.   SECOND STUDY

Since the relatively practiced subjects of the first study had performed at a surprisingly high level, a larger group of naive subjects was studied in a single half-hour session to test the generality of the initial findings. Eighteen subjects from an introductory psychology course were tested. Two others began the experiment but did not finish, one due to a power failure, and the other when a language deficiency became apparent.

As in the previous experiment, the marble game was used to facilitate understanding. The auditory signals were the words "marble" and "no" spoken by the experimenter, instead of dots and dashes controlled by the computer. The subjects responded by vocalizing the name of the letter, rather than using a teletype. In a first series of practice tests the letters X, H, T, L, U, and Y were presented upright in a single matrix, followed by knowledge of results after the subject's response. Then 12 tests of the same letters in a variety of orientations in a single matrix were given, again with knowledge of results. Finally, the letter I was shown in several positions involving three matrices or planes of the marble game.

There followed 12 experimental tests on the same letters with no knowledge of results. Each of the letters occurred once in each block of six tests in a random order for each subject. Over the two blocks each letter was used once in each of the two interposition conditions, *hidden* and *open*. Patterns were described at a rate of approximately one word per second, save that between groups of three there were 2 sec, and between sets of nine signals there were 3 sec. The experimenter waited for the subject to either vocalize the name of a letter or indicate his failure to discover the pattern.

The proportion of correct responses for the *hidden* condition was .65, while that for the *open* condition was .72. There was no significant difference in the mean proportions correct, $t(17) = 1.30$, $p > .05$. Thus, the small superiority of the *open* condition over the *hidden* condition could very easily have been due to chance variation.

A variable that was found to be significantly related to correct identification of the letter patterns was number of positive positions in the pattern. Two of the patterns were formed by four positive elements, two by five elements, and two by seven elements. The proportions correct in order of increasing number of elements were .79, .72, and .54. An analysis of variance of numbers of correct identifications for these differing numbers of positive elements produced significant results, $F(2,34) = 6.02$, $p < .01$.

The limit on capacity in this experiment seemed to be related to number of positive elements, rather than size of the frame of possible positions. The framework was stable, a relatively permanent part of memory; the positive positions were transient and subject to forgetting. Of course, some of the errors may have been failures to place the elements correctly rather than forgetting after they had been placed. It took a fair amount of concentration to listen carefully while 27 signals were given over a period of half a minute.

Note that to recognize an angle the subject had to make use of the dimension of depth. Angles were not identifiable in any single matrix. One could not add an angle from one matrix to a line from another in an additive combination of features. There had to be preservation of positions from all the matrices to form a pattern. Only when the second and third matrices were combined with the first was there an integrated pattern. It is possible that a fair guess about the identity of the letter could be made in some cases after two matrices had been described. In any event, the task involved some intriguing combinatorial properties that call for further study.

The failure to find an effect of interposition in visual imagery is not surprising. The point of view of the observer can readily be changed so that a hidden object or part of a pattern is no longer behind the interposing object. In visual perception one can move to see behind something, but it is accomplished faster in the case of internal imagery. Indeed, this is the hallmark of imagery; one can rotate objects or whole scenes. A part of a scene can be enlarged, if it is of particular interest. Objects can be removed from their usual contexts and imagined in a bizarre setting.

VII. Experiment V:
Recognition of Previously Unseen Patterns

The previous experiments demonstrated that subjects are able to identify familiar patterns which have not been presented visually. Experiment I indicates that nonsense patterns are not particularly useful as mnemonic aids. This section reports the extent to which visual nonsense patterns can be recognized in a tachistoscopic exposure even thought they have never been seen before.

A. REHEARSAL STUDY

A delayed recognition test was given following presentation of binary auditory signals describing a nonsense pattern in an imaginary matrix. The delay was necessitated by the consideration that a test immediately after presentation would be influenced by the availability of signals retained in auditory memory. During the retention interval the subject counted backward by threes to minimize rehearsal of the signals.

The binary signals in the recognition studies were sequences of the terms "black" or "white" spoken by the experimenter at a rate such that nine signals took about 6 sec. Again the signals were grouped into three sets of three. The pattern in this case was to be imagined as made up of black squares against a white background.

The tachistoscopic exposure showed four or five black squares drawn on a white card. Half of the recognition tests exposed a single pattern which was that which had been described by the sequence of blacks and whites. The other half of the tests used a pattern differing from the one described by displacement of one black cell of the matrix. The empty cells of the matrix were not outlined in the tachistoscopic exposure. There was one pattern exposed in each recognition test.

The recognition test was cued by the experimenter saying, "ready," after which the subject pressed a telegraph key which operated the tachistoscope for a 500-msec exposure of the test

TABLE III

PROPORTIONS OF CORRECT RECOGNITIONS
AFTER DIFFERING TIMES FOR REHEARSAL

	Retention interval	
Amount of rehearsal	0 Sec	10 Sec
2 Sec	.91	.86
7 Sec	.98	.91

figure. Subjects responded "same" or "different"; 15 sec elapsed between tests. Appropriate practice was given separately in imagining letter shapes from auditory signals, imagining unfamiliar shapes, using the tachistoscope, and counting backward. Practice was also given on combining all of the operations into an integrated test.

The initial study was a 2 × 2 factorial design in which amount of rehearsal time following presentation of the binary signals was either 2 or 7 sec, and the retention interval filled with backward counting was either 0 or 10 sec. Eleven naive subjects were given four tests in each of the four experimental conditions in a mixed order.

The proportions of correct recognitions are shown in Table III. The main finding is that recognition was quite accurate, even with minimal rehearsal followed by 10 sec of counting. The small superiority of 7 sec of rehearsal is not statistically significant, nor is the decrement over the long retention interval. There is no doubt that subjects were recognizing patterns never seen before. However, their efficient performance seems to have produced a ceiling effect, so that rehearsal could not improve their recognition accuracy by very much. Recognition memory for pictures has also been found to be resistant to forgetting.

B. INTERFERENCE STUDY

A second study was designed to make recognition of a previously unseen unfamiliar pattern more difficult. A possible source of interference was introduced by having the subjects construct two nonsense shapes in relatively rapid succession. Since either of the shapes in the double presentation could be tested, there were three experimental conditions. In the *single* condition only one shape was described in binary signals by the experimenter. As in the rehearsal study, there was a 2-sec pause for the subject to rehearse his image, and then 12 sec of backward counting followed. In the *double first* condition two shapes were described, and the first shape was tested at a retention interval equal to that of the *single* condition. Specifically, nine words were spoken, there was a 2-sec pause, nine more signals were given over a 6-sec period, there was another 2-sec pause, and the subject counted backward for 4 sec. The retention interval was in this way filled with presentation of a second pattern plus a period of counting. The introduction of the second pattern suggests a retroactive interference paradigm. In the *double second* condition two shapes were similarly described, but the second shape was tested. To equalize the retention interval there was 12 sec of counting after the end of the 2-sec rehearsal period that followed presentation of the second pattern.

Fourteen naive subjects were obtained from the usual population. They never knew before a given test how many shapes would be described, nor which one would be tested after the double presentations. They did not have to indicate whether the test item had been first or second during presentation on positive tests. Nine tests were given, three in each condition in a mixed order after practice tests similar to the earlier experiment. For half the subjects there were five "same" items and four "different" items. With the other half same and different tests were interchanged. In a final attempt to increase the difficulty of the task the tachistoscopic exposure was reduced to 200 msec.

The mean proportions correct for the *single, double first,* and *double second* conditions were .88, .81, and .57, respectively. An analysis of variance indicated that the conditions differed significantly, $F(2,26) = 10.69$, $p < .01$. There was little forgetting after 12 sec of counting backward when only one nonsense pattern was presented. Nor was there much retroactive interference when a second pattern followed shortly after the first. There was a substantial effect of a previous pattern on recognition of a shape presented second. The recognition of this shape was little better than chance.

Why was there such a marked inferiority in recognition of the second shape? To say that proactive interference produced forgetting does not go far in explaining it. It could also be called a primacy effect, but again naming it does not suffice. A similar finding has been reported in short-term retention of two paired-associates (L. R. Peterson & Peterson, 1962), in which the response presented first was recalled better than the second. In the present case there is no reason to believe that competition at time of test was a factor, since it was a recognition test and the subject did not have to choose between first and second tests. A difference in effectiveness of coding seems the most likely reason for this primacy effect. The first pattern was given more careful attention than the second, or lingering effects of the first pattern may have disrupted coding of the second pattern. Such an explanation could apply to both the imaginal and verbal cases.

It does not seem reasonable, however, to explain the recognition performance of the current experiment by memory for the words used to describe the matrix. Short-term retention studies of words suggest memory for nine words over 12 sec of counting backward would be quite poor. Nevertheless, to check on the possibility five control subjects were tested under three conditions similar to those of the present experiment. Recall of the verbal signals was required instead of the recognition test. The proportions of sequences correctly recalled for the *single, double first,* and *double second* conditions were 0, .13, and .07, respectively. It seems clear that students in the recognition experiments would not have been successful by checking the tachistoscopic exposure against a remembered set of the original signals.

We conclude that subjects stored information about the imagined matrix that they constructed in response to the binary signals. They stored the pattern. Not that the storage of labels describing the pattern might not have helped them; indeed, in remembering pictures we may store labels identifying them. Even nonsense forms tend to elicit verbal labels in many instances. It seems plausible that both verbal and imaginal information contributed to the recognition. These verbal labels were not the signals given originally, but labels elicited by the imaginary pattern.

A final point to be made is that the retention of previously unseen patterns extended over activity that would seem to rule out simple rehearsal of the imaginary pattern. Conceivably the pattern could have been rehearsed during counting, since it was a dissimilar activity. But for the *double first* condition, the construction of the second pattern should have insured disruption of continuing rehearsal of the first pattern. Therefore, something of the nature of learning resulted from the imaginary construction of a pattern.

VIII.   Experiment VI:
Concurrent Vocal and Imaginal Rehearsal

The previous experiments have examined the construction of imagery in visual–spatial memory, a process which is hypothesized to have some characteristics differing from auditory–verbal memory. From this point of view there is no single short-term store, but two or more systems can support short-term retention. These systems are not defined in terms of physiological structures, but are characterized as having independent functional organization. They are not separate from general memory, but are portions of that memory that are currently active.

To the extent that two systems are appropriately organized, they may be active concurrently on different tasks. Memorizing can occur while the subject is engaged in irrelevant vocalization (Murray, 1968; L. R. Peterson, 1969). One can count or repeat a syllable over and over while one looks at other symbols to memorize, add, or solve an anagram. In general, one can function quite well at two concurrent symbolic activities, if one of these is an overlearned routine.

The possibility of performing two memory tasks concurrently is an intriguing possibility. A demonstration of this has been reported by Baddeley and Hitch (1974, p. 69ff.). At the same time that subjects listened to a list of words which were to be recalled later, they alternated between looking at groups of digits and writing down their memory for them. Not only were subjects able to perform these two tasks concurrently, but the typical recency effect of free recall emerged in the serial-position curve. Concurrent storage and recall of the digits did not disrupt whatever mechanism is responsible for the recency effect in free recall of the words.

The present experiment examined a single task, free recall, when subjects had been trained to engage in two kinds of processing of the words concurrently. Continuous vocalization of some of the words went on at the same time that the other words were processed in the imagination. The 16 naive subjects were given practice tests on rehearsing aloud continuously, adding a new word to the string of previously presented words, until at the end of a list four words were being rehearsed. They were also given practice in forming images that would integrate previous words that had been presented with the current word. Further practice combined the two tasks into one concurrent task.

Ten lists of eight common words were presented in a memory drum at a 4-sec rate in the experiment that followed the practice. Words were alternately typed in black or red. Words of one color were to be recycled continuously aloud in an ever-lengthening sequence as new words became available. Words of the other color were to be viewed but not vocalized as rapid recycling of the other set continued unabated. The set of words assigned to a given condition was counterbalanced over subjects. Subjects were tested individually. They were given an immediate, written, free recall test during a 1-min period after each list. After 10 lists had been tested, subjects were given an unexpected final free recall test on all of the words that had been presented.

In the immediate recall tests 92% of the vocalized words were recalled, while only 66% of the imagined words were recalled. The difference in mean number recalled is significant, $t(15) = 4.35$, $p <$ .01. In the final-recall test, this difference was reversed: 47% of the imagined words were recalled compared with only 26% of the vocalized words. Again, the means of the numbers recalled are significantly different, $t(15) = 4.25$, $p < .01$.

A number of investigations have found that rote repetition provides high immediate recall of words, but that it is inferior to other forms of processing at longer retention intervals (Craik & Watkins, 1973; Mazuryk & Lockhart, 1974). The point of interest in the present experiment is that a single class of verbal items was divided and processed differentially during the same period of time. Evidence for the differential processing includes the two kinds of instructions, the kind of vocal behavior observed during the list presentation, and the corresponding differences in retention. It is strong evidence for the concurrent operation of two independent functional systems with idosyncratic features.

It should be noted parenthetically that the imagery in this experiment is not necessarily the same as that constructed in the binary matrix studies. Imagining the referents of words is not the same as imagining positions in two- or three-dimensional space. Investigators studying modality-specific interference have inserted visual or verbal interfering tasks into the retention interval following a visual or auditory task. Interference between tasks in the same modality is sometimes found and sometimes not. Thus, visual tasks during a retention interval interfere with spatial memory for an earlier task (Salthouse, 1975). On the other hand, a visual task during the retention interval does not necessarily interfere with memory for words coded by imagery (Kosslyn, Holyoak, & Huffman, 1976). Furthermore, a concurrent visual task during presentation of a list of words does not have a greater interfering effect on concrete words than on abstract words (Baddeley, Grant, Wight, & Thomson, 1975). The concurrent visual task in the latter study was pursuit tracking, and pairs of words were presented aurally as the other task. The last three pairs of words were never tested first, to eliminate recall from primary memory. The failures to find modality-specific interference raise interesting questions, but they probably do not bear on our current interest in possibilities for avoiding interference between two kinds of processing. Failures to find interference suggest independence of two systems, in the above-mentioned experiments independence within a modality. There seems to be no reason from our point of view why a visual and a spatial task could not be carried out independently of one another when there was no great similarity between the two apart from their modality being shared. Deutsch (1975) has found interference from tones on memory for a previous tone, but no interference from digits presented in the auditory mode. Reitman (1974) has found more interference on memory for words with interpolated detection of syllables than with detection of tones. Thus, similarity within a modality has to be considered in interpreting attempts to produce modality-specific interference.

IX. Memory Systems

The imagery which has been examined in this chapter may be described as having been constructed in active visual–spatial memory. The latter has many characteristics similar to auditory–verbal memory, as well as some characteristics which are different. From one point of view, the two could be called *functional stores,* but only with the understanding that they are active portions of general memory rather than discrete physiological structures (L. R. Peterson & Johnson, 1971). The concept of THE short-term store says too much and it says too little. It says too much in suggesting a physiological structure which is independent of a long-term store. It says too little because there is more than one system which actively maintains information for short intervals of time. The auditory–verbal system is only one such system; the visual–spatial system is another. The auditory–musical system may be another (Deutsch, 1975). These general systems normally interact with one another, but they can also act independently with minimal interference in special circumstances. Whether some innate mechanisms are specific to each of them is an interesting question, but there is little doubt that past learning has left them well integrated.

The visual–spatial memory system of the adult is the end product of a long history of learning experiences. The imaginary binary matrix is learned as a subsystem of the more general system, just as verbal mnemonic devices of memory experts build upon the verbal system. Of course, mnemonists also make liberal use of visual imagery, so it might be asked whether it is necessary to postulate two systems where one might be more parsimonious. The answer is that to the extent that they can be experimentally separated, it is useful to distinguish between them.

X. Visual–Spatial Memory

A summary of the characteristics of visual–spatial memory will begin with a number of commonalities with auditory–verbal memory.

1. Visual–spatial memory has a limited capacity. It can be measured in terms of number of discrete positions that may be held in a spatial framework for immediate report. The limits seem to be of the same order of magnitude as the magic number 7 found with verbal immediate memory. Performance is high with four or five positions, lower with seven as in the three-dimensional study, and lower yet with 8 and 10 in Experiment I. When random patterns were tested in Experiment I, positions in space were not reported any more accurately than sequences of sounds.

2. Capacity is greater when spatial positions can be integrated into familiar patterns. Chunking is also a well-known aspect of verbal memory, where the chunks consist of words and phrases. Furthermore, verbal memory can provide a label for a pattern in visual memory, an example of coordination of visual and verbal memory.

3. Information can be maintained by rehearsal for an indefinite period in visual–spatial as well as auditory–verbal memory. Convincing evidence for this comes from the three-dimensional experiment, where upward of half a minute was required for all of the signals to be presented during which time the earlier positions had to be maintained while new positions were established.

4. Retention beyond maintenance rehearsal occurs following activity in the visual–spatial memory, just as in verbal rehearsal. The best evidence for this was found in the interference experiment when introduction of a second shape after the first did not materially affect recognition of the first. It is doubtful that rehearsal of the first could have continued during presentation of the second, and therefore something other than continuing rehearsal was the basis for recognition. Again, in verbal memory there is retention after intervening activity has cut off rehearsal during a delay period.

5. A primacy effect can be found in visual–spatial memory which has its counterpart in auditory–verbal memory.

6. Entry of information into either visual–spatial or auditory–verbal memory can be cross-modal, indicating constructive imagery occurs for both.

It could be argued that with all of these common characteristics there is no need to distinguish two kinds of active memory. There are information-processing mechanisms that operate on whatever task is presented the student. Different tasks require differing degrees of involvement of the various processing mechanisms, and hence there are some superficial differences in performance reflecting the various kinds of tasks which are presented to the subject. But to say there are different memories is misleading.

On the other hand, there are some further considerations that suggest it is useful to distinguish at least two memory systems. Chief among them is:

1. The nature of organization of visual–spatial memory, the positioning of information in three-dimensional space. Not that there is a one-to-one correspondence between an imagined object and its counterpart in the external world. There is instead a second-order isomorphism in the representation of spatial objects, to use Shephard's terminology (1975). The brain constructs a model of the outside world, in a "sandbox in the head" to use a metaphor of Attneave (1972). In visual perception a third dimension is added to the two-dimensional image on the retina, and activity in this system is what we refer to as visual–spatial memory. The same constructive mechanisms are used in imagery as in perception.

2. The three-dimensional nature of visual–spatial memory permits operations such as rotation of representations relative to the orientation of the framework in which the representations are positioned.

3. A further consequence is limited parallel access to portions of the spatial field in contrast to the serial access of verbal memory. As a result representations based on spatial relationships can be interpreted in ways that have only a remote indirect counterpart in verbal memory. Differential readouts of images are readily carried out.

4. Visual–spatial memory has no direct output which can easily be observed, which is quite different from verbal memory, in which articulatory mechanisms provide rapid, direct output. The articulatory coding in the case of verbal memory provides phonemic features, even when a nonauditory input has occurred. When articulation is irrelevant to the verbal message, then phonemic similarity is no longer a factor if the input was visual (L. R. Peterson & Johnson, 1971). Therefore, the modal characteristics in verbal memory are

associated with the output, whereas visual–spatial memory lacks a direct output so that visual–spatial features must be incorporated in some other way.

5. The total capacity of immediate memory is an additive combination of the capacities of the verbal and visual–spatial subsystems. Sanders and Schroots (1969) found that when verbal and spatial tasks were performed in succession, the total amount remembered was greater than the contribution of either task measured separately. Indeed, there was little loss due to an added task from a different modality. This is a neglected aspect of studies of modality-specific interference. Perhaps it could be called *modality-additive capacity*. The concept refers to total capacity of memory being the sum of the capacities of individual subsystems.

6. Rehearsal in visual–spatial memory can proceed concurrently with rehearsal in its verbal counterpart. This is the most dramatic indicator of the utility of postulating two independent functional stores or subsystems in active memory. Once again, a failure to find interference is intriguing, and it seems to be most naturally handled in terms of local autonomy of separate organizational systems.

7. In spite of disclaimers that any physiological differences are necessary to establish different functional systems, there remains the possibility that such differences exist. It is generally accepted that there is specialization of function in the cerebral hemispheres, with the left processing verbal information, and the right processing visual and spatial patterns among other things. Tests of reaction time have shown differences depending on whether the right or left visual field is stimulated and on whether a picture or a letter is presented (Klatzky & Atkinson, 1971). The cogency of the reasoning is somewhat diminished by the need to assume that the letters in that experiment were coded spatially and the pictures coded verbally. Nevertheless, the specialization of function in the two hemispheres remains a suggestive consideration.

8. The reliable findings of modality differences in short-term retention after brief intervals provides some support for two systems of active memory (Penney, 1975). It is generally found that auditory presentations of verbal materials result in better retention than visual presentations. Taken by itself this could mean that a single memory store with phonemic coding features was in use for both auditory and visual presentation, but that it operated more efficiently when the auditory mode was used. However, when this superiority is coupled with the example of a patient whose short-term memory for visually presented items was fairly normal in spite of deficient

memory for items from auditory presentations, the argument from modality differences in retention becomes more convincing (Warrington & Shallice, 1972).

The conclusion we reach from these considerations is that two major systems of active memory can be differentiated. The evidence suggests a strong visual–spatial system that can function independently of the auditory verbal system. There may be other major systems, for instance, an auditory–musical system (Deutsch, 1975). Furthermore, there are minor functional systems within the major systems. Some are designed for storage, as is the case with mnemonic devices of professional mnemonists. Others have storage as a byproduct, as in subsystems dealing with operations on numbers. It seems reasonable to assume that any information-processing routine practiced to the point of automaticity can in some sense serve a short-term storage function.

REFERENCES

Anders, T. R., & Lillyquist, T. D. Retrieval time in forward and backward recall. *Psychonomic Science*, 1971, **22**, 205–206.

Anderson, J. R., & Bower, G. H. *Human associative memory*. New York: Winston-Wiley, 1973.

Attneave, F. Representation of physical space. In A. W. Melton & E. Martin (Eds.), *Coding processes in human memory*. New York: Winston-Wiley, 1972.

Baddeley, A. D., Grant, S., Wight, E., & Thomson, N. Imagery and visual working memory. In P. M. A. Rabbitt & S. Dornic (Eds.), *Attention and performance V* New York: Academic Press, 1975.

Baddeley, A. D., & Hitch, G. Working memory. In G. H. Bower (Ed.), *The psychology of learning and motivation* (Vol. 8). New York: Academic Press, 1974.

Bower, G. H. Mental imagery and associative learning. In L. W. Gregg (Ed.), *Cognition in learning and memory*. New York: Wiley, 1972.

Brooks, L. R. Spatial and verbal components in the act of recall. *Canadian Journal of Psychology*, 1968, **22**, 349–368.

Conrad, R. Interference or decay over short retention intervals? *Journal of Verbal Learning and Verbal Behavior*, 1967, **6**, 49–54.

Craik, F. I. M., & Watkins, M. J. The role of rehearsal in short-term memory. *Journal of Verbal Learning and Verbal Behavior*, 1973, **12**, 599–607.

Deutsch, D. The organization of short-term memory for a single acoustic attribute. In D. Deutsch & J. A. Deutsch (Eds.), *Short-term memory*. New York: Academic Press, 1975. Pp. 108–151.

Fernald, M. R. The diagnosis of mental imagery. *Psychological Monographs*, 1912, **14**(Whole No. 58).

Garner, W. R., & Clement, D. E. Goodness of pattern and pattern uncertainty. *Journal of Verbal Learning and Verbal Behavior*, 1963, **2**, 446–452.

Glanzer, M., & Clark, W. H. The verbal loop hypothesis: Binary numbers. *Journal of Verbal Learning and Verbal Behavior*, 1963, **2**, 301–309.

Johnson, N. F. Organization and the concept of a memory code. In A. W. Melton & E. Martin (Eds.), *Coding processes in human memory*. New York: Winston-Wiley, 1972, Pp. 125–159.

Klatzky, R. L., & Atkinson, R. C. Specialization of the cerebral hemispheres in scanning for information in short-term memory. *Perception & Psychophysics*, 1971, **10**, 335–338.

Kosslyn, S. M. Information representation in visual images. *Cognitive Psychology*, 1975, **7**, 341–370.

Kosslyn, S. M., Holyoak, K. J., & Huffman, C. S. A processing approach to the dual coding hypothesis. *Journal of Experimental Psychology: Human Learning and Memory*, 1976, **2**, 223–233.

Kroll, N. E. A. Visual short-term memory. In D. Deutsch & J. A. Deutsch (Eds.), *Short-term memory*. New York: Academic Press, 1975. Pp. 153–179.

Mazuryk, G. F., & Lockhart, R. S. Negative recency and levels of processing infree recall. *Canadian Journal of Psychology*, 1974, **28**, 114–123.

Moyer, R. S. Comparing objects in memory: Evidence suggesting an internal psychophysics. *Perception & Psychophysics*, 1973, **13**, 180–184.

Murray, D. J. Articulation and acoustic confusability in short-term memory. *Journal of Experimental Psychology*, 1968, **78**, 679–684.

Neisser, U., & Kerr, N. Spatial and mnemonic properties of visual images. *Cognitive Psychology*, 1973, **5**, 138–150.

Paivio, A. Perceptual comparisons through the mind's eye. *Memory & Cognition*, 1975, **3**, 635–648.

Penney, C. G. Modality effects in short-term verbal memory. *Psychological Bulletin*, 1975, **82**, 68–84.

Peterson, L. R. Concurrent verbal activity. *Psychological Review*, 1969, **76**, 376–386.

Peterson, L. R., Holsten, J., & Spevak, P. Spatial coding of auditory signals. *Memory & Cognition*, 1975, **3**, 243–246.

Peterson, L. R., & Johnson, S. K. Some effects of minimizing articulation on short-term retention. *Journal of Verbal Learning and Verbal Behavior*, 1971, **10**, 346–354.

Peterson, L. R., & Peterson, M. J. Minimal paired-associate learning. *Journal of Experimental Psychology*, 1962, **63**, 521–527.

Peterson, M. J. The retention of imagined and seen spatial matrices. *Cognitive Psychology*, 1975, **7**, 181–193.

Pylyshyn, Z. W. What the mind's eye tells the mind's brain: A critique of mental imagery. *Psychological Bulletin*, 1973, **80**, 1–24.

Reitman, J. S. Without surreptitious rehearsal, information in short-term memory decays. *Journal of Verbal Learning and Verbal Behavior*, 1974, **13**, 365–377.

Salthouse, T. A. Simultaneous processing of verbal and spatial information. *Memory and Cognition*, 1975, **3**, 221–225.

Sanders, A. F., & Schroots, J. J. F. Cognitive categories and memory span: III. Effects of similarity on recall. *Quarterly Journal of Experimental Psychology*, 1969, **21**, 21–28.

Shepard, R. N. Form, formation, and transformation of internal representations. In R. L. Solso (Ed.), *Information processing and cognition*. New York: Erlbaum-Wiley, 1975, Pp. 87–122.

Simon, H. A. *The science of the artificial*. Cambridge, Mass.: MIT Press, 1969.

Warrington, E. K., & Shallice, T. Neuropsychological evidence of visual storage in short-term memory tasks. *Quarterly Journal of Experimental Psychology*, 1972, **24**, 34–40.

Weber, R. J., & Harnish, R. Visual imagery for words: The Hebb test. *Journal of Experimental Psychology*, 1974, **102**, 409–414.

ATTENTION AND PREATTENTION[1]

Howard Egeth

THE JOHNS HOPKINS UNIVERSITY, BALTIMORE, MARYLAND

I. Introduction

The field of attention is in a state of flux. Early research strongly supported the notion that man's information processing channel was quite "narrow" and easily overloaded since subjects in those studies often had grave difficulty attending to as few as two things at once. Moreover, much of the early evidence seemed to suggest that the bottleneck existed at a fairly early stage of processing, i.e., at or

[1] The research reported in this chapter was supported in part by a grant from the National Science Foundation (BMS 76-01227), and in part by a contract between the Office of Naval Research (Engineering, Psychology Programs) and The John Hopkins University. I would like to thank Alfonso Caramazza, James Pomerantz, and Steven Shwartz for valuable ideas and assistance.

before the stage of perception or recognition of signals rather than at the level of response selection or execution. This extensive literature has been reviewed by, among others, Broadbent (1958), Egeth (1967), Egeth and Bevan (1973), Kahneman (1973), Neisser (1967), and Treisman (1969).

All along, however, there have been hints that there may *not* be a processing bottleneck at or before the level of perception or recognition. For example, when a message in an unattended ear is preceded by one's name, one is more likely to hear the subsequent message than if there is no such premonitory cue (Moray, 1959). There are numerous other examples of messages on "unattended" channels capturing attention. Clearly this could not happen if unattended messages were not receiving any perceptual analysis at all. In fact in recent years the pendulum seems to have swung in the other direction. As I shall describe in subsequent sections, many investigators are reporting data that suggest there is no attentional bottleneck impeding perceptual processing. These recent findings suggest a model of processing that has the following characteristics: (*a*) Perceptual processing may proceed on several independent channels simultaneously; (*b*) An input receives the same perceptual analysis regardless of whether or not it is "attended"; and (*c*) Stimulus encoding is effortless; capacity limitations in human information processing are due to stages subsequent to encoding. Since we are talking here about stages prior to an attentional bottleneck, we may, in fact, be referring to characteristics of what Neisser (1967) called *preattentive processing.*

The balance of this chapter is devoted to a discussion of evidence pertaining to these three propositions. In addition to a selective review of the existing literature, several previously unreported studies from my laboratory are also presented. To provide a glimpse ahead, the evidence I review suggests that the first two propositions are reasonable first approximations to reality, although there appear to be important circumstances in which these principles are incorrect. The third proposition is more troublesome. My analysis of the literature suggests that the methods that have been used to test the proposition are generally inappropriate. What little clear evidence there is suggests encoding is not effortless.

Before launching into a discussion of the literature I should say that the three propositions above are highly interrelated and so, at times, the decision about where to bring in a specific study was arbitrary.

II. The Independent Channels Hypothesis

A. MULTIELEMENT VISUAL DISPLAYS

Several recent lines of evidence have suggested that several visual stimuli may be processed simultaneously and independently. For example, Egeth, Jonides, and Wall (1972) had subjects indicate whether or not a target character was present in the visual field. The independent variable of chief interest was the number of nontarget "noise" elements in the field. Reaction time (RT) to detect the presence of a target character was unaffected by the number of noise elements (varied over the range 1–5). This was true even when the target was defined as "any digit" and the noise elements were a heterogeneous assortment of letters. (In that paper we suggested that it was not a special property of digits and letters that led to the independence of RT and display size, and that similar results would obtain whenever target and noise elements belong to mutually exclusive, easily remembered sets. Shiffrin and Schneider (1977) have now shown that this position is essentially correct.)

The independence of RT and display size was taken as disconfirming any plausible serial model for visual detection. This result would also seem to rule out a limited-capacity parallel model of the type proposed by Rumelhart (1970). The data were taken to mean that each stimulus element was processed by a separate channel and that the channels were independent.

Measuring accuracy rather than latency, C. W. Eriksen and Spencer (1969) and Gardner (1973) have obtained results consistent with an independent channels model. For example, in Gardner's study, when target elements (T's and F's) were dissimilar to nontargets (0's) accuracy of detection was independent of the number of nontargets in the display. However, when the nontargets (hybrid T-F's) were confusable with the targets, detection accuracy declined as display size increased. In Gardner's model this display size effect is attributed to confusion at the decision stage rather than to a capacity limit in perceptual analysis. The logic is as follows. Suppose that with a single nontarget stimulus in the field the probability of making a false-positive response (i.e., mistaking a nontarget for a target) is p_1. If M nontargets were presented the probability of a false positive would *increase* to $1 - (1 - p_1)^M$, just on the assumption that the M locations were processed independently and without assuming any limit on processing capacity.

Despite its success in handling these (and other) results, the independent channels model of visual detection now appears to be inadequate in several respects. Perhaps the most serious problem is that it is not completely general. Specifically, it is clear that the "channels" (whatever they may be) that are assigned to detect stimuli are independent only when the stimuli themselves are sufficiently separated spatially (say by 1° of visual angle). Elements that are closer together interact in various ways, perhaps in the fashion of generalized lateral masking, or perhaps through inhibitory or facilitatory processes that depend on the features of the specific target and noise elements used in a particular condition (e.g., Estes, 1972; Gilmore, 1975; Pomerantz, Sager, & Stoever, in press). The independent channels model may be seen as a special case of some more general interactive channels model in that it applies only for sufficiently separated stimuli. In any case, the interactive channels models that have been proposed so far may also be characterized as spatially parallel.

How do these data bear on the notion of preattention? I think they are supportive but only in an indirect and general sense. Preattentional processes are supposedly parallel (Neisser, 1967, p. 89). Thus, it is nice to know that processing in at least some well-defined experimental tasks exhibits the requisite property of spatial parallelism. I do *not* think that the failure of strict independence among channels found in some of the visual detection experiments means that processing was not preattentive in those studies. Nonindependence was not necessarily forced by a lack of capacity. Pomerantz *et al.* (in press) have argued that nonindependence may occur as the result of feature-specific inhibition that serves to separate figure from ground. They argued further that the operation of such inhibition is both fast and automatic. These two properties would appear to be the crucial hallmarks of preattention, rather than simple independence of channels.

In closing this section, it is well to point out that our notion of preattentive processing may be criticized on at least two grounds. First, it might be argued that the term means little more than "easy processing" (cf. Norman & Bobrow, 1975). Second, Neisser (1967) has given the following warning:

> Much cognitive activity in daily life is preattentive. That is one reason why tachistoscopic research often seems so inappropriate to psychologists concerned with everyday cognition. A subject paying sharp attention to a fading iconic blur, in an effort to decide which of the 26 letters it represents, is

functioning very differently from a man who "recognizes" the familiar sights of his office as he enters in the morning, or notes out of the corner of his eye that his secretary has already come in. Such a man can easily be deceived—the picture on the wall may have been changed, the secretary may be a substitute—and he will be in for a surprise when he notices the deception. His response will then be the redirection of attention, together with appropriate orienting responses as he focuses on the newly interesting object. (Ulric Neisser, *Cognitive Psychology*, © 1967, p. 92. Reprinted by permission of Prentice-Hall, Inc., Englewood Cliffs, New Jersey)

In short, it is liable to be difficult to get preattention under experimental control. While it is important to keep this caveat in mind, it is perhaps prudent not to let it serve as an excuse for not trying to explore the concept at all.

B. MULTIMODAL AND MULTIDIMENSIONAL
    STIMULATION

There are several experiments using stimuli drawn from differing sensory modalities or sensory dimensions that lend support to the independent channels hypothesis.

One important experiment was conducted by Eijkman and Vendrik (1965). They presented signals independently and randomly to the eye and to the ear. The signals were increments in the intensity of a light and a tone. In a divided-attention condition subjects were instructed to judge independently if a visual and/or auditory signal had been presented. In selective-attention control conditions the subjects monitored and responsed to just one modality at a time. In the unattended modality the background tone or light was present, but no increments were presented. The results showed that the eye and ear acted as independent detectors of signals. Moreover, performance was the same in the divided- and selective-attention conditions.

A similar result was obtained by Moore and Massaro (1973) who had their subjects judge the loudness and quality of auditory signals. They used a divided-attention condition and a selective-attention condition and found performance to be equal in the two conditions. In other words, when subjects has to judge just the loudness of a set of tones that varied in both loudness and quality, they were no more accurate than when they had to judge quality in addition to loudness.

In contrast to these findings is a whole host of experiments that show that performance in divided-attention conditions is worse than performance in selective-attention conditions, suggesting that subjects cannot handle two signals as well as one. For example, Egeth and Pachella (1969) had subjects make absolute judgments about various aspects of visual stimuli. In one experiment subjects had to report the horizontal and/or vertical position of a dot presented in a square white field. When subjects had to report just one dimension, performance, as measured by information transmission, was significantly better than when they had to report both. This was true for both .1- and 2.0-sec exposure durations. In another experiment subjects had to identify the color, size, and eccentricity of an ellipse presented for .1 or 1.0 sec. Information transmission was significantly worse when subjects had to report all three dimensions than when they had to report just one dimension. This was true for both .1- and 1.0-sec exposure durations.

Similar decrements in multimodal or multidimensional report conditions have been reported by Massaro and Kahn (1973) for judgments of duration of a visual stimulus and tone recognition, and by Taylor, Lindsay, and Forbes (1967) and Lindsay (1970) for judgments of vertical position of a dot, horizontal position of a dot, pitch of a tone, and intensity of a tone. The results of all of these experiments appear to be contradictory to the independent channels hypothesis.

In the realm of dichotic stimulation, there is also evidence embarrassing to the independent channels hypothesis. Sorkin, Pohlmann, and Gilliom (1973) and Ostry, Moray, and Marks (1976) have shown that the detectability of a signal is dependent on the nature of the contralateral event occurring at the same time. For Sorkin et al., signals were pure tones, while for Ostry et al., signals were defined semantically (targets were digits, nontargets were letters). A result common to both studies is that a signal is more likely to be missed if it occurs at the same time that a subject has a "hit" (correct detection) on the other ear. Additionally, in both experiments performance under divided-attention instructions was worse than under selective-attention instructions. Thus these results suggest a limitation to the independent channels hypothesis: Although it may not be possible to fully process two simultaneous signals as efficiently as either one alone, it is possible to *monitor* two channels as well as one. Gilliom and Sorkin (1974) have proposed what they call a high-level interrupt model. It incorporates the notion of independent monitoring of several channels, but allows for interactions at the cognitive level. For example, on a given trial the inputs of more than one channel might exceed some preset criterion. In this case the subjects' processing capacity is directed to the strongest input first. In consequence, processing of other inputs is interrupted; they are held in a short-term store until they can be processed. But of course information is lost rapidly in such a store. This mechanism forces the important finding: Correct detections on one channel tend to decrease the probability of correct detections on other channels. The authors note that this kind of interaction among channels should be construed as decisional rather than perceptual.

In an effort to save the independent channels hypothesis, Shiffrin and Grantham (1974) suggested that those studies that were inconsistent with the independent channels model suffer from problems that cloud their interpretation. The gist of their criticism is that the independent channels model is a correct description of perceptual processing and that deviations from the model are: (*a*) due to artifact, or (*b*) occur later than perceptual encoding in the processing sequence. An example of potential artifact is that in the Taylor *et al.* (1967) and Lindsay (1970) studies, in the selective-attention conditions the unattended dimensions were held constant from trial to trail, whereas in the divided-attention condition all dimensions varied from trial to trial, thus the stimuli were not identical in the divided- and selective-attention conditions. An example of an interpretation of a divided-attention decrement being postperceptual is Shiffrin and Grantham's argument that the duration judgments used by Massaro and Kahn require short-term memory and decision capacity, neither of which can be divided without loss. Judging the duration of the visual signal may take processing time, so that relevant information concerning the tone is lost before a judgment can be made.

It is not obvious to me whether the Egeth and Pachella experiment can be criticized on these grounds, since multidimensional judgments were poorer than unidimensional judgments even with exposure durations as long as 1 sec (color, size, eccentricity experiment) and 2 sec (dot location experiment). Furthermore, our nonattended dimensions did vary from trial to trial. In the absence of independent estimates of the time required for the judgments in this and other related experiments, there appears to be no a priori way of determining whether interference between dimensions occurs perceptually or postperceptually.

C. SENSORY DOMINANCE

A clear refutation of the independent channels hypothesis is implicit in the notion of sensory dominance, or, more specifically, of visual dominance over audition. As a case in point, Colavita (1974) obtained data which, taken at their face value, suggest that we cannot see and hear at the same time.

In Colavita's experiments subjects were presented with a series of suprathreshold stimuli consisting of a brief tone and a brief light flash in random alternation. They had two response keys, one for the tone and one for the light. Thus, the experimental sequence was much like that of a conventional choice RT task. However, on occasional trials both stimuli were presented simultaneously. When this happened, although the subjects should have pressed both keys, they in fact usually pressed only the light key. Moreover, on some trials some subjects seemed totally unaware that the tone had also been presented. This was the case when the tone and the light were equated in subjective intensity, and even though on preliminary simple RT trials, the tone was responded to more quickly than the light.

Experiment 1: Sensory Dominance

Larry Sager and I have conducted a series of experiments on visual dominance. Our initial goal was to verify the existence of the effect. Succeeding in this, we next tried to determine the locus of the effect, i.e., whether it is actually a sensory phenomenon such as some form of masking, as opposed to, say, a decisional or response phenomenon. Our logic in this effort was to assume that if the dominance occurred at an early, sensory stage of processing it would be unaffected by manipulations (e.g., of response mode) that presumably affect later, more cognitive stages. These experiments will be reported more fully elsewhere, and so I will give just a brief summary here.

In the first experiment the tone and light were not brief as in Colavita's study; instead each was terminated when the appropriate response button was pressed. Subjects first equated the intensity of the light until it matched the tone. A series of simple RT trials confirmed the usual finding that with such equated stimuli auditory RT (288 msec) is faster than visual RT (320 msec), $t(9) = 2.62, p < .05$.

Following the simple RT trials the subjects received 30 "choice" trials in which the tone and light were randomly sequenced. Randomly interspersed among these 30 trials were five additional dual stimulation trials on which the light and tone occurred simultaneously. Subjects were told that such trials would occur and they were instructed to press both keys on those occasions. The mean RT's on choice trials were 427 and 429 msec for tone and light respectively, $t(9) > 1$. The important results are that on dual trials the light response was made first 34 out of 50 times (10 subjects, five dual trials each), and that 9 of 10 subjects made the light response first on a majority of their dual trials, $p < .05$ by sign test.

These results support Colavita's finding that on dual stimulation trials a visual stimulus dominates a matched auditory stimulus. Of course, since this particular method involved presenting signals until termination by a key press, we were only interested in comparing RT's to tone and light; there was not reason to expect any reports of unawareness.

In our first experiment visual dominance was manifested in a tendency to respond to light before responding to tone. If visual dominance is "sensory," so that, e.g., a light slows down the processing of a simultaneous tone, it should also manifest itself even if we remove the requirement to respond to the light. In several of our succeeding experiments we did just that; subjects were instructed to ignore the light and respond only to the tone. We took as our index of dominance the difference in tone RT between the situation in which tone was accompanied by light and the situation when tone alone was presented. These experiments differed from the first in that subjects served for much longer periods and received some 300 trials. We also systematically manipulated the proportion of light, tone, and dual trials.

Without going into too much detail, I can report the main result as follows: When subjects responded to just tones, there was no experimental condition in which mean RT on dual stimulation trials was longer than on tone-only trials. Thus, by this measure, visual dominance failed to obtain. Several other control conditions had to be run to rule out some (to us) uninteresting interpretations of the data, but we now feel confident that visual dominance as obtained by Colavita reflects postperceptual processing. The dominance effect seems to be a manifestation of our general difficulty in producing two separate responses to two closely spaced stimuli. Of course these comments do not explain the asymmetry between vision and audition. Posner, Nissen, and Klein (1976) have recently addressed this issue.

D. SUMMARY

The independent channels model is consistent with a wide variety of data. Upon close examination even some apparent contradictions, such as Colavita's (1974) demonstration of sensory dominance, dissolve. However, recent evidence is making it clear that the model is wrong in detail. Experiments on visual detection suggest the need for a model in which there is interaction among elements. A related observation is that with dichotic stimulation: Events on one channel appear to affect the detectability of events on the other channel. However, there may well be a difference in the two cases in that the interactions in visual detection seem to be at the perceptual level, while those in dichotic listening may stem from decisional factors.

The preceding seems relatively clear. What is less clear is the cumulative impact of the results we have reviewed on the notion of preattention. I argued above that strict independence (among visual stimuli) did not seem to be a necessary condition of preattention. In addition, I shall argue that the fact that two simultaneous signals cannot always be processed to the point of recognition does not seem terribly embarrassing to the general idea of preattention. What does seem relevant to the concept of preattention is that when a subject monitors the environment for signals, his efficiency does not decline the more channels he must monitor. Several recent studies converge on this conclusion, and thus lend credence to the notion that in at least some situations processing can meaningfully be called preattentive.

III.   Attentional Control of Perception

In this section I shall review some of the arguments for and against the proposition that an input receives the same perceptual analysis regardless of whether or not it is attended. These arguments have commonly been based on data from two paradigms. The first paradigm explores the conditions under which nominally irrelevant information receives analysis to the point of recognition. A classic example, used in refutation of Broadbent's (1958) filter model, is Moray's (1959) demonstration that a message presented to the unattended ear in a dichotic listening task may be heard if it is preceded by the subject's name.

In the other paradigm of interest we ask whether perceptual processing becomes more efficient as the subject is given more precise foreknowledge concerning that stimulus. For example, suppose a subject is asked to detect the presence of a light. In a "single-set" condition he might be told in what location the light will occur (imagine that eye movements are controlled). In a "multiple-set" condition he might be told that the light will occur in four possible locations. It is usually assumed that if there is no performance difference between the single- and multiple-set conditions, then this indicates that attention cannot be allocated to spatial locations, and vice versa. In other words, the perceptual analysis of the spot of light is independent of whether the subject tries to focus his attention on one location or divide it among four locations.

A. FAILURE OF ATTENTIONAL SELECTIVITY IN THE
   SPATIAL DOMAIN?

In the studies by Egeth et al. (1972), C. W. Eriksen and Spencer (1969), and Gardner (1973), the spatial location of the target was variable and not known in advance. Thus, one might argue that subjects should have deployed attention widely over the area of potential target locations in all conditions. Consequently, these experiment might speak to the issue of whether or not multiple stimuli are processed in independent channels, but they do not necessarily speak to the issue of whether attention can be deployed voluntarily to specific regions of the visual field. There are several studies that have been directed to this important question. Grindley and Townsend (1968) showed that subjects could detect the orientation of a dimly illuminated T-shaped figure no better when they were told shortly in advance of the stimulus display in which of four possible widely separated locations the target would appear as when they were not told the location. One plausible interpretation of these data is that subjects cannot voluntarily attend to one location in the visual field at the expense of others, at least in the absence of eye movements. (In this as in the other studies cited here, the design of the experiment makes it unlikely or impossible for eye movements to account for the results.) It is interesting to note that prior information concerning target location *was* useful when (and only when) several noise elements were presented along with the target. This finding was attributed to selective readout from a short-term visual store, which is the same interpretation that has been frequently given to Sperling's (1960) results.

Shiffrin, Gardner, and their colleagues have pursued the issue of voluntary control of attention. In the first of a series of papers, subjects identified which one of two target letters was presented in a square four-letter array (Shiffrin & Gardner, 1972). In the simultaneous condition, all four letters were displayed concurrently for a brief duration (t msec). In the sequential condition, letters were presented one at a time for t msec each, each letter being preceded and followed by a masking field. In another sequential condition, the two letters along each of the two diagonals were displayed together, one diagonal being presented after the other, again for t msec each. Subjects always knew the order of onset of the letters in sequential conditions. If attention can be voluntarily deployed selectively to the relevant locations in sequential conditions, then the sequential conditions ought to result in higher accuracy than the simultaneous condition. This did not obtain; the simultaneous and sequential conditions were equal. Thus, Shiffrin and Gardner (1972) concluded that the initial stages of information processing, up to at least the stage of letter recognition, take place both without capacity limitation and without attentional control.

Shiffrin, McKay, and Shaffer (1976) found that the accuracy of detecting the presence of a dot at the center of the visual field was the same regardless of whether observers could attend solely to the center location or whether they also had to monitor eight surrounding locations or 48 surrounding locations. They concluded that "... perceptual processing is automatic, not under subject control, and that selective attention is the result of subsequent processes in short-term memory" (p. 210).

Experiments II, III, and IV: Failures of Spatial Selectivity

What the preceding studies suggest is that subjects can monitor several signal sources or channels as well as they can monitor a single source when only a single signal is presented and responded to on a given trial. Thus, these studies tend to indicate that subjects can attend to several information sources simultaneously. There also exists evidence that subjects are frequently unable to ignore irrelevant information sources even when it is to their distinct advantage to do so. One classic example of this is the Stroop color-word test. We have recently done some work on a similar phenomenon, using a paradigm developed by Eriksen and his colleagues to study the spatial selectivity of vision. On a trial, one of two targets is presented at a specified location and the subject must indicate which target was presented. The target character might appear alone (no noise) or, in addition to the target character, some other elements may also be present in the display. These other elements might be repetitions of the target (compatible noise), or they might be the character associated with the other response (incompatible noise), or a character not associated with any overt response required in the experiment (neutral noise). The logic of the design is that if a subject cannot restrict his attention to the specified location and ignore elements at other locations, and if the incompatible noise is processed to the point of recognition, it may engender response competition thus reducing the speed and/or accuracy of the response to the target. Since the physical separation between the target location and noise locations may be manipulated, the method may be able to give us a quantitative index of the size of the field of visual attentional selectivity. (The neutral and compatible conditions serve as a control for nonspecific interference effects such as lateral masking.)

In a study by C. W. Eriksen and Hoffman (1972) the stimuli were letters presented around an imaginary circle centered at the fixation point. By keeping distance from the fovea equal for all stimuli, this method assures the stimuli will be approximately equally visible. The target location varied from trial to trial and was incicated by a bar marker. The chief finding was response latency decreased markedly as the separation between the target and incompatible noise elements was increased up to 1° but there was no further decrease in RT as the separation was increased to 1.4°. In a study by B. A. Eriksen and Eriksen (1974) a nonsearch paradigm was used in which the target was always centered in a horizontal array. Again RT decreased as the separation between the target and the flanking noise elements was increased. At the maximum separation of 1° the interference effect was only about 17 msec.

The two paradigms used by Eriksen and his colleagues have complementary virtues. On the one hand the use of a circular display keeps target and noise elements equally visible, but the necessity of determining the target location by locating the bar marker on each trial presents additional perceptual and cognitive problems. On the other hand, while the use of a nonsearch paradigm with centered linear displays may make target location easy, the design confounds interelement separation and acuity. That is, subjects may have successfully "ignored" elements more than 1° from the foveal target simply because they couldn't see them clearly. As we were interested in determining the extent to which interference might occur with interelement separation in excess of 1–1.4°, but with the localization problem minimized, we used the nonsearch paradigm with large characters to try to overcome reduced acuity.

In our first experiment (carried out by Peter Whitehouse, Patricia Somers, and me) 16 paid volunteers each participated in a single session. There were eight different stimuli as shown in Table I. They

TABLE I

STIMULI, MEAN REACTION TIMES (RT), AND ERROR RATES IN EACH CONDITION

Condition	Stimuli	Mean RT	Percentage of errors
No flankers	2 3	406	2.4
Neutral	0 2 0 0 3 0	412	1.7
Compatible	2 2 2 3 3 3	411	1.7
Incompatible	3 2 3 2 3 2	448	5.9

were composed of dry transfer numerals on white cards. At the viewing distance of 58 cm, the digits subtended approximately 1.9° in height, 1.2° in width, and were separated by 2.0° edge to edge.

The subjects were instructed to attend to and respond on the basis of the stimulus appearing at the center of the display. Testing was preceded by eight practice trials. To indicate that a 2 was present at the center of the display the subject pressed a button with his left index finger; in indicate a 3 was present, he pressed a different button with his right index finger. Stimuli were presented for 200 msec in a Gergrands two-field mirror tachistoscope. A small fixation point was present at the center of the field between trials. Response latencies from the onset of the stimulus were measured to the nearest millisecond.

Mean RT for correct responses and error rates are shown in Table I. Analysis of variance carried out on the latency data indicated that the effect of conditions was significant, $F(3, 45) = 9.46$, $p < .001$. Post hoc Scheffé tests confirmed what seems obvious in Table I; i.e., the no-noise conditions did not differ from the neutral and compatible conditions ($p > .1$), while the incompatible condition did differ from the others ($p < .001$). The most conservative index of interference due to response incompatibility is 36 msec (448–412 msec), which is larger than the interference effect found by B. A. Eriksen and Eriksen (1974) at 1° separation. The error data were consistent with the conclusions drawn above: The incompatible condition was more difficult than the others, which did not differ among themselves.

To ensure that the flanking elements were clearly visible in all conditions, several additional subjects were recruited and asked to report the entire array in left to right order after it was shown for 200 msec. These subjects performed with 100% accuracy.

These data indicate that subjects cannot (or at least do not) ignore incompatible information that is as much as two degrees away from a known target location.

In a subsequent experiment (carried out by Suzanne Gatti and me) we explored still wider separations. The stimuli and design were similar to the preceding experiment, the chief change being that displays incorporating 1°, 3°, and 5° separations were presented together in a mixed sequence. Eight new subjects participated in this experiment.

Mean RT's appear in Fig. 1B. It is clear that no interference is found at 3° or 5° separation.

On the basis of our first two experiments, we might conclude that perception is partially under attentional control in that subjects *can* restrict their perceptual processing, but only with a tolerance of approximately 2°. The obvious problem that stands in the way of easy acceptance of this conclusion is that the stimuli that caused interference at 2° may not have been large enough to compensate for the acuity falloff at 3° or 5°. Rather than attempt to calibrate stimulus size to obtain noise elements that would be effective at 3° and 5°, we decided to turn to an entirely different source of response competition—the Stroop effect.

In our third experiment (Fig. 1A) on spatial selectivity (carried out by Gatti and me), subjects were presented with a color patch (red, blue, or green) at the center of the viewing field and were asked to name the color shown on each trial. Color patches appeared either alone or flanked above and below at separations of 1°, 3°, or 5° by noise stimuli. As before, the noise stimuli were compatible (e.g., red patch with the word RED above and below it), incompatible (e.g., red patch with the word BLUE above and below it), or neutral (e.g., red patch with XXXX above and below it).

Our subjects received 351 trials randomly mixed with respect to target—noise separation and compatibility. The latency of the vocal naming response was measured on each trial. Sixteen subjects participated in the experiment.

A somewhat similar experiment (Experiment IV, Fig. 1B) had been performed earlier by Dyer (1973), who showed interference with a 4° separation between the color patch and the interfering color name. However, there is one crucial difference between our study and Dyer's study. In his study the color patch and word appeared

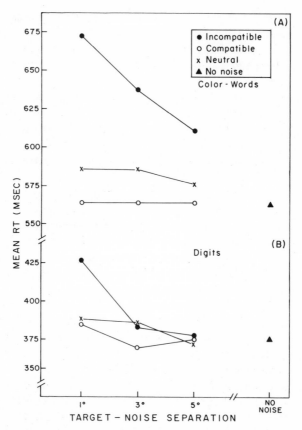

Fig. 1. Experiments III (B) and IV (A): Mean RT's for each condition as a function of the separation (in degrees of visual angle) between targets and flanking noise elements. •, Incompatible; ○, compatible; x, neutral; ▲, no noise.

one to the left and one to the right of fixation, but their relative positions varied randomly from trial to trial. Thus, his subjects could not attempt to focus attention at one location in the visual field and ignore other locations as they could in our study.

The data appear in Fig. 1A. Unlike the preceding experiment, there was substantial interference at all three separations used. Even at 5° the 35 msec difference between the incompatible and neutral conditions was significant, $t(15) = 5.25$, $p < .001$.

I suspect that if appropriate compensation could be made for the reduction in acuity (and transmission speed) at eccentric retinal locations, interference could be shown for substantially greater inter-stimulus separations. However, as it seemed that unpleasant technical difficulties might stand in the way of such further demonstrations, this line of research has not been pursued further.

At this point we may stop to consider what we have learned from our series of studies using response competition as a tool to study spatial selectivity. The chief finding is that subjects cannot focus attention sufficiently to entirely gate out stimuli as far as 5° from a centrally located target. This finding is certainly consistent with the idea that perceptual processes operate without attentional control, but it by no means proves the case. The problem is that we cannot conclude from such data that subjects cannot filter (in the sense of attenuate) irrelevant information. It may be that our subjects *were* filtering the noise to some extent and that the interference effects we have observed were less than they would have been if subjects had not been able to attend selectively. The data do not permit us to decide if this is the case. Of course, this conclusion also applies to other studies in which "unattended" stimuli are shown to capture attention or otherwise disrupt processing of attended material. Such demonstrations abound in the auditory literature. As one example, Lewis (1970) found shadowing was disrupted by concurrent words in the unattended message that were semantically related to words in the shadowed message. As another example, Corteen and Wood (1972) showed that words conditioned to an electric shock caused GSR deflections when they were presented in the unattended ear during a shadowing task. Both of these studies have been interpreted to mean that all inputs receive full perceptual analysis even when they are unattended. Two points need to be made about these experiments. First, the mere fact of interference does not in any way prove that a stimulus receives the *same* analysis when unattended as when attended. Second, at an empirical level, recent studies have cast grave doubt on the initial observations themselves. Wardlaw and Kroll (1976) made a strenuous effort to replicate Corteen and Wood, but failed. Treisman, Squire, and Green (1974) replicated Lewis's experiment but found that the unattended words impaired shadowing only occasionally; there was no evidence that unattended words were routinely fully analyzed. I shall turn now to some research which does suggest that perception may be under attentional control.

B. ATTENTIONAL CONTROL IN THE SPATIAL DOMAIN

Eriksen and his co-workers have reported a series of experiments in which attentional focusing mechanisms have been demonstrated. Perhaps the most striking such demonstration was one in which in direct contrast to Grindley and Townsend's (1968) and Shiffrin and Gardner's (1972) data, subjects performed better when they were given foreknowledge of where the target would appear (C. W. Eriksen & Hoffman, 1974). On each trial a single letter was presented somewhere on the circumference of an imaginary circle surrounding the fixation point. Just prior to the display of the letter an indicator was shown near the spatial location that the letter would occupy. The warning interval varied from 1 to 150 msec. (Note that warning intervals of up to 150 msec would not permit an eye movement to occur.) The latency to identify the letter was up to 40 msec faster with the precue than when the indicator appeared simultaneously with the target letter. This effect is above and beyond any general alerting properties of the precue, since an informationless precue was used as a control. The fact that no facilitation was found with the simultaneous precue could be interpreted in several ways (e.g., lateral masking of the target by the cue); the important finding is that there was an advantage for the informational bar marker over the informationless dot at intervals greater than zero. (In fact, there is another study that did show sensitivity improvements with simultaneous cueing and single-stimulus presentation, namely that of Van Der Heijden & Eerland, 1973.)

Another demonstration of attentional control in vision has recently been provided by Posner, Nissen, and Ogden (1975). They showed that simple RT to detect the onset of a spot of light depends on whether or not the light occurs where the subject expects it to occur. Subjects fixated at the center of the visual field, and the spot of light appeared either to the left or right of fixation. The probability of occurrence at the locations was imbalanced in some conditions (e.g., 20% left, 80% right). Mean RT was faster when the light appeared in the more probable location.

Experiment V: Focusing of Attention

The study reported here was carried out by Steve Shwartz and myself; it follows a pilot experiment run in 1970 by Jeffrey Epstein, an undergraduate assistant in my laboratory. The question at issue is whether performance under conditions of focused attention is superior to performance under conditions of distributed attention. The procedure we used was similar to that used by Shiffrin *et al.* (1976) in that we compared performance at the center of the field when that was the only possible target location with performance at the center of the field when more peripheral locations also had to be monitored. Note that this design is addressed to a somewhat different point than was addressed by the experiment of C. W. Eriksen and

Hoffman (1974). In that study, attention was presumably centered at the beginning of each trial and then shifted to the location indicated by the bar marker. So the experiment speaks to the issue of whether attention can be moved as if it were an internal eye. The present experiment, like the Shiffrin *et al.* (1976) experiment, is addressed to the question of whether attention, while directed at a central locus, can be "expanded" or "contracted" (like a zoom lens) to meet the demands of the task.

On each trial a single letter was presented on a computer-controlled CRT. Prior to each trial a fixation field was presented for 500 msec. This field contained nine dots, one at the center of the display and eight others equally spaced around the perimeter of an imaginary circle. At the end of 500 msec a single dot was extinguished and immediately replaced by a letter that remained on for 200 msec. At the end of the 200-msec exposure the letter and the eight remaining dots were extinguished simultaneously. In separate blocks of trials subjects had to discriminate a T from an L or a T from a T tilted 45° to the right of vertical. In the focused condition the diameter of the circle of dots was 3.8°; however, target stimuli appeared only at the center of the display. The distributed-small condition also used a 3.8° diameter fixation circle. Targets appeared in the center location on 20% of the trials and in each of the eight peripheral locations on 10% of the trials. The distributed-large condition used the same distribution of trials but the diameter of the fixation circle was 12.0°.

Two groups of six subjects each were employed. The subjects in the first group served in a single session in which they received the six conditions of the experiment (two discriminations × three degrees of focusing of attention) in separate 125-trial blocks, in an order that was balanced over subjects. The subjects in the second group served in two sessions, one devoted to the T-L discrimination, the other to the T-tilted T discrimination. Each day they received three blocks of 150 trials each corresponding to the three attentional conditions. The order of discrimination tasks and of attentional conditions was balanced over subjects. The data from the two groups of subjects appear in Fig. 2. The most important finding is that mean RT for targets appearing at the central location increased as subjects had to distribute their attention more widely. For the first group, $F(2, 10) = 13.27$, $p < .005$; for the second group, $F(2, 10) = 13.52$, $p < .005$.

Where does this result leave us? It seems quite clear that choice RT is dependent upon locational certainty, even when the data are examined for the same retinal location across conditions. This find-

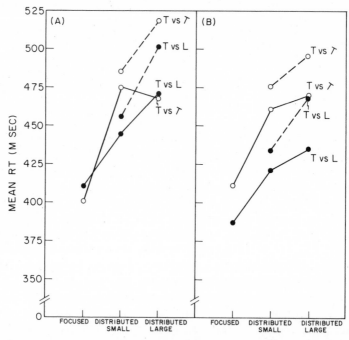

Fig. 2. Experiment V: Mean RT's for discriminating T from L and T from tilted T, for central and peripheral stimulus positions, as a function of the degree of focus of attention. (A) Data for six subjects who served for a single session. (B) Data for six subjects who had the T-L and T-tilted T discriminations in separate sessions. (——), Center (---), periphery.

ing is at odds with several previous studies, including one quite similar in design (Shiffrin *et al.*, 1976). It isn't entirely clear why. On the one hand, there may be something wrong with our experiment. On the other hand, there may be something wrong with the Shiffrin *et al.* experiment. In fact, that study has been criticized by Keren and Skelton (1976) on several counts, perhaps the most pertinent being that targets occurred at the central location so often that subjects had little incentive to distribute their attention in any condition. Since targets only occurred at the center on 20% of the trials in the Egeth and Shwartz experiment reported here, it seems that our subjects would have had an incentive to distribute attention. In any case, it is too early to tell if Kerem and Skelton have correctly identified the reason for the apparent failure of attentional selectivity in the Shiffrin *et al.* study.

Before leaving this experiment I should mention at least briefly the purpose of the two discrimination tasks. Beck and Ambler (1973) had shown that in the visual periphery under conditions of distributed attention a T-tilted T discrimination was much easier than a T-L discrimination, even though there was little difference between these discriminations when attention was focused. In their experiment eight letters appeared around the perimeter of an imaginary circle 18.2° in radius. Before the array appeared, one or more dots were presented that served to indicate the location(s) the target element might be in on a particular trial. Focused attention refers to a condition in which just one location was specified, while distributed attention refers to conditions in which two or eight different locations were specified. Thus, in the extreme, distributed attention meant that the subject had to consider stimuli at all eight possible locations in his search for the disparate element (i.e., an L among T's or a tilted-T among T's). Shwartz and I were interested in seeing if the same superiority for the discrimination based upon line slope rather than line arrangement would manifest itself when attention was distributed largely over empty space rather than over nontarget letters. As is evident in Fig. 2 A and B, the T-tilted T discrimination was not any easier than the T-L discrimination, even at the periphery of the large circle. (The apparent superiority of the T-L discrimination in the periphery was not significant.) What this means is that an important determinant of the relative ease of the two discriminations is processing load rather than literal spatial "distribution" of attention. Of course, with a 200-msec exposure duration, our subjects may have been able to accomplish some degree of rapid redistribution of attention before responding. Further tests involving post-stimulus masking fields to control effective exposure duration should help clarify this issue.

C. ATTENTIONAL CONTROL IN THE NONSPATIAL DOMAIN

Experiment V showed that detection performance was improved by increasingly specific foreknowledge of *where* a target element would appear on a particular trial. A closely related issue is whether or not detection performance depends on foreknowledge of *what* the target element will be. This topic is traditionally included under the rubric of "set" in the psychological literature.

The earliest report I have been able to track down of an attentional effect on performance was reported by Wundt (1880). He had subjects respond as soon as they detected the presence of a light, a tone, or a touch. He noted that RT was very noticeably retarded when the subject was ignorant of the modality of the forthcoming stimulus even though the paradigm measured simple, not choice RT. A more complete report is available of an early study by Mowrer, Rayman, and Bliss (1940). Subjects had to release a key as soon as they detected the onset of either a light or a tone. By use of instructions and specially designed stimulus sequences they were able to compare performance when, say, the light was expected but the tone was actually presented. Subjects were slower to respond to such unexpected signals than to expected signals. This result may be taken to mean that subjects are able to direct attention voluntarily to one modality or the other as a function of expectancy.

An example of a set effect where the dimensions of stimulus variation are not so clear has been provided by Corcoran and Rouse (1970). Subjects named words presented tachistoscopically. There were two pure-list conditions; in one the words were printed and in the other they were handwritten. In the other condition a mixed-list was used; printed and handwritten letters appeared equally often in a random order. Accuracy of report was significantly greater in the pure-list conditions than in the mixed-list conditions. Ginger Berninger and I have recently showed a similar set effect on response latency. Letters were presented one at a time for naming. They were either uppercase or lowercase, and the two cases were presented in either pure lists (all uppercase or all lowercase) or a mixed list (half uppercase, half lowercase in random order). Although the mean difference in RT was only 11 msec, 14 of 16 subjects were faster in the pure-list than in the mixed-list condition. (p = .004 by sign test).

In contrast, there are several experiments in which foreknowledge did not affect performance. For example, Doehrman (1974) had subjects detect the presence of a briefly illuminated line segment that could vary in orientation. Different conditions were characterized by different degrees of uncertainty regarding the orientation of the line. The result of chief interest to us is that variation in the number of possible orientations of the line produced only slight changes in detection performance.

There are of course many other studies of set, indeed too many to discuss here. Simply to keep this section within reasonable bounds, I shall omit large sections of this literature. In particular, I shall not discuss the substantial body of research in which the identification of complex objects is called for and in which stimulus alternatives are presented before or after the exposure of the target stimulus (e.g., Egeth & Smith, 1967; Pachella, 1970). Instead I shall limit myself chiefly to those studies in which differential amounts of foreknowledge are provided about relatively simple stimulus attributes.

1. Experiment VI: Set for Color and Size

In the Wundt and the Mowrer, Rayman, and Bliss experiments, subjects could evidently not monitor two or more channels as effectively as one. This finding is inconsistent with the independent channels hypothesis and, considering some later data, is actually rather surprising. For example, as mentioned before, there are several experiments that suggest that subjects can not only monitor several channels simultaneously, but can sometimes even render independent judgments about the contents of the several channels on a given trial (e.g., Eijkman & Vendrik, 1965; Shiffrin & Grantham, 1974).

Several possible explanations of the apparent inability to monitor two channels as well as one have suggested themselves. One possibility is that this occurs when the component tasks are themselves so demanding that they cannot be handled preattentively. While it isn't clear why the detection of e.g., a tone or light wouldn't be easy enough to be classified as preattentive, it is possible that some aspect of the stimuli or of the task led subjects to process stimuli more deeply than was necessary. The purpose of the present experiment, conducted by Mark Bradshaw and myself, was to determine if a set effect could be obtained when care was taken to insure that the component tasks were themselves preattentive. There are not widely accepted grounds for deciding whether or not a task is preattentive, and there is even some dispute about whether the term means anything more than "easy" (cf. Norman & Bobrow, 1975). In any case, in line with the discussion earlier in the chapter, it seemed to us reasonable to require, at a minimum, evidence of spatial parallelism before we would classify a task as preattentive.

The subjects' task was to decide whether a display was homogeneous or heterogeneous. Homogeneous displays consisted of two, four, six, or eight small black disks .42° in diameter irregularly spaced around the perimeter of an imaginary circle 3.58° in diameter. Heterogeneous displays also consisted of two, four, six, or eight elements; they were like the homogeneous displays except that in the place of one of the small black disks there was an element that differed from the others either in size (.84° in diameter) or color (red). There were two pure-list conditions and one mixed-list condition. In the pure-size condition there were 48 homogeneous displays and 48 heterogeneous displays, each of which contained a single size-discrepant element. There were equal numbers of homogeneous and heterogeneous displays at each display size. The pure-color condition was similarly constituted. The mixed-list display consisted of 96 homogeneous displays and 96 heterogeneous displays (48 color-discrepant and 48 size-discrepant) in a random order. Again, there were equal numbers of each stimulus type at each display size.

Eight subjects served in this experiment, each participating in two 1-hr sessions on consecutive days. Half of the subjects served in the two pure-list conditions on Day 1 and in the mixed-list condition on Day 2, while the order was reversed for the remaining subjects. The order of the two pure-list conditions was also balanced over subjects. On each trial subjects indicated their decision (heterogeneous or homogeneous) by pressing one of two response keys.

The chief results are shown in Fig. 3. The first point to note is that detection of color and size discrepancies both appear to be handled by a spatially parallel process since detection latency doesn't increase with display size. For the overall display size effect, F (3, 21) = .436, $p > .25$; in addition, display size did not interact with either dimension (color vs. size), $F(3, 21) = 1.27$, $p > .25$, or set condition (pure list vs. mixed list), $F(3, 21) < 1$. Thus, in lieu of any better definition we shall tentatively conclude that we have designed a task and a set of stimuli that lend themselves to preattentive processing. Having established this, we may examine the effect of set or foreknowledge. The pure-list condition led to faster detection than the mixed-list condition by 39 msec, $F(1, 7) = 5.7$, $p < .05$; It was also the case that the effect of set was more pronounced for size

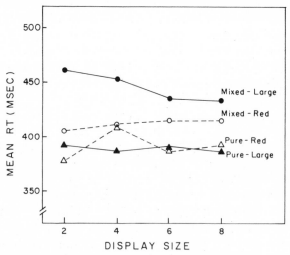

Fig. 3. Experiment VI: Mean RT for the detection of color or size discrepancies in pure or mixed lists as a function of number of display elements.

discrepancies (a 57-msec effect) than for color discrepancies (a 20-msec effect), $F(1, 7) = 8.77$, $p < .025$, although we have no particular interpretation to offer for this finding.

In sum, even presumably preattentive discriminations can be influenced by set. Although color and size discrepancies appear to "pop out" at the observer, they apparently pop out more readily when the subject is fully prepared (pure lists) than when he is not (mixed list). These results point to an internal contradiction in the conception of preattention that I outlined briefly in the Introduction; I shall return to this point later.

A follow-up experiment was conducted by Hazel Dunnigan to determine if set effects decrease with practice. She used the four-element display from the preceding experiment, and ran subjects in the pure-list and mixed-list conditions on each of four successive days. Six new subjects participated in this study.

The mean RT difference between the mixed and pure lists was only 21 msec in this study, but the effect was reliable nonetheless, $F(1, 5) = 8.39$, $p < .05$. Moreover, the magnitude of the set manipulation did not change across days, $F(3, 15) = 1.27$, $p > .25$.

2. Experiment VII: Size Invariance in Perception?

Corcoran and Rouse (1970) presented lists of handwritten or printed words one at a time in a tachistoscope and determined the probability of correct recognition. Recognition accuracy was higher when words were blocked with respect to being handwritten or printed than when they were mixed together in an unpredictable sequence. It is instructive to compare this finding to some findings recently obtained by Ginger Berninger and myself.

We were interested in the general issue of size invariance in perception. Common sense, buttressed by the results of some research on transfer in animal discrimination learning (e.g., Sutherland & Carr, 1963), suggest that, ". . . there must be some process which extracts shape independently of size" (Corcoran, 1971, p. 129). However, there is at least one finding that seems contrary to the spirit of this assertion. Bundesen and Larsen (1975) had subjects compare random forms with respect to the identity of their shapes. They found that mean RT's for both same and different judgments increased linearly with the size ratio of the forms being compared. Thus, e.g., two identical small forms would be judged "same" 100 to 200 msec faster than two forms of the same shape in which the larger one was four times larger than the smaller one. The findings were suggestive of a size transformation prior to matching similar to the kind of rotational transformation studied by Shepard and Metzler (1971).

The apparent failure of perceptual invariance over size differences may, of course, be unique to the use of unfamiliar random forms. What is the case with overlearned stimuli such as alphanumeric characters? To find out, we used Bundesen and Larsen's procedure, but we displayed digits instead of random shapes. Twelve subjects judged whether pairs of digits presented side by side were the same or different with respect to name (i.e., a small 2 and a large 2 should be called "same"). Half of the pairs were same and half were different. In all cases the digit on the left subtended approximately .5° in height. On one-fourth of all same trials, the digit on the right was the same size; on one-fourth of all same trials, the digit on the right was the same size; on one-fourth it subtended about 1° in height; on one-fourth about 1.7°, and on the remaining fourth about 2°. So size ratio varied from 1:1 to 1:4. The stimuli were dry transfer numerals that varied in "point" size; thus stroke width of the numerals also increased as height increased. Mean "same" RT increased in a negatively accelerated fashion as size ratio increased. This is somewhat different from Bundesen and Larsen's finding of a linear increase. More strikingly different were our results for "different" judgments. In our study, mean RT actually *decreased* (in a negatively decelerating fashion) as size ratio increased. This finding suggests a two-factor model. Specifically, it may be that when comparing familiar stimuli, subjects encode identity information and size information in parallel, and the implicit judgment of size may facilitate or compete with the explicit name judgment (cf. Egeth, 1966). In short, the same–different paradigm may not be the clearest way of studying size invariance in perception. It was this conclusion that prompted us to use a set paradigm to explore the possible independence of shape perception and size.

3. Experiment VIII: Set for Size

Subjects simply had to name digits (from 0 to 9) as they were presented one at a time in a tachistoscope. There were three conditions. In the pure-small condition the digits all subtended .5° in height. There were 50 trials in this condition. In the pure-large condition the digits were all 2° in height. Again there were 50 trials. In the mixed condition there were 50 small and 50 large digits in a random order. Presentation time was 200 msec. Vocal reaction time was obtained in each of these three conditions for 16 subjects. Half of the subjects received the mixed condition first, half received both pure conditions before the mixed condition. The order of presentation of the large and small pure conditions was balanced.

For the small stimuli, mean RT was 447 msec in the pure condition and 450 msec in the mixed condition. For the large stimuli, mean RT was 440 msec in the pure condition and 435 msec in the mixed condition. Clearly, there was no significant set effect for either large or small stimuli.

This absence of a set effect is consistent with the hypothesis of size invariance in perception. The data suggest that, unlike the situation comparing written and printed words, humans have a single "program" for recognizing large and small stimuli at least when the stimuli are familiar.

D.   INTERPRETATION OF SET EXPERIMENTS

In interpreting set experiments, it is commonly assumed that if performance declines as stimulus uncertainty increases (e.g., going from single-set to multiple-set conditions), then subjects cannot monitor several channels as effectively as one. This in fact was the assumption on which our set experiments were based. It turns out, however, that a decline in performance with increasing stimulus uncertainty is not necessarily inimical to the independent channels model; on the contrary, that model would seem to demand such a decline in performance under certain circumstances. This issue was discussed in Section II, A in connection with Gardner's analysis of the display size effect in visual detection. The point is that when subjects must make a single "yes" or "no" response on each trial, the response represents an integration of the information from all of the channels that are relevant on a particular trial. The more channels that are relevant, the greater the chance that noise in a channel not containing the target will trigger a response. Thus, even an ideal observer that does not have limited attentional capacity would be expected to show a performance decrement as the number of channels to be monitored increases.

An experiment by Lappin and Uttal (1976) shows the value of explicitly considering this prediction of the independent channels model. The experiment was designed to determine whether the detectability of visual targets embedded in random visual noise was affected by the number of alternative targets. The targets were four evenly spaced dots in a straight line, presented on a background of 35 other randomly spaced dots. The eight potential targets locations may be described as the evenly spaced spokes of a wheel; thus, they differ in orientation and position. There were three levels of stimulus uncertainty; $M = 2$ (12 and 6 o'clock), $M = 4$ (12, 6, 3, and 9 o'clock), and $M = 8$. The task required just detection, not identification. The decline in accuracy with increasing stimulus uncertainty followed closely the prediction of the independent channels model.

Lappin (1976) has argued further that an effect that shows up as a change in accuracy in a detectability paradigm should show up as a change in latency in a speeded-response paradigm. Therefore, the independent channels model should also predict an increase in RT with increasing stimulus uncertainty. The curves labeled IC (for independent channels model) in Fig. 4 depict the hypothesized effects of stimulus uncertainty on accuracy and latency. Note that the shape of the RT function is not precisely specified by a particular theory in this figure; it is simply monotonically increasing.

Although Lappin's argument is plausible, it depends on subsidiary assumptions that may be incorrect. I don't think it is *necessary* to predict that RT increases with stimulus uncertainty. In any case, the problem is that in too few set experiments have the full implications of the independent channels model been taken into consideration. This is especially true of studies using RT as the chief independent variable. Progress will require more than careful experimentation. It will also require the development of models based on the independent channels hypothesis that are capable of predicting RT.

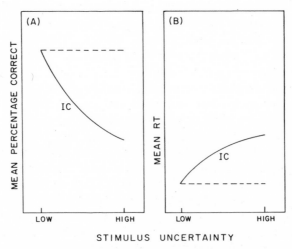

Fig. 4. Theoretical predictions of the effects of stimulus uncertainty on latency and accuracy of response, according to the independent channels model (IC).

Must we conclude that the existing data are either consistent with the independent channels model or inadequate to test it? I think not. Note that the independent channels model may be disconfirmed either by performance that is worse than expected or better than expected, although the implications of these two outcomes are different. We have already seen several cases where performance is better than would be predicted. Specifically, the independent channels hypothesis cannot readily account for RT or accuracy remaining unchanged, or only slightly changed as stimulus uncertainty is varied (see flat functions in Fig. 4A and B). For example, in direct contrast to Lappin and Uttal's (1976) study, Doehrman (1974) found little if any change in performance as he increased the number of possible orientations in which a target line could be presented.

1. Experiment IX: Set for Orientation

I have recently investigated orientation uncertainty using an RT measure. In this study, stimuli were black lines inscribed on white cards. Exposure duration was 200 msec. Three levels of stimulus uncertainty were used in three counterbalanced blocks: $M = 1$ (vertical); $M = 2$ (vertical or horizontal); $M = 4$ (vertical, horizontal, or either diagonal). Only RT's to the vertical target were analyzed in each condition. To prevent subjects from responding simply to the onset of the white card itself, 20% of the presentations were catch trails in which a card with no lines was shown. Twelve subjects each received 200 trials. Mean RT's to the vertical targets were, for $M = 1$, 286 msec; for $M = 2$, 286 msec; and for $M = 4$, 285 msec. Reassuringly, the false alarm rate on catch trials was less than 5%.

2. Speculations on Set

In an effort to make some sense of the inconsistencies among set experiments, I shall offer some post hoc speculations and comments. In the first place, a set effect would be expected if the outputs of detectors sensitive to irrelevant stimulation (e.g., irrelevant orientations of a line) could be ignored by higher order decision mechanisms. A set effect would *not* be expected if the outputs of both relevant and irrelevant detectors are passed on to the decision mechanism for examination. This latter point is, of course, the basis for the expectation of what would occur if processing were handled preattentively.

The line of reasoning sketched here provides a way of determining whether or not perception is invariant with some particular transformation. For example, the lack of a set effect in Experiment VIII shows that stimulus identification is unaffected by size variation. This is a reassuring finding since pattern recognition is usually supposed to be invariant over size transformations, within reasonable bounds (e.g., Corcoran, 1971, chap. 5). By contrast, Corcoran and Rouse (1970) found that word identification was dependent upon whether or not the subjects knew in advance whether the stimuli were printed or handwritten. This suggests that different sets of detectors are utilized for the two kinds of materials and that perception is not invariant over this particular "transformation." To put the matter differently, the distinction between "A" and "a" can hardly be considered a perceptual transformation at all.

The second speculation I would like to offer concerns the nature of noise and centers on the discrepancy between the results of Lappin and Uttal (1976) on the one hand, and Doehrman (1974) and my Experiment IX on the other hand. I shall argue that in the Lappin and Uttal study, the task was what Garner (1974) has called *process limited* in that the target (four dots in a straight line) and the noise (35 randomly positioned masking dots) were inherently confusable. One could do such an experiment with a 10-sec exposure duration and there would still be errors. In other words, there need have been no *perceptual* problem at all in that experiment, and so the fact that the authors were able to predict performance with a decisional model should not be surprising. However, this still does not explain why Doehrman and I found virtually no set effect as orientation uncertainty increased. I suspect the resolution of this discrepancy may reside in the nature of the detectors that were stimulated in these three line-detection studies. In Doehrman's study and in my study, since lines were presented, it is reasonable to think that line detectors were stimulated. On the further assumption that line detectors of varying orientation may indeed converge on a higher order detector regardless of their relevance, the lack of a set effect is "explained." However, it is possible that the dots used by Lappin and Uttal to constitute their stimuli may not have excited line detectors. Thus, subjects could at best make judgments about the colinearity of sets of dots, but they may not actually have "seen" lines at all. In this case it is quite reasonable to believe that subjects could make use of prior knowledge to limit their judgments to just relevant portions of the display.

The failure to take into account the predictions of the independent channels model causes the most serious interpretive problems where performance gets worse as stimulus uncertainty increases. If we knew, for example, that the increase in RT with increasing stimulus uncertainty was greater than predicted by the model, we could draw a definitive conclusion: Monitoring efficiency declines with task demands. This could be taken as an argument against the concept of preattention at least as defined in this chapter. However, in the absence of a specific model, it is not clear that, say, the RT increases caused by the multiple-set condition in Experiment VI reflect division of processing capacity.

My intuition has been that results such as those of Experiment VI do demonstrate an inability to monitor two "channels" (in that study, color and size) as well as one. However, I recognize several problems with this conclusion, in addition to the obvious fact that it is only an unsubstantiated guess right now. One problem is that it may be unreasonable to expect a set effect (i.e., a decline in monitoring efficiency) with strong signals when such effects have not been found with weak signals (e.g., Eijkman & Vendrik, 1965). Another related problem is that it is possible that whatever the results may be, they may tell us more about response latency than about the division of preceptual processing capacity.

E. SUMMARY

Many of the studies that have addressed the proposition that inputs receive the same perceptual analysis whether or not they are attended to have not been decisive. For example, I argued earlier that studies based on an interference paradigm (e.g., Experiments II, III, and IV of the present chapter, or dichotic listening studies showing some semantic processing of "unattended" messages) can show that unattended inputs can reach high levels of perceptual analysis. However, they cannot show that the perceptual analysis is as thorough as it would be if the input were attended to.

In the interference paradigm two or more inputs are presented simultaneously. Thus interference may be due in part to a limitation on overall processing capacity rather than on perceptual capacity per se. In the set paradigm only one target stimulus is presented at a time; however, subjects have to monitor a variable number of input channels. Under these circumstances there is evidence that subjects can monitor several channels as efficiently as one—which may be thought of as another way of saying that inputs receive the same perceptual analysis whether or not they are attended to. Further research will be necessary to determine whether exceptions to this rule such as Experiments V and VI are real or just apparent.

IV. Effortless Encoding

It is obvious that man has a limited capacity for processing information. The interesting question is *where* is capacity limited. Several
theorists have maintained that capacity limitations come into play
only after stimuli have been encoded, i.e., made contact with their
representations in memory (e.g., Deutsch & Deutsch, 1963). Further,
some theorists have adduced evidence to support the contention that
information processing up to and including the encoding stage may
be effortless, i.e., require no processing capacity (e.g., Keele, 1973;
Posner & Boies, 1971).

Posner and his colleagues (e.g., Posner & Boies, 1971; Posner &
Klein, 1973) have used a probe task to measure the demands of the
various stages of information processing, including encoding. In the
Posner and Boies (1971) experiment the subjects' primary task was a
sequential letter match. A 1-sec interval separated the onset of the
first letter from the onset of the second letter. The subject made a
"same" or "different" response as soon as he could after the presentation of the second letter. The secondary task, which measured
residual processing capacity, was to make a simple key press response
to a brief auditory probe that might be presented at any one of a
number of temporal positions during a letter-match trial. The relevant finding was that probe RT was no slower shortly (150 msec)
after the first letter was presented than before it was presented.
Another finding in that same paper was that encoding of the first
letter took up to 500 msec. Together, these results suggest that
encoding does not require processing capacity. This conclusion is not
simply the result of the probe task being insensitive to processing
demands, because probe RT was markedly elevated at several points
during the primary task, e.g., shortly after the second letter was
presented. This latter finding suggests that subjects have trouble
processing the probe during the response phase of the letter-match
task.

We (James Pomerantz, Steven Shwartz, and I) have recently conducted some experiments that attempt to determine the capacity
demands of encoding. The logic of these studies is somewhat similar
to that of the Posner and Boies experiment; however, there are
enough differences to demand additional background material.

One of the stages of processing that does seem to require capacity
is active rehearsal of the contents of memory. In fact, the effects of
varied memory loads on simple discrimination tasks have been examined in numerous experiments. To convey the flavor of the research

on this topic, we shall discuss three illustrative studies. One, by Wattenbarger and Pachella (1972), involved a memory scanning task in which size of the memory set of letters was varied from one to five. On occasional, unpredictable trials, a probe consisting of an arrow pointing left or right was presented (instead of a letter probe), and the subject was to respond with a left or right button press, respectively. With such high stimulus–response compatibility, memory load for the arrow discrimination should have been minimal. The important finding was that RT to the arrow presentation was independent of memory set size. Thus, a discrimination we would have supposed to be preattentive was, in fact, not interfered with by a simultaneous memory load that did require processing capacity. Shulman and Greenberg (1971) required subjects to make a simple discrimination of line length while at the same time retaining a set of consonants in memory. Discrimination RT was not affected by memory loads of fewer than six digits, but greater loads slowed RT's substantially. Finally, Connor (1972) used a "same–different" judgment task in which from 3 to 12 letters were presented simultaneously. The task was to decide if all the letters were the same or if one differed from the rest. At a variable interval before the letter display, a display of 0 to 4 digits was presented, which the subject would have to recall later. Connor found that RT's in the letter discrimination task increased with greater memory loads, particularly when the time interval between the digit and letter displays was brief. But regardless of the memory load, RT's were independent of the number of letters displayed.

Note that these results are not entirely consistent with one another. Wattenbarger and Pachella found no interference of a memory task on a perceptual task. Shulman and Greenberg did find interference, but only with large memory loads. Connor found interference even with small loads, but this interference did not interact with the number of elements to be processed in the perceptual task. There were procedural differences among these studies that could account for the apparent discrepancies. For example, Connor's task required *encoding* as well as retaining the memory load during the perceptual task; her results could be explained if subjects delayed beginning the perceptual matching task until encoding of the digits was completed. (In fact, she found that when a long interval separated the memory load array and the to-be-matched array, only minimal interference obtained.) Shulman and Greenberg's perceptual task was not a particularly easy one and so may not have been handled preattentively. Finally, Wattenbarger and Pachella's experiment lacked a control condition in which there was no memory load during the perceptual task. Their subjects may have adopted the strategy of first deciding whether the test stimulus was a letter or an arrow and then processing accordingly (although the authors argued against this possibility).

It would probably be premature to attempt to draw any firm conclusions from this set of experiments. Further experiments are necessary to elucidate the relationships among the crucial experimental factors. Three such experiments are reported below.

A. EXPERIMENTAL STUDIES OF THE EFFORTLESS ENCODING HYPOTHESIS

1. Experiment X: Simple RT and Memory Load

This experiment is similar to those of Shulman and Greenberg (1971), Wattenbarger and Pachella (1972), and Connor (1972). However, instead of requiring a choice RT or a subtle discrimination, the subjects simply had to press a button when a plus sign (+) appeared at the center of a CRT screen.

At the beginning of each trial, a number (0, 4, 8, or 12) appeared at the center of the screen indicating the number of consonants that were to follow. The number remained on for 5 sec and served as a warning signal. Then the consonants were presented at the center of the screen, each letter remaining on the screen for 1 sec, with 1 sec between letters. A grid of dots was presented 1 sec after the offset of the last consonant in the series to signal the beginning of a 30-sec retention interval. At the end of the retention interval a question mark appeared on the screen; this was the subject's signal to write down as many of the consonants as he could, in the correct order.

During the retention interval the subject was also required to press a button whenever a plus sign appeared at the center of the screen. The plus sign appeared at unpredictable times and remained on for 200 msec. More specifically, the probability was .25 that a plus sign would occur for each of the 30 1-sec intervals that constituted the retention interval. Thus the number of signals requiring a response on each trial followed a binomial distribution.

Each of the six subjects received 36 trials. The initiation of each trial was self-spaced. As in the Posner and Boies (1971) study, the subjects were told to consider the probe RT task to be secondary in importance to the other task. Thus, simple RT should serve as a measure of residual processing capacity.

Mean probe RT increased with memory load: 0 letters, 412 msec; 4 letters, 418 msec; 8 letters, 464 msec; 12 letters, 474 msec; $F(3, 15)$ = 5.88, $p < .01$. We would like to conclude that encoding (of the plus sign) does take capacity since probe RT was influenced by memory load. The obvious problem with this interpretation is that even as simple a task as pressing a button when a clear, bright signal appears has several components in addition to encoding. For example, memory is involved in that the subject must remember to do something when he detects the signal. And since subjects were to respond as quickly as possible, the response execution stage is also implicated. Thus, we cannot conclude that the encoding stage requires capacity; memory load may have affected RT through interaction with some other stage of processing. It is instructive to compare the interpretive problem raised by this experiment with the interpretive problem raised by a similar experiment done by Reitman (1974). This study was a follow-up to earlier studies (Reitman, 1971; Shiffrin, 1973) that showed that faint signals could be detected just as accurately with a memory load as without a memory load. In her 1974 paper Reitman increased the difficulty of the memory task over what she had used in her 1971 study and found out that detectability of probe signals was reduced by the simultaneous requirement to remember a list of words. It may be that the response requirements are in some sense weaker in an unspeeded detection task than in a speeded probe RT task. Thus, a probe task with accuracy as the dependent variable may provide a purer measure of the capacity requirements of encoding. The problem, however, is that such a method can only be used with weak or degraded stimuli that are detected less than 100% of the time. While information about the encoding demands of weak stimuli are obviously of interest to a general theory of perception, they may not be relevant to the study of preattentive processes which may be concerned only with the detection of relatively intense stimuli. In summary, we need a new method if we wish to study the processing requiremens of the encoding stage for strong signals. The approach we took was to use the logic of the additive factors method (e.g., Sternberg, 1969) to isolate the encoding stage and then to see how memory affected the duration of that particular stage.

2. Experiment XI: Additive Factors Analysis of RT

Before proceeding with a determination of the capacity demands of the encoding stage, we (Shwartz, Pomerantz, & Egeth, in press) had to devise a manipulation that could plausibly be said to affect

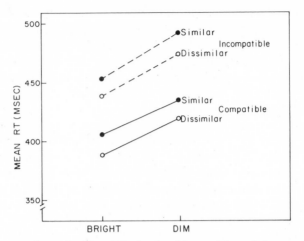

Fig. 5. Experiment XI: Mean RT's for the eight conditions of the experiment.

just the encoding stage of processing. We did this in the context of a larger effort in which we found three factors which affected three distinct stages of processing. More specifically, using a two-choice discrimination paradigm, the effects on RT of stimulus intensity, stimulus similarity, and stimulus—response compatibility were found to be additive. The task was to discriminate the direction in which an arrow pointed and to respond by pressing one of two buttons. One variable was stimulus intensity: The arrows were either bright or dim. Another variable was stimulus similarity: The two arrows pointed in either grossly or slightly different directions. The final variable was stimulus—response compatibility: The subject had to respond by pressing either the button toward which the arrow pointed or the opposite button.

Twenty undergraduates participated in this experiment, 10 in the high-compatibility and 10 in the low-compatibility condition. After some practice, each subject was tested in 40 trials, each lasting 30 sec, with a 10-sec rest between trials. For each of the 30-msec intervals within a trial there was a .33 probability that an arrow would occur, with the restriction that a minimum of 1.5 sec elapsed between the onset of two consecutive arrows. Each arrow remained on 200 msec.

Mean probe RT's are shown in Fig. 5 for each condition. Analysis of variance showed all main effects of interest to be significant; for compatibility, $F(1, 18) = 5.36$, $p < .05$; for similarity, $F(1,18) = 57.89$, $p < .001$; and for intensity, $F(1,18) = 104.95$, $p < .001$. None of the interactions approached significance (p's $> .25$). While the three main effects accounted for 29% of the total variance, the three double interactions and the triple interaction together accounted for less than .02% of the total variance. Following Sternbert's (1969) logic, additivity of the mean RT's of the three factors strongly supports the hypothesis of three functionally independent stages of processing.

3. Experiment XII: Effects of Memory Load on Stimulus Encoding

This experiment was essentially a combination of the preceding two studies: The stimulus and response conditions of Experiment XI were used on conjunction with a task-irrelevant memory load of 0, 4, 8, or 12 items, as in Experiment X. Each of 20 subjects was tested in nine blocks of four trials each. Each block consisted of one trial at each of the four levels of memory load, in randon order. On each trial the subject was presented with a warning digit indicating the size of the memory load. He was then given 0, 4, 8, or 12 consonants, followed by a 30-sec retention interval, during which he performed the discrimination task. A recall period followed the discrimination task. Ten subjects wer assigned to the high-compatibility condition and ten to the low-compatibility condition. Subjects were told that memory task was much more important than the discrimination task. Each subject received one block of practice trials before the start of the experiment. The session lasted about an hour.

Mean RT's for the conditions of chief interest are shown in Fig. 6. All experimental manipulations produced significant main effects; for memory load, F (3, 54) = 31.64, $p < .01$; for similarity F (1, 18) = 7.08, $p < .05$; for degradation, F (1, 18) = 101.70, $p < .01$; for compatibility, F (1, 18) = 6.40, $p < .05$. However, none of the interactions in the experiment approached significance (F's < 1).

We find these results surprising. On the assumption that one or more stages require processing capacity from the same central pool required by the retention taks we expected at least some factors to interact with memory load. Our initial expectation was that the factor affecting encoding (stimulus intensity) would *not* interact with load, thus providing evidence of effortless encoding. But we did not expect the factors affecting comparison and response selection also to be additive with memory load. What, then, are we to make of the pattern of significant main effects in the absence of any interactions? Pomerantz, Shwartz, and I now believe that the simplest interpretation of these data is that subjects do not simultaneously rehearse and attempt to process probes, but instead delay response to

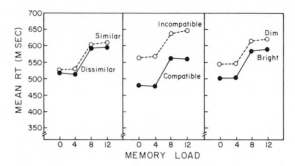

Fig. 6. Experiment XII: Mean RT as a function of memory load for the various conditions of the experiment. Each panel illustrates the (lack of) interaction between a particular factor and memory load.

the secondarily important probes until such time as they can interrupt rehearsal. We do not know if our results imply that subjects cannot handle the two tasks simultaneously or if they simply choose not to do so.

At this point we were perplexed. Posner and Boies (1971) had apparently found that encoding and probe processing could take place at the same time without mutual interference. In our Experiment XII, the shape of the function relating probe RT to memory load was the same for bright and dim stimuli, i.e., these factors did not interact. Following the logic of the additive factors method, one possible conclusion is that encoding (of the probe) and memory load affect separate stages which means, in turn, that rehearsal and probe processing may not take place at the same time.

A resolution to this apparent discrepancy may reside in the seemingly trivial fact that we used a visual probe while Posner and Boies used an auditory probe. The plausibility of such a resolution was established in an experiment done by Shwartz (1976) in which he extended the original Posner and Boies experiment. In Shwartz's study, two matching tasks were used in different conditions, one involving single-letter displays (as in Posner and Boies's experiment) and the other involving four-letter displays. Also, probes could be either auditory (as in Posner and Boies's experiment) or visual. Both of these manipulations were designed to provide a sensitive test of the hypothesis that encoding is effortless. If no capacity is required to encode one letter, then no capacity should be required to encode four letters (4 × 0 = 0). And if no capacity is required to encode a letter, then the encoding process should not interfere any more with a visual probe than with an auditory probe. The data showed that there was in fact no difference in the effect on probe RT of one vs.

four-letter arrays. However, for both one and four letter arrays there were large differences between the visual and auditory probes. The auditory data were much like Posner and Boies's; however, the visual probe showed a sharp increase in probe RT shortly after the presentation of the first array (i.e., during encoding). These results indicate that some capacity is demanded by the encoding process.

In the absence of further evidence, it is not clear whether the difference between auditory and visual probes simply reflects the difference between general and modality-specific interference (e.g., Segal & Fusella, 1970) or whether it indicates a basic difference in the way auditory and visual material is processed. We incline to the latter position. Posner and his colleagues (Posner *et al.*, 1976) have recently argued that auditory signals are more alerting than visual signals and that alerting based on visual signals requires effort whereas alerting based on auditory signals does not, or at least requires much less effort than visual alerting.

This line of reasoning prompts the following comments on the endeavor to ascertain the processing demands of encoding with a probe RT task. On the one hand, if it is true that auditory encoding requires no effort (i.e., capacity), then it would not be appropriate to use an auditory probe as a secondary task to determine if some primary task does or does not require capacity. On the other hand, if it is true that a visual probe is not particularly alerting, such probes may simply be held in a very short-term buffer until the presumed rehearsal cycle has reached some point where it can be interrupted with minimal disruption. In short, there is no conclusive evidence that the available methods have forced subjects to handle two effortful tasks as once. Thus, we cannot yet draw firm conclusions about the processing demands of encoding.

An objection that may occur to the reader is that the auditory probe task cannot be effortless because the matching task does not interfere with it when the auditory probe is presented close in time to the second stimulus of the to-be-matched pair. Note, however, that the claim is only that the *encoding* of auditory signals is effortless; the requirement to make a rapid response to the probe would still require capacity. Thus, interference with probes presented near in time to the second stimulus could be due to competition for limited capacity in the response system.

B. SUMMARY

Reitman's (1974) experiment showed that signal detectability was reduced by a concomitant memory load. If we assume an unspeeded detection task minimizes the importance of respone selection and execution stages, then it seems reasonable to conclude that stimulus encoding requires processing capacity (although it *is* possible that it is the memory for the criterion that is affected by memory load rather than signal processing per se).

Attempts to determine the capacity required to encode more intense signals have used RT measures. It is easy to show mutual interference between speeded response tasks. However, it has proven to be considerably more difficult to assess the degree to which interference occurs at specific stages of processing in those tasks. In particular, it is not yet clear whether the encoding stage does or does not require processing capacity.

V.   Concluding Remarks

It would be nice to be able to end on a decisive note, either strongly supporting or strongly refuting the three propositions characterized in Section I. However, it seems to me that the data dictate a more judicious finale.

The independent channels model appears to be an excellent first approximation to reality. Many of the existing data are consistent with it, and upon close examination even some apparent contradictions, such as Colavita's (1974) demonstration of sensory dominance, dissolve. However, it is becoming increasingly clear that in detail the model is wrong. For example, the results of studies on letter detection seem to require a model in which there is interaction among stimuli at the perceptual level. In studies of dichotic listening, events on one channel do appear to affect the detectability of events on the other channel (e.g., Ostry *et al.*, 1976). Thus, even the two ears may not serve as completely independent channels. To be fair, however, it may well be the case that the interference effects found in dichotic listening actually stem from decisional factors and not from an inability to *monitor* two or more channels independently. In any case, perhaps it is only when different modalities or grossly different stimulus dimensions are tested that subjects can both monitor and respond independently to two channels (e.g., Eijkman & Vendrik, 1965). Even then, to demonstrate independence, care must be taken not to overload the response system (cf. Colavita, 1974; also our Experiment I).

One of the useful directions for further research would be to develop a solid basis for exploring channel independence with strong signals. But, of course, detectability per se is not a problem with strong signals, and so the method of choice in such studies has been RT. The problem here is that models of RT appropriate to multichannel detection tasks are few and far between.

The hypothesis that inputs receive the same perceptual analysis whether or not they are attended seems to me to be not decisively refutable on the basis of existing evidence. As we have seen, there are circumstances in which the independent channels model leads us to expect a performance decline. Further research will have to address two related questions. First, are there circumstances in which performance decrements are greater than predicted by the independent channels model (thus implying an attentional effect)? Second, why is it that in some circumstances performance does *not* decline with increasing stimulus uncertainty?

As for the hypothesis of effortless encoding, my colleagues and I found it difficult to devise a satisfactory test. The reason is that we have used techniques that measure the degree of mutual interference between tasks, based on the assumption that the two tasks are being performed simultaneously. However, we have been unable to convince ourselves that subjects were in fact performing the two tasks simultaneously.

One can imagine that further work in this area could be directed along two very different paths. On the one hand, one can envision a methodological breakthrough that will insure that subjects work on two tasks at once. On the other hand, one can envision a theoretical breakthrough that simply dispenses with notions of capacity, fixed or otherwise, and will lead us to radically different kinds of experiments. The "correct" path is not yet obvious.

REFERENCES

Beck, J., & Ambler, B. The effects of concentrated and distributed attention on peripheral acuity. *Perception & Psychophysics,* 1973, **14**, 225–230.

Broadbent, D. E. *Perception and communication.* Oxford: Pergamon, 1958.

Bundesen, C., & Larsen, A. Visual transformation of size. *Journal of Experimental Psychology: Human Perception and Performance,* 1975, **1**, 214–220.

Colavita, F. B. Human sensory dominance. *Perception & Psychophysics,* 1974, **16**, 409–412.

Connor, J. M. Effects of increased processing load on parallel processing of visual displays. *Perception & Psychophysics,* 1972, **12**, 121–128.

Corcoran, D. W. J. *Pattern recognition.* Baltimore: Penguin Books, 1971.

Corcoran, D. W. J., & Rouse, R. O. An aspect of perceptual organization involved in the perception of handwritten and printed words. *Quarterly Journal of Experimental Psychology,* 1970, **22**, 526–530.

Corteen, R. S., & Wood, B. Autonomic responses to shock-associated words in an unattended channel. *Journal of Experimental Psychology*, 1972, 94, 308–313.

Deutsch, J. A., & Deutsch, D. Attention: Some theoretical considerations. *Psychological Review*, 1963, 70, 80–90

Doehrman, S. The effect of visual orientation uncertainty in a simultaneous detection–recognition task. *Perception & Psychophysics*, 1974, 15, 519–523.

Dyer, F. N. Interference and facilitation for color naming with separate bilateral presentations of the word and color. *Journal of Experimental Psychology*, 1973, 99, 314–317.

Egeth, H. E. Parallel versus serial processes in multidimensional stimulus discrimination. *Perception & Psychophysics*, 1966, 1, 245–252.

Egeth, H. E. Selective attention. *Psychological Bulletin*, 1967, 67, 41–57.

Egeth, H., & Bevan, W. Attention. In B. Wolman (Ed.), *Handbook of general psychology*. Englewood Cliffs, N.J.: Prentice-Hall, 1973.

Egeth, H., Jonides, J., & Wall, S. Parallel processing of multi-element displays. *Cognitive Psychology*, 1972, 3, 674–698.

Egeth, H. E., & Pachella, R. Multidimensional stimulus identification. *Perception & Psychophysics*, 1969, 5, 341–346.

Egeth, H. E., & Smith, E. E. Perceptual selectivity in a visual recognition task. *Journal of Experimental Psychology*, 1967, 74, 543–549.

Eijkman, E., & Vendrik, A. J. H. Can a sensory system be specified by its internal noise? *Journal of the Acoustical Society of America*, 1965, 37, 1102–1109.

Eriksen, B. A., & Eriksen, C. W. Effects of noise letters upon the identification of a target letter in a nonsearch task. *Perception & Psychophysics*, 1974, 16, 143–149.

Eriksen, C. W., & Hoffman, J. E. Temporal and spatial characteristics of selective encoding from visual displays. *Perception & Psychophysics*, 1972, 12, 201–204.

Eriksen, C. W., & Hoffman, J. E. Selective attention: Noise suppression or signal enhancement: *Bulletin of the Psychonomic Society*, 1974, 4, 587–589.

Eriksen, C. W., & Spencer, T. Rate of information processing in visual perception: Some results and methodological considerations. *Journal of Experimental Psychology Monograph*, 1969, 79 (No. 2, Part 2).

Estes,W. K. Interactions of signal and background variables in visual processing. *Perception & Psychophysics*, 1972, 12, 278–286.

Gardner, G. T. Evidence for independent parallel channels in tachistoscopic perception. *Cognitive Psychology*, 1973, 4, 130–155.

Garner, W. R. *The processing of information and structure*. Potomac, Md: Lawrence Erlbaum Associates, 1974.

Gilliom, J. D., & Sorkin, R. D. Sequential vs. simultaneous two-channel signal detection: More evidence for a high-level interrupt theory. *Journal of the Acoustical Society of America*, 1974, 56, 157–164.

Gilmore, G. C. *The interaction among letters in a visual display*. Unpublished doctoral dissertation, Johns Hopkins University, 1975.

Grindley, G. C., & Townsend, V. Voluntary attention in peripheral vision and its effects on acuity and differential thresholds. *Quarterly Journal of Experimental Psychology*, 1968, 20, 11–19.

Kahneman, D. *Attention and effort*. Englewood Cliffs, N.J.: Prentice-Hall, 1973.

Keele, S. W. *Attention and human performance*. Pacific Palisades, Calif.: Goodyear, 1973.

Keren, G., & Skelton, J. On selecting between theories of selective attention. *Perception & Psychophysics*, 1976, 20, 85–88.

Lappin, J. S. *The relativity of choice behavior and the effect of prior knowledge on the speed and accuracy of recognition*. Paper presented at the Conference on Mathematical and Theoretical Psychology, Bloomington, Indiana, April 1976.

Lappin, J. S., & Uttal, W. R. Does prior knowledge facilitate the detection of visual targets in random noise? *Perception & Psychophysics,* 1976, **20**, 367–374.

Lewis, J. L. Semantic processing of unattended messages using dichotic listening. *Journal of Experimental Psychology,* 1970, **85**, 225–228.

Lindsay, P. H. Multichannel processing in perception. In D. I. Mostofsky (Ed.), *Attention: Contemporary theory and analysis.* New York: Appleton, 1970.

Massaro, D. W., & Kahn, B. J. Effects of central processing onauditory recognition. *Journal of Experimental Psychology,* 1973, **97**, 51–58.

Moore, J. J., & Massaro, D. W. Attention and processing capacity in auditory recognition. *Journal of Experimental Psychology,* 1973, **99**, 49–54.

Moray, N. Attention in dichotic listening: Affective cues and the influence of instructions. *Quarterly Journal of Experimental Psychology,* 1959, **11**, 56–60

Mowrer, O. H., Rayman, N. N., & Bliss, E. L. Preparatory set (expectancy)—An experimental demonstration of its "central" locus. *Journal of Experimental Psychology,* 1940, **26**, 357–371.

Neisser, U. *Cognitive psychology.* Englewood Cliffs, N.J.: Prentice-Hall.

Norman, D., & Bobrow, D. G. On data-limited and resource-limited processes. *Cognitive Psychology,* 1975, **7**, 44–64.

Ostry, D., Moray, N., & Marks, G. Attention, practice, and semantic targets. *Journal of Experimental Psychology: Human Perception and Performance,* 1976, **2**, 326–336.

Pachella, R. G. *The nature of the effect of set on tachistoscopic recognition.* Unpublished doctoral dissertation, Johns Hopkins University, 1970.

Pomerantz, J. R., Sager, L. C., & Stoever, R. J. Perception of wholes and of their component parts: Some configural superiority effects. *Journal of Experimental Psychology: Human Perception and Performance,* in press.

Posner, M. I., & Boies, S. J. Components of attention. *Psychological Review,* 1971, **78**, 391–408.

Posner, M. I., & Klein, R. M. On the functions of consciousness. In S. Kornblum (Ed.), *Attention and Performance IV.* New York: Academic Press, 1973.

Posner, M. I., Nissen, M. J., & Klein, R. M. Visual dominance: An information-processing account of its origins and significance. *Psychological Review,* 1976, **83**, 157–171.

Posner, M. I., Nissen, M. J., & Ogden, W. *Attending to a position is space.* Paper presented at the meeting of the Psychonomic Society, Denver, November 1975.

Reitman, J. S. Mechanisms of forgetting in short-term memory. *Cognitive Psychology,* 1971, **2**, 185–195.

Reitman, J. S. Without surreptitious rehearsal, information in short-term memory decays. *Journal of Verbal Learning and Verbal Behavior,* 1974, **13**, 365–377.

Rumelhart, D. E. A multicomponent theory of the perception of briefly exposed visual displays. *Journal of Mathematical Psychology,* 1970, **7**, 191–218.

Segal, S. J., & Fusella, V. Influence of imaged pictures and sounds on detection of visual and auditory signals. *Journal of Experimental Psychology,* 1970, **83**, 458–464.

Shepard, R. N., & Metzler, J. Mental rotation of three-dimensional objects. *Science,* 1971, **171**, 701–703.

Shiffrin, R. M. Information persistence in short-term memory. *Journal of Experimental Psychology,* 1973, **100**, 39–49.

Shiffrin, R. M., & Gardner, G. T. Visual processing capacity and attentional control. *Journal of Experimental Psychology,* 1972, **93**, 72–82.

Shiffrin, R. M., & Grantham, D. W. Can attention be allocated to sensory modalities? *Perception & Psychophysics,* 1974, **15**, 460–474.

Shiffrin, R. M., McKay, D. P., & Shaffer, W. O. Attending to forty-nine spatial positions at once. *Journal of Experimental Psychology,* 1976, **2**, 14–22.

Shiffrin, R. M., & Schneider, W. Controlled and automatic human information processing: II. Perceptual learning, automatic attending, and a general theory. *Psychological Review*, 1977, **84**, 127–190.

Shulman, H. G., & Greenberg, S. N. Perceptual deficit due to division of attention between memory and perception. *Journal of Experimental Psychology*, 1971, **88**, 171–176.

Shwartz, S. P. Capacity limitations in human information processing. *Memory & Cognition*, 1976, **4**, 763–768.

Shwartz, S. P., Pomerantz, J. R., & Egeth, H. E. State and process limitations in information processing: An additive factor analysis. *Journal of Experimental Psychology: Human Perception and Performance*, in press.

Sorkin, R. D., Pohlmann, L. D., & Gilliom, J. D. Simultaneous two-channel signal detection III. 630- and 1400-Hz signals. *Journal of the Acoustical Society of America*, 1973, **53**, 1045–1050.

Sperling, G. The information available in brief visual presentations. *Psychological Monographs*, 1960, **74**(11, Whole no. 498), 1–29.

Sternberg, S. The discovery of processing stages: Extensions of Donder's method. *Acta Psychologica*, 1969, **30**, 276–315.

Sutherland, N. S., & Carr, A. E. The visual discrimination of shape by octopus: The effects of stimulus size. *Quarterly Journal of Experimental Psychology*, 1963, **13**, 225–235.

Taylor, M. M., Lindsay, P. H., & Forbes, S. M. Quantification of shared capacity processing in auditory and visual discrimination. *Acta Psychologica*, 1967, **27**, 282–299.

Treisman, A. M. Strategies and models of selective attention. *Psychological Review*, 1969, **76**, 282–299.

Treisman, A., Squire, R., & Green, J. Semantic processing in dichotic listening? A replication. *Memory & Cognition*, 1974, **2**, 641–646.

Van Der Heijden, A. H. C., & Eerland, E. The effect of cueing in a visual signal detection task. *Quarterly Journal of Experimental Psychology*, 1973, **25**, 496–503.

Wardlaw, K., & Kroll, N. E. A. Automatic responses to shock-associated words in a nonattended message: A failure to replicate. *Journal of Experimental Psychology: Human Perception and Performance*, 1976, **2**, 357–360.

Wattenbarger, B. L., & Pachella, R. G. The effect of memory load on reaction time in character classification. *Perception & Psychophysics*, 1972, **12**, 100–102.

Wundt, W. *Grundzuge der physiologischen Psychologie* (2nd ed., Vol. 2). Leipzig: Engelmann, 1880.

SUBJECT INDEX

A

Abstractive memory, 5
Amplification, use of sentence operators for, 74–77
Analog models, of symbolic comparison, 118–130
And, use of, 49–51
Associations, cognitive, in classical conditioning, 216–217
Associative models, of symbolic comparison, 117–118
Attention
  control of perception by, 286–287
  experimental data, 303–307
  failure of selectivity in spatial domain, 287–293
  in nonspatial domain, 297–303
  in spatial domain, 293–297
  effortless encoding and, 308–316
  independent channels hypothesis
  multielement visual displays and, 279–281
  multimodal and multidimensional stimulation and, 281–283
  sensory dominance and, 283–285
Availability principle, symbolic comparison and, 115–117

B

Blocking, in classical conditioning, 227–228

C

Categorical models, of symbolic comparison, 118
Choice, in semantic-coding model, 145–155
Classical conditioning
  blocking in, 227–228
  cognitive associations and, 216–217
  differential, 228–230
  expectancy potentials in, 220–221
  extinction in, 222–226
  generalization in, 217–220
  random partial reinforcement in, 226–227
  relearning in, 222–226
  spontaneous recovery and, 222–226
  stimuli and, 215–216
  terminology and theory of, 205–211
  theoretical deficiencies, 231–232
Comparison, *see* Symbolic comparison
Comprehension, constructive processes during, 4–8
Conditioning, *see* Classical conditioning
Context, sentence operators and, 58–63, 86–88

E

Encoding
  Bartlett's theory of, 16–17, 34
  effortless, 308–316
  elaborative, 14–16
  experimental data on, 17–33
  levels of processing, 13–14, 35
End-anchor effects, symbolic comparison and, 113–114
Expectancy potentials, in classical conditioning, 220–221
Experience, long-term memory and, 168–170
Extinction, in classical conditioning, 222–226

G

Generalization, in classical conditioning, 217–220